# The Utopian Function of Art and Literature

*The essential function of utopia is a critique of what is present.*

## Studies in Contemporary German Social Thought
Thomas McCarthy, General Editor

# The Utopian Function of Art and Literature

Selected Essays

Ernst Bloch

translated by Jack Zipes and
Frank Mecklenburg

The MIT Press
Cambridge, Massachusetts
London, England

Second Printing, 1989

This book was set in Baskerville by Asco Trade Typesetting Ltd., Hong Kong, and printed and bound by Halliday Lithograph in the United States of America.

Library of Congress Cataloging-in-Publication Data

Bloch, Ernst, 1885–1977.
The Utopian function of art and literature.

(Studies in contemporary German social thought)
The first essay, Something's missing, was originally published in German in Gespräche mit Ernst Bloch; the other essays are from Bloch's Ästhetik des Vor-Scheins.
Includes index.
1. Aesthetics.  2. Utopias.  I. Title.  II. Series.
B3209.B753U87  1988      700′.1      87-4068
ISBN 0-262-02270-2

# Contents

Contents

# Notes on the Translation and Acknowledgments

With the exception of the interview between Bloch and Theodor W. Adorno, the essays were taken from Ernst Bloch, *Ästhetik des Vor-Scheins*, ed. Gert Ueding, 2 vols., Frankfurt am Main, 1974. They were originally published in different volumes of Bloch's collected works, and in some cases, they were rearranged or abridged by Ueding with Bloch's permission. The original titles of the interview, the essays, and the books in which they appeared are as follows (note that the date in parentheses indicates the essay's first date of publication in a journal, newspaper, or first edition of a particular book):

1. "Something's Missing: A Discussion between Ernst Bloch and Theodor W. Adorno on the Contradictions of Utopian Longing"— "Etwas fehlt ... über die Widersprüche der utopischen Sehnsucht," in *Gespräche mit Ernst Bloch*, eds. Rainer Taub and Harald Wieser, Frankfurt am Main: Suhrkamp, 1975.

2. "Art and Society" ("Kunst und Gesellschaft")

"Ideas as Transformed Material in Human Minds, or Problems of an Ideological Superstructure (Cultural Heritage)"—"Ideelles als das im Menschenkopf umgesetzte Materielle oder Probleme eines ideologischen Überbaus (Kulturerbe)," in *Das Materialismusproblem*, Frankfurt am Main: Suhrkamp, 1972.

"The Wish-Landscape Perspective in Aesthetics: The Order of Art Materials According to the Dimension of Their Profundity and Hope"—"Die Wunschlandperspektive in der Ästhetik; Rang der Kunststoffe nach Massgabe ihrer Tiefen- und Hoffnungsdimension," in *Das Prinzip Hoffnung*, Frankfurt am Main: Suhrkamp, 1959.

3. "Art and Utopia" ("Kunst und Utopie") "The Creation of the Ornament"—"Erzeugung des Ornaments" (1918), in *Geist der Utopie*, rev. ed. Frankfurt am Main: Suhrkamp, 1973.

"The Conscious and Known Activity within the Not-Yet-Conscious, the Utopian Function"—"Die bewusste und die gewusste Tätigkeit im Noch-Nicht-Bewussten, utopische Funktion," in *Das Prinzip Hoffnung*, Frankfurt am Main: Suhrkamp, 1959.

"The Artistic Illusion as the Visible Anticipatory Illumination"—"Künstlerischer Schein als sichtbarer Vor-Schein," in *Das Prinzip Hoffnung*, Frankfurt am Main: Suhrkamp, 1959.

4. "Marxism and Poetry"—"Marxismus und Dichtung" (1935), in *Literarische Aufsätze*, Frankfurt am Main: Surhkamp, 1965.

5. "The Fairy Tale Moves on Its Own in Time"—"Das Märchen geht selber in der Zeit" (1930), in *Literarische Aufsätze*, Frankfurt am Main: Suhrkamp, 1965.

6. "Better Castles in the Sky at the Country Fair and Circus, in Fairy Tales and Colportage"—"Bessere Luftschlösser in Jahrmarkt und Zirkus, in Märchen und Kolportage" (1954), in *Das Prinzip Hoffnung*, Frankfurt am Main: Suhrkamp, 1959.

7. "Building in Empty Spaces"—"Die Bebauung des Hohlraums," in *Das Prinzip Hoffnung*, Frankfurt am Main: Suhrkamp, 1959.

8. "On Fine Arts in the Machine Age"—"Über bildende Kunst im Maschinenzeitalter" (1964), in *Literarische Aufsätze*, Frankfurt am Main: Suhrkamp, 1965.

9. "On the Present in Literature"—"Über Gegenwart in der Dichtung" (1956), in *Literarische Aufsätze*, Frankfurt am Main: Suhrkamp, 1965.

10. "The Stage Regarded as a Paradigmatic Institution and the Decision within It"—"Die Schaubühne, als paradigmatische Anstalt betrachtet und die Entscheidung in ihr," in *Das Prinzip Hoffnung*, Frankfurt am Main: Suhrkamp, 1959.

11. "A Philosophical View of the Detective Novel"—"Philosophische Ansicht des Detektivromans" (1960), in *Literarische Aufsätze*, Frankfurt am Main: Suhrkamp, 1965.

12. "A Philosophical View of the Novel of the Artist"—"Philoso-

phische Ansicht des Künstlerromans" (1961), in *Literarische Aufsätze,* Frankfurt am Main: Suhrkamp, 1965.

13. "The Representation of Wish-Landscapes in Painting, Opera, and Poetry"—"Dargestellte Wunschlandschaft in Malerei, Oper, Dichtung" (1949), in *Das Prinzip Hoffnung,* Frankfurt am Main: Suhrkamp, 1959.

Not all the essays included in Ueding's edition have been printed here. I have selected those that, I believe, will enable English-speaking readers to obtain a comprehensive view of Bloch's aesthetics. They cover the period from 1918 to 1972 and represent his most significant views on music, art, architecture, theater, film, and literature. Bloch did not develop a systematic theory of aesthetics. Rather, he sought to comprehend how the apparent generic differences in art and literature were related to basic ontological and political questions underlying humankind's quest for utopia. The essays published in this volume can also be considered signs or traces of Bloch's own struggle to reformulate aesthetic questions for the purpose of preserving the cultural heritage that he considered necessary for humankind's survival and realization of utopia. They were meant to intervene in the dominant discourse of aesthetics, to provoke, and to jar.

In translating Bloch, Frank Mecklenburg and I used an interpretative approach and sought to clarify Bloch's ideas as much as we could without simplifying or misrepresenting them. We also endeavored to capture his elliptical and metaphorical style, but where his syntax and formulations were confusing and baffling, we were compelled to employ clearer sentence structure and straightforward terminology to express the intent and content of his phrases, that is, what we thought comprised the intent and content. Due to the fact that it is sometimes impossible to understand Bloch, even when one has a firm command of German, there are no doubt mistranslations. One is never on firm ground when reading Bloch. Many of the Blochian terms we have conceived, such as "anticipatory illumination" (*Vor-Schein*), "upright gait" (*aufrechter Gang*), "non-synchronous" (*ungleich-zeitig*), and "indelible" (*unausgegolten*), will contradict existing translations of these concepts. Yet, with Bloch there is always room for multiple interpretation and translation, and we have translated his concepts and terms anew with the purpose of reutilizing them for the cultural heritage in keeping with his spirit.

The essay "A Philosophical View of the Detective Novel" was first translated by Roswitha Mueller and Stephen Thaman and appeared in *Discourse* 2 (1980). I revised and reworked their translation with their kind permission and wish to thank them for their help. In the course of the translation I reworked all the essays several times.

During the work on the translation and introduction, Tom McCarthy and Larry Cohen gave me invaluable advice and support. In addition, I also benefited greatly from the suggestions and criticism of Bob D'Amico, Andy Rabinbach, and Greg Ulmer in writing the introduction. Last but not least, without Frank Mecklenburg's collaboration on the translation and his substantial discussions about Bloch's philosophy, the project would never have been brought to fruition.

Jack Zipes
Gainesville, 1987

# Introduction: Toward a Realization of Anticipatory Illumination

## Jack Zipes

Ernst Bloch's disturbing contradictions have always made it difficult to write about this philosopher of Marxist humanism and revolutionary utopianism. Bloch assumed many roles and positions during his long life. He was consistently unconventional, upredictable, and provocative. His curiosity and thirst for knowledge were insatiable, and it seemed like he was always in motion, always searching for clues to a lost world that anticipated the future. He retained everything he read, heard, or observed. He was as passionate about Karl May's westerns, the fairy tales of the Brothers Grimm, the *Arabian Nights*, and the comic strips of the *Boston Globe* as about the works of Goethe, Schiller, Hoffmann, Keller, Kafka, and Brecht. He could play and recite entire operas and could discourse with authority on physics, architecture, psychology, theater, sociology, and, of course, philosophy. Like many intellectuals of his generation, he was a "perfect" product of the *Bildungsbürgertum*, the incarnation of all the bourgeois liberal ideals of the nineteenth century, and in fact he placed great stock in those ideals. But at the same time, he sought to break out of this bourgeois tradition, to turn it inside out and compel it to live up to the promises made by those revolutionary movements that had established the rule of the middle classes.

It was against the domination of the middle classes and the ossification of bourgeois idealism that Bloch rebelled, and he sought to ground his rebellious urges by postulating the possibility of a life without oppression and enslavement. At first he sought to develop this possibility from his study of phenomenology and German idealism mixed with a blend of anarchist, pacifist, and mystical notions. After World War I it was Marxism that became the ground of all his thoughts, and his disturbing contradictions cannot be unraveled unless one understands that Bloch sought to revitalize Marxism without totally abandoning his bourgeois heritage and that he believed in the necessity of establishing a real communist society in order to bring about a genuine democracy and humanitarianism. Unfortunately, Bloch often used the terms Marxism, socialism, and communism crudely in opposition to fascism, capitalism, and imperialism, and he made many mistakes and unmediated assertions in his political analyses. Aware of his own shortcomings, though never apologetic, Bloch dealt with his contradictions and those of his time by continuously trying to locate the basic needs of oppressed groups and elaborating a Marxist critique of alienation and exploitation. In the process he maintained his optimistic belief in the potential of art to provide not only hope for a better future but also illumination toward the realization of this goal. In a 1968 interview Bloch stated:

In every age two threads intertwine: first, "the cultural heritage" [Engels], that is, religion, art, and philosophy; and second, ideology. Ideology is just a coloration of the awareness that stands and falls with the ruling class power. "The dominant ideas of an age are the ideas of its ruling class" [Marx]. The Bible is made an excuse for its cheap imports; preservation of the purity of communism is a pretext for the occupation of Czechoslovakia. Nothing has changed. The slogans and alibis circulating in the Soviet Union today are pure ideology, and the best that can come from them is the warning: This is not the way to act. What has cultural value expresses more than the goal of one age or one class: It speaks for the future. Any significant philosophical or artistic work contributes to future maturity. Therefore great achievements in the superstructure no longer belong completely to their age. The Parthenon cannot be written off just because it was built by a slaveholding society. Its social mission at the time is no longer the important thing. What interests us now is its meaning for later generations living under a changed general situation. Only progress and the progression of time therefore bring out the full value of the past heritage—and that never completely.... The 18th century had no eye for Gothic art; we understand it because the parallax is greater from where we stand. But in the future we will see yet more. The receptive subject of culture grows with socialism; his entire richness will flourish only in socialist society.[1]

Bloch's own growth as a "receptive subject of culture" came through his intense concern with questions of aesthetics and the cultural heritage and against the grain of institutionalized bourgeois aesthetics and ideology in practically every phase of his life. Thus it is important to place Bloch historically, to consider how he developed his disturbing political and personal contradictions, because his notions about the utopian function of art and literature were in part an endeavor to resolve them. Aesthetics was a way of life for Bloch, which meant that he had no interest in becoming a disinterested spectator of culture. In fact, Bloch intervened in almost all the crucial philosophical and aesthetic debates of his time, and his interventions left scars that need tracing if we are to realize their value for a critique of contemporary cultural developments.

# I

Ernst Bloch was born in 1885 in Ludwigshafen.[2] His parents were assimilated, well-to-do Jews who had clear but narrow expectations for their son. His father was a senior official of the Imperial Railways and treated his son with a firm hand. For the most part he seemed concerned more with respectability than with helping the boy develop his talents. Bloch in turn felt his parents' imposition of stultifying regulations as a direct impingement on his personal freedom. In his rare remarks about his youth, Bloch always stressed his desire to break away, and he hardly mentioned his parents in his later years. Nor was Ludwigshafen itself conducive to his childhood dreams and desires. At the end of the 19th century, the city was a dreary industrial center in which the living conditions of the workers were decrepit and the life style of the bourgeoisie was boring and predictable. Compared with the neighboring city of Mannheim, which was more affluent and had a more varied cultural life, Ludwigshafen, the "proletarian" city, stood as a constant reminder to the young Bloch of the social and political inequities that would disturb him throughout his life.

To a certain extent, it was the contradiction between Ludwigshafen and Mannheim that gave rise to Bloch's early political consciousness. Here was a clear instance of what he would call nonsynchronism: Mannheim was a modern society (*Gesellschaft*) moving with the times toward secularization and cosmopolitanism, while Ludwigshafen was still underdeveloped and harbored strong 19th-century notions of community (*Gemeinschaft*). The nonsynchronous breach between the cities later helped Bloch grasp why fascism, which paid heed to the basic yearnings and customs of the lower classes and did not dismiss them as communism did, had such great appeal for the German people.

In his youth, however, Bloch was more bothered by the void in his own life, which he came to realize was also connected to the contradiction between Ludwigshafen and Mannheim. That is, his home was characterized by what he called "mush," dreariness, and lack—lack of love, understanding, and stimulation. He filled the void as he could with daydreams, voracious reading, music, theater, letter-writing to eminent philosophers, rebellion against traditional schooling, and concern for social democratic politics.

Bloch left Ludwigshafen in 1905 to study philosophy and German literature at the University of Munich; he then moved on to the University of Würzburg, where he studied experimental psychology, physics, and music and took an intest in the Cabbala and Jewish mysticism. After receiving his doctorate in philosophy in 1908 with a dissertation on Heinrich Rickert under the direction of Hermann Cohen, he moved to Berlin to study under the renowned sociologist Georg Simmel. It was in Simmel's seminar that he met Georg Lukács, who became one of his best friends and later one of his foremost philosophical antagonists. Bloch studied with Simmel until 1911 and was strongly influenced by Simmel's *Lebensphilosophie*, which stressed the "lived moment" and the impossibility of knowing the immediate. More important, Simmel was one of those remarkable intellectuals who believed that a philosopher must be concerned with everyday occurrences and small events. He had a broad range of interests and expounded on everthing he encountered. He was a man after Bloch's own heart, and he left a lasting impression even after Bloch broke with him over Simmel's defense of German patriotism.

The period between 1909 and 1914 was a time of major changes in Bloch's life. Like other young Jewish intellectuals such as Martin Buber, Walter Benjamin, Siegfried Landauer, Kurt Hiller, Salmo Friedländer, and Theodor Lessing, Bloch took a strong interest in the question of Jewish identity and Zionism, and he reflected on these issues in an essay entitled "Symbol: Die Juden" (1912/13).[3] As Anson Rabinbach points out,

Bloch's and Benjamin's confrontation with Buber and with Zionism affirmed a different Jewish idea that was both secular and theological—and which represents an intellectualist rejection of the existing order of things. The messianic idea, though more pronounced in Bloch's early writings than in Benjamin's . . . still comes through in their common emphasis on the limits of rationalism, the need to transcend ordinary modes of perception and experience through utopia and the restorative nature of the "language-work" of the intellectuals.... The purpose of philosophy or criticism is not merely to point to the failure of rationalism to grasp the totality—it is to reveal through language the missing dimension of cultural experience, to restore the ellipse of reason.[4]

Bloch also began studying Christian mysticism at this time in deference to the religious convictions of Else von Stritzky, a gifted sculptress from Riga whom he married in 1913. It was also in 1913 that Bloch moved to Heidelberg, where he participated in Max Weber's seminar. It was not so much Weber who drew Bloch to Heidelberg as it was Georg Lukács, with whom he shared a concern with developing a philosophy that would transcend the rationalism of the Enlightenment and provide more intuitive means for understanding experience and dealing with such problems as alienation. In Heidelberg there was also a group of pacifist intellectuals, including Karl Jaspers and Gustav Radbruch, who were to stimulate Bloch's political thinking. Most important for Bloch at this time was his work on what he called the *noch-nicht-bewusst* (the not-yet-conscious) and the *noch-nicht-geworden* (the not-yet-become). Here he began to connect messianic ideas with the study of everyday phenomena, art, literature as a means of criticizing existing social conditions.

It is not by chance that some of Bloch's most radical philosophical categories were conceived near the outbreak of World War I, which compelled him to link questions of individual awareness and cognition with the need to transform, if not revolutionize, sociopolitical conditions. Given his opposition to the war, Bloch found few opportunities to earn a living or make his ideas known. In 1917 he emigrated to Switzerland with his wife, who was suffering from an ailment that would take her life in 1921. In Bern, Bloch undertook a study of utopian currents and political strategies for the journal *Archiv für Sozialwissenschaft und Sozialpolitik*. He had also hoped to earn money as a political journalist, but the possibilities were more limited than he had expected. He and his wife lived as they could on a small subvention from a wealthy businessman.

Bloch's contact with Hugo Ball at this time reinforced his own position of religious anarchism and led him to explore the ideas of Franz von Baader and Thomas Münzer. In addition, he wrote numerous articles against the war and German militarism (often under pseudonyms) while also conceiving his first major philosophical publication, *Geist der Utopie* (*Spirit of Utopia*). Poor living conditions often caused Bloch to act in desperate ways, and this book became his concrete means of countering harsh social and personal realities.

*Geist der Utopie* was published in 1918 and then revised and expanded in 1923. The book marked out the path Bloch was to pursue during the 1920s. It was an expressionist effusion that rejoiced in the apocalyptic ending of Wilhelminian rule and the breakdown of the alienating conditions that had existed in Germany. According to Bloch, this apocalypse might allow a "warm" messianic redemption, one that depended on communal action:

Life is going on all around us and does not know where it is going. We ourselves are still the lever and motor. The external and especially the revealed sense of life is faltering. But the new ideas have finally broken out, into the full adventures, into the open, unfinished, dreaming world, into Satan's rubbles and darknesses, providing the cutting off itself. Life also goes around girded with despair, with our spiteful presentiment, with the tremendous power of our human voice, to name God and not to rest until the innermost shadows are expelled, until the world is doused with that fire that is behind the world or shall be ignited by it.[5]

This passage is typical of the elliptical, metaphorical, and prophetic style that Bloch was to use for the rest of his life. It was his way of cultivating the "form of the inconstruable question" that would need art and literature to illuminate the way toward utopia. At the same time, as indicated by the last chapter of the book entitled *Karl Marx, Death, and the Apocalypse*, Bloch was turning more and more toward Marxism to provide the framework in which he would pose questions about ontology, aesthetics, and utopia.

In fact, despite his mystical and expressionist leanings, Bloch became a hardline communist during the 1920s. His attempt to blend religious mysticism and communism can be seen most clearly in his study *Thomas Münzer als Theologe der Revolution* (*Thomas Münzer as Theologian of Revolution*, 1921), in which he depicted Münzer as a forerunner of Marxism by interpreting the chiliastic aspects of Münzer's thinking in terms of the Marxist notion of a classless society. This unorthodox interpretation opened new approaches to both religion and Marxism. All of Bloch's writings from 1919 to 1933, even the numerous articles he wrote for newspapers and journals, were now focused on an elaboration of Marxist principles that was disturbing to most orthodox Marxists, particularly Bloch's friend Lukács, whose thinking at the time was expressed in his *History and Class Consciousness* (1923).

The period from 1921 to 1933 was a trying one for Bloch, both personally and professionally. After the death of his wife, he went through a long period of depression. A desperate and unhappy marriage to Linda Oppenheimer in 1922 lasted less than a year. He also worried that his work had had an impact only on a small group of intellectuals, which included Walter Benjamin, Theodor Adorno, Gerschom Scholem, and Siegfried Kracauer. He wanted a wider audience because he was supremely confident in the importance of his philosophical revision of Freud and Marx. To his acquaintances he sometimes seemed arrogant and pretentious, though they always expressed admiration for his "genius."

Like Walter Benjamin, Bloch was curious about seemingly incidental events and cultural artefacts, and he studied them with an uncanny understanding and appreciation of their significance. His reverence for the small as well as the great drew him to Bertolt Brecht, whom he met in Berlin, and he became one of Brecht's avid champions and interpreters.

During the 1920s Bloch sought to learn from politically active expressionist writers and painters, and he adopted the montage technique and elliptical symbolism in his own writings to induce estrangement from the familiar. He wanted to provoke his readers to break away from whatever prevented them from becoming conscious of what they were missing, of things they would have to define for themselves. Bloch's techniques were similar to Brecht's, and in this sense Brecht's plays were models of anticipatory illumination.

During the 1920s it seemed as though Bloch was trying to act out his philosophy of distancing and estrangement: He kept breaking out of Berlin, traveling between 1924 and 1926 to Italy, France, and North Africa. He even lived for a while in Paris, but he kept returning to Berlin, the city that had become the center of cultural experimentation in Europe and that kept challenging him to expand his philosophical and political ideas. On one of his forays he met Karola Piotrkrowska, an art and architecture student, and this attachment seemed to give his work a new vitality.

In 1930 Bloch and Karola took an apartment in a "red district" in Berlin, where numerous writers and artists of various left-wing persuasions lived and mixed. Both took an increasing interest in practical politics, especially as the danger of fascism grew and daily life became more violent. Karola drew closer to the Communist party, which she joined in 1932, while Bloch continued to maintain a critical distance from the party. Indeed, Bloch felt that one reason why the fascists were able to gain control in Germany was that the communists spent more time attacking the social democrats and spreading meaningless, rhetorical progaganda than addressing the needs, dreams, and wants of the German people. He wrote numerous insightful articles on mainstream politics and culture, often criticizing the inadequacy of bourgeois art and literature and the dangers of Nazi ideology and practice while at the same time trying to analyze why it was that the National Socialism had captured the imagination of the people.

On March 5, 1933, when the Nazis legally took power in Germany, Bloch was in Ludwigshafen. He received a phone call from Karola telling him that his name was on a list of enemies and that he was scheduled to be arrested. The next day Bloch fled to Switzerland, where Karola soon joined him. In Zurich they were active in resistance groups, but this was frowned upon by the Swiss authorities, who expelled them in 1934. Just before the expulsion, Bloch completed *Erbschaft dieser Zeit*, a penetrating study of fascism in which he elaborated the categories of synchronism and nonsynchronism to explain the attractions of fascist movements. Bloch emphasized the failure of left movements to recognize the huge gaps that modern technology and industrial change had created in people's lives. He maintained that "progress" brought about disorientation, especially for the agrarian and petit-bourgeois classes, and that the longing for bygone days, for the old ways of life, for solid traditions, was a direct result of this disorientation and not simply reactionary. He called for creative and inventive communist programs that confronted modernism in all its forms, so that the masses would not feel left out or left behind. Since the Communist party and other left organizations relied on empty slogans and called for paternalistic programs that failed to speak to basic human needs, it was no wonder that people turned to National Socialism with its mythic ideology and concrete welfare programs. Bloch sought to expose the regressive policies of the Nazis while keeping alive the genuinely revolutionary impulse for change in socialism. He insisted that the communists and socialists could only combat fascism if they recognized the different types of contradictions they had to resolve:

Thus, it is our task to extend the agitated Now. First, one must distinguish the falsely from the genuinely nonsynchronous contradiction, the latter from the synchronous contradiction, and then, in both of them, the objective and the subjective factors of the contradiction. *The subjectively nonsynchronous contradiction is pent-up anger, the objectively nonsynchronous one is unsettled past; the subjectively synchronous one is the proletariat's free revolutionary act, the objectively synchronous contradiction is the impeded future contained in the Now, the impeded technological benefaction, the impeded new society, with which the old one is pregnant in its productive forces.* The basic factor in the objectively synchronous contradiction is the conflict between the collective character of the productive forces developed within capitalism and the private character of their antipathy.... It is our task now to locate within contradiction a possible force even when it does not go beyond the nonsynchronous rift. The latter remains favorable to the Now of capitalism only as long as the nonsynchronous people lack the leadership or even the magic spell spurring them to march into the present-day battlefield. The task is to extrapolate the elements of the nonsynchronous contradiction that are capable of antipathy and transformation, that is, those hostile to capitalism and homeless in it, and to refit them to function in a different context. Consequently, what remains is the "triple alliance" between the proletariat and the immiserated peasants and the immiserated middle class, under proletarian hegemony.[6]

As we can see from these remarks, Bloch advocated a common front between communists and socialists even before the *Volksfront* became the official policy of the Communist party. One can also see a tendency here to hypostatize the proletariat in a way that would eventually lead Bloch to support Stalinist politics. But at the same time there was a politics of signs that emanated from Bloch's book *Spuren* (1930) and contradicted his other political observations. Crucial in *Spuren*, an unusal collection of anecdotes, stories, political commentaries, and essays, is the designation and detection of traces in everyday events and cultural artefacts of the past and present that are harbingers of a better future. Bloch pursued these traces, but he became caught up in his own contradictions because of his eagerness to identify with the *potential* of revolutionary change that was symbolized, he thought, by the Soviet Union.

During the years 1934–1988 Bloch married Karola and they both worked for the popular front—Bloch as unorthodox critic and Karola as courier for the Communist party. In 1935 they moved to Paris, after stops in Switzerland and Austria, in time for Bloch to participate in the International Congress for the Defense of Culture. There he gave a speech on "Literature and Socialist Objects" in which he introduced his notion of *Vor-Schein*, or anticipatory illumination, and spoke against the pessimism of those writers who doubted that Marxism could combat the expansion of fascism. According to Bloch, "truth is not the reflection of facts but of processes; it is ultimately the indication of the tendency and latency of that which has not yet become and needs its activator."[7] Literature and art contain the anticipatory illumination of that which has not yet become, and the role of the writer and artist is similar to that of a midwife who enables latent and potential materials to assume their own unique forms. At this point in his life, Bloch was committed both philosophically and aesthetically to Marxism as the *only* critique that could clarify what was missing in life, what obstacles had to be overcome before a classless society could come into its own, and what direction *we* had to take, for the realization of individual autonomy was only possible if the "we" came into its own as the collective agent of its own destiny.

In Paris, Bloch began a book on materialism, wrote numerous philosophical and cultural essays, and did what he could to support the antifascist resistance. His stance toward the Soviet Union at this time was complex and contradictory. On the one hand, he became the chief opponent of orthodox cultural politics through his debate with Georg Lukács about the artistic merits of expressionist art.[8] On the other hand, while he knew that conditions in the Soviet Union had worsened since the late 1920s, and while he had never been a proponent of state socialism, he felt obliged to portray the Soviet Union in a positive manner in light of the fascist threat. For Bloch, the Soviet Union had gradually become a symbolic beacon pointing toward socialism and a classless society, and as long as that beacon shed light, no matter how dim, he argued that it was the duty of committed socialists to keep it going in every possible way. As a result, he defended the Moscow Show Trials (1936/37) and refused to distinguish the cause of socialism from that of Stalinism. This position was untenable, as Bloch was to learn through bitter experience.

Given his attacks on the cultural politics of the Soviet Union during the 1930s and his generally unorthodox Marxist position, Bloch's defense of Stalin seems astonishing. Moreover, he never evinced any desire to seek "refuge" in the Soviet Union. In 1937, when the Blochs moved to Prague because Karola had been given a new assignment, they kept hearing gruesome stories from friends who had escaped from persecution in the Soviet Union. Bloch was relieved when the trials came to an end in 1937, but he still rationalized them as a drastic measure to prevent the rise of fascism in the East. He was realistic enough, though, to perceive that the Soviet Union would not harbor an unorthodox Marxist of his kind, and when it came time to think of leaving Prague—Karola gave birth to their son Jan in 1937 and the fascists were about to invade Czechoslovakia—the Blochs chose the United States as their refuge.

The Blochs spent eleven years in the United States, 1938–1949, the first three in New York and New Hampshire and the last eight in Cambridge, Massachusetts, where Bloch worked in Harvard's Widener Library on *The Principle of Hope* and *Subjekt-Objekt*. It was practically impossible for Bloch himself to earn money. He was shunned by members of the Frankfurt School, particularly by Max Horkheimer, because of his defense of the Soviet Union, and his former friends refused to help him obtain teaching or publishing jobs. Karola became the breadwinner of the family, working first as a domestic and then in a Boston architect's office. Meanwhile Bloch wrote political articles for the journal *Freies Deutschland* and became a member of the National Committee for a Free Germany. His major preoccupation, however, was the further elaboration of his primary categories of the not-yet-conscious and not-yet-become in relation to hope, utopia, and wishful thinking. Since Bloch's English remained limited, and since there was virtually no audience for his works, Bloch felt isolated most of the time and longed for a situation in which his philosophical teachings might have some effect.

By 1945 both Karola and Bloch had obtained American citizenship. However, many of their close friends were already under surveillance by the FBI and had been called before the House Committee on Un-American Activities. Brecht, Hanns Eisler, and Alfred Kantorowicz, among others, had already returned to the Soviet Zone of Germany. In 1948 Bloch, who was 63 years old and had never lectured at a university, received an offer to assume the chair of philosophy at the University of Leipzig. Knowing that he might face attacks from the orthodox communists, Bloch insisted on absolute freedom to teach what he wanted. He received such a guarantee from Werner Krauss, a leading Marxist scholar and Bloch's chief supporter in Leipzig, and the Blochs moved to East Germany in 1949.

Now, for the first time in his life, Bloch was able to have a direct impact on students and to play a role in the development of a university. Leipzig at that time possessed some of the finest Marxist scholars in East Germany. Aside from Krauss, whose specialty was French literature, Hans Mayer taught German literature and Fritz Behrens economics, while Georg Meyer had assumed the post of rector. From the outset Bloch was perceived by the students as playing an oppositional role to the official politics of the state and the SED (Sozialistische Einheitspartei Deutschland), the new communist party of the German Democratic Republic. His lectures, books, and essays contained indirect criticisms of Stalinism insofar as it represented a mechanical base-superstructure position and disregarded the vital role that culture played in the formation of social relations. Moreover, Bloch always stressed the dialectics of individual and social freedom and placed great emphasis on creative experimentation and the *unfinished* nature of the socialist project. On the other hand, Bloch continued to defend the Soviet Union and Stalinism as real, existing socialist formations that set the material conditions for the qualitative development of communism. Without carefully studying the political history of either the United States or the Soviet Union, Bloch continued to make hardline materialist pronouncements about both countries. Through 1953, Bloch associated the United States with fascism and imperialism and called it a threat to world freedom, whereas the Soviet Union was the guarantor of genuine freedom throughout the world. He rationalized the police measures and restrictions in the Soviet Union and in East Germany just as he had the Show Trials. He believed that if only the Soviet Union were not theatened by the imperialist tactics of western capitalism, it would be able to get on with the socialist experiment and allow greater civil liberties.

Bloch was convinced that the American invention and use of the atomic bomb, the communist witchhunts, the onset of the Cold War, and the Korean War indicated that the western nations were out to sabotage the communist cause. Therefore, Bloch publicly showed solidarity with the communists, while in intimate circles—and sometimes within the university—he was outspoken in his criticism of Stalinism and pushed for reforms wherever he could.

Aside from schooling numerous students in dialectical Marxism and utopian thinking, students who went on to assume important roles in the party and state leadership, Bloch helped found the journal

*Deutsche Zeitschrift für Philosophie* with the help of his old friend Georg Lukács, and one of his prize pupils, Walter Harich, became editor-in-chief. In addition, his major works began to be published. *The Principle of Hope* (whose three volumes appeared in 1952, 1954, and 1959) established Bloch as the foremost unorthodox Marxist philosopher in perhaps the most Stalinist of the Eastern Bloc countries. In this enormous work Bloch mapped out the formations of the not-yet-conscious as they take shape in daydreams, wish-landscapes, and religious, scientific, political, and artistic events of signification. The signification can be traced in the anticipatory illumination and is determined by the manner in which it gives rise to hope within the cultural heritage. The centrality of art and literature in Bloch's chiliastic Marxism, that is, the emphasis he placed on the possibility of the transformation of the material base through superstructural developments, is apparent throughout the three volumes.

*The Principle of Hope* contains crude criticisms of "fascist America" and bombastic statements about the proletariat, communism, and the Soviet Union. Yet the overall thrust of Bloch's utopian project was and is subversive in view of developments in *both* the United States and the Soviet Union. Despite its inconsistencies and ramblings, *The Principle of Hope* is important because it focuses our attention on concrete moments in history that point the way toward an actual transformation of the material world. The luminous aesthetic quality of these concrete moments, even though they are fragmentary, allows them to be utilized and reutilized for realizing what has not yet become but can become, namely the classless society. Insofar as the aesthetic formations illuminate what is missing and might still come, they instill hope in viewers or readers and provide the impetus for individual and collective change.

Bloch felt himself caught in the contradictions of his positions the more he came into contact with the reality of GDR socialism. By 1955 he had received numerous awards from the government and felt more confident about openly criticizing the state, its rigid form of teaching, and the limitations it imposed on individual freedom and human rights. In 1956, after Khrushchev had launched the criticism of Stalinism, Bloch thought that the hour for major democratic reforms had finally come. However, he did not believe that the mistakes that had been made in the East Bloc were caused solely by cults of personality. He saw them as stemming from the dogmatic tendencies of the party and the rigid bureaucratic system.

Bloch tried through discussions and articles to foster changes in the university and government, but he had overestimated the extent of Kruschchev's break with Stalinism and did not perceive how the new Soviet policy would be used to legitimize the interests of the new oligarchies within the Soviet Union and reinforce the power of Walter Ulbricht in East Germany. Thus, as Bloch began to speak out more openly for reforms, the German Democratic state and party leadership, which had tolerated him as long as he had served their propagandistic purposes and kept his voice low, came to view Bloch as an enemy who had to be isolated.

The SED seized its opportunity in 1956. Under the leadership of Walter Harich, a group of intellectuals in Berlin had begun planning a coup. Bloch knew about these plans but refused to join in. The government discovered the plot and sentenced Harich and several other collaborators to prison terms. Bloch himself now came under attack in the newspapers and magazines. In January 1957 he was forcibly prevented from continuing a series of lectures at the university, and throughout the year public conferences denounced the errors and faults of his philosophy while articles attacked his notions of Marxism. Finally Bloch was forced to retire and was banned from holding public talks. His present and former students were obliged to break with him or recant his teachings. Some fled to West Germany; some lost their jobs; one committed suicide; and some protected their careers by turning against him.

Though Bloch endeavored to remain active by participating in meetings of the section of philosophy at the Academy of Sciences in East Berlin, he was for all intents and purposes silenced and isolated by 1958. Thereafter, aside from privately trying to help some of his students, Bloch concentrated his energies on publishing and lecturing in West Germany. Though he could have remained in the West, Bloch did not want to give up the struggle for civil rights and socialism in East Germany, nor did he want to abandon the friends who had sided with him. However, during the summer of 1961, while the Blochs were vacationing in Munich after Bloch had lectured at Tübingen and Bayreuth, they learned about the building of the Berlin Wall, and they decided not to go back.

This decision caused a great sensation in the German newspapers.

In the East, Bloch was attacked as a traitor, while in the West he was generally mocked for having had "hope" in communism and scorned for his defense of Stalin and the Soviet Union. Due to his outspoken criticisms of West German society, Bloch was considered by many to be an unwelcome guest in the Federal Republic, and it was only with great difficulty that his supporters obtained a special position for him as professor of philosophy at the University of Tübingen.

On November 17, 1961, Bloch gave his inaugural lecture to a packed audience at the university, significantly entitled "Can Hope Be Disappointed?" Bloch's reply to his own rhetorical and politically provocative question: Even a well-founded hope can be disappointed; otherwise it would not be hope. In fact, hope never guarantees anything. It can only be daring and must point to possibilities that will in part depend on chance for their fulfillment. Thus, hope can be frustrated and thwarted, but out of that frustration and disappointment it can learn to estimate the tendencies of countervailing processes. Hope can learn through damaging experiences, but it can never be driven off course. The substance of its goal is "real humanism," [9] and since this goal is not present, one can neither speak about it out of experience nor formulate it completely. To do so would be pure invention, not definition. Still, it is possible to determine the direction toward real humanism, a direction that is invariable and unconditional; it is "indicated precisely in the oldest conscious dream (*Wachtraum*) of humankind: in the overthrow (instead of the hypocritical new installation) of all conditions in which the human individual is a humiliated, enslaved, forsaken, despised creature." [10] Bloch also stressed that "even when the contents of this 'true being' as one that is still in the form of latency are not already manifest and articulated, they are still sufficient to determine what is *not* humanism and also to determine its exact opposite, namely Hitler or the later Stalin, in other words to determine altogether what the primordial phenomenon of Nero is." [11] In conclusion, Bloch maintained that "the world process has not yet been won anywhere, but it has not been thwarted anywhere, and human beings can be on earth the indicators of their decisive way toward salvation that has not yet come or toward damnation that has also not yet come. The world remains in its entirety the same highly laboring laboratory *possibilis salutis*. . . . Hercules says: 'Whoever does not hope for the unhoped-for will not find it." [12]

From 1961 until his death in 1977 at the age of 92, Bloch wrote, spoke, and fought unceasingly in the name of a hope that could be disappointed and could err but could never be eradicated as long human beings live on this earth. Hope had always been for Bloch a religious, ontological, and political matter, and it continued to be such more than ever in West Germany, where he became a symbol of integrity for the protest movements that emerged during the 1960s. While lecturing throughout Europe, Bloch again became involved in political struggles. He supported the Social Democratic party in West Germany, attacked the right-wing Springer Press monopoly, criticized the introduction of professional proscription of civil servants in West Germany, and took positions against nuclear armament, German anti-Semitism, the Vietnam War, the Soviet invasion of Prague, and the terrorism of the Baader-Meinhof Group. Though he was critical of Israeli militarism, he also defended the right of Israel to exist in a 1967 public statement and refused to have anything to do with the anti-Zionist forces in West Germany. His political position became more discriminating and clearer, and the centrality of aesthetics in his political philosophy was often reiterated, as in the following statment from a 1968 interview with Michael Landmann:

Aesthetics should not be confused with contemplation or considered disinterested. Often, certainly, the true, the good, or the beautiful, or rather what is proclaimed as such, has nothing to do with daily life and so serves the purpose of deception, as an opiate of the people. . . . Stage and story can be either a protective park or a laboratory; sometimes they console or appease, sometimes they incite; they can be a flight from or a prefiguring of the future. The stage is not just illusion; it can also be an anticipation of what is to come, for in it the resistance of the empirical world is eliminated. Brecht made the stage a laboratory for new models. On the problem of whether a man can be sacrificed to the group, he first writes a "Yes-sayer" then a "No-sayer" and he could have added a "Maybe-sayer." Art retains its anticipatory function even after the revolution. The image of Greek man, the citizen, was first delineated in art. Likewise, architecture first creates real space against the obstacles with which the earth is full. Were the inflammatory elements of art eliminated in the classless society, that would be proof that reality had remained a petit-bourgeois society in which art becomes a palliative ideology instead of a clarion call. True art, including nonrevolutionary art, is always a clarion call and a challenge.[13]

Although he was half blind during the last ten years of his life, Bloch continued to hold his seminar for students of philosophy and managed to finish the revisions for the 17-volume edition of his complete works.

In his *Politische Messungen*[14] he altered some of his older essays to make them more critical of Stalinism; he justified this by arguing that his works were part of a process of change and reflection and that his entire philosophical project would always remain unfinished in the same way that the human project on earth would remain unfinished. Bloch continually tried to learn from his errors and contradictions and reworked his former views if proven wrong by historical developments. In doing this, he clung to a personal ethics of the *aufrechter Gang*, the upright gait. According to Bloch, humankind had not yet learned to take full possession of its natural rights and to walk upright with dignity. Humans still had to learn to become like God and take destiny in their own hands, that is, to make history for the first time. What is envisioned as home (*Heimat*) in childhood is in actuality the goal of the upright gait toward which human beings strive as they seek to overcome exploitation, humiliation, oppression, and disillusionment. The individual alone cannot attain such a goal, which is only possible as a collective enterprise. Yet the measure of the individual's ethical backbone can be determined by his or her struggle to stand and walk upright and contribute to the collective goal. The relative historical gains, revolutionary transformations and formations, what Bloch called "concrete utopias," were stepping stones and indications of what the human individual and the world could become. In this regard, Bloch's contradictions until his death in 1977 should be regarded as unique individual traces in a struggle to realize philosophy as part of a collective praxis.

## II

From the outset, Bloch saw his task as part of an ongoing endeavor to name the unnameable final destination, to construe the unconstruable question about the meaning of human existence. In his essay "Poesie im Hohlraum" (1931), he phrased it succinctly:

The entire being of the world (*Weltsein*) is a questioning of its meaning and looks with a thousand eyes, in a thousand ways of predisposed mediation, at the speakers for more thorough information, at the searchers for the key to disclosure. Whereby it cannot easily have that interior so defined or have materials in the empty space of the present alienation, materials in which it could feel well or with which it could already come out of the twilight every place where the revolutionary struggle against alienation is concerned.[15]

Conscious that his task, which was intrinsically tied to that of the *Weltsein*, would remain unfulfilled during his lifetime, Bloch elaborated principles to explain why it must remain unfulfilled, and he cultivated a language commensurate with his task. The formation of this language was closely connected to the substance of his thought and his personal development. Form implied human intention for Bloch. That is, embedded in form was human creative activity that sought to make its mark and march toward a better world. The experience of World War I, the collapse of the monarchy, and the October Revolution in Russia served to reinforce his belief that bourgeois philosophy, art, and literature could no longer express the questions and problems necessary for pushing forward the socialist experiment. But by no means was the bourgeois heritage to be dismissed. Rather it was to be reutilized (*umfunktioniert*) in a manner that would allow its utopian undercurrents to be realized. Only through the reorientation, revitalization, and reutilization of language, and only through experimentation with what had already been designed to fill humankind's deeply felt lack could the socioeconomic crisis of ossification, staleness, and degeneration be overcome. Bourgeois capitalism itself had created what Bloch called the *Hohlraum*, the empty space, the hollow gap, and it was imperative that progressive intellectuals, artists, and politicians fill the void with substantially new forms and content.

Bloch believed that the relativistic thinking elaborated in the work of Ernst Mach and other leading physicists would provide some sparks for revolutionary political action as well as the radical advancement of technology and the natural sciences. It also generated a teleological possibility for concretizing the impulses of these momentous changes in the direction of a world free of oppression. In *Erbschaft dieser Zeit*, Bloch argued that

the real fruit of "relativism" is montage, not objectivity (*Sachlichkeit*), for it *improvises* with the context that has been exploded. Out of those (exploded) elements that have become pure and are made into rigid facades by objectivity, montage creates variable temptations and attempts in the empty space. This empty space originated precisely because of the collapse of bourgeois culture. Not only does the rationalization of a different society play in it, but one can see a new formation of figures arising out of the particles of the cultural heritage that have become chaotic.[16]

In effect, montage is what replaces the empty space:

The montage of the fragment out of the old existence is here the experiment of its reutilization (*Umfunktionierung*) into a new one. Mechanistic, dramaturgical, or even philosophical montage is certainly not completed by a more or less quick reutilization, that is, with the use of short and disposable models.... Montage in the late bourgeois period is the empty space of the bourgeois world, filled with sparks and overlaps of a "history of appearance" that is not the right one; yet in this instance it is a mixed place of the right one. Also it is a form to ascertain the old culture: viewed from the journey and perplexity, no longer from education.[17]

Bloch's own philosophical language combines the language of expressionism with a reformulation of traditional systematic European thought, primarily German idealism, one of the reasons why Jürgen Habermas called Bloch a "Marxist Schelling."[18] Moreover, he elaborated and expanded Marxist categories with notions of Messianism, Christian mysticism, and the Judaic commandment against creating graven images. Thus Bloch employed images, comparisons, implications, connotations, provocations, aphorisms, fables, and anecdotes to form and reform philosophical categories. Like other expressionist artists and writers, Bloch wanted to "shock" his readers into an awareness of their own inner needs so that they would break out of themselves and break down those reified conditions that prevent communication and collective action. Bloch's metaphorical use of montage techniques included a conscious juxtaposition of crude expressions with chiliastic images and euphoric pronouncements. Though his use of such technique, was at times naive, he purposely relied on them to break with the instrumental manipulation typical of traditional philosophy and of Marxism as well. Bloch wanted to estrange both himself and his readers; distance had to be gained from the immediate experience of life and from those customary forms that locked life into blocks of classifications and categories. Like his thought processes, Bloch's language never stood still. He constantly played with images and categories to refine them and to endow them with the very anticipatory illumination he endeavored to trace and analyze in works of art and everyday cultural phenomena.

Though it is often difficult to read Bloch, it is a challenging and tantalizing experience that can open up new horizons of thought. He forces his readers to rethink the purpose of philosophical language and thought. More than anything else, Bloch placed great faith in art and literature to raise the not-yet-conscious to a point where it could grasp the direction humankind would have to take to bring about the fulfillment of those needs, wants, and wishes that he saw scattered in dreams and daydreams. As already noted, Bloch never developed an aesthetic theory, for he was convinced that aesthetics along with ethics and politics should not be separated from fundamental philosophy but actually formed the inner core of all philosophical thought. Thus, at a time when aesthetic questions are treated either in a rigorous scientific manner or in a manner that eliminates the subject and intentionality from all consideration, Bloch's writings on art and literature may appear quaint. Yet his anthropocentric approach to art and literature and his emphasis on the utopian function of art and literature lead to a useful substantive questioning of those "poststructural" and "postmodern" positions that so often become bogged down in their own discourses. As Gérard Raulet has pointed out,

the self-stabilization of the system is certainly not the ideal of postmodernism. However, it is satisfied with substantiating the impossibility of overcoming alternatives. . . . Through the historical and relativistic citing of all possible fragments from the past in postmodern architecture or through Lyotard's "atomization of the social in the supple system of language games," the specific is not saved at all but surrendered to total reification despite all the ostensible richness of experience. The appropriate answer to this paradox is its reversal—the saving of the specific requires that one take into consideration its dependence and constraints in order to grasp it as something that has already always been mediated. Benjamin's *Denkbild* (image of thought), Adorno's *Konstellation* (constellation), and Bloch's *Auszugsgestalt* (processual figure) all have this as their goal.[19]

Indeed, Bloch's philosophical aesthetics is an antidote to that pessimism and helplessness often expressed by the intelligentsia in both the West and East, where the creator as the subject of art and literature apparently no longer counts. Bloch returns our gaze to the tensions and mediations between the intender, tendency, and intention in the reception and use of works of art. Important here is the fact that both author and receiver are intenders who come together through the work of art to form the substance and *Novum* of the cultural heritage.

Bloch's unorthodox Marxism consisted in his making the human being the center of all things, and he placed his hope in the potential of human beings to mold and shape themselves into "godlike" creatures. This entelechical development could only occur through a dialectical relationship with nature, whereby art and literature mediated the relationship of human beings to one another and to the material world around them. To grasp how Bloch conceived the function of art and literature impelling human beings to move forward in the direction of utopia, it is important to consider Bloch's basic philosophical categories, which are often intended to startle us in a mysterious and mystical sense. Bloch liked to generate a sense of *Staunen* in his readers. In German, *Staunen* implies not only startlement but astonishment, wonder, and staring, and the formation of his philosophical categories compels us to pause and reconsider what we think, where we are, and what we want to look for. Most of all, Bloch's *Staunen* as conveyed in his philosophical discussions of art and literature convey a reverence for human creation and nature in all their aspects.

## III

Under the heading "Intention," Bloch's first book, *Geist der Utopie*, begins this way:

I am. We are.
   That is enough. Now it is up to us to begin. Life is placed into our hands. It has long since become empty. It sways back and forth, but we stand firm, and thus we want to give it its first and goals.[20]

Writing in 1918, at the end of World War I, Bloch signaled that the time had come for human beings to take life into their hands and shape their destiny, but it would not be easy, as he wrote in the very next section of the book, "The Self-Encounter":

*Too Near*
I am on top of me.
   That I walk, speak, is not there. Only directly afterward can I hold it out in front of me. While we live, we do not see ourselves in it; we flow onward. So what happened in the process, what we actually were in it, will not coincide with what we can experience. It is not that which one is and certainly not what one means.[21]

Despite our intention and despite the fact that we exist, we cannot realize who we are and what we mean until we penetrate the "darkness of the immediately experienced moment." To illuminate this darkness, Bloch introduced the philosophical category of the not-yet-conscious as a supplement to Freud's unconscious. "Since we, however, have never yet seen ourselves, we cannot recall things about us. What was never conscious cannot become unconscious. Neither our

'wanting' as 'such' nor the entire remaining darkness of the immediately experienced moment is a given. We live ourselves, but we do
not experience ourselves, and it is thus clear that we possess ourselves
on top of ourselves neither in the ostensible present nor above all in
any section of the memory." [22] This being the case, Bloch argued that
humans have a type of consciousness, formed by the impulse of hope,
in which inklings of what they might become manifest themselves.
For the individual, the not-yet-conscious is the psychical representation of what has not-yet-become in our time and its world. Signs of the
not-yet-conscious are found primarily in daydreams, where individuals have presentiments of what they lack, what they need, what they
want, and what they hope to find. Unlike dreams, which house
repressed and forgotten desires and experiences, daydreams can be
productive for the formation of individuals and the world since they
occur in semiconsciousness and point to real, objective possibilities. It
is by moving away from the darkness of the immediately experienced
moment and toward the intimations of a better world sighted in the
not-yet-conscious that the darkness will become clarified and we shall
know what we experience. Important here is Bloch's notion of the
presentiment (*Ahnung*) that arises in the not-yet-conscious.

This presentiment is also in its usual appearence the meaning for that which
paves the way ahead. If the presentiment is productive, it will connect itself
with the imagination, particularly with the imagination of that which is
objectively possible. The presentiment that is capable of working is intellectual productivity, now regarded as *work-forming* (*werkbildend*). Productivity
sets itself into what is next to it as a triple extension triply growing into that
which has not come: as incubation, as so-called inspiration, as explication.
All three belong to the capacity to go beyond the former borders of consciousness and to move forward. [23]

It is at this point that art and literature assume their utopian
function, for they are the means through which human beings form
themselves, conceive their questions about themselves, and portray
the possibility of attaining their objectives. Daydreams by themselves
remain unproductive. They can only provide the impetus to move out
of oneself to come into oneself if they are shaped into images that deny
ideology's hold over humankind. In this regard, all art and literature that have anything to say to humankind are utopian. As Gert
Ueding, one of Bloch's foremost interpreters, has argued:

Literature is utopia in the very wide sense of course that it is not identical
with the reality that faces us as nature and society. It is utopia in the very

precise sense that its connection to this reality is like that of fulfillment to lack.... Literature as utopia is generally encroachment of the power of the imagination on new realities of experience. It means discovering with lots of plans and rich imagination and activating the productive capacity of the human individual in the aesthetic image and critical rejection of an inhibiting reality. In addition, its temporal point of reference is the future. However, it does not withdraw from the reality principle merely to place an ethereal and empty realm of freedom in place of the oppressive realm of necessity. Rather it does this intentionally to test human possibilities, to conserve human demands for happiness and playfully to anticipate what in reality has not at all been produced but what dreams and religious or profane wish-images of humans are full of. On this definition, literary activity becomes a special form of dream work.[24]

Obviously not all of literature and art is utopian. The utopian quality of a work of art is determined by its *Vor-Schein* or anticipatory illumination. The anticipatory illumination is an image, a constellation, a configuration closely tied to the concrete utopias that are lit up on the frontal margins of reality and illuminate the possibilities for rearranging social and political relations so that they engender *Heimat*, Bloch's word for the home that we have all sensed but have never experienced or known. It is *Heimat* as utopia—and here Bloch specifically reutilizes a Nazi term—that determines the truth-content of a work of art, and it is through the anticipatory illumination of the work of art that we are able to gain a sense of truth in reality. Bloch argued that

the question as to the truth of art becomes philosophically the question as to the possibly available depictability of beautiful illusion, as to its degree of reality in the by no means single-layered reality of the world, as to the location of its object-correlate. Utopia as object-determination, with the degree of existence of the real possible, thus encounters in the shimmering phenomenon of art a particularly fruitful problem of probation. And the answer to the aesthetic question of truth is: Artistic illusion is not only mere illusion, but a meaning that is cloaked in images and can only be described in images, of material that has been driven further, wherever *the exaggeration and narrative stucturing depict a significant anticipatory illumination, circulating in turbulent existence itself, of what is real*, an anticipatory illumination that can specifically be depicted in aesthetically immanent terms. What habitual or unblunted sense can hardly still see is illuminated here, in individual processes as well as social and natural ones. This anticipatory illumination becomes attainable precisely because art drives its material to an end, in characters, situations, plots, landscapes, and brings them to a stated resolution in suffering, happiness, and meaning. Anticipatory illumination is this attainable thing itself because the métier of *driving-to-the-end occurs in dialectically open space*, in which any object can be aesthetically depicted. Aesthetically depicted means: immanently more achieved, more thoroughly formed, more essential than in the immediate-sensory or immediate-historical occurrence of this object. This thorough formation remains illusion even as anticipatory illumination, but it does not remain illusive. Instead, everything that appears in the artistic image is sharpened or condensed to a decisiveness that the reality of experience in fact only seldom shows, but that is most definitely inherent in the subjects.[25]

Another way of defining the anticipatory illumination can be found in Ueding's introduction to the original German collection of essays about the aesthetics of *Vor-Schein*:

The not-yet-become of the object manifests itself in the work of art as one that searches for itself, shines ahead of itself in its meaning. Here anticipatory illumination is not simply objective in contrast to subjective illusion. Rather, it is the way of being, which in its turn wakes utopian consciousness and indicates to it the not-yet-become in the scale of its possibilties.[26]

Here it is important to clarify further what Bloch meant by anticipatory illumination by distinguishing it from *Schein* (illusion) and *Erscheinung* (appearance).

As he did with Freud, Bloch also sought to expand ideas taken from bourgeois philosophical idealism and reutilize them according to basic Marxist tenets and his principle of hope. In this case, Bloch converted epistemological concepts that had been primarily developed by Kant and Hegel. In the *Critique of Pure Reason*, Kant made an important distinction between appearance and illusion: Only appearance formed the object of knowledge because it was constituted in part of our forms of space and time. On the other hand, illusion emanates from reason's endeavor to go beyond the given bounds of our experience. Illusion is self-deceiving; but it has another side in that it can function as transcendental illusion, which operates as a moral postulate to regulate experience. Thus, for Kant, illusion could deceive through its intangible nature, and yet, in its transcendental metaphysical condition, it could serve as a corrective on reality and point to a way in which one might extend the bounds of experience.

It was the double nature of illusion that appealed to Hegel, who endeavored to elaborate the dialectics between illusion and appearance. In his *Encyclopedia of the Philosophical Sciences*, he demonstrated that the essence of a thing must appear. It does this through *Scheinen* or shining, and the shining determines how being assumes its form as existence. Thus, when the shining of being is fully developed, its essence appears and can be known in its phenomenological form. In other words, there is a dialectics between illusion and appearance: The essence of a being is not only illusory as it appears but is also illuminated through a shining that allows the essence of being to appear. It is through the dialectics of illusion and appearance that we can achieve knowledge of a thing, but this dialectics is historical, tied to a given moment, and bound by the totalizing concept that it engenders.

Kant provided Bloch with the basis for an ethical and political ideal in the illusion that could act as a corrective in regard to reality, while Hegel demonstrated that illusion as a process of shining was actually a historical objectification of the subject as appearance. Burghardt Schmidt summarizes succinctly how Bloch combined the Kantian and Hegelian notions of illusion and appearance in an innovative manner:

Anticipatory illumination mediates through the working, realizing subject that which is still only illusion about him with that which could become appearance. To be sure this is no longer appearance in the Kantian transcendental sense but in the materialist sense of a qualitative reality that has been requalified. Illusion is moved through anticipatory illumination to a realizable future that is reachable no matter how far away. However, it remains problematic as a more-than-this future. Anticipatory illumination is not the process of systematization according to the idea as a "subjective maxim," but rather it is subjective anticipation of something that is objectively realizable that provides the measure for the anticipation to experience its real criticism. Otherwise, anticipation would be mistaken for planification. It is only as anticipation, however, that anticipatory illumination is the fundamental category of utopian philosophizing.[27]

I have several reasons for choosing the phrase "anticipatory illumination," rather than "preappearance," to translate *Vor-Schein*.[28] First, it is clear from the discussion of Kant and Hegel that Bloch did not associate *Schein* with appearence or *vor* with the prefix "pre," which connotes something coming before its time. The *Schein* in Bloch's *Vor-Schein* must be distinguished from both appearance and illusion as a real artistic configuration that sheds light ideally on what we might anticipate to be the goal of all humankind. It has an element of enlightenment in it. In this regard, the word "illumination," which contains a sense of *shining* and enlightenment as a real manifestation of human anticipation, is to my mind preferable to the term "appearance." Moreover, "anticipatory" is clearly what Bloch had in mind when he chose the prefix *vor* to qualify the nature of the *Schein*.

In general, Bloch's anticipatory illumination compels us to focus on works of art in relation to human productive activity that is bound up with the way we define ourselves and the world. It also demands that we become detective-critics in our appeciation and evaluation of such works. It is up to us to determine what the anticipatory illumination of a work is, and in doing this we make a contribution to the cultural heritage. That is, the quality of our cultural heritage and its meaning are determined by our ability to estimate what is valuable and utopian in works of art from all periods. According to Bloch, it is decisive for a work of art to have an *Überschuss* or surplus for it to be truly utopian. Literally translated, *Überschuss* means overshot. For Bloch, the meaningful artist tries to go beyond himself or herself in projecting subjective wishes and needs, and thus the creation contains not only what the artist means but more—the surplus that continues to hold meaning for us today because of its *Vor-Schein*. Historically, the surplus of a work of art enables us to grasp the conditions and tendencies of the times during which the artist worked, for it critically formulates what was lacking and needed during its period of conception and realization. This surplus is also the objectification of shared human values and possibilities that provide us with the hope that we can realize what we sense we are missing in life. By cultivating different forms of human creation, we constitute our cultural heritage, and in this constitution we also redefine and reformulate what we hold to be the truth-content of reality and ideologies.

The shape of a work of art, according to Bloch, depends on the specific techniques used by artists to bring about an encounter with the self and with the world whereby certain truths might be gleaned through anticipatory illumination. The task of the reader/viewer as critic is to trace the formation of genres and the innovative means that artists and writers employ as part of their own journey toward self-discovery and self-realization. Criticism is essay, the endeavor to locate one's place in a historical development that must be pushed forward in light of the anticipatory illumination in the work of art. The critical reader learns through the anticipatory illumination not to accept passively what has been culturally served up as classical and standard, as necessity. The reception of the work of art is a selective and active renewal of the cultural heritage. Personal choice and taste have sociopolitical ramifications. We read, view, and listen with hope for new impulses, whether the work is old or new, whether it is given high marks by elite critics or is considered mere entertainment of the colportage kind.

Bloch was fond of the term *colportage*, which refers to the cheap materials sold by the colporteur or traveling bookseller of the seventeenth through nineteenth centuries. The colporteur carried bibles, chapbooks, cookbooks, primers, medical books, calendars, manuals, prayerbooks, romances, fairy tales, and adventure books. By the nineteenth century most of his materials catered to the dreams and wishes of lower-class readers who looked for something totally outside their ordinary routines. Though the works were of dubious ideological character—often sexist, militaristic, and sadistic[29]—Bloch refused to dismiss them as reactionary because they addressed the hunger of the imagination of people whose wants he felt must be respected.

The drive for the new is obviously conditioned by fashion and market demands, but it also represents a constant hope for something more than the market can offer, something that exceeds society's limits. Bloch used the term *Novum* in various ways to demarcate the horizon line drawn by works that open up genuinely new possibilities to move forward in the world experiment. The *Novum* as the startling and unpredictable new is always at the forefront of human experience and indicates the qualitative reutilization of the cultural heritage. It is through the *Novum* that we orient ourselves and reshape the inconstruable question about the nature of human existence in concrete ways so that we can see more clearly the direction of utopia.

Genres of art and literature result from the differing means artists use to break away from convention to form anew what they sense they cannot answer or find. Bloch revered all genres and forms and refused to establish hierarchies or canons, though he did make qualitative distinctions. Anticipatory illumination could be found in fairy tales, the circus, adventure novels, detective novels, opera, classical music, and cartoons. In particular, Bloch constantly referred to the fairy tale as the common denominator of all utopian art, and often his remarks about the fairy tale reveal how he made distinctions about the utopian or nonutopian role that genres play in fostering anticipatory illumination. For instance, in his essay "Das Riesenspielzeug als

Sage" (The Gigantic Toy as Legend), Bloch commented:

Fairy tale and legend are so close and smooth next to each other as though they did not depict a totally different time. As though they did not draw a totally different world: the *fairy tale*, illuminating the way into colportage, designates revolt; the *legend*, stemming from myth, designating tolerated fate. If there is rebellion of the small person in the fairy tale, and if it means breaking and clearing up the magic spell, before there was one, then the *legend* reports calmly about the irrevocable.[30]

Key here is whether a genre and work of art is enlightening in the sense of illuminating:

The fairy tale is just as much the first enlightenment as it, in its proximity to humankind, in its proximity to happiness, forms the model of the last enlightenment. It is for all times a childlike story of war about cunning and light against the mythical powers. It ends like a fairy tale about human happiness, like reflected being as happiness.[31]

Bloch's views of the detective story, the novel of the artist, the stage as paradigmatic institution, the horror novel, and colportage all manifest the same concern with the subjective unraveling of the question concerning the meaning of human existence as an objectified formation oriented toward exposing false illusion (often referred to as *Kitsch*) and illuminating the way toward *Heimat*. For example, the detective novel's peculiar form involves tracing clues, exposing crimes, revealing false signs, all with the purpose of bringing the truth to light. Yet truth is not the major theme of detective novels, but rather the process by which one endeavors to get at the truth:

In all other narrative forms both deeds and misdeeds develop before the omnipresent reader. Here, on the contrary, the reader is absent when the misdeed occurs, a misdeed which, though brought home in a neat package, shuns the light of day and lingers in the background of the story. It must be brought to light, and this process itself is the sole theme. The dark occurrence is not even portrayed in a prelude, for it is as yet portrayable, except through a process of reconstruction from investigation and evidence.[32]

As the philosopher of the utopian function of literature, Bloch was attracted to genres and forms that question and dissolve conventions and rigid notions of life. If the detective novel is concerned with exposing evidence of the past that can be productive for the future, then the novel of the artist, a genre that, like the detective novel, emerges with the rise of the bourgeoisie, distinguishes itself by its concern with questions of genuine art and by exposing what is new on the horizon. Implicit in all novels concerned with the development of the artist is the fact that the artist's growth is hindered by bourgeois society. The artist always strives to rewrite and break prescriptions that confine the imagination. Thus wishful thinking and hope constitute the productive imagination of the artist. It follows naturally that wish-images and wish-landscapes are formations conceived by artists to measure the distance we have yet to go to achieve happiness. The wish-landscapes seem to transcend reality yet, in fact, leave indelible marks in our consciousness and in cultural artefacts: They are the traces of utopia that constitute the cultural heritage, and the continual production and reutilization of wish-landscapes point to the ultimate realization of a promised land that has yet to find its appropriate form:

Franz Marc has said that pictures are our own surfacing in another place, and here, in the placelessness in which interior and perspective merge and permeate themselves with a dissolved other world, *a whole existence* surfaces *in the other place*; here there is nothing more than the wish-landscape of this everywhere, of this permeatedness with home. A limit of art is also reached here of course, if not ventured beyond; for religious art is none at all insofar as it is always on the point of doing away with the appearance which exists for all the senses, without whose appearance nothing can be portrayed aesthetically. Wish-landscapes of beauty, of sublimity as a whole, remain in aesthetic anticipatory illusion and as such are attempts to contemplate the world without its perishing. Such virtual perfection, the object of every iconoclasm and itself perforated in religious art: *this rises, suo genere geographically, in the wish-landscapes, placed far ahead of painting, opera, and literature.* They are often mythologically cloaked and disguised, but they never remain settled and sealed in this; for they intend human happiness, a sense of its space having been well placed and having turned out well, from the idyllic to the still mystical space. Anticipatory illumination provides this aesthetic significance of happiness at a distance, concentrated into a frame.[33]

Bloch maintained that it was up to socialist art and by implication a socialist society to see to it that "the auroral feature" of the wish-landscape takes hold in reality. Indeed, he talked about the "reddening dawn" that must be cultivated in the cultural heritage, playing upon the *red* of the dawn.[34] It is too easy to dismiss Bloch's attitude as that of a naive idealist or a crass communist. The realization of wish-landscapes will never depend upon a state but upon the struggle of human *individuals* acting together to bring about what is necessary to live without a state. Of course, for Bloch this meant communism, but like Marx before him, he refused to paint a picture of the communist society. He preferred to elaborate philosophical categories that would further the world experiment. As Ernst Fischer, one of Bloch's "comrades-in-arms," always stressed, "Art is necessary in order that man should be able to recognize and change the world. But art is also necessary by virtue of the magic inherent in it." [35]

To write, to compose, to paint. To read, to listen, to view. These are human acts of hope. Their forms are manifold. Bloch cherished these acts, no matter how small and common, and sought to trace their origins with an eye to the future. To a certain extent, his views prefigure those of Jacques Derrida in that he ignored the distinction between philosophy on one side and literature and art on the other. He did not try to treat literature and art *as* philosophy, but rather treated philosophy as a kind of "work" motivated by the same principle as artistic creation. Unlike Derrida, however, his philosophical emphasis on fragmentation, the unfinished character of all intellectual work, did not involve an endless displacement of meaning. For Bloch, writing leads to a self-authentication that is ultimately dependent on the transformation of the material conditions of society. Such conditions cannot be totalized or reduced by writing or philosophical conceptualization. Yet Bloch maintained that, as humans make their marks on the world, they leave behind specific traces and formations of intended meaning that serve as signposts toward ultimate truth. The reading of the signposts that would take into consideration the tendency of human intention must approach writing, nature, and human experience in much the same way as the writer does, in a collaborative effort to form tentative meanings measured by what Bloch called the invariable direction toward a society without oppression. Interpreting and understanding meaning was part of Bloch's conceptualization of a new relation between theory and practice. He refuted all theoretical programs of negativity that might be used to justify abstinence from action, and he also deplored dogmatic Marxist theory that rationalized the vested interests of ruling groups through categories of closure. For Bloch, interpreting and understanding meaning formed part of the uncontrollable relation between political struggle and the deep impulses and wishes embedded in and generated by works of art and intellectual projects such as Marxism. Reading and interpreting were political acts of detection, pointing toward resolution while demonstrating how this resolution is related to the ultimate mystery that is still in need of illumination.

The hermeneutic of Bloch's philosophical views was grounded in a historical assessment and appreciation of each work of art, but it was essentially—and crucially—informed by his search for the anticipatory illumination that would propel us home. As Fredric Jameson has remarked, "the world is (for Bloch) an immense storehouse of figures, and the task of the philosopher or critic becomes a hermeneutic one to the degree that he is called upon to pierce this 'incognito of every lived instant,' and to decipher the dimly vibrating meaning beneath the fables and the works, the experiences and the objects, which surrounding us seem to solicit our attention in some peculiarly personal fashion." [36] The discovery of the "incognito of every lived instant" involved for Bloch the aesthetic formation of the home to come within his own philosophical works, and in this respect his philosophical categories were shaped and took the form over the course of a turbulent century of a trajectory that moves toward and urges us toward the realization of the anticipatory illumination.

## Notes

1. Michael Landmann, "Talking with Ernst Bloch: Korčula, 1968," *Telos*, 25 (Fall 1975), 183–84.

2. My remarks on Bloch's life are based on my reading of several important works: Arno Münster's edition of six interviews with Bloch, *Tagträume vom aufrechten Gang* (Frankfurt am Main: Suhrkamp, 1978); Karola Bloch's autobiography, *Aus meinem Leben* (Pfullingen: Neske, 1981); Wayne Hudson's critical study *The Marxist Philosophy of Ernst Bloch* (New York: St. Martin's Press, 1982); Peter Zudeick's fine biography, the most exhaustive todate, *Der Hintern des Teufels. Ernst Bloch—Leben und Werk* (Moos & Baden-Baden: Elster, 1985).

3. This essay first appeared in the 1918 edition of *Geist der Utopie* but was omitted in the edition of 1923. Instead it appeared in the 1923 edition of essays entitled *Durch die Wüste*. See Ernst Bloch, *Durch die Wüste. Frühe kritische Aufsätze* (Frankfurt am Main: Suhrkamp, 1964).

4. "Between Enlightenment and Apocalypse: Benjamin, Bloch and Modern German Jewish Messianism," *New German Critique*, 34 (Winter 1985), 101–102.

5. *Geist der Utopie. Unveränderter Nachdruck der bearbeiteten Neuauflage der zweiten Fassung von 1923* (Frankfurt am Main: Suhrkamp, 1964), p. 217.

6. "Non-synchronism and the Obligation to its Dialectics," *New German Critique*, 11 (Spring 1977), 35–36. This essay was originally written in 1932 and published as part of *Erbschaft dieser Zeit* (1935). I have slightly modified the translation that appeared in *NGC*.

7. "Dichtung und sozialistische Gegenstände," *Literarische Aufsätze*, in *Gesamtausgabe*, vol. 9 (Frankfurt am Main: Suhrkamp, 1977), 141.

8. See Hans-Jürgen Schmitt, ed., *Die Expressionismusdebatte. Materialien zu einer marxistischen Realismuskonzeption* (Frankfurt am Main: Suhrkamp, 1973) and *Aesthetics and Politics*, tr. Ronald Taylor with an afterword by Fredric Jameson (London: New Left Books, 1977).

9. "Kann Hoffnung enttaüscht werden?" *Literarische Aufsattze,* in *Gesamtausgabe,* vol. 9 (Frankfurt am Main: Suhrkamp, 1977), 389.

10. Ibid., p. 390.

11. Ibid.

12. Ibid., p. 391.

13. "Talking with Ernst Bloch: Korčula, 1968," p. 184.

14. The book in question is *Politische Messungen, Pestzeit, Vormärz* (Frankfurt am Main: Suhrkamp, 1970). The second book, which appeared without Bloch's changes and with an interesting afterword by Oskar Negt, was *Vom Hasard zur Katastrophe. Politische Aufsätze aus den Jahren 1934–1939* (Frankfurt am Main: Suhrkamp, 1972). For a discussion of this incident, see Zudeick, *Der Hintern des Teufels,* pp. 296–299.

15. *Literarische Aufsätze,* in *Gesamtausgabe,* vol. 9 (Frankfurt am Main: Suhrkamp. 1977), 119.

16. *Erbschaft dieser Zeit,* in *Gesamtausgabe,* vol. 4 (Frankfurt am Main: Suhrkamp, 1977), 214–215.

17. Ibid., p. 228. Bloch uses the word *Bildung* for education, implying that traditional or institutionalized education will no longer suffice or help determine the contours of the genuine, socialist cultural heritage.

18. See "Ernst Bloch: A Marxist Schelling" in Jürgen Habermas, *Philosophical-Political Profiles,* tr. Frederick G. Lawrence (Cambridge: MIT Press, 1983), 61–78.

19. "Schweigen mit Hintergründen. Blochs Spur in Frankreich," *Spuren,* (July 1985), 64.

20. *Geist der Utopie* (Frankfurt am Main: Suhrkamp, 1964), p. 11.

21. Ibid., p. 17.

22. "Über das noch nicht bewusste Wissen," *Die weissen Blätter,* 6 (1919), 355.

23. Ibid., p. 355.

24. "Literatur ist Utopie" in *Literatur ist Utopie,* ed. Gert Ueding (Frankfurt am Main: Suhrkamp, 1978), 7, 10.

25. *Das Prinzip Hoffnung,* vol. I (Frankfurt am Main: Suhrkamp, 1970), 247–248. This translation is based on the one in *The Principle of Hope,* trs. Neville Plaice, Stephen Plaice, and Paul Knight, vol. I (Cambridge: MIT Press, 1986), 214–215. I have changed some of the terminology in the translation.

26. "Bloch's Ästhetik des Vor-Scheins" in Ernst Bloch, *Ästhetik des Vor-Scheins,* ed. Gert Ueding, vol. 1 (Frankfurt am Main: Suhrkamp, 1974), 21.

27. *Ernst Bloch* (Stuttgart: Metzler, 1986), 126–127.

28. The translators of *The Principle of Hope* use "preappearence," as does Wayne Hudson in *The Marxist Philosophy of Ernst Bloch.* Fredric Jameson employs the curious term "ontological anticipation" in *Marxism and Form* (Princeton: Princeton University Press, 1971), 150.

29. See Rudolf Schenda, *Volk ohne Buch* (Frankfurt am Main: Klostermann, 1970).

30. *Erbschaft dieser Zeit*, in *Gesamtausgabe*, vol. 4 (Frankfurt am Main: Suhrkamp, 1977), 182.

31. Ibid., p. 184.

32. "Philosophische Ansichten des Detektivromans," *Literarische Aufsätze* in *Gesamtausgabe*, vol. 9 (Frankfurt am Main: Suhrkamp, 1977), 247.

33. *Prinzip Hoffnung*, in *Gesamtausgabe*, vol. 5 (Frankfurt am Main: Suhrkamp, 1977), 980–981.

34. Ibid., p. 981.

35. *The Necessity of Art* (Baltimore: Penguin, 1963), 14.

36. "Ernst Bloch and the Future," in *Marxism and Form* (Princeton: Princeton University Press, 1971), p. 145.

# The Utopian Function of Art
# and Literature

# Something's Missing:
# A Discussion between Ernst
# Bloch and Theodor W. Adorno
# on the Contradictions of
# Utopian Longing

Horst Krüger (moderator): Today the word 'utopia' does not have a good sound to it. It has been depreciated and is used primarily in a negative sense to mean "utopian." There is something anachronistic about our theme and our term as well.

Theodor W. Adorno: If I may be allowed to say something first, even though I may not be the correct person to begin, since my friend Ernst Bloch is the one mainly responsible for restoring honor to the word 'utopia' in his early work *The Spirit of Utopia (Geist der Utopie)*, I would like to remind us right away that numerous so-called utopian dreams—for example, television, the possibility of traveling to other planets, moving faster than sound—have been fulfilled. However, insofar as these dreams have been realized, they all operate as though the best thing about them had been forgotten—one is not happy about them. As they have been realized, the dreams themselves have assumed a peculiar character of sobriety, of the spirit of positivism, and beyond that, of boredom. What I mean by this is that it is not simply a matter of presupposing that what really is has limitations as opposed to that which has infinitely imaginable possibilities. Rather, I mean something concrete, namely, that one sees oneself almost always deceived: the fulfillment of the wishes takes something away from the substance of the wishes, as in the fairy tale where the farmer is granted three wishes, and, I believe, he wishes his wife to have a sausage on her nose and then must use the second wish to have the sausage removed from her nose. In other words, I mean that one can watch television today, look at things that are far away, but instead of the wish-image providing access to the erotic utopia, one sees in the best of circumstances some kind of more or less pretty pop singer, who continues to deceive the spectator in regard to her prettiness insofar as she sings some kind of nonsense instead of showing it, and this song generally consists in bringing together "roses" with "moonlight" in harmony. Above and beyond this one could perhaps say in general that the fulfillment of utopia consists largely only in a repetition of the continually same 'today.' In other words, when it means for Wilhelm Busch "it's also beautiful somewhere else, and here I am at any rate," then this word begins to assume a horrifying meaning today in the realization of technological utopias, namely, that "and here I am at any rate" also takes possession of the "somewhere else," where the great Mister Pief*,1 with the great perspective has wished himself to be.

Krüger: Mr. Bloch, do you also believe that the depreciation of the term 'utopia' is connected to—how shall I put it?—'the perfection of the technological world?'

Ernst Bloch: Yes and no—it has something to do with it. The technological perfection is not so complete and stupendous as one thinks. It is limited only to a very select number of wish dreams. One could still add the very old wish to fly. If I recall correctly, Dehmel[2] wrote a poem concerning this in which he said, "And to be as free as the birds"—the wish is in there, too. In other words, there is a residue. There is a great deal that is not fulfilled and made banal through the fulfillment—regardless of the deeper viewpoint that each realization brings a melancholy of fulfillment with it. So, the fulfillment is not yet real or imaginable or postulatable without residue. But it is not only this that brings about the depreciation of utopia. Incidentally, I believe that this depreciation is very old—the slogan "That's merely utopian thinking" reduced as depreciation to "castle in the clouds," to "wishful thinking" without any possibility for completion, to imagining and dreaming things in a banal sense—this depreciation is very old, and it is not our epoch that has brought it about. I do not know for sure, but it may be that our epoch has brought with it an 'upgrading' of the utopian—only it is not called this anymore. It is called 'science fiction' in technology; it is called grist to one's mill in the theology, in which the "principle of hope" that I have

* Chapter notes, which are cited by superior Arabic numerals, appear at the chapter's end.

treated with great emphasis plays a role. It begins to play a role optatively with the "If only it were so," which overtakes the role of reality—something is really so and nothing else. All this is no longer called utopian; or if it is called utopian, it is associated with the old social utopias. But I believe that we live not very far from the topos of utopia, as far as the contents are concerned, and less far from utopia. At the very beginning Thomas More designated utopia as a place, an island in the distant South Seas. This designation underwent changes later so that it left space and entered time. Indeed, the utopians, especially those of the eighteenth and nineteenth centuries, transposed the wishland more into the future. In other words, there is a transformation of the topos from space into time. With Thomas More the wishland was still ready, on a distant island, but I am not there. On the other hand, when it is transposed into the future, not only am I not there, but utopia itself is also not with itself. This island does not even exist. But it is not something like nonsense or absolute fancy; rather it is not *yet* in the sense of a possibility; *that* it could be there if we could only do something for it. Not only if we travel there, but *in that* we travel there the island utopia arises out of the sea of the possible—utopia, but with new contents. I believe that in *this* sense utopia has not at all lost its validity in spite of the terrible banalization it has suffered and in spite of the task it has been assigned by a society—and here I would agree with my friend Adorno—that claims to be totally affluent and now already classless.

Adorno: Yes, I support very much what you have said, and I want to use the objection that you have implicitly raised to correct myself a little. It was not my intention to make technology and the sobriety that is allegedly connected to technology responsible for the strange shrinking of the utopian consciousness, but it appears that the matter concerns something much more: it refers to the opposition of specific technological accomplishments and innovations to the totality—in particular, to the social totality. Whatever utopia is, whatever can be imagined as utopia, this is the transformation of the totality. And the imagination of such a transformation of the totality is basically very different in all the so-called utopian accomplishments—which, incidentally, are all really like you say: very modest, very narrow. It seems to me that what people have lost subjectively in regard to consciousness is very simply the capability to imagine the totality as something that could be completely different. That people are sworn to this world as it is and have this blocked consciousness vis-à-vis possibility, all this has a very deep cause, indeed, a cause that I would think is very much connected *exactly* to the proximity of utopia, with which you are concerned. My thesis about this would be that all humans deep down, whether they admit this or not, know that it would be possible or it could be different. Not only could they live without hunger and probably without anxiety, but they could also live as free human beings. At the same time, the social apparatus has hardened itself against people, and thus, whatever appears before their eyes all over the world as attainable possibility, as the evident possibility of fulfillment, presents itself to them as radically impossible. And when people universally say today what was once reserved only for philistines in more harmless times, "Oh, that's just utopian; oh, that's possible only in the land of Cockaigne. Basically that shouldn't be like that at all," then I would say that this is due to the situation compelling people to master the contradiction between the evident possibility of fulfillment and the just as evident impossibility of fulfillment only in *this* way, compelling them to identify themselves with this impossibility and to make this impossibility into their own affair. In other words, to use Freud, they "identify themselves with the aggressor" and say that *this should* not be, whereby they feel that it is precisely *this* that *should be*, but they are prevented from attaining it by a wicked spell cast over the world.

Krüger: Professor Bloch, I would like to ask the following question: What is actually the content of utopias? Is it happiness? Is it fulfillment? Is it—a word that has just come up in our discussion—simply freedom? What is actually hoped for?

Bloch: For a long time utopias appeared exclusively as social utopias: dreams of a better life. The title of Thomas More's book is *De optimo statu rei publicae deque nova insula Utopia*, or *On the Best Kind of State and the New Island Utopia*. The "optima res publica"—the best state—is set by Thomas More as a goal. In other words, there is a transformation of the world to the greatest possible realization of happiness, of social happiness. Nor is it the case that the utopias were without an "itinerary" or "time schedule." With regard to their content, utopias are dependent on social conditions. Thomas More, who lived during the period when British imperialism was beginning, during the Elizabethan period, set liberal conditions for the feeling among his islanders. One hundred years later, during the time of Philip II and the Spanish domination of Italy, during the atmosphere of the Galileo Trial,[3] Campanella conceived a countermodel to freedom in his Sun State. He said that all conditions could only be brought to order if the greatest possible order reigned, if everything is "patched up," as the extremely sensible and well-known expression puts it. But the goal of More and Campanella was always the realm of conscious dreaming, one that is more or less objectively founded or at least founded in the dream and not the completely senseless realm of daydreaming of a better life. In addition, the technological utopias made their first imprint in Campanella's work and then most clearly in Bacon's *Nova Atlantis*. His 'Templum Salomonis' is the anticipation of a completed Technical University, in which there are monstrous inventions, a complete program of inventions. Yet, there is still a much older level of utopias that we should not forget, that *we least of all* should not forget—the fairy tale. The fairy tale is not only filled with social utopia, in other words, with the utopia of the better life and justice, but it is also filled with technological utopia, most of all in the oriental fairy tales. In the fairy tale "The Magic Horse," from the *Arabian Nights*, there is even a lever that controls the up and down of the magic horse—this is a "helicopter." One can read the *Arabian Nights* in many places as a manual for inventions. Bacon addressed this and then set himself off from the fairy tale by saying that what *he* means, the real magic, relates to the oldest wish-images of the fairy tale as the deeds of Alexander relate to the deeds of King Arthur's Round Table. Thus, the content of the utopian changes according to the social situation. In the nineteenth century the connection to the society at that time can be seen clearly, most clearly in the works of Saint-Simon and Fourier, who was a great, exact, and sober analyst. He prophesied the coming of monopoly as early as 1808 in his book *Théorie des quatre mouvements*. In other words, in this case it is a negative utopia that is there, too. The content changes, but an invariant of the direction is there, psychologically expressed so to speak as longing, completely without consideration at all for the content—a longing that is the pervading and above all only honest quality of all human beings. Now, however, the questions and qualifications begin: What do I long for as optimal? Here one must "move out" of the "home base" (*Stammhaus*) of the utopias, namely the social utopias, on account of the totality, as you say, in order to see the *other* regions of utopia that do not have the name "technology." There is architecture that was never built but that was designed, wish architecture of great style. There is theater architecture, which was cheaply set up with cardboard and did not cost much when money was lacking and technology was not far advanced. In the Baroque Age, most of all in the Viennese Baroque Theater, there were tremendous buildings that could never be inhabited because they were built out of cardboard and illusion, but they nevertheless made an appearance. There are the medical utopias, which contain nothing less than the elimination of death—a completely foolish remote goal. But then there is something sober, like the elimination and relief of pain. Now, that is in truth much easier and has been accomplished with the invention of anesthesia. The goal is not only the healing of sickness, but *this*, too, is to be achieved—that people are healthier after an operation than they were before. In other words, there is a reconstruction of the organism in exactly the same way as there is a reconstruction of the state. Above all there is, as I said at the beginning, the utopian in religion. This is indeed the divine realm, that which appears at the end, or that which announces, that which the Messiah, which Christ brings—distant wish-images, with tremendous content and great profundity, which appear here, so that, I believe, one must also look at the social utopias and at what resounds in them and is set in motion by these wish-images. However, these kinds of wish-images can be discussed individually according to the degree to which present conditions allow for their realization—in other words, in space, in the topos of an objective-real possibility. The possibility is not treated poorly as a 'stepchild' among the categories for nothing and also not clearly named—the possibility . . .

Adorno: . . . even Hegel treats this poorly.

Bloch: Yes, even Hegel treats this poorly. He had to treat it poorly on account of this old notion: There is nothing possible that is not real. If it were not real, it would not be possible. In other words, the possibility is absolutely a subjective-reflective category in Hegel's writings.[4]

Adorno: That's why it gets a "slap in the face."

Bloch: And it gets a "slap in the face." But when the ocean of possibility is much greater than our customary land of reality, which one could thus name the present-at-hand (*Zurhandenheit*)[5] without calling up associations—if I may beg your pardon . . .

Adorno: Please!

Bloch: . . . without placing stress on the "authenticity" (*Eigentlichkeit*),[6] then we can see that the possibility has had a bad press. There is a very clear interest that has prevented the world from being changed into the possible, and it has been poorly treated and, as was mentioned, has been insufficiently brought into the philosophical range not to mention the insults it has received, which have run parallel to the insults directed at the utopian.

Adorno: Yes, and here I would like to return to the question posed by Mr. Krüger about the content of the utopian. I believe, Ernst, that you have unrolled a whole series of—how shall I put it—of very different types of utopian consciousness. That has a great deal to do with the topic because there is nothing like a single, fixable utopian content. When I talked about the "totality," I did not at all limit my thinking to the system of human relations, but I thought more about the fact that *all* categories can change themselves according to their own constituency. Thus I would say that what is essential about the concept of utopia is that it does not consist of a certain, single selected category that changes itself and from which everything constitutes itself, for example, in that one assumes that the category of happiness alone is the key to utopia.

Krüger: . . . not even the category of freedom?

Adorno: Not *even* the category of freedom can be isolated. If it all depended on viewing the category of freedom *alone* as the key to utopia, then the content of idealism would really mean the same as utopia, for idealism seeks nothing else but the realization of freedom without actually including the realization of happiness in the process. It is thus within a context that *all these* categories appear and are connected. The category of happiness always has something wretched about it as isolated category and appears deceptive to the other categories. It would change itself just like, on the other hand, the category of freedom, too, which would then no longer be an end in itself and an end in itself of subjectivity (*Innerlichkeit*) but would have to fulfill itself.

To be sure, I believe—and it moved me very much, Ernst, that *you* were the one who touched on this, for my own thinking has been circling around this point in recent times—that the question about the elimination of death is indeed the crucial point. This is the heart of the matter. It can be ascertained very easily; you only have to speak about the elimination of death some time with a so-called well-disposed person—I am borrowing this expression from Ulrich Sonnennmann, who coined and introduced it. Then you will get an *immediate* reaction, in the same way that a policeman would come right after you if you threw a stone at a police station. Yes, if death were eliminated, if people would no longer die, that would be the most terrible and most horrible thing. I would say that it is precisely this form of reaction that actually opposes the utopian consciousness most of the time. The identification with death is that which goes beyond the identification of people with the existing social conditions and in which they are extended.

Utopian consciousness means a consciousness for which the *possibility* that people no longer have to die does not have anything horrible about it, but is, on the contrary, *that* which one actually wants.

Moreover, it is very striking—you spoke about close-handedness (*Zurhandenheit*) before—it is very striking that Heidegger to a certain degree had already cast aspersion on the question about the *possibility* of an existence without death as a mere ontic question that concerns the end of existence (*Daseinsende*), and he was of the opinion that death, as it were, would retain its absolute, ontological, thus essential dignity only if death were ontically to disappear (that is, in the realm of the existing)—that this sanctification of death or making death an absolute in contemporary philosophy, which I at any rate regard as the absolute anti-utopia, is also the key category.

Thus I would say that there is no *single* category by which utopia allows itself to be named. But if one wants to see how this entire matter resolves itself, then this question is actually the most important.

Krüger: Mr. Bloch, would you accept what has been elaborated up to this point, that, to a certain degree, it is actually people's fear of death, a fear that they must die, that is the most profound and also the most legitimate root of their utopian thinking?

Bloch: Yes. The concern with death appears in two areas: in one instance, in medicine, where it is practical, empirical, or vocational, so to speak; in the other, in religion. Christianity triumphed in the early centuries with the call, "I am the resurrection and the life!" It triumphed with the Sermon on the Mount and with eschatology. Indeed, death depicts the hardest counter-utopia. Nailing the coffin puts an end to all of our individual series of actions at the very least. In other words, it also depreciates the before.

And when now there is nothing else? There is a picture by Voltaire of despair—the total despair of a shipwrecked man who is swimming in the waves and struggling and squirming for his life when he receives the message that this ocean in which he finds himself does not have a shore but that death is completely in the now in which the ship-wrecked man finds himself. That is why the striving of the swimmer will lead to nothing, for he will never land. It will always remain the same. To be sure, this strongest counter-utopia exists, and that must be said to make things more difficult. Otherwise, there would not be that Heideggerian 'creature' (*Wesen*) at all, if there were not something here in the reality that is unavoidable and has no history up till now and no change in the real process—thus, if this reality itself did not ward itself so extraordinarily from the test case.

And here we touch on the area of the feeling of freedom. It is related to the "dreams of the better life," which portray the social utopias, but it also distinguishes itself from them. In the social utopias, in particular, the best possible communal living conditions are deter-mined either through freedom or through order. Here freedom is a variable or auxiliary for the best possible life. Freedom as feeling does not appear in utopia but in natural law, and to be sure, in the liberal natural law of the eighteenth century in connection with the upright gait, in connection with human dignity, which is only guaranteed by freedom. *William Tell* and the dramas of Alfieri are filled with great freedom figures, who stand independently and cry out, "In tyrannos!" Here one finds natural law, and it also lies within the realm of objective and real possibility, but it is not the same as social utopia. In other words, there are two utopian parts: the social utopias as constructions of a condition in which there are no laboring and burdened people; and natural law, in which there are no humiliated and insulted people. It is the second one that I attempted to depict in my book *Natural Law and Human Dignity*. Now there is also a third. However, it is not the miracle but death, which is faith's dearest child, and that is the best way to express it. Still, it is necessary to have a miracle to remove death from view. This means, then, the resurrection of Christ, that is, faith, or "Who will save me from the jaws of death?" as stated in the Bible, in the New Testament. This is transcendental. This is something *we* cannot do. So we need the help of baptism, Christ's death, and resurrection. In the process the utopian is transcended in the choice of its possible means. And, nevertheless, it belongs to utopia.

Adorno: Yes, I believe that, too. Indeed, the matter here does not concern conceiving of the elimination of death as a scientific process in such a way that one crosses the threshold between organic and inorganic life through new discoveries. To be sure, I believe that without the notion of an unfettered life, freed from death, the idea of utopia, the idea of *the* utopia, *cannot* even be thought at all. On the other hand, there was something you alluded to about death that I would say was very correct. There is something profoundly contradictory in every utopia, namely, that it cannot be conceived at all without the elimination of death; this is inherent in the very thought. What I mean is the heaviness of death and everything that is connected to it. Wherever this is not included, where the threshold of death is not at the same time considered, there can actually be no utopia. And it seems to me that this has very heavy consequences for the theory of knowledge about utopia—if I may put it crassly: One may not cast a picture of utopia in a positive manner. Every attempt to describe or portray utopia in a simple way, i.e., it will be like this, would be an attempt to avoid the antinomy of death and to speak about the elimination of death as if death did not exist. That is perhaps the most profound reason, the metaphysical reason, why one can actually talk about utopia only in a negative way, as is demonstrated in great philosophical works by Hegel and, even more emphatically, Marx.

Bloch: "Negative" does not mean "in depreciation . . . "

Adorno: No, not "in the depreciation of utopia," but only in the determined negation of that which because that is the only form in which death is also included, for death is nothing other than the power of that which merely *is* just as, on the other hand, it is also the attempt to go beyond it. And this is why I believe—all this is now very tentative—the commandment not to "depict" utopia or the com-

mandment not to conceive certain utopias in detail as Hegel and
Marx have . . .

Bloch: Hegel?

Adorno: Hegel did this insofar as he depreciated the world-reformer
in principle and set the idea of the objective tendency in opposition—
this is what Marx adopted directly from him—and the realization of
the absolute. In other words, that which one could call utopia in
Hegel's works, or which one *must* call utopia in his youth, originated
right at this moment. What is meant there is the prohibition of casting
a picture of utopia actually for the sake of utopia, and that has a deep
connection to the commandment, "Thou shalt not make a graven
image!" This was also the defense that was actually intended against
the cheap utopia, the false utopia, *the* utopia that can be bought.

Bloch: I agree with you completely. This leads us back again to the
first actual question, so to speak, and the actual state of affairs where
utopia becomes diffused, in that I portray it as being (*seiend*) or in that
I portray it as achieved even if this is only in installments. As install-
ment of having been achieved is already *included* when I can portray
it in a book. Here it has at least become real already and, as you said,
"cast into a picture." One is thus deceived. It is diffused, and there is
a reification of ephemeral or non-ephemeral tendencies, as if it were
already more than being-in-tendency, as if the day were already
there. Thus, the iconoclastic rebellion against such reification is now
in this context completely correct. And displeasure must keep on its
guard, for which death most certainly provides a continual motiva-
tion. Indeed, death is not "Now he must go," as the old Schopenhauer said; rather it disturbs one constantly so that one cannot be
satisfied, no matter how great the satisfaction is and no matter how
many economic miracles and welfare states there are. But *that* continues to exist, an 'it-should-not-be' of the utopian, of the longing for
a 'coming-in-order' or an 'in general,' where freedom would be,
where everything would be right or together in a much deeper sense,
a more comprehensive sense than the social utopia portrays it. Such
yearning is present, and there is—to come back to death—the
human fear of death, which is entirely different from the animal fear
of death. In other words, there is this fear of death that is actually cast
into a picture and is based on rich experience that humans have had

and the feeling that multiple goals break down. For there is no such thing as utopia without multiple goals. In a non-teleological world there is no such thing. Mechanical materialism can have no utopia. Everything is present in it, mechanically present. Thus, the fact that there is such a sensitivity about an 'it-should-be' demonstrates that there is also utopia in this area where it has the most difficulty, and I believe, Teddy, that we are certainly in agreement here: the essential function of utopia is a critique of what is present. If we had not already gone beyond the barriers, we could not even perceive them as barriers.

Adorno: Yes, at any rate, utopia is essentially in the determined negation, in the determined negation of that which merely is, and by concretizing itself as something false, it always points at the same time to what should be.

Yesterday you quoted Spinoza in our discussion with the passage, "Verum index sui et falsi."[7] I have varied this a little in the sense of the dialectical principle of the determined negation and have said, Falsum—the false thing—index sui et veri.[8] That means that the true thing determines itself via the false thing, or via that which makes itself falsely known. And insofar as we are not allowed to cast the picture of utopia, insofar as we do not know what the correct thing would be, we know exactly, to be sure, what the false thing is.

That is actually the only form in which utopia is given to us at all. But what I mean to say here—and perhaps we should talk about this, Ernst—this matter also has a very confounding aspect, for something terrible happens due to the fact that we are forbidden to cast a picture. To be precise, among that which should be definite, one imagines it to begin with as less definite the more it is stated only as something negative. But then—and this is probably even more frightening—the commandment against a concrete expression of utopia tends to defame the utopian consciousness and to engulf it. What is really important, however, is the will *that* it is different. And it is most definitely true that the horror that we are experiencing today in the East is partly connected to the fact that, as a result of what Marx in his own time criticized about the French utopians and Owen, the idea of utopia has actually disappeared completely from the conception of socialism. Thereby the apparatus, the how, the means of a socialist society have taken precedence over any possible content, for one is not allowed to say anything about the possible content. Thereby the theory of socialism that is decidedly hostile toward utopia now tends really to become a new ideology concerned with the domination of humankind. I believe I can remember the time when you had conflicts in Leipzig, when Ulbricht—I do not want to quote this because I am not sure that my memory is correct—made a statement against you at that time: Such a utopia cannot at all be realized. Now this was exactly a philistine phrase, i.e., that we do not *want* at all to realize it.

In contrast to all this, we should bear *one* thing in mind. If it is true that a life in freedom and happiness would be possible today, then this one thing would assume one of the theoretical forms of utopia for which I am certainly not duly qualified, and as far as I can see, neither are you. That is, neither of us can say what would be possible given the present standing of the forces of production—this can be said concretely, and this can be said without casting a picture of it, and this can be said without arbitrariness. If this is not said, if this picture cannot—I almost would like to say—appear within one's grasp, then one basically does not know at all what the actual reason for the totality is, why the entire apparatus has been set in motion. Excuse me if I have taken the unexpected role of the attorney for the positive, but I believe that, without this element, one could do nothing in a phenomenology of the utopian consciousness.

Krüger: Mr. Bloch, may I ask you once again: Would you accept what Mr. Adorno has said about the utopian element having entirely disappeared from the socialism that rules the eastern world today?

Bloch: With the amendment that it has *also* disappeared in the West and that similar tendencies exist that reproduce the unity of the epoch despite such great contrasts.

Adorno: *D'accord.*

Bloch: West and East are *d'accord.* They are sitting in the same unfortunate boat with regard to this point: nothing utopian should be allowed to exist. But now there is a difference between the commandment against casting a picture and the warning or command to postpone doing this. The mandate, or rather, the work principle, which was necessary for Marx, not to say much more about the utopian—this principle was only to be polemical some period of time, short or long; it was directed against the abstract utopians, who were the forerunners, and who believed that one only had to speak to the conscience of rich people and they would begin to saw off the branch on which they were sitting. Marx objected to the over-estimation of the people's intellect, an over-estimation that was characteristic of the utopian socialists. In other words, interest played a role here as well as the Hegelian look (*Blick*) for concreteness. This was surely necessary as medicine against rampant speculative thinking, against the rampant speculative spirit of that time. Without it, *Das Kapital* (*Capital*) would probably never have been written and perhaps could not have been written.

The turn against utopia that has been conditioned by the times has certainly had terrible effects. Many of the terrible effects that have arisen are due to the fact that Marx cast much too little of a picture, for example, in literature, in art, in all possible matters of this kind. Only the name Balzac appears; otherwise there is mainly empty space instead of Marxist initiatives to reach a higher culture that would have been possible. I consider this a condition that can be explained historically and scientifically, and that at the moment when this historical-scientific situation no longer lies before us, when we no longer suffer from a superabundance of utopianism, it will become devoid of meaning. The consequences that arise from this have been terrible, for people in a completely different situation have simply regurgitated Marx's statements in a literal sense.

It is from the Marxist viewpoint definitely necessary to act like a detective and to trace and uncover what each case is about—without any kind of positivism. By doing this, one can set things aright, but one must not forget that other thing—the utopian. For the purpose of the exercise is not the technocratic . . .

Krüger: *What* would the purpose of the exercise be?

Bloch: We talked before about the totality on which everything depends. Why does one get up in the morning? How did such an especially striking situation arise already right in the middle of the nineteenth century enabling Wilhelm Raabe to write the following sentence?: When I get up in the morning, my daily prayer is, grant me today my illusion, my daily illusion. Due to the fact that illusions are necessary, have become necessary for life in a world completely devoid of a utopian conscience and utopian presentiment . . .

Adorno: The same motif also appears in Baudelaire's work where he glorified the lie in a very similar way, and yet, there are very few other parallels between Baudelaire and Raabe.

Bloch: There would not have been a French Revolution, as Marx stated, without the heroic illusions that natural law engendered. Of course, they did not become real, and what did become real of them, the free market of the bourgeoisie, is not at all that which was dreamed of, though wished for, hoped, demanded, as utopia. Thus now, if a world were to emerge that is hindered for apparent reasons, but that is entirely possible, one could say, it is astonishing that it is *not*—if such a world, in which hunger and immediate wants were eliminated, entirely in contrast to death, if this world would finally just "be allowed to breathe" and were set free, there would not only be platitudes that would come out at the end and gray prose and a complete lack of prospects and perspectives in regard to existence here and over there, but there would also be freedom from earning instead of freedom to earn, and this would provide some space for such richly prospective doubt and the decisive incentive toward utopia that is the meaning of Brecht's short sentence, "Something's missing." This sentence, which is in *Mahagonny*, is one of the most profound sentences that Brecht ever wrote, and it is in two words. What is this "something"? If it is not allowed to be cast in a picture, then I shall portray it as in the process of being (*seiend*). But one should not be allowed to eliminate it as if it really did not exist so that one could say the following about it: "It's about the sausage." Therefore, if all this is correct, I believe utopia cannot be removed from the world in spite of everything, and even the technological, which must definitely emerge and will be in the great realm of the utopian, will form only small sectors. That is a geometrical picture, which does not have any place here, but another picture can be found in the old peasant saying, there is no dance before the meal. People must first fill their stomachs, and then they can dance. That is a *conditio sine qua non* for being able to talk earnestly about the other without it being used for deception. Only when all the guests have sat down at the table can the Messiah, can Christ come. Thus, Marxism in its entirety, even when brought in in its most illuminating form and anticipated in its entire realization, is only a *condition* for a life in freedom, life in happiness, life in possible fulfillment, life with content.

Adorno: May I add a word? We have come strangely close to the ontological proof of God, Ernst . . .

Bloch: That surprises me!

Adorno: All of this comes from what you said when you used the phrase borrowed from Brecht—something's missing—a phrase that we actually cannot have if seeds or ferment of what this phrase denotes were not possible.

Actually I would think that unless there is no kind of trace of truth in the ontological proof of God, that is, unless the element of its reality is also already conveyed in the power of the concept itself, there could not only be no utopia but there could also not be any thinking.

Krüger: That is actually *the* concept I wanted to introduce to conclude our discussion. We already touched on it, Professor Adorno. We had already said that utopia refers to what is missing. So the question to pose at the end is, to what extent do human beings realize utopia? And actually here the word "hope" is due. Here we could use an explanation of what hope actually is and what it is not.

Bloch: In hope, the matter concerns perfection, and to that extent it concerns the ontological proof of God. But the most perfect creature is posited by Anselm as something fixed that includes the most real at the same time. Such a tenet is not defensible. But what is true is that each and every criticism of imperfection, incompleteness, intolerance, and impatience already without a doubt presupposes the conception of, and longing for, a possible perfection. Otherwise, there would not be any imperfection if there were not something in the process that should not be there—if imperfection did not go around in the process, in particular, as a critical element. One thing is certainly against it, and once we take care of some misunderstandings, we shall be in agreement here: hope is the opposite of security. It is the opposite of naive optimism. The category of danger is always within it. This hope is not confidence . . .

Krüger: Hope can be disappointed.

Bloch: Hope is not confidence. If it could not be disappointed, it would not be hope. That is part of it. Otherwise, it would be cast in a picture. It would let itself be bargained down. It would capitulate and say, that is what I had hoped for. Thus, hope is critical and can be disappointed. However, hope still nails a flag on the mast, even in decline, in that the decline is not accepted, even when this decline is still very strong. Hope is not confidence. Hope is surrounded by dangers, and it is the consciousness of danger and at the same time the determined negation of that which continually makes the opposite of the hoped-for object possible.

Possibility is not hurray-patriotism. The opposite is also in the possible. The hindering element is also in the possible. The hindrance is implied in hope aside from the capacity to succeed. But I employ the word 'process,' which has many meanings—chemical, medical, legal, and religious. There would not be any process at all if there were not something that should not be so. In conclusion, I would like to quote a phrase, a very simple one, strangely enough from Oscar Wilde: "A map of the world that does not include Utopia is not even worth glancing at."

## Notes

1. The great Mister Pief is a character in Wilhelm Busch's book *Plisch und Plum* (1882). Busch wrote the following poem about him: "Zugereist in diese Gegend/ Noch viel mehr als sehr vermögend/ In der Hand das Perspektiv/ Kam ein Mister namens Pief/ "Warum soll ich nicht beim Gehen"/ Sprach er, "in die Ferne sehen?/ Schön ist es anderswo/ Und hier bin ich sowieso." (Just arrived in this region/ Much more than very rich/ In his hand a telescope/ Came a mister by the name of Pief/ "Why shouldn't I look,"/ Said he, "into the distance as I walk?/ It's also beautiful somewhere else/ And here I am at any rate.")

2. Richard Dehmel (1863–1920) was an important precursor of expressionism in Germany.

3. The trials of Galileo took place in Rome in 1615/16 and 1633.

4. The subjective-reflective category denotes the reflection of a subject in contrast to a category (matter) that is present in the "object" in the reality itself.

5. *Zurhandenheit* (present-at-hand) is a term developed by Heidegger to describe the things with which people deal in their daily lives, for example, instruments.

6. Bloch is referring here to Adorno's book *The Jargon of Authenticity* (*Jargon der Eigentlichkeit*, 1964), in which he sharply criticized Heidegger's language and the ideology of existentialism.

7. The true is the sign of itself and the false.

8. The false is the sign of itself and the correct.

# Art and Society

## Ideas as Transformed Material in Human Minds, or Problems of an Ideological Superstructure (Cultural Heritage)

After one has enjoyed the first taste of Marxist criticism, one will never again be able to stand ideological hogwash. But it could be said just as well that it is precisely because Marxism places an emphasis on everything economic and on all transcendental elements (the creative-postulative), which are continually latent but remain hidden, that it approximates the critique of pure reason, which has yet to be supplemented by a critique of practical reason.

*The Spirit of Utopia*, 1918

### Drudgery with Trimming

Lower and upper, until now they have been largely held together by business. Their consolidation is manifested in the economic-minded humans by the way in which they act and express themselves. The so-called upper regions of the sublime in which they express themselves, or in which the sublime reveals itself on order, may conceal the foremost significance of economics. The sublime may also enhance the major concerns of humankind in such a way that artistic and scientific forms arise that no longer seem to have a connection to the economic animal domain. Yet, this separation is deceptive. Postulated in this manner, the sublime only veils business. And such sublime veiling is not self-engendered anyway, nor is it self-perpetuating. Rather, its origins can be traced to economic behavior and its corresponding attitudes. Today the veiling is no longer subjectively honest on the part of the business employer. He uses great and noble words quite cynically to conceal interests that are not allowed to be said aloud. It is already easier to sell something if the customer advertises the service: the exploiter is represented as benefactor if he succeeds in providing bread for a continually growing number of workers. And one only exports articles because one is humanely motivated by the hungry children "over there." Otherwise, business and the sublime are kept quite separate, especially in those areas where the sublime appears as high art. Business and the sublime are set in rigid opposition to each other, particularly in the degree to which work becomes more dreary or the exploitation more unabashed, or in the degree to which the capitalist economy as a whole, even for the profitmakers, becomes more alienating. On such occasions the sublime is not supposed to remind anyone at all of business. Fraud or flight to the muses is recommended. Even the employees, especially these people, do not want to accept the truth that Sunday, part of the sublime higher region, is most closely connected to the workday, particularly because it provides escape from the workday. In no way should it become known that leisure time only serves to regenerate labor power, to make people fit again for the crippling workday. Drudgery and the sound of music seem to have become two completely different things. Apparently even the same wind does not propel them. The employee suffers, the employer commands the economy. The only real forces causing false consciousness, which the employee has, and which the employer for the most part spreads, are to be found up above. The exploitative person, along with his victims, stands behind these forces just as he keeps his close connection to business deals and also stands right behind the arts, which apparently entrance him. A binding breath of air goes through the workday and Sunday. This is precisely why they like to support each other so much.

Marxist Interpretation and the Expansion of Economic Material

It is that into which the inhabitants of the earth are born that makes them really fat or lean. This is why we must take a fundamentally penetrating look at business and investigate the ways it might be changed. Obviously such an economically dry explanation of history differs greatly from the previous accounts, which focused on biological factors. And it does this in such a way that the economic penetrates history completely, colors and determines it materialistically, and does not simply depict one part next to another. Both the bourgeois interest and the bourgeois division of labor, which continually destroy connections, have isolated the economic aspect. They have degraded it to the status of a shoemaker who is supposed to work within his limits. Since the division of labor has also emerged in the sciences, the different areas of capitalist life, which anyway have been torn asunder and reified, have also become distinct areas for specialized study. This is the way in which so-called disciplines arose, among them the bourgeois economy as an especially particular and circumscribed system. It does not take much to show that this kind of "economy" is not the real one—according to Marxist terms—that fundamentally lies at the basis of the superstructure; yet, the bourgeoisie does not conceive of its economy or its earlier economy in this way. This is also true of Ricardo's and Smith's concept of economy. Even then, the period of the emerging bourgeoisie, the *homo economicus* was considered self-sufficient and separate. At the same time, his capitalist economic form was considered to have finally been discovered and pronounced eternally natural. Ever since the overt interest of capitalism was promoted to a discipline, it has forfeited even its own categories in certain places: the word profit has disappeared from its literature in the course of the past century. Once again it conceals surplus value with its theory. And instead of the word crisis, one encounters the term "the tidal movements of economic life" more and more frequently. Here, for the most part, bourgeois economy has become ideology itself, an apology, and this is understandable since there is no real depiction of what really constitutes the base. Such particulars as those of reports and, until recently, statistics, the sociologically interesting materials, may still be used in a cautious way. However, as Marx said, in endeavoring to kill two birds with one stone, the intensified class struggle "sounded the knell of scientific bourgeois economy. From then on it was no longer a question of whether this theory or that was true, but whether it was useful or harmful to capital, expedient or inexpedient, legal according to its own laws or illegal. In place of disinterested inquirers, intellectual pimps were hired to conduct research; in place of open scientific research, bad conscience and the evil intention of apologetics became the rule" (*Afterword* to the second German edition of *Capital*).

Yet, the bourgeois economic system would not have been mediated by the superstructure even then if it had not been in the interest of capital. As Marx remarked, "the use value as use value already lies beyond the radius of observation of bourgeois political economy" just as the contents of the human-social totality do. In view of this, Marx's *concept* of the political economy was already radical and different in his time: it had nothing to do with a system of division or with a separate commodity circulation based on a self-sufficient system of commodities. Marx's concept was distinguished largely by its comprehensiveness and its dialectical relationship to life, and this has far-reaching ramifications. In *The Poverty of Philosophy*, Marx remarked that "the economists explain how production takes place in the relations given, but they do not explain how these relations themselves are produced, that is, the historical movement which gave rise to them." And Marx expanded upon his ideas about the way the economy functions more clearly in *Capital*: "If we study all the connections, the capitalist process of production or of reproduction does not only produce commodities and surplus value. It produces and reproduces the capitalist condition itself: on one side, the capitalist, and, on the other, the wage-earner." Or as Engels defined it in his review of the *Critique of Political Economy*: "The economy does not revolve around things but rather around the relations between people and in the final analysis between classes." And again to cite Marx in *The Poverty of Philosophy*: "Economic categories are only the theoretical expressions, the abstractions of social relations of production." In short, an economy comprehended as connected to the social system—and this has nothing to do with the plain existing bourgeois economy, which determines and reflects everything—means that we take into consideration the process of production and reproduction of a (particular) *society as a totality*. Instead of the different reifications (commodity, interest, capital), which are fetishized by bourgeois economics, and which all appear to take precedence over and above the people who first produce them, the focus here is on work, the work process. The knowledge about the work process and, more generally, about the "relations of humans to humans and to nature" is such that it is simultaneously knowledge about the entire history with its superstructure and ideology, with all the ways "humanity" is formed. This is why Marx asserted that economy had no such thing as its own history, and this is also true of law, art, philosophy, etc. Rather, all things considered, "History is the product of humans through human labor."

Here the sharp and exact contours characteristic of economic existence are not blurred by those functional subject-object connections. The economic system itself is categorized according to its place within the social totality, which has been called slaveholder society, feudalism, capitalism, and later socialism, and thus it is not isolated when viewed this way, but rather its essence can be grasped by perceiving how it functions in the interest of profit accumulation and by revealing the ways in which ideologies seek to legitimize this interest by veiling it in an idealistic way. And the nonisolated economic system also remains part of the reciprocal relations that it influences as social base with the superstructure in that it takes part in the contemporaneous events of a totality just by being included in the term "epoch" itself. The difference here is that the separation is gone, the same kind that did not allow economic categories to be connected to the labor process or to the ideologies of the society as a whole. To think of the economy as part of the social totum does not minimize the explosive charge of the economic-materialist notion of history. In particular, it is the philosophical total view of Marxism that enables it to expose capitalist society with economic precision; it is certainly not due to vulgar Marxism and pure economicism. All this does not occur in a so-called "impartial," disconcerned sociological manner of studying the context of things. Rather, it occurs with the finalizing view of the totum, which is socialist, partial, and practical and is directed toward transcending the mere "pre-history" of humankind, which has been our experience to date. This is why the expansion in Marxism remains completely aggressive. The fierce quality in scientifically founded Marxism is due to the badness recognized in the "way capitalism conducts itself in the world" (even while emphasizing its former progressive, somewhat sombre-progressive function). *It is precisely due to the fact that Marx expanded the economic categories and used them*—alienation, self-production, the alienation of humans from each other, the reification of humans and things, etc., concepts that cannot occur in bourgeois economics concerned only with partial aspects, concepts that require a critical and evaluating look at the total nature of the entire existence of humankind—*that this critique becomes as precise as though it were in the very material itself.* Thus, in view of the capitalist relationship of humans to other humans: "The propertied class and the proletarian class represent the same human alienation. But the former feels well and self-confirmed in this self-alienation. It knows this alienation and sees in it its own impotence and the reality of an inhuman existence" (*The Holy Family*).

But, in regard to the capitalist relationship to nature, this condition is also the same and is brought about by means of the property rent or the machine constructed for profit. "Private property does not only alienate the individuality of humans but also that of things" (*German Ideology II*). Such a view of the totality is lacking in bourgeois economics for the most part, and this is also true of the research in the so-called humanities that followed later. All these approaches move barely more than a meter beyond their reified and special objects of study. Unfortunately, specialized histories of economics are still being produced, just as there are specialized ones of law, art, religion, and intellectuals immersed in their problems and works continue to reproduce themselves up in the clouds beyond economics, high above the material world like the echo of a bell, high above the means of production and exchange as a parthenogenesis of ideas. However, it has become clear that the history of property in Roman society was the real secret history, the base and context of everything, as Marx says. It has become clear that capitalist society is based on the unlimited profit motive and price quantification of all of its objects, and thus it is the commodity category that rules all relations, including the mathematical natural sciences and even all the "irrational" diverging ideologies. It has become clear that the capitalist superstructure is filled with commodity ideas just as the capitalist base is filled with corresponding abstractions and calculating considerations. All of these insights flowed first from the critique of political economy as a total critique and from economic materialism, which was in no way viewed economically in an isolated way. Capitalism is capitalist all over, not only in its factory owners and export quotas. Feudalism is feudal all over, not only in its ideas of loyalty, honor, and adventure. It manifests itself in all its forms of relations and objects, with thousands of mediating figures from the tithe collector up to the lord of the castle. And it is only vulgar Marxism with its partiality to economics adapted from bourgeois economics, not from Marxism, that disregards the power of ideological infusion, even in the mode of economics itself. For philosophical economics, this infusion is the essence of the social-material itself. When Kautsky explained that the Reformation was "nothing but the ideological expression of profound changes on the European wool market," then he was making just the same kind of rigid, narrow-minded and nonsensical claim as that idealistic bombast that views the Reformation as emanating only from the Germanic soul. Instead of this, Marx continually asserted that the heart of the matter was "the relationship of human beings to each other and to nature" with the respective modes of production and exchange as the "foundation" or "the final decisive factor." Here Marx was still pointing instructively to the relationship of human beings to nature, to one that was not simply economic in kind and that was still unquestionably materialist. Vulgar Marxism would have worked itself out of its un-Marxist narrow corner much more easily, even after it had barred itself from analyzing the economic totality of relationships, if it had at least grasped the other components that Marx, in order to preclude any economistic misunderstanding, had linked to the "pure economic" components—those of *technology*. It is not surprising that all reactionary criticism of Marx also suppresses this technological component of the materialist conception of history. It is easier to assert that Marx "focused only on economics," and this allows idealistic, small-minded critics to pursue their anti-Marxism in a better way.

But it is precisely the relationship of human beings to nature that Marx stressed as basic, and this relationship clearly included a notion of technology just as Marx presupposed technology in each individual case as continually exercising an influence on changes in the mode of production and exchange. "The hand mill produces a society with feudal lords, the steam mill, one with industrial capitalists." Marx defined productive power itself as "that part of inner and outer nature which human beings know how to control." The manner in which the controlled natural forces (animals, human beings, wind, water, fire, etc.) are disposable indicates the fundamental principles with which human beings produce and reproduce their lives. The manner in which they are disposable is such that even dim-witted people can envision an "expansion" of the free economy, except for the essential one constituted by the social totality. Or, according to the Marxian principle, which must always be applied with the definition of the base in mind: "Technology contains the active relation of human beings to nature; it contains the immediate process of production in their lives, and along with this their social relations and their intellectual notions which spring from all these relationships." In sum, from this standpoint Marx's concept of economics can essentially be explained by the concept of work and the conditions of work. First and foremost, work is for Marx the cradle of history—and it is not a fetishized and specialized condition with an abstract *homo economicus*. This latter definition must be considered indefensible from a Marxist point of view since it disassociates technology from its base as Stalin at one time dictated, and it shifts it (along with language as well) to a strange third place next to the base and superstructure. This would mean that in precisely the most important concern of Marxism, namely, the changing of the world, the human intervention aimed at changing what was and what little has been achieved would be deprived by this of its most visible genetic instrument. The material of historical materialism is by and large the fastest and most readily convertible in the world. And it alone has given rise to a material position of the superstructure created in and through human beings, and this position is fully new, hardly discovered, and very unsettling. It is virtually a second nature, a hylopneumatic one. In terms of society this amounts to the two levels of base and superstructure whereby the latter rises from the material one, here still in its usual businesslike sense.

Transitions between Economy and Ideology: The Problem
Concerning the Production of Culture

The question here is how everything becomes shifted around. How does business alone move into the limelight? Certainly not by itself. There must have been first a social class that had time for it. As Engels has said about the beginnings, "it is easiest to approach this matter from the standpoint of division of labor." Hunting societies did not have a division of labor, other than perhaps those that were figurative or natural such as sexual intercourse and different kinds of corporeal power. The genuine division of power began first with grazing societies, with the ownership of herds, later with the ownership of property, and, along with the rise of classes, the economy began to be separated from the ideological forms above it. "Society," Engels concluded, "produces certain common functions which it needs. The people who are appointed to certain positions form a branch of the division of labor within the society. Thereby they receive special interests even *vis à vis* their mandates. They become independent of them, and the state comes into being." Consequently, they represent the first appearance of the superstructure, with chiefs and laws yet to be written down but that subconsciously make distinctions and serve the upper classes. The state did not and does not exist among the primitive communist tribes. Rather, the state is determined by the division of labor and the oppositions that are directly engendered by this division. It functions as the powerful suppressor of these contradictions in exactly the same manner that the respective intellectual forms of the superstructure do: the conscious ideological forms had to emerge as the apparent compromise of these contradictions—as their whitewash or their attempted solution on a "sublime level." (Life is serious, art will elevate you.) The decisive factor in all of this was the separation of manual and intellectual work brought about by the division of labor, that is, by the emergence of a leisure class. It was exactly at this point in history that Marx placed the actual origins of the *intellectual* superstructure, which was still in the process of being formed above the state. And, to be sure, this superstructure was filled largely by a false and perverted consciousness: "From this moment on consciousness can really imagine itself something other than the consciousness of the prevailing practice. It can really conceive something without conceiving something real. From this moment on consciousness can emancipate itself from the world and proceed to form pure theory, theology, philosophy, ethics, etc." (*German Ideology I*). Thus, such forms are different from the state. They are on a more "sublime level," just as the state is, in turn, different from society, even from the bourgeois society, in that it represents the committee that manages society's business. Engels makes the following perceptive remarks with regard to this state, distinguishing it from "those lofty domains which float in the clouds": "It is by no means a power which has been imposed upon society from the outside ... it is the admission that this society has become entangled in an insoluble contradiction within itself and has become split into irreconcilable antagonisms which it is powerless to dispel. But in order to prevent these antagonisms and classes with conflicting interests from consuming themselves and society in fruitless struggle, it became necessary to have a power seemingly standing above society that was supposed to alleviate the conflict and keep it within the limits of order. And this power that has arisen from society but has placed itself above it and has increasingly alienated itself from it is the state" (*The Origin of the Family*). Accordingly, Engels concluded that the state will perish in an economic system that is no longer antagonistic and will transform itself from a government over people into an administration of things. Thus, the state is the product of class society in a process that is not very complicated; the political superstructure stands rather directly on the base and reacts directly to the tensions in it by either suppressing them or concealing them by means of an ostensible constitutional state (*Rechtsstaat*). It was fascism that clearly brought to light once again the genuine oppressive nature of the state, which had been kept exceptionally hidden and had been relatively latent. The semblance of a "constitutional state," which was still possible to maintain with minimal class contradictions, was completely broken down. If the bourgeois state was "nothing more than a mutual insurance company of the bourgeois class to guard itself against its own members as well as against the exploited class," according to Marx and Engels, it has become solely an insurance company to guard against the exploited in the monopoly-capitalist stage, that is, after the disappearence of free competition under the bourgeoisie. Only if the class contradiction is not formidable, in other words, if the proletariat sleeps, only in this anomalous situation is it possible for the state to pretend to be the prime organizer of class struggle from above. So everywhere that things occur for the Right instead of for the Left, the legal superstructure must occupy itself with oppression; that is, the *facultas agendi* of civil law will be increasingly replaced by criminal law and its norm of oppression. These are the ways and means by which the material business rationalizes itself ideologically in each case as a creation of the state and as part of the legal system. They are small enough to be retracted almost overnight when the conditions demand it, right back to the starting point—the class contradiction. To be sure, it follows from this that the superstructure is not merely placed upon the base externally like the masthead is attached to the ship and passively conforms to all its movements. This dualistic notion stems from vulgar Marxism. It forgets that the economy, which can never be isolated, is made by human individuals, as is politics, which can never be isolated. If they are not made by the same individuals, then they are nevertheless made by those who are just as much ruled and directed by the upper class as this upper class is dependent on the work of its subjects. All that pertains to the state does not originate externally; rather it arises immanently from the economy itself. Both the economy and the state are human products and still are in accord with the material movement without difficulty, in this case the human movement of work. Both classes, the masters and the servants, in all subsequent societies (the primitive, oriental, ancient, feudal, modern, bourgeois) experience a related self-alienation that spreads and grows due to the prevailing category of exchange value. This is why Marx could say, "The propertied class and the proletarian class represent the same human alienation." The contentment of the former class and the bitterness of the latter class do not make *this kind of 'sameness,' that of the ruling economic and ideological category of relations*, false. This sameness provides the fertile ground on which the economy and state meet, and they reveal this convergence distinctly anyway. This is also where the political-legal system's "capacity to react" to production and commerce emanate—a point to which Engels referred time and time again. And it was in opposition to economicism and its one-sided, undialectical causality that lacked totality that caused him to make the following remarks: "According to the materialist conception of history, the ultimately determining element in history is the production and reproduction of real life. Neither Marx nor I have ever claimed more than this. If, then, somebody twists this around to mean that the economic element is the only determining one, he changes the sentence so that it becomes a meaningless, abstract, nonsensical phrase. The economic situation is the basis, but the various elements of the superstructure—political forms of the class struggle and its results—constitutions established by the victorious class after a successful battle, etc.—juridical forms, and even the reflexes of all these actual struggles in the minds of the participants, political, legal, philosophical theories, religious views and their further development into systems of dogmas—also exercise their influence upon the course of the political struggles and in many cases prevail in determining their form. There is a reciprocal effect caused by all these elements in which, among all the possible contingencies, the economic movement finally asserts itself as the necessary factor" (letter to J. Bloch, 1890). The reciprocal effect assumed by Engels clearly requires something relatively common between the mode of production and consciousness, which may possibly still be backward and illusionary. Meanwhile, that which is structurally common between the economy and the political-legal superstructure —like the contractual relationship of the owners of commodities with each other and the contractual ideology of the bourgeois liberal state, as is also the case with monopoly capitalism and the growing fascist tendencies of the state—can be clearly seen. Despite its particularly deceptive character and the illusion it evokes of harmonizing the economic contradictions, even political ideology is not just illusion of the same kind as religious ideology—which is frequently less deceptive—can be. Therefore, it is imperative to prove that it would not be appropriate to deduce the mode of production from the type of state of an epoch when even we no longer have information about the mode. For example, the spotted map of the medieval period reveals a number of small economic centers constituting a village and city economic system; the tight centralization of the great kingdoms of the seventeenth century reveals a period that had manufacturing as its base while production and agriculture were expanding. Often one can see the type of state being formed in each economic mode—and not merely the contents of that which the political ideologies then reflect in a vague or idealistic way. Thus, free enterprise or the emancipation of the growing productive forces from the limitations of the guilds and their reglimentation on the one hand, and the idealized bourgeois domain of human rights on the other, were made from the same wood—not to mention, spirit. The reflection of a liberal superstructure activated the basis here with particular clarity; that is, it even activated the free enterprise economy on its own. The transition here is not all that complicated given the minimal difference between the basis of business and the structure of the state. Its complexity is hardly much greater than the equation of a second or third degree of difficulty at the most.

However, everything cannot be so easily shifted around everywhere. Business does not only assume a nationalized form, but, whenever the transformation occurs in "lofty domains," it also becomes more difficult to perceive this, and the *mediations* are vast and more subtle. Certainly even the political superstructure cannot be seen by its very own constituents right then and there, especially when its manifestation is too beautiful to be true. In the nineteenth century it was still possible for the entrepreneur or the lawyer to imagine subjectively that he was acting mainly in behalf of humanity. The

bourgeoisie had not yet become cynical, so that the ideological reasons that they presented for their motives could appear as their own
and as the starting point of their actions. It is relatively easy to grasp
the equation economy = state, to be sure, not according to the way
the beneficiaries at the time understood it, but according to Marxist
terms. However, with regard to the fields of *art*, *religion*, and *philosophy*,
the components predicated on the same illusory givens cannot be
explained directly by the Marxist analysis or even partly by the base.
The cultural forms with which human beings become aware of social
conflicts, engage in them, or surpass them, such forms could only
be developed in a well-intentioned manner. Thus, the cultural-
ideological change is just as imperceptible from the Marxist analytical viewpoint as is the political shift. This is due to the fact that the
cultural shift shows a creative, reflecting consciousness that demonstrates manifold ways of transformation. This distinction evaded the
materialist analysis itself, especially when it tended to take art, etc.,
too lightly. The economic schematism could not have been more
inappropriate in dealing with Pushkin or even with Tolstoy, in the
early days of the Soviet Union. In this way, the Soviets robbed
themselves of their great writers. Each one of them was labeled with
an economic tag: Gogol was the "literary representative of the land-
owners," and Tolstoy stood for the "realism of the worldly aristoc-
racy," and that was that. Even Dostoievsky, the troublesome genius,
was reduced completely to the representative of a reading public,
which itself was schematized to resemble a symphony that could be
played upon a comb. "Dostoievsky became and is partially the writer
of the romantic anti-capitalist, petty bourgeois, intellectual opposition, a class which vacillates between the Right and the Left, with a
wide-open, paved road toward reactionaryism in the direction of the
Right, and a narrow, difficult road toward revolution in the direction
of the Left." *C'est tout, c'est Dostoievsky.* Or, in other words, this would
be the essence of Prince Mishkin, or the Grand Inquisitor's scene, or
Ivan Karamazov, whose problems would lead in the direction of the
wide-open, paved road. The heyday of this schematism is now gone.
By caricaturing literature, such schematism has shown how dangerous it can be, especially when Thersites is made to seem proud of
economic materialism. Consequently, one could learn from the lack
of mediations that became apparent in the schematism due to the
methodological rashness that was also not irrelevant. Even Franz

Mehring's diligent analyses of the superstructure revealed this weakness. In his time Georg Lukács correctly demonstrated that Mehring's analyses in his book *Die Lessing-Legende* were profound and sensitive "when they dealt with the organization of the state and army in the time of Frederick the Great or Napoleon. However, they have much less validity and depth as soon as he deals with the literary, scientific, and religious constellations of the same epoch" (*History and Class Consciousness*, 1923). Kautsky, who employed economistic methods to study the history of ancient Christianity, the Orient, and, in part, Thomas Münzer, was much worse. Even Lukács in his later Marxist literary essays was not able at times to avoid schematism in contrast to his interpretation of Hölderlin as the lost *citoyen*, as the poet who wrote about the utopia of the *citoyen*.

Here is a case in point: the observer who enters the halls of art and wisdom is moved by a sublime feeling, and there is a reason for this. This feeling marks the difference in greatness, the difference in mediating between Athens as a place of commerce and as a place for the Parthenon, which arose in solemn peace as did Athens. The difference in mediation also contributes to the shock of idealists and the pleasure of materialists when the economic reasons for the sonatas, tragedies, temples, etc., are revealed. The idealists want to disregard such mediation, while the materialists want to comprehend it from top to bottom. Now, to be sure, the problem of this mediation, in other words, of *the production of culture*, cannot be treated dualistically in any way. Nothing is accomplished by continually dismembering the economic body, or the ideological ghost of the soul. The very best that can be derived from this method consists of mysterious dilutions, vaporizations, or sublimations of the economic material so that it becomes like ideological clouds in the sky. Such attempts to derive the production of culture from isolated economicism recall similar dualistic dilemmas that Baroque thinkers underwent when searching for the transitions between the "substances," body and soul, *extensio* and *cogitatio*, spaciousness and consciousness. The alleged "fluids of the nerves" that were thought at that time to be the conductors of everything between the "expanded and thinking substance" were figures of speech, nothing more. They formed the body-soul relationship, which Descartes had called a "powerful combination," and were not fluid and flexible themselves. In their dilemma the thinkers of that time groped for a transcendental mediation, for one created by

God out of matter and spirit that were allowed to function independently of one another like two clocks in Geulincx's writings. Such a transcendental mediation is naturally unthinkable for economicism. It resorts to the easiest reduction, the easiest etherealization (*Entrealisierung*) of the cultural superstructure—that which does not exist does not have to be explained in detail. In short, reification and mediation exclude each other particularly in cultural problems, in which is understood to be the transition from the economic mode to cultural ideology. Here they are most hopeless. Economics by itself cannot explain cultural history, just as the intellect alone is incapable of doing this—as if a piano did not need a player, as if the origins of consciousness were in the brain. It is here, too, that totality must be grasped, for it is only in the totality that the intellect has a place "to transform material into ideas," this intellect, which can be comprehended neither by economicism nor by mechanism. Here is the point: human beings make the economy together with the superstructure, which does not always have a hazy reflection; in turn, the economy and the superstructure together make human beings again in the totality of the subject-object relationship, without the undialectical antagonisms derived from abstraction.

Hegel says that "to sublate such antagonisms which have become firm is the major concern of reason." And this sublation also reoccurs constantly for the economic-cultural problem as we comprehend the work process, the changing relationship of human beings to one another and to nature in history, the diapason of a time and its society that cause everything to be related. Here, too, the work process is the primary as well as the true "final judgment." Not only does it account for the shift at one time between the economy and ideology, between the interaction of base and superstructure from the beginning of history, but it continually accounts for all the shifts, even up to the point at which the work process reflects itself in a hazy but also idealistic way that leads to the formation of an ideal picture based on the division of labor. And it is exactly here that the *cultural* superstructure establishes itself as product and place of this reflection. To be sure, something new begins with this reflection as with every starting point of another mediation of the base, namely, *the topos of a superstructure itself.* To what extent it can really be considered something new can be answered by slightly changed phrase from Leibniz, who added a footnote to Locke's "nihil est intellectu quod non fuent in sensu."

Leibniz commented sarcastically on Locke's statement, as well as perceptively, in his *Nouveaux essais*: "nisi intellectus ipse." And here Leibniz's *intellectus* provides a striking parallel, for the superstructure as such is not contained in the base by definition. It appears as its own *topos*. Certainly, it is not as if the pervasive, common social substance were to be thrown off course by the *novum* superstructure. The basic perspective of historical materialism remains. Insofar as the *topos* deriving from the senses (and thus it is not estranged) appears and is set forward according to and because of the division of labor, it also expands and fills itself culturally with each basic category of the work relationship, which lies at its root in the base. It expands according to the form, fills itself according to the substance with the contradictions in the relations of work and in the illusion of the solution that had already been prepared in the base but had not been developed and hypostatized. The basic category of commodity has run through the economy since the seventeenth century just as it has run through the quantifications of mathematical natural sciences and the opposing ideologies, which provide the explosive potential for utopias in their opposition. And, on the other hand, the free competition of commodity-owners has substantially gilded the great, desirable individuals of the moral and literary superstructure itself as well as the subject of self-realization or of the titanic person, the entrepreneur. Laissez-faire has made them important. And the same tendency that undermined the hierarchical levels of the feudal estate society brought about a change even in a field that seems to be the very opposite of the base. This is the case with music, where there was a new shift from the horizontally corporate-structured fugue to the free movement of voice and thematically dialectical activity of the sonata symphony. This is the way the form of the superstructure is and remains different from the base. And it is by no means an empty form; rather, it fills and nourishes itself in regard to its contents with the common social temper that emanates each time from the base. Yet, even when it is now ready for expression, that which has been creatively transformed in the cultural superstructure and assumes a particular form does not exhaust itself in the final account. This is revealed just by the very different nature of the historical transitoriness of the transformed content of the superstructure, partly in the legal and political structures and partly in the cultural. The ancient slave and feudal societies no longer exist, but this is not the case with Greek and medieval art. Both have experienced numerous revivals in history that bring out new problems and continue to show their validity. Marx himself emphasized this "non-synchronous development." He considered Greek art an eternal and even incomparable model. In other words, there is a relative return of the cultural superstructure even when the base disappears, and this return is subsumed by the so-called cultural heritage quite independently of preservation through censorship or imitation. Such a "return" demonstrates the difference between the ideologically unreflected base and culture and the creatively postulated transformations in a more or less pointed manner. Of course, the transformations have an advantage: the sublimating medium is in a surprising, better, and instructive position to find ways of shifting, whereby the process of change, according to Marx, occurred most readily in the oldest part of the cultural superstructure and reflection—in mythology. The mediations that have continued and have become increasingly richer emerged at first with especially strong illusions, blossomed with transpositions and harmonization of the social contradictions. "It is well-known," Marx said in the introduction to *The Critique of Political Economy*, "that Greek mythology was not only the arsenal of Greek art, but was also its fundament . . . . Greek art has Greek mythology as its prerequisite; this means nature and the social form already elaborated by the imagination of the people in an unconscious, artistic form." So, even after mythology has disappeared or has dried up through the rational, subject-object relationship, even since the Renaissance, the artistic transformation still lives from mythological elements that are recollected. This is the case with Raphael and Rembrandt, not to mention Shakespeare and Goethe. This is also true of Jakob Böhme as it is of Hegel. And this is possible (even if we take into consideration the first false consciousness to which mythology contributed many times) because the mythology that preceded art (even the pre-Greek) was the first and most prevalent medium of change (*Umschaltung*). This was not due to the fact that "a higher level of immediacy was reproduced," as Lukács has asserted in *History and Class Consciousness*, but among other things, it was due to the fact that at this level of undeveloped relations of production it was still relatively easy to transpose and transcend the harmonization of social contradictions. Moreover, the relations of production under which the mythology formed itself were not strongly developed and had not yet been rationalized. So, the "imagination of the people" (*Volksphantasie*), as Marx labeled it, had its formative period invigorating nature when a life of nature was not very far from one of rationalism. Aside from the harmonizing elements, there were elements of rebellion depicted throughout, and they were inescapable in the mythological exaggerations, as in the Prometheus myth or in the *Eritis sicut deus* right in the midst of the ruling class ideology. And last the relations of production, which were not fully developed, caused the mythology to hold on to corresponding archetypes of primitivism, those archetypes of imagination without which great writing and a worldly philosophy are impossible. The work relationship is filled with such archetypes: master and servant. Almost half of mythology consists of just these kinds of hierarchical relations designated by rank and file: the stranger, the native, the master, etc. Here there is still something surprising to note: the first appearances of mythology precede the starting point of the division of labor and the formation of classes. They can be found in primitive communism itself and in later, increasing elements of rebellion, which recall primitive communism. At that time it was not the task of mythos to convey and normalize social contradictions in an imaginative way. Rather, myth tended to convey the fear and tension in relation to nature that was felt to be eerie: all the outstanding archetypes have their origins here, especially the later distinctively rebellious myths. For instance, Prometheus brings fire and light from the gods to humankind. And it is just this utopian and bright impact, this wish-scenery in the mythology, that allowed the cultural ideology nourished by mythology to become *one that could be culture* and not only one of beautifully colored evil, of the *toto coelo* soluble illusion. As we shall presently see, this is decisive for the surplus, which distinguishes culture from mere ideology. That which is itself untrue in the mere mythological as such is the hypostatization of its conceptions and also of its wish-sceneries in a *rigid and existing postulated transcendence*. But that which remains, even if it is *not yet true* in the mythological, can be the indicated *utopian overtaking* in it. To be more exact, it can be that sequence of hope—the night-light that cultural consciousness decisively adopted from the arsenal and fundaments of mythology. And such a thing is not to be invalidated, even when there may no longer be a business life to switch around any more, even when the ideologues of false consciousness yield to the clear recognition of what is and, above all, what will be. Here is where cultural production can finally preserve and concretize itself, even though or because the capacity for mythological transformation according to its imagination has become dried up or unnecessary. On the other hand, ethics without ideology and without property, aesthetics without illusion, dogmatism without superstition, and free imagination would ultimately like to and could take root here.

Genius and Ideological Surplus

The same nectar knows how to flourish over and beyond business. This does not depend solely on money that cultivates the seeds of the fruit and lets them grow, for whatever flourishes, sings, and writes in a meaningful way, whatever becomes significant beyond its own way, extends itself into the wide blue yonder beyond what economics has assigned it. This is the direction a significant thinker takes in order to move and operate, somebody who subjectively does not at all belong to business. The great capacity to express things and the ultimate form of the expression itself carry with them false consciousness about the real forces and processes in society in an immediate way just as the insignificant ideologies do. But, there is something more here. Whatever more has to be transformed out of this and its ideological surplus allows for a so-called true consciousness to form itself in the mere false consciousness of ideology at least in regard to the particular epoch. Actually, this is not ideology but rather something that surpasses the particular epoch in a utopian way. This new mode of transforming accomplished by a person for the first time in a mythological way at the beginning is called *genius*.

It is well known that the superstructure revolutionizes itself more slowly than the base, but the duration of the actual surplus in its productive late stage is completely different from the lethargy in the revolution. The period of the surplus distinguishes itself from the general, unselective lethargy of the superstructure by its connection to that which is significant. It is not the customary but the uncustomary that continually distinguishes individual works of the superstructure. Marx would have been the last one to break with the materialist notion of history. Yet, in spite of this, he maintained that there were careers of genius that were connected to historical materialism. "The difficulty does not consist in understanding that Greek art and epics are connected to certain social forms of development. The difficulty is that they still provide artistic pleasure for us and to a certain extent are considered as standards and incomparable models." Childlikeness, one can also say youthfulness, which Marx noted as a special feature of the Greek superstructure, has been a characteristic of genius for ages. To be sure, on the basis of historical materialism, Marx rejected both the sober as well as the exaggerated appraisal of the individual person. It is not the so-called chosen men who make history that calls forth and finds its Cromwells and Napoleons when it needs them, nor is history itself called forth or created by the Cromwells and Napoleons. But the role of genius itself cannot be invalidated because the bourgeoisie has given great men laurels and made statues out of them *post festum*. Cromwell and Napoleon were powerful figures, who not only carried out history but also made it. Marxism itself, which appears to dethrone people, is named after the mighty person of its founder, and Marxism is what it is because the great moment found a great specimen, not just a Proudhon or even a Lassalle, for example. In other words, geniuses are indeed historical forces of production, as political as they are ideological, which is especially important in the present context. This means that they make their mark on culture as it shifts around. Even when the generals Cromwell and Napoleon could have been replaced by others from the same camp, it is hardly conceivable that the same thing could have occurred in the field of *cultural surplus*, the production of which is our present problem and theme. Nor did the same thing ever happen. Creative geniuses are not replaceable when they have not been there.

There are many centuries that objectively provided important possibilities and tasks for poetry or philosophy. However, when the specific talents necessary for the tasks were missing, the tasks went unfulfilled. The possibility remained empty. For example, such an empty spot arose when German painting became stale after Dürer and Holbein and became nothing when their works were sold out. There is another even more apparent empty spot—and this is astonishing—when one considers that there is no further development of the requiem text of the *dies irae oratorium* with the text of St. John's revelation about the origins of the divine Jerusalem (*apocalypsis cum figuris*), even though there were many painters and artists from Dürer onward who treated this theme. (Thomas Mann based his novel *Doctor Faustus* right on this remarkable empty spot *post festum*.)

I have drawn attention to other cultural gaps that arose because the Homers and Dantes were missing in my book *Das Materialismus-problem* (*The Problem of Materialism*), and here I mean the well-formed epic based on the great gnostic myth about the divine journey of the soul (a myth that is no less than that of *The Divine Comedy*). Works of this kind have not always found their creators even when the cultural possibility was definitely there, and the missing artist was by no means replaceable. A cultural tendency without a creative genius remains a kind of blank page within the mere genre—an empty spot. In any case, the tenable essence does not appear in culture without the creative person—a work with surplus that has a continual impact, a work of genius.

Though no genius has ever floated completely above his times, it is certainly true that the cultural light that raised itself above the ideology of its times and floated above it continues to shine, and it is through this light that the productive power called genius expresses itself, mediates, transforms, and stimulates. Here it is clear that the category of genius should no longer be used ideologically or be misunderstood. Genius does not produce cultural surplus because it is especially personal (in the entrepreneurial sense of master) or because it is especially atavistic or archaic, like a shaman from primitive times who has arisen in broad daylight. Neither would have much of a significant continual impact. At best, the first would result in a sharply chiseled profile (like the so-called artistic princes who were not exceptions, as other princes have shown). The other would yield a magical patina (as they can be found more commonly in the works of Swedenborg than in those of Goethe or Hegel). The surplus that genius engenders is much more like something that has a continual impact, is valid and utopian: *ideological surplus arises according to the utopian function in the formation of ideology and above this ideology.* Thus, great art or great philosophy is not only its time manifested in images and ideas, but it is also *the journey of its time and the concerns of its time if it is anything at all,* manifested in images and ideas. From this vantage point, it is new for its time. From the vantage point of all times, it is that which is not yet fulfilled. It is from this element of utopia alone, which ultimately must be prepared in advance by the phenomenon of genius, that the continual impact of the surplus is derived and goes beyond the particular ideology of an epoch. Most of all, it is this element that produces the valid, eternal, genuine quality and the transformed and transforming truth of this surplus that accounts for the continual impact in the midst of its mere ideological character, that is, false consciousness in the immediate present and beyond it.

To be sure, the good newness is never completely new, for long before its existence in history there is what Marx has called the "dream about a thing." However, the articulated newness itself appears as a breakthrough each time, and this breakthrough is what constitutes its passport or seal of newness—right there in the successful work of genius, and certainly not only in art, but also in those new oceans that are definitely linked to it and on which Kant sailed with the term transcendental production, and that Hegel sighted when he first distinguished the dialectics as explosive powder in the relation of a production that was no longer formal. Even religion in its long changing history in which only the names of the gods are ideological has experienced the decisive breakthrough of that "Look, I'm making everything new" that it has made not-exchangeable up through the present with the mere *religio* = re-alignment. If the mythological element, that is, the archaic element of primitive times, was the ground and arsenal for this throughout the centuries, then it became reutilized by the essential function of genius itself. For genius is primarily a view into the world, which has become lost. And that which continues to be of significance keeps itself fresh and above all of the ideologies of time thanks to the power of genius—even if Hecuba, who was most concerned with ideology in her time and place, is long forgotten and no longer even remembered by the poem about her. Instead of regression, the work of genius produces more of a projection, and its figures and situations themselves—above all as an aesthetic work—give expression to the essential lines of extension that are part of its driving force. The ideology in a great work reflects and justifies its times, the utopia in it rips open the times, brings them to an end, brings them to that end where there would no longer be a mere past and its ideology, but rather where it could be shown: *tua propria vera res agitur.*

If we no longer need to embellish, then our concern will present itself clearly everywhere. This is the case with the classless society insofar as master and servant disappear, that is, when neither the master nor the servant has cause to reproach each other anymore. False consciousness, the illusory cultural solution of social contradictions, will be eliminated along with these two roles themselves.

They will perish. But then the question arises, How will the rose blossom without dung? How will the ideological surplus blossom without ideology? To be sure, it is unfortunately somewhat premature to ask this question, one that is unfortunately not on the agenda in our ideological times. However, the question has already been posed sarcastically by anti-Marxist lovers of the philosophical lie and has been just as sarcastically dismissed by vulgar-Marxist lovers of insipidity. We have seen that the major function of ideology is the premature and illusory solution of social contradictions, the opposite of research into materialism. The illusory solution gives rise to false consciousness, which an epoch has about itself. Moreover, it fills the figurative formation of the cultural, of culture's capacity to contemplate itself. However, it has already become evident that not every cultural work of the past has necessarily been bound by this kind of ideological harmonization. For example, as a musician of an ideology that was still revolutionary, Beethoven obtained significantly less ideology in a static-harmonious sense than he did in a dashing utopian sense. Even if this dashing utopian spark was connected to the economic mode that allowed more freedom for the individual, it was nevertheless that which constituted the gripping nature of the *Eroica* and is undoubtedly that which filled it with different implications when heard: greatness without oppression, enthusiasm without narcotics, freedom without the entrepreneurial verve: All this makes art like that of Beethoven's thinkable even without the ideological prerequisites. To be sure, Beethoven would not have composed his work the way he did without the French Revolution in mind, but he would have also composed without the false consciousness of the French Revolution, without the actual entrepreneurial ideology that cloaked itself in freedom, equality, and brotherhood. To be sure, the case is much more complex when we consider cultural works of a non-dynamic or non-revolutionary ideology, but rather works of a static ideology—for example, works by Giotto and Dante. No matter how great, or particularly illuminating and eternal, the surplus of these creations are, they are nevertheless bound by the corporate estate society of their times and the static ideology. Its structural formation and ostensible equanimity are transmitted in these great works—as really structured, structural formations and equanimity.

But is the feudal society with its church really transmitted by what

Giotto and Dante had in mind? Are there not also implications in their works that do not need the Middle Ages to be understood and brought to light? For example, are the great implications of "equanimity," "order," and "hierarchy" sufficiently explained by and limited to the feudal estate society? If they are missing in Cézanne's works, are they unproducible and impossible to find in a classless society? Certainly not. Rather, the same utopia of "equanimity," which as such gave the estate society its cultural surplus, will allow or have to allow the formation of an unreactionary anticipatory illumination that is not self-evident and is unsettling. It is here that excitement finds peace, time becomes space and looks upon this as if everything had found its place—I am talking about an anticipatory illumination that could never be realized in an ideology of the status quo but, rather, has been connected to it like an explosive, as though it could always engender the most stimulating surplus beyond the ideology. By not receding to a metaphysical plus, the elimination of a class ideology enables the entire novum of surplus to become one that no longer needs to be one beyond ideology or one above false consciousness, which only portrays objective falsehood, even in its best form. Instead of this, a surplus is needed *beyond the elimination of social contradictions that has really begun.* This means a surplus beyond the possible concretization of a partial solution produced by a vulgar Marxism, which is conceivable even in a classless society. Vulgar Marxism is already haunting the world in a kind of petit bourgeois communism, or, to put it in a less paradoxical way, it sees the main goal of communism in triviality such as an electric refrigerator for everyone, or art for everyone. It is exactly against such red philistinism that the new surplus, free of ideology, establishes and launches its utopian essence, its most central concern. It is the surplus of the utopian conscience and concern in a world, which itself has not arisen with the classless society, free from antagonisms and antagonistic contradictions. Nor is this surplus finished with the contradiction of the subject and its own objectifications to which it is still tied as to a stranger. Nor is the surplus finished with the contradiction in which the totality of the actual exists as one that has not yet become and stands in relation to everything that has become inadequate.

Both contradictions—the first as motor of the remaining dialectic, the second as its alluring final goal—are ultimately one contradiction or the basic contradiction that will keep the world process going until the due result comes about. Yet, insofar as this basic contradiction pervades the entire tendency as well as the latency of the world process and the illumination process of the world material, it is not accordingly resolved as such in the classless society. Rather, the classless society is only the elimination of its dreariest part—the class contradiction along with its illusion of premature harmony that is hypostatized as complete. But the thorn remains, the restlessness of the utopian function remains, and of the works—not their illusion, but their structured anticipatory illumination. This function, which now arises completely free of ideology, does not at all stop once ideology and its foundation perish; rather, it now begins to be free and ordered, conscious and concrete. To prepare the essence of what is due to be realized—of the individual who is no longer to be humiliated, enslaved, forsaken, scorned, estranged, annihilated, and deprived of identity—this is not the goal or end of the classless society, which resolves the major contradictions in a relative way. On the contrary, it is the beginning of its work. Consequently, the production itself of genius can first attain the power of its complete force of production in the world only after the elimination of ideology and all interest in illusion.

The possibility for a socialist cultural heritage only indicates the sphere of receptivity of what is already happening in the productive sphere much beyond the platitude of "Good for you that you're following in your grandfather's footsteps," and the possibility for a socialist heritage can only continue to arise in a more emancipatory way: beauty without falsehood, faith without delusion, mystery without mist. Realism that unfolds in this way is certainly not mechanical realism. Moreover, the shattering of illusion related to realism does not preserve itself or prove itself in the least by annihilating the anticipatory illumination and/or by becoming disconsolate. Such disconsolation itself belongs to the unreal, somewhat distorted mechanical materialism of the previous century and to that passive pessimism that played a decisive role in Schopenhauer's works, where it found its most genial manifestation, only because it cuts out time, process, and latency from the world, throws it away, and renounces it. However, realism cannot at all exist if it does not do justice to the enormous arsenal of the possible, that is, also to the hope, which is the correlate to the world that has not yet been thwarted. In this sense one may rest completely assured about the continual possibility for an aesthetics without illusion and aesthetics of truth that can hardly be endangered by a pessimism of continual gray. Of course, it remains to be seen whether the concrete utopia, which is free of ideology and abstraction, one which is no longer cultural surplus beyond ideology, can be given a name, can still be included in the category of "culture." Culture is creative. Culture has a contemplative quality. Culture has distanced itself quite a bit from the original etymological meaning of cultivation (*Bebauung*), namely, of human beings and not only of his fields of observation. Another kind of "economy," one in which interest and idea no longer stand in contrast to another or collide, has little room for the reification of the creative element, particularly of the powerless creative element. Disconcertment and observation exclude one another. This was already involved in those impulses behind iconoclasm, even though it was so mythical or inner-mythical, beginning with baptists. Nevertheless, culture of the past that really existed must be distinguished from reified imitation, that is, from the term culture consisting of statues, laurels, and museums from the past century, and now also from the doubly reified term of commodity culture and the cultural market, just as clearly as the socialist heritage must be distinguished everywhere from the cultural heritage of the bourgeoisie. The socialist cultural heritage belongs to the classless society as work, cultural work and its universal quality—culture. As cultivation, it will definitely be continued without ideology, particularly without reification, without the double reification that also remains historicism. Here, too, the result is that because of the continual utopian function in the work of genius, the connection of the transmitted culture to false consciousness of its time is capable of being dissolved. This is as true in regard to the productive heritage as in regard to the structured anticipatory illumination, which need not be productively tied to the ideological illusion. Thus, the withdrawal of ideology from the consciousness of the classless society need not be regretted by either side. That which remains, like the possible true element, had already been produced before this, not from ideology. It had been produced from the utopian function that worked within it and continues to operate. Today, ideology does not even produce long-lasting delusion, but it persists in manipulated fashions and their cheaply and interestingly made distractions, and the changes occur so rapidly and are so washed out that the dead dog of yesterday can run around in the park and romp just as merrily as the dangerous lion of today or tomorrow. Everything is relaxed, everything administered and made trivial; in short, everything is cashed in by capitalism. Utopia continues to be indelible. Thus, it allows one to remember in a productive way and to allow truth to be produced with realism, which is the realism of the process that has understood the urgency to produce that which is really new.

### Ideological Surplus in the Superstructure and the Genuinely Made Cultural Heritage

To do one thing and drop the other is very often advisable when one undertakes something. Lions do not attempt to circle and strike from all sides. Their course of action is the direct leap. Too much circling makes one indecisive. A buyer who makes a quick decision never lets himself be diverted. Rather, the narrow vision helps one accomplish one's goal more effectively. Even the wise man, just so he remains satisfied, extols the principle that Charles Ramuz presented in his *Story about the Soldier*: one should not seek to add something already owned to what one owns. But are these maxims really pertinent for the different ways and means by which the past is employed? Are they not really pertinent only for those ways that one does not use? If so, are they not a heavy, superfluous burden to carry around? And do these teachings not rely upon the opposite of the lions, namely, on weak subjects and times, totally different from the direct leap and fastest way?

In fact, it is in opposition to heritage as mere historicism that the truth addresses and concentrates on weak subjects and times, and only on them. It warns against all kinds of stipulations that could be carried over from the nineteenth century in regard to cultural heritage—against the ossified heritage of the past and the lifeless copies of mere facades against the dried-out wreaths and the decline of real historical thinking to pure epigonism. It was during this very time of decline that Ludwig Feuerbach wrote the following critique (and he wrote it against that school of history that was becoming much too historicist): "The chariot of world history is a tiny chariot. So, just as one cannot climb into it if one is too late, one can only obtain a place if one abandons some of the commodities of the old historical household utensils—and only takes along the most unsaleable, necessary, and essential things. For those who emigrated with the Greek sage Bias from Priene and dragged with them their household utensils, the Bias of *omnia mea mecum porto* must have seemed very abstract and negative."

Such a statement is a warning even today when unproductive groups comprehend the past only as clinging to the past and knowledge only as a recollection of humankind about that which they were. A significant architect, Gottfried Semper, realized more than a century ago quite correctly that style is the harmony of the appearance of a work of art with its historical origins. However, it was exactly because Semper lived in the time of caricature, the time of historical masquerades, that he drew the wrong conclusion from his observations, which were nearly faultless. Thus, he actually prevented the kind of productivity he was discussing by asserting that the previous history of architecture had already provided the essence of all buildings—the theater as Roman theater, the halls of justice as Palladian architecture, the military barracks as feudal fortress, the synagogue as masonic temple, and of course, the church as gothic edifice. Thus, the architect became the actor of history, that is, of its so-called treasure of forms, its "eternal patterns." Naturally, these patterns are not only limited to architecture and the history of art, and unfortunately, not only to the epigonism of the past century. Each and every reification of the "epochal," of the "tragical" and other pedantic schemes reveals this historical sickness.

In contrast, Feuerbach's anti-historical principle, so to speak, reveals the unstructural truth; it is against everything that contributes to seeing tradition only as tradition. Against that which endows heritage with the role of custodian of the past and not as master, avenger, and executor primarily of the revolutionary tradition and also of that which has not yet become in the great works of the past. Just as it was impossible in Feuerbach's time to bring about a total agreement between the ideology of power and the equilibrium of its statics, it was also impossible to accomplish an agreement in the victory march of the next ruling class. The only possibility would have been to recall socage (*Fron*), but not in a contemplative way, which created the possibility for the pure world of luxury in culture. This adds a new kind of iconoclasm to the term cultural heritage and amounts to eliminating the luxury of the victors in it. Here Benjamin hit the mark in his comments about this in his *Theses on the Philosophy of History* even though he tended to be too derisive in his generalizations. "Accordingly, empathy with the victor always benefits the rulers. The historical materialist has addressed this point sufficiently. Up to the present whoever has triumphed has marched in the victory parade which leads the contemporary rulers to step over those people who are downtrodden. As has always been the custom, the spoils are carried in the victory parade. They are called the cultural treasures. They will have to reckon with a detached observer in the form of the historical materialist. For whatever he examines as cultural treasures . . . is never a document of culture without simultaneously being one of barbarism." However, on the other hand, Benjamin said something before this about spiritual matters. "In spite of this, the latter (spiritual things) make their presence felt differently in the class struggle than as the spoils which fall to the victor. They are alive as confidence, courage, humor, cunning, and fortitude, and they have a retroactive effect as time moves along. They call into question each victory of the ruling class time and time again."

In addition, cultural heritage only becomes what it is when the heir does not die along with the benefactor, when he stands on the side of the future in the past, when he stands with what is indelible in the cultural heritage and not with the takeover of parasitical rulers. Cultural heritage will stop being a victory march with the spoils as loans on security—it will stop being a funeral watch, or monument as soon as the earth possesses the power to transform what has been transmitted by the past into something immortal and, if necessary, in spite of itself, to transform what is anticipated that continues to be an element in it and constitutes the surplus—the surplus not only beyond the former ideology but also beyond that which mere contemplation envisions as *refined completion* of the great work of culture and engenders silence. If the utopian function (in its most visible form, in the function of genius) produced the cultural surplus from the ideology of then and there, then the same function continues to operate in the productive cultural heritage that is no longer refined. It operates as the *successive continuation of the implications* in the cultural constellations of the past gathered around us as non-past. This is just the same thing as the emphasis on the future in the past that is significant and continues to be significant to the degree that the genuine agent (*Täter*) of cultural heritage reaches into the past, and in this very same act the past itself anticipates him, involves and needs him. Thought cannot forge itself into reality when reality does not forge itself into thought. This Marxist principle of knowledge is also valid for the reality, which is present as cultural heritage. *Omnia mea mecum porto*: the chariot of world history only carries that with it that forges itself forward out of the past. It carries only that luggage that can be used actively and in a worthwhile way for the future, not that which is antiquated. It carries only that which has an order to be sealed. To be sure, the chariot is part of a process that carries this living heritage of history with it by necessity. Otherwise, there would only be abstract putsches instead of concrete revolutions, ephemeral news of the day instead of—world history.

As we have seen, the weak person is not fit to bear this heritage. He is overwhelmed by it. He does not invent anything; rather, at best, he lets things out or produces the weaknesses of those things he imitates. However, it should be added here that, if the epigone does not have the strength to continue the heritage, this is also true of the other seemingly more active kind of parasite—the plunderer, the historical pirate. This latter type appears where the spirit of the rulers takes over history only for the purpose of falsifying it. The Nazi desecration of the past was constituted in this way. Rosenberg only carried everything that Joseph de Gobineau and Houston Stewart Chamberlain had started *ad absurdum*. Of course, the sublime and pretentious explanation of history was also constituted in this way by the Stefan George Circle, those poets who encompassed the beautiful mountains of culture from Pindar to Hölderlin, from Frederick the Second of Hohenstaufen to Napoleon and Goethe, in order to proclaim their own scant powers. Walter Benjamin had good reason for calling something like Gundolf's biography of Goethe "a monumental testimony to his own statuette." Whenever or wherever this occurs, there is no assumption of heritage, but rather, a falsification of pedigree; that is, the simulation of the past occurs along with the right to complete the task. All this only amounts to the opposite picture of heritage since historicism involves the sterile incarceration of history. Of course, this is the complete opposite of sterility itself; yet, they are connected to each other. Historicism, insofar as it was self-conscious and not presumptuous—maybe it was bombastic at times but it was not supercilious—still possessed a good side by seeking to develop that new art of reading, namely, philology, which the "mountain climbers" of history had completely lost. Philology is or was the endeavor to discover the opinion of the author himself in the text that he authentically produced. This "art" gradually became dissipated by the late bourgeois legacy hunters, by the pretenders, who interpreted the text in such a way to make their own ineffective wishing most important. It is amazing to see what Heidegger himself with his pseudo-philology and pseudo-interpretation read out of Hölderlin, Anaximander, Parmenides, Plato, and Kant. The mountains endure labor pains only to give birth to a private sphere of interests. The profundity of culture is interpreted by ideologies of decadence. The mountain climbing of history is done in such a way that it becomes the opposite of a concrete heritage like epigonism, and furthermore, it becomes its caricature. Genuine heritage is and remains precise and progressive transformation, and to be sure, a transformation of that immanent material in the material of heritage intended for completion without ideology, with implication. This is how that which is not just remembered originates. Goethe discussed this in his essay *Wiederholte Spiegelungen* (*Repeated Reflections*, 1823), and to be sure, with ever increasing significance: "A drive unfolds from all of this, a drive to charm and to realize everything out of the past that is possible . . . . If one now considers that repeated moral reflections not only keep the past alive but even raise it to a higher life, then one will keep in mind the entophytic phenomena whose reflections do not wane but rather flare up at the right moment, then one will attain a symbol of that which has often repeated itself in the history of the arts and sciences, the church, and even in the political world, and still repeats itself every day."

In addition to this, there is an element of revenge in the assumption of culture insofar as it restores that which had been beaten to the ground or deprived of recognition in its day, and justice will now be done. There is something executory in the assumption of heritage in that it disdains that which had been called famous in its own time without due reason, disconnects that which had been famous in its own time with good reason based on evidence from the ideology of that time and now continually fills it with the true evidence of its implications. In this way posterity takes just as much fame as it continues to transmit in a more substantial form. All this depends on the material to be transmitted insofar as it has its indelibility in the past and makes itself useful. It cooperates with heritage insofar as it lives up to its potential and continues to develop after its final conception. In fact, the historical material is continually transformed in the mere contemplative recollection. No work of history from one epoch appears to be the same as one of the next epoch, and nothing reveals the influence of history so much as the descriptive studies of history themselves. One hundred evenings of thorough work on Sophocles or Plato, on Dante or St. Thomas Aquinas, do not exclude the possibility that what has become clear one year will not return to trouble one the next, that what was unclear will transform itself because of an imperceptible shift of the value system in connection with the guiding lights. As always the social changes of entire epochs nurtured the particular ideology of the epoch with ideas of the past that were accommodable, and this was also the case with the reception of Greece in Germany, developed in the different images of Winckelmann, then Hölderlin, and Nietzsche. Yet, how will things be when, for the first time, there is no subject for ideology to make repeated reflections with, but rather, when the transformation moves toward complete liberation of the cultural surplus? Here I mean the cultural surplus beyond any kind of ideology, that is, *even beyond the antiquated reification of culture*, in short, cultural surplus that stems from the utopian function in the creation of culture and fills the horizon of times with such surplus. That which could originate in this classless process would not only be transformed heritage, but also the rectified heritage. It would be *transformation as the revelation of truth*. It would be, like all fruitful criticism, the mortification of the works, which means to view them as if one were viewing ruins and fragments instead of finished products, glistening works that had been given the final touch. It would be, like all fruitful rebirth, the taking seriously of that anticipatory illumination, which would no longer make the great works useful for precipitous harmony in the service of ideology; rather, it would make them useful information of justice that would arise. If this anticipatory illumination, as structured illumination, has nothing in common with embellishment—rather, if it is based more on the tendency and latency of the time and on the unknown essence (*das Eigentliche*) in which the world (not art) could attain its aim—then this is realism. To be sure, though, it is certainly not naturalism. It is that realism of tendency and latency (the realism that touches on both) that includes the latent frames of the powerful reality of Velasquez, Balzac, and Tolstoy, just as it has made the widest reality of the powerful latency of Goethe's *Faust*. And the continual and effective *conversion* of the material into the hypothetical in the cultural heritage, that is, *in the utopian surplus* as both *heritage and anticipatory illumination*, sublates the material in such a minimal way that it opens up its potential in the most vigorous manner and articulates its horizon. Due to this process, material is not left idealistically or even surpassed. Rather, it continues to enlighten, opens itself up *more and more to us, to the coming foundation of the consensus*, to that which has not yet become, that which has still not been accomplished, but which has not been thwarted in existence *(Sein)*, in existence as realm. Thus the difference between tradition and producing the future is dissolved; certainly the contrast is dissolved. The revelation of truth in the cultural heritage is a territory with boundary lines stripped away in the wider territory of the anticipatory illumination that is to be articulated in a responsible and concrete way. The commodity category of alienated past comes to a halt in this productivity, and the extreme category of contemplative historicism no longer has a place here: the indelible of history stands upright in the middle of the process of production and articulation on the front instead of laying on its back. Now this would be real cultural heritage, with tradition of the future.

Despite the fact that Hegel was so antiquarian in regard to his contemplation, he himself had an anticipatory illumination concerning the hope of heritage because of his utopian dialectic, which was against the denial of cryptic-utopian totality. This is why he stated, "History depicts what is changeable, what is past, what has disappeared in the darkness of the past, what is no longer here." Then later on in the same connection: "What each generation has engendered in science and in intellectual endeavors is an heirloom, which former ages accumulated, a relic, in which all species of humankind gratefully and cheerfully hung up, something that helped them through life, something that they garnered from the profound reaches of nature and spirit. This inheritance is both the reception and assumption of heritage ... and at the same time this received legacy is reduced to material lying about that which is metamorphized by the intellect." The same thing is expressed in the unity of the dialectical process: "The intellect, consuming the shell of its existence, does not merely assume another shell, nor does it only rise rejuvenated from the ashes of its shape, but it goes forth exalted, transfigured, a pure spirit from the shell. To be sure, it emerges against itself, consumes its existence (*Dasein*), but in the process of consumption, it assimilates its existence, and its process of formation becomes the material from which its work raises itself to a new formation."

Everything must be able to begin in such a way, with a new quality. One does not discover new parts of the world if one does not have the courage to lose sight of familiar shores. But everything that is alive from the old shores comes along in the process of the new, of the essential, and sails toward something that is no less Jacobin, no more deliberately conservative than concrete revolution. It is even possible that only that novum will emerge in the process that was intended in the past—as tendentious. Then the maxim reads as follows: if the way is begun, then the revolution completes it. Or, to put it in Marx's formulation of the same thing: "the reformation of consciousness only consists in letting the world enter one's consciousness, in waking up the world from the dream about itself, in explaining its own actions to itself. . . . Then it can be shown that it does not concern a large hyphen between past and future but the completion of the idea of the past" (letter to Ruge, 1843). And it is precisely this "dream about a thing" that transforms history from the temple of memory into an arsenal. With recollection, the cultural heritage only begins, but there is no point at which the heritage is circumscribed by recollection nor exhausted by it. Rather, *hope comes primarily from cultural work.* Only hope understands and also completes the past, opens the long, common highway. With Hitler way in the rear, in a dark hole, with Spartacus and Münzer nearby on the side; with the actual trash in buried nothingness, but with the great works as a symbolic chorus announcing the coming existence.

Three Stages, also Three Types in the Surplus without Ideology
(Factors That Make for Heritage in the Rise, Flourishing, and
Decline of Epochs)

Not everything presents itself in the same way to conscious inheritors for the purpose of transformation. They themselves have paid close attention to the past and know how many beautiful things originated in a nefarious way. They know how much poverty luxury required and needed to attain its glory and to be considered as beautiful art history. Forgotten is the torment of the slaves and serfs, forgotten are the persecution of the Jews and the witchhunts: *non olet*, nothing stinks anymore. And undoubtedly the factors that make for heritage have to be qualified even with all their surplus beyond the past costs of production and ideology: the Jacobin cap and whatever is connected to it are easier to obtain than the crown and its consequences.

Altogether there are three stages that make for heritage, that is, that make for the possible meta-ideological surplus: the first stage is always that of the revolutionary rise, then that of the sanctimonious flourishing, and finally the stage of spotted decline, which until now has often been overlooked. As far as the *first* stage is concerned, that of the *revolutionary rise*, it is the one with which we have more of an elective affinity, and it is obviously the least questionable. A proletariat as rising class readily took over people, symbols, and slogans from the struggles of liberation of former oppressed classes and used them for its purposes. Even when the uprising did not lead to the formation of a class with a future orientation, there was some identification here and there, namely, with the will of the revolt itself, against the bestial rulers. This was the case with the rebellion of the Roman slaves. The revolutionary transmission comes into its own only after the really new forces of production set themselves free, and this began between the twelfth and thirteenth centuries. This is where those words of Georg Büchner originated: "Down with the palaces, restore peace to the huts!" This is where those recollected guidelines come from—those with which Nikolaus Lenau closes his poem *Albigenser*, which actually does not close—probably the only poem that ends with an etcetera:

Den Albignesern folgen die Hussiten
Und zahlen blutig heim, was jene litten;
Nach Huss und Ziska kommen Luther, Hutten
Die dreissig Jahre, die Cevennenstreiter,
Die Stürmer der Bastille, und so weiter.

The Hussites follow the Albigensians
And what those others suffered, they pay back with blood;
After Huss and Ziska come Luther, Hutten,
The thirty years, the struggles of Cevennes,
The storming of the Bastille, etcetera.

Revolutionary times have always welcomed their ancestors by discovering them anew and certainly by understanding them in a new way. They have done this just as well as, and, for the most part, better than, reactionary times, which reflected themselves in the castles of knights, in the emperor's court, or in the chapel of the church. And yet, everything must be soundly converted here, too, so that the heritage becomes one, and so that its birth is commemorated by the subtraction of the alien class contents—in this case, the bourgeois. The joyous reliance on earlier revolutions must be almost more cautious here than the assumption of sedate and great cultural goods from the classical epoch of a society. The best example for such caution is provided by the French Revolution with its kind of freedom, equality, and brotherhood, with its human rights. At that time the liberation of the individual was a powerful and inspiring impulse. Thus, even when the bourgeoisie was destined to begin everything in a beautiful way and to end it horribly, even when bourgeois freedom, in what was once revolutionary America, a country born out of revolution, could become the pretext for the strongest tyranny of capitalism, human rights were still never excluded insofar as they were postulated by the bourgeoisie and made into a program. Their freedom contained that of the merely formal one of property owners; their realm of reason became, as Marx said, the idealized realm of the bourgeoisie.

The Marxist critique of human rights evaluates not only their consequences, that is, the concrete democracy instead of the mere formal kind; it also stresses most clearly and points toward the socialist "freedom from profit" versus the "freedom of profit," which has long since stopped being progressive. Only after a great and substantial reutilization of the surplus of the French utopia of revolution does it emerge beyond its former class ideology. To be sure, then it emerges as a holiday of the revolutionary heritage, as the first broad "point of departure of human beings from dependency brought about by their own fault," according to Kant's definition of enlightenment. The bold act that succeeds is sufficient enough to make use of pure reason from Lessing to Goethe's *Faust*, from Kant to Hegel's *Phenomenology*, from the cheerful fairy-tale music of Mozart to Beethoven's *Eroica* and the joy of the Ninth Symphony. Here we can see the difference between the bourgeois revolutionary heritage and those evenly balanced, sedate great works, for the bourgeois revolutionary heritage is marked by movement, by disturbance and the process with the upright gait, which unites Spartacus with all of the Promethean works. Such is the heritage at its point of revolutionary outbreak.

Now, as far as the *second* stage of the heritage is concerned, how and where does the revelation of truth contained in the works of the *sanctimonious flourishing* of a society that are cut off from the origins have a place, especially those of the Middle Ages? After all, the Jacobin cap is fundamentally red, but the crown is white with gold in each and every aspect—that is, it represents domination, has been usurped, and is not merely anticipated harmony. Here we can attain a consciousness of form even in the usurped harmony in spite of its sedate nature. We can attain a consciousness of form on the strength of its equanimity, which is still more or less hostile to agitation that is obviously related to radical change. It is not necessary to be cautious about the really traditional structures, but one must have the courage and sovereign power to grasp everything not with a view to the past, but with a view concerned with surplus. In the chorale and fugue, in the architectural staidness and in the spirit of the medieval *summa*, in these eminently ordered constellations, there are the attitude and the composure, the equanimity and the crystal clarity, there is the intended architectural style of an eternity, which radiates passively from the Byzantine mosaics and reaches its pinnacle in the domes. It is in here that the element of gravity, gravity itself, which appears as the most austere pattern in Egypt, is to be found, is being (*Sein*) that has become geometrical. In Europe Giotto, Dante, and St. Thomas Aquinas belong to this world. The Christian movement decided here in favor of torpid figures of destruction, in favor of sedate figures of salvation. In a demonstrative way the primacy of equanimity pre-vailed over the movement of the primacy of space in which all things had their designated place and prevailed over the changing times. Naturally, there was still a pure reflection of class society that existed in these hierarchical works. As it passed away, so did the works—the Bach fugue was its last expression in Europe. However, the belief in a prescribed and canonized *Ordo sempiternus rerum*, which each epoch only had to make visible, continued to pose a problem for a long time thereafter and in a different way than just having a reactionary effect. It still constituted the unhistorical allure in Spinoza's system. It even maintained a systematic conscience that had been both tried and proven in the paradox of an open system. But how does that which is so hostile to process and openness relate to concrete utopia? What is the connection between concrete utopia and that which seems to belong so overwhelmingly to the ideology of a given ruling class, to the apologetics of the hierarchical structure and the established gravity? The problem of an irrefutable affinity even with the existing status quo and with a complicated affinity filled with simplifications is simplified by a specific element of hope that benefited it beyond its ideology and apologetics and endowed it with surplus. The assertion of the *Ordo sempiternus rerum*, which was always only a conjuration and never evident in the existing things, made no exception with its hypostatized perfect figures of this utopian essence. In the sanctimonious order there was a transitional social order, which was not only idealized in transition as eternal, but anticipated an available attainment that was due only as possibility and experimented with itself here. Thus, the Marxist thesis according to which not only the exploited but also the ruling class are alienated, even though the latter feels comfortable and confirmed, remains valid—the profundity of this thesis remains valid *cum grano salis* even in the fanatical pictures of equanimity marked by social class. For it is just this alienation, the entire exteriorization (*Aussersichsein*) of the individual human being that has not been socially exhausted, that gives the ideology of domination a work lacking something (*Vermissens-Werk*), a work that will propel it to its very end. Consequently, it is one in which the wish-fulfillment landscape has a place, in which utopia of the being-in-order (*In-Ordnung-Sein*) resides more or less illusorily. In my book *Geist der Utopie* (*The Spirit of Utopia*), and especially in my book *Das Prinzip Hoffnung* (*The Principle of Hope*), I gave numerous examples of such wish-fulfillment landscapes in the sedate works. A great deal can be learned from them about the affinity between heritage and equanimity. Thus, here, too, there is a possible revelation of truth. That is to say, the best possible revelations of truth can be attained here, namely, those of the free situation (*Situationslosigkeit*).

The final stage concerning the red heritage can even be seen in bourgeois decadence, which I have already emphasized and documented in my book *Erbschaft dieser Zeit* (*Heritage of Our Times*), 1934. Here we are touching upon the third stage of heritage. After the revolutionary phase, after the relatively sedate high period, we now come to the *bourgeois final phase*, one that is not only horrible but instructive. All this may sound unusual; yet, *Heritage of Our Times*, which dealt with the 1920s, had already introduced the problem: "It is precisely here that the richness of a time that is falling apart is great, the collapsing times of the 1920s mixed with dawn and dusk." The luster of the surface during that time exploded with Joyce, with Proust, Musil, Kafka, and others. There was a bunch of non-synchronous contents, that is, contents that stood askew if not archaically in relation to bourgeois reason (*Ratio*); a bunch of encounters, montages, which were not only objectively but subjectively possible, made out of rashness, interruptions, and fragments, between phenomena and elements, which had been miles apart until that time. *Heritage of Our Times* examined such phenomena, recorded them, recommended that we give them due consideration. This was intended not only for the present consciousness of that time, which was also distorted, but for the consciousness that grasped tendencies, that penetrated under the surface, that is, especially under the surface that had cracked. And in no way should the problem of heritage be rejected *a priori* on the grounds that, ever since Goethe, Hegel, and Feuerbach, it is no longer necessary to belong to the bourgeoisie. According to this viewpoint, the highest attainments of bourgeois civilization were also the best, and the cultural decline with all its splits, fiery images, relativism and paradoxes does not even deserve our attention. The apriorism and schematism in this division of the heritage, of the pure problem of heritage, are obvious, even when it is falsely postulated by Marxists here and there. Such schematism does not at all belong to Marxism, for it prevents itself from being exposed to dialectics in the decline. It belongs more to the diatribes of someone like Spengler, which can be seen in his work on contemporary history. He was forced to maintain his schematism in regard to what was happening in his time. According to Spengler in *The Decline of the West*, the only thing left is "a dangerous art, embarrassing, cold, sick, for those with wrought nerves ... it is the *Satyricon* to the great oil painting from Leonardo to Rembrandt." It is quite clear that such rejection of the problem of heritage regarding the final period is not appropriate for Marxists, although orthodox Marxists have at times taken this position. Rather, it is more appropriate for the bourgeois cultural reaction itself and can be driven to the point of absurdity by Spengler's conclusions.

In point of fact, the most advanced consciousness will not blind itself to the signs of the dissolution of bourgeois culture or overlook the many possible blows that it receives that fall dialectically between evening and morning. In no way does the bourgeoisie produce its own apology while it is falling apart. It is no longer in a position to do this.

Its mere polemics become more and more transparent as pure fraud, and, in addition, more and more boring. But it is right here that the crashes reveal boredom as its most significant fault, and these phenomena cannot be circumvented. It is self-evident that nothing can be adopted directly from all of this. Here the most complicated problem is the revelation of truth. Everything about Joyce is itself a problem and not a solution. However, we find here unusual material that had not appeared until this time and also a montage experiment that tries to do justice to this material. And finally, as far as even archaic regressions in surrealism are concerned, which could previously be seen in the work of some expressionists, with the beautiful as the beginning of the terrible—even this indelibility arose originally from the decline. To be sure, it arose from the leaky connection of the pure artificial surface, one that broke in a different way from the previous normal bourgeois view, calling urgently for its own new reason (*Ratio*).

Here we are confronted with a warning signal and a wide angle about which the nineteenth century, in spite of romanticism, knew nothing, and philosophy must overcome its paralysis and deal with this problem. Its task is to hear what has become loud in the final phase of bourgeois rationalism. This is its own executive duty in the heritage: to reutilize that which is breaking down so it becomes another kind of Apollo. The allure of the old-fashioned had already belonged to the "regression" in the period of decline, that uncanny-homey element of the gaslight era, plush and drapery aura from the time of one's parents, that is, the archaic times of today's contemporaries. The effectiveness of archaic archetypes belongs here in a distant way. Even the pure historical categorization of the material of heritage, the order (revolutionary rise, sedateness, and decadence) produces the effect in this last "regression" of being left behind. For there is something subliminal and explosive, something that in no way belongs to a known culture X, something similar to the so-called indestructible smile of Mona Lisa in spite of all familiarity that breaks through, overwhelms in the midst of all the calm solutions and structures—it does this even because of them. But even doubts about the explicit archetypical heritage, when glimpsed in a utopian and rational way, selected and reutilized, were not the worst that dissolved in the period of bourgeois decline. In spite of a misuse of archetypical heritage, which was also definitely the worst, there was, of course, a misuse that would have been scarcely possible on such a large scale without the neglect of the archetypical.

In sum, the Marxist assumption of heritage is based on the pioneer work of Engels, who stated, "One can only become a communist when one enriches one's memory with the knowledge of all those riches that humankind has cultivated." This does not pertain only to "German classical philosophy." The Marxist assumption was instigated by this, but it did not limit itself to philosophy, nor was it limited by it. With *docta spes* it delves into the entire treasure house of humankind, discarding whatever the moths and rust have eaten away. It accomplishes this with such energy that it does not have to envy the culture of any past epoch. It accomplishes everything with a new energy and unity made up of production and salvation, utopia and tradition at the same time. Rudolf Lotze, a fine epigone of philosophy, not an inheritor, once said that the graciousness of the present, its lack of envy via-à-vis the future is one of the most remarkable attributes of human nature (*Gemüt*), even when one takes into consideration how selfish individuals are. Insofar as this statement is not just the pure rhetoric of epigonism, it means that there is no envy of the future and its heritage because it was always intended that it would become a house at one time that would be bright and friendly for all human beings. This is why there is no envy of this future, but rather expectation: the future assumes a heritage that has become classless as legitimatized and concretized from what had been lacking and anticipated until then. Here its own historical material is converted into surplus and employed as result and historical profit, which no longer needs to have anything in common with the desire for profit and its basic premises. In the final analysis, cultural heritage means the knowledge of what is missing that propels one to culture; separation of utopia from the ideology in cultural works; keeping the promise of culture, which means building its house. It is precisely here that we find, not only in the contemporary activation of the base through the superstructure but above all in the successive development of the superstructure, the way, and with this, of course, the way of the problem, the aporia of being-consciousness (*Sein-Bewusstsein*), even from a new side, one of the starting point of culture. And it is here that we can find how it would never come into being without the base, and yet exists as its own act and topos of the surplus thereafter with its light especially radiant with anticipatory illumination.

Coda: The Problem of the Heritage That Is Still Partially Indelible
and Based on Earlier Images of Nature That Are Still Transmitted
Mythologically

But there are many other things that are still lying around the house,
endeavoring to be developed historically. Hunger creates fields. A
great many things were formed from that which is outside us and
made into things for us. The enormous world that is sometimes
helpful, sometimes hostile, sometimes indifferent, had to be understood as such for better or for worse. Thus, the real object of human
research was never just humankind. Human beings could not afford
this. They were constantly on an exchange basis with nature. Heroic
epics were always close to magic; belletristic literature was always
close to science. Thus, the images of nature that emerge one after the
other historically with their different social interpretations of nature
also belong to culture. They belong to it more than fifty percent in
spite of the independent human material that is so strongly embedded
in the socially determined notions of nature.

There have been all sorts of *natural-animistic, oriental-magical, class-
qualitative images of nature* that preceded the bourgeois qualitative-
mechanistic images. And the question within the problem of heritage
that must now be pursued to an end is, *Is there a possible heritage here as
well?*

This question had seemed senseless because of the quantitative-
mechanistic worldview from Galileo to Robert Mayer, which had
formed a closed system and had triumphed over other approaches. It
had seemed senseless so long as the phenomena of life explained by
Du Bois-Reymond's statement had been considered indisputable:
anything that cannot be explained by physics is not scientifically
comprehensible. As is well known, however, the belief in mechanistic
causality as the be all and end all of everything, even the belief in the
Newtonian three-dimensional space in which it occurs, has been
shaken many times since then. Certainly the decline of bourgeois
society and its seemingly tight-knit view of the world fell apart here.
So gaps opened up, even in physics. At the very least, bourgeois life,
which had become generally insecure, became sensitive to subatomic
connections of insecurity, to mesocosmic monstrosities. Once again a
vast homelessness (*Unzuhause*) opened itself up in the world, and in
un-known human relations. All the previous physical models were

exploded or limited to a narrow mesocosmic observation room. Of course, it had been impossible up to that point to find a crack between the Newtonian world and the Planck-Einstein world. To do away with any kind of observation, the non-Euclidian geometry, the time-space continuum—all of these things were very complicated and new, but their beginnings go back to Leibniz and his debate with Clarke and Newton. Even Newtonian physics is still valid in un-changed form for our world of observation or the mesocosmic world between the atomic and the astronomic. In spite of this, a gap has arisen in the connections through which nature not only generates puzzles once again, but also through which pre-bourgeois images of nature return transformed. The most impressionable since Galileo, Bruno, and Newton are those of the closed space in contrast to the infinite and decentered ones. Thus, Hermann Weyl was on safe ground in his book *Philosophie der Mathematik und Naturwissenschaft* (*The Philosophy of Mathematics and the Natural Sciences*) when he noted a connection between Dante's closed space (minus pole and counter pole) and Einstein's curved space. Even in the new discoveries of the natural sciences, which are in contrast mere miscellaneous matters like those of the law of organic composition, we can find a long-forgotten, even direct connection to the old system of the four humours. Such "recollections" would have been considered im-possible in the previous century and would have been dismissed, with some exceptions, as mere play. For example, there were numerous "aesthetic" or even romantic-natural philosophical reactions against the quantitative worldview. They did not gain any power over the quantitative perspective because of the developing and existing solidity of the quantitative-mechanistic way of thinking in capitalist society, but they did continually bring the heritage of earlier images of nature into the restless beginnings of modern natural science, among the founders themselves.

The Renaissance world is partly animistic, partly oriental-magical. It also reveals the influence of cabalism, which is connected to the Pythagorean symbolism of numbers, and this is all the more troublesome since this leads directly to the insight that the book of nature was written in numbers, the insight of Galileo. It was widely known that Kepler's thought was originally tied to the animistic, especially to the class and qualitative past and essence of nature, and has never been completely rejected. Beauty and perfection, those hierarchical questions, like those about the "status of the earth," took up a great deal of space in Kepler's work that was carried over from the previous century. He was very reluctant to give up the orbit of the planets as the most perfect in favor of "the secondmost perfect," the ellipse. He never abandoned the teaching of the five regular cosmic bodies from the Platonic *Timaeus* or the ancient harmony of the spheres. Thus, there is not even a sharp distinction between this mythical heritage and the new mathematical quantitative calculus to be seen in his thinking, or in his method. The geometrical determination that governs the distances of the planets according to the scheme of the five regular bodies is tied to the law of music, which regulates their movements and makes them harmonious. For Kepler, there had to be a connection that prevailed between the speed of a planet, which could change according to its own laws, and the middle values of speed of different planets, which is analogous to those between the frequencies of oscillations of harmonious tones. And it was precisely by following the ramifications of these analogies, which are not at all modern, that Kepler was able to discover his third law, which determines the amount of time it takes planets to circle the sun as a function of their distances from it. Here we can see that Kepler was not unaware of heritage, but rather that he had one in mind that was remarkably reutilized. The following statement from his *Harmonices mundi* reveals this: "Yes, I stole the golden receptacles of the Egyptians in order to erect a holy shrine for my God—far, far away from the borders of Egypt."

It was a different story during the period of romanticism when consciousness was, of course, not reutilized. However, the romantic, and not only the romantic recollection of quality, as in the case of Goethe, Schelling, and Hegel, emerged with a warning sign against the absolutizing of physical nature that was to be considered only on the basis of quantitative physics. Naturally, in the case of Novalis, the regression, which took the form of qualities and the corresponding formation of qualitative analogies, was often grotesque. In contrast, Goethe's theory of color yielded a heritage of the qualitative relations of nature worth observing beyond Newton, since it contained a real, applicable symbolism of color. Here again Marx's evaluation of the relationship of nature in *The Holy Family* is more valid than that of Newton or Hobbes: in a totally sensuous gleam material looks right at human beings. Hegel's philosophy of nature not only absorbed

Schelling's thinking and touched upon the ideas of Paracelsus and Böhme, but also borrowed the qualitatively determined hierarchical structure of nature from the class and qualitative order of Aristotle and St. Thomas Aquinas. Without this there would not have been any room whatsoever for a dialectical transformation of quantity into quality, since physics as a whole was not at all familiar with quality. If ice, water, and steam were purely physical conditions of accumulation, if everything qualitative about them were only sensuous illusion, then this alone would have accounted for all of Hegel's dialectics having played itself out, almost more than Schelling's. Light and sound are only subjective and ideal in physics, nothing but the contents of emotions. In no way are they the objective contents of nature. This is entirely different in the naive and pre-calculatory opinion that haunts the thinking of Goethe and Hegel, that is, explodes and emerges in a strange way. For instance, there is this sentence in Hegel's work (and here it is not a matter of whether this is a point for discussion): "In life, light is completely the master of gravity, so that what is alive is this individuality which has subjectivized the other special features of gravity in it and is active in itself." This statement and other qualitative assessments such as the "water realm of plants" and the "fire realm of animals" had already stopped appearing by the time of Paracelsus and Böhme. Without a doubt, modern natural science has gone beyond this as though it were an aberration and has dealt with those things that were really on the agenda. But this agenda was what Gustav Fechner, the physicist and also last descendant of the romantic philosophy of nature, called a pure "night view," that is, one of an ethereal world of oscillations comprehended without light and sound. Yet, in order not to remain entirely outside the realm of discussion, that is, to take the bull by its powerful horns, we must ask the question, What is the situation of pre-capitalist heirlooms and thus the situation of the qualitative elements in dialectical materialism?

Of course, dialectical materialism is very much up-to-date. Modern research into nature itself is its most preferred material of heritage. And, nevertheless, it does not at all reject the dialectical and qualitative thought of Hegel in its observations of nature. Dilthey maintained quite correctly, "There is a similar thesis which emerges in the work of Kepler, Galileo, and Descartes, namely that it would be foolish to think that, if the goal of the universe lay in the human

being, then the way we interpret the world would be fully changed."
However, is not the old humane goal (*Mensch-Pointe*), which Dilthey
calls Christian, reproduced implicitly in dialectical materialism? As
far as nature is concerned, does not dialectical materialism rely on a
depiction of nature like Engels' depiction in *Dialectics of Nature*, which
goes back beyond Hegel to Aristotle's stages of nature with its entirely
own qualitative groups of a physical, chemical, and organic kind and
its own spheres? Do we not find here the results of Aristotle's and St.
Thomas' ideas, such as quantitative movement, addition and de-
duction, the movement of place or the change of place, qualitative
movement or transformation? All this can be detected in sentences
like the following (italics are Engels'): "In the work of natural scientists, movement is always self-evident, as though it were physical
movement, assumed to be a change of place. This view came from the
pre-chemical eighteenth century and makes it difficult to have a clear
understanding of how everything works. Applied to matter, movement is *any kind of change*. It is from this same misunderstanding that
the intense desire arises to reduce everything to the physical movement whereby the specific character of other forms of movement is
obfuscated. This is not to say that none of the higher forms of
movement may always necessarily be connected to a really physical
one, whether it be external or molecular. Just as the higher forms of
movement also produce others at the same time, chemical action is
not possible without the change of temperature and electricity, and
organic life is not possible without physical, molecular, chemical,
thermetic and electrical change, etc. However, the pressure of these
ancillary forms does not exhaust the essence of the respective major
form" (*Dialectics of Nature*). The changing form of movement, which
Engels establishes here—and, to be sure, a movement in which the
physical, chemical, and organic merge with another—clearly
contains a pre-bourgeois, non-quantitative heritage. This is also the
case with the change of quantity into quality as a change that would
nevertheless be one in a nature without quality, one without a
physical, chemical, organic gradation, one without an object. Thus,
dialectical materialism has such a thing as a heritage of pre-capitalist
connections to nature, even though it is an exemplary objective
heritage, that is, one without any kind of antiquated and mystical
magic.

It was due to this that the linear movement forward comprising the dominant scientific exclusivity of the quantitative concept of nature was sublated. It seems that there was much more of the indelible in the earlier ideologies of nature, almost like those ideologies that referred to *humaniora*. The earlier connections to nature were now no longer continually hidden in the mere junk room of history without the problem of heritage in them. Rather, they revealed a parallel to the heritage in cultural images if the maturation of a concept could be found. Thus, the entire colorful way of the dialectical change from quantity into quality and the dialectical sublation of the Newton-Goethe debate that was still important, that is, the antinomy of quantity-quality, remained within the context of the aporia of being-consciousness, but it resulted in a significant way from the tension of the base-superstructure made only by human beings. Pre-calculable images of nature sharpen and also invigorate daily experience so that nature does not consist of qualities but so that the world is capable by itself of being one of "day view" (*Tagansicht*).

This is evident only when something corresponds objectively to the old images, when they do not merely contain archaic and beautiful charming aspects like those that had been dressed up in a fancy way by the enemies of the Enlightenment. They are not to be considered except as a warning. The legitimate question raised in the previous sections was headed in another direction: Is there, was there, a possible heritage in the earlier images of nature? This question was answered in the affirmative with a reference to the numerous receptions that have occurred within history. Now, however, the question to be raised is as follows: Is there also a possible objective heritage, i.e., one that is not only within history but also a heritage of the non-ideological kind, one not only of the culturally humanistic surplus but also one that concerns the cognition of objective nature itself? Accordingly, this heritage does not only belong to the history of humankind, does not belong to nature as a purely social category; consequently it does not belong to the determinedness of natural scientific expressions through social relations or to nature as raw material in the production process of social existence but to the unmarketed nature, which is still independent of human beings. Therefore, this heritage places material objects above that kind of object quality embedded in each and every connection of human beings to the non-human world in an external human way. The problem of heritage conceived in this way has already been posed in

*Heritage of Our Times*: "Mustn't there also be a problem of heritage in nature? Doesn't it take the form of designating and informing those outstanding elements of the great tendencies in the essence of nature and in the individual concepts of nature which emerged historically—the primitive, animistic, magical, qualitative—beyond ideology? ... The mechanistic relativism of today, as the decline of physics from the point of view of the object, produces a sensitivity for the possibility of earlier absolutes as relative absolutes in nature so that the dialectics of nature would contain not only the mechanistic natural science of yesterday but also certain earlier elements, particularly the qualitatively graded elements, as the element to be sublated, as the sublated element, where physics would not have surplus material."

Time and again, however, doubt arises as to whether the earlier connections to nature might not have been entirely within history. Perhaps they actually belong to the history of human imbecility like magic or even astrology? Or, to take an illustrious example, where in the history of mathematics is the Pythagorean symbolism of numbers halfway so seriously treated, so distant from the pertinence of the matter, as in the history of philosophy? Now is the time to ask the opposite question: How is it that so much of the physical objectivity or all of it corresponds to the mathematical natural science of capitalist society? Is not the pulse of nature being taken here in a way similar to that in which an ideological pulse would be taken so that the pulse of nature can hardly be counted without being disturbed? Does not bourgeois society necessarily meddle with its commodity form in the theoretical relationship to nature, and are there not particular consequences as well? Is the calculatory and abstract thinking, which is characteristic of the bourgeoisie, in fact the final conclusion of the knowledge of nature? Is the quantification of commodity thinking the commodity connection, which in the final instance is nothing but the most expedient formalization of the mere functional connections without content and viewpoint, the final conclusion? Does the reification, that reification that is economically and culturally incapable of bringing about an awareness of the process in nature, possess an exclusive correlate? There are some natural scientists who have made important attempts to break away from the mere quantification thinking in regard to nature. For instance, the Swiss physicist Heitler has written, "The world, including all living creatures, is made into a meaningless, mechanical and quantitative operating machine, which is once and for all there and does not call for any change. But this viewpoint does not only mean an over-estimation of the quantitative but simultaneously also a degradation of everything which is not quantitative, that is, of humankind as well. In the extreme case it is a degradation to the point of absolute zero.... In contrast to this, the actual phenomena of nature, which are strongly governed by qualities, and which are excluded by physics, are not understood for the most part. Of course, this is not to say anything against the direction of research *per se* in this field.... Obviously there are areas that scientific research has hardly touched or even entered until now. In these areas everything that is not quantitative must appear, in other words, the qualities of color, sound, smell, etc. Everything must also appear that concerns the connection of physical, chemical, and material processes with the animal and human internal life—and much more" (*Der Mensch und die naturwissenschaftliche Erkenntnis* [The Human Being and the Knowledge of Natural Sciences], 1961, p. 21).

Here is just the place where we can locate a real ecology, which has become so urgent in our time. This means the discovery of a con-stitutive connection between an inner household of plants and animals, and one that corresponds to the landscape. This landscape is one that is of a geographic kind and a category constituted by different types and even characters, and it legitimizes itself precisely with ecology and in ecology, not only as aesthetic phenomenon but also as one made up of a real qualitative context. One that also becomes even more urgent today as the balance of the symbiosis becomes increasingly more visible through its industrial destruction. Whatever can be destroyed in such a way must have been quali-tatively and concretely present before this, even though it does not occur in pure quantitative physics, which has become more and more abstract. And, furthermore, just as that essence that is hostile to quality was blind to the balance in the house of nature, landscape of past times, so it was also blind to that which was emerging and open and still possible in nature. Here the remarks of the Tübingen min-eralologist Engelhardt are pertinent: "The human being in scien-tifically known nature is in a world which is not yet finished, in an open world, a world in the process of becoming, a world under the aspect of hope.... The exploitation of the experimental research by private capitalist industry and the state was only the first phase of the development of human life set in motion by the research of nature.... The research of nature makes human beings freer in that it releases the world of nature from the modality of that which is available and that which enters into the modality of becoming and possibility.... Thus, it can be shown that research is not only the way to inquire into the composition of the world which is simply available, but it is also the discovery of a world of new quality" (*Was heiss und zu welchem Ende treibt man Naturforschung?*) [*What Does Research into Nature Mean and What Is Its Purpose?*]).

There is no doubt that there has been enormous progress made toward a real understanding of nature since the sixteenth century. Moreover, due to the growth of mathematics in the natural sciences, technology has celebrated one victory after another. And, insofar as the proof is in the pudding, that is, insofar as praxis is the proof of theory, technological praxis, which has been made possible by the mathematical natural sciences, has indeed given bourgeois calculation a great deal of legitimation in this field. Yet, bourgeois technology has also increased accidents, and the technological accident corresponds methodologically to the economic crisis. This means that even mathematical calculation is still related to its object in an abstract way and is still not mediated with it in a materialist and concrete way. Here is a more detailed statement about this point: "If the fire is only tamed and watched over, it remains isolated. Its own track, upon which it continues, is thus a completely dangerous one, even when its continued force is supposed to be under better control than it was. In the contemporary extant society there is nothing dependable that can be recognized from a related spirit which turns its visage toward us right in the midst of the fire. There is a specific fear of the engineer going too far, penetrating too far in uncertainty. He does not know those forces with which he may have to contend. And it is from such non-mediation that the most obvious effect of the ommitted content is ultimately derived: the technological *accident*. It is this accident above all which demonstrates how the content of the forces of nature which is not mediated enough with us cannot be abstracted without great damage. In the process there is a remarkable similarity which occurs simultaneously in all the accidents encountered by humans and which teaches us a great deal: *the technological accident is not completely unrelated to the economic crisis, the economic crisis not completely unrelated to the technological accident.* Certainly, the differences between both are more visible, in certain places even larger than their relatedness, and therefore, the comparison sounds paradoxical. The technological accident appears as a coincidental crossing of regular movements, as their external, unforeseeable intersection. On the other hand, the economic crisis develops in a completely predictable way within the production and exchange system of the capitalist economy itself, as one of its constant contradictions which is becoming harder and harder. And, nevertheless, both catastrophes correspond to each other in a profound way, for both stem ultimately from a *poorly mediated abstract relationship of human beings to the material foundation of their actions"* (*The Principle of Hope*).

There is one thing here to be stressed above everything else: dialectical materialism is ultimately not only the dialectical understanding of the mathematical natural sciences, not only its supervening consciousness. But it is all of this by itself because dialectical materialism gives the transformation of quantity into quality a great deal of room by completely sublating the rigidity of set categories. Such transformation should not have any kind of mechanistic household law, and dialectical materialism does not in any way place a roof on that which has been reified and made static. There were few writers more critical of the mere mechanical limitation of nature as Engels, few who had such complete disdain for the form that mechanical materialism took in the nineteenth century. In *Dialectics of Nature* he noted, "Hegel's summary and rational grouping of the natural sciences amounted to a far greater accomplishment than all the materialist idiocy taken together." Thus, the abstract-quantitative concept of nature was at least relativized by Marxism instead of being made into ultimate wisdom. By reducing quantitative thinking about nature to the exclusive dominant commodity form in the relations of bourgeois society and its consciousness itself, Marxism restored a proper perspective regarding the absolute superiority of bourgeois natural science, that is, the alleged objectivity of bourgeois natural science, which is ahistorical.

Due to the fact that doubts could arise from a socio-historical perspective about the total objectivity of the quantitative connection to nature since Galileo's time, it would still be conceivable that the exclusive supremacy of the partly or only qualitatively grasped Pythagoreanism about the qualitative images of nature would be questionable, or, at the very least, full of gaps. The old qualitative images of nature could still show remnants here and there of a concreteness that had become homeless, remnants that had fallen out of a *natura non-naturans* that had become much too anorangic, and all this has been neglected here.

In point of fact, even the earlier connections to nature, the primordial animistic, the oriental-magical, even the class-qualitative revealed a theory about objects that is not to be completely rejected even if it is also quite a mess, and these connections are not entirely submerged in mere ideology, in mere prelogistical mythology, in primeval imbecility—despite caution or consternation about this in all great philosophy. In regard to this point, Aristotle stated that a great sector, which is much more real and to a degree more determining, has been opened up by the present mathematical natural sciences. However, in the complete cycle of nature, there are other, previous "moments" or "elements," which were not left out, even entire segments, which were not easily accessible to mechanistic natural science, the natural science of abstract laws about isolated factors that break out of the process. The mechanistic connection may touch one sector that is still abstract in nature. Nature itself has ostensibly an area of reification in itself, a surface of shells made out of external necessity, that which is designated by commodity thinking as not completely reflective. The concept of this external "ananke" is itself old and can be found early in Democritus' work and allowed Democritus to triumph over Aristotle, especially the qualitative history of development aspects, just at a time when the bourgeoisie was emerging as the dominant class. Yet, the great natural basis is not placed at our feet with this physics, nor is nature as the enormous cosmic vault of human historical space certainly at an end or determined to its end. The cosmogony itself is not yet at an end with the second heat movement, entropy as the freezing to death of the world. Along with the notion of the universe as a mere carousel of planets or as a desert of fixed stars, there is the humanly intended, mythologically reorganized human mediation, the humanization of nature that cannot remain therefore without reflection *ab ovo*, or *a fine*, or even remain untrue because it does not guard itself from being more constructive than entropy. Just as human essence, as pure tendency not as *fixum*, experiments in different ways in different societies and has become more or less summarized, so can a hypothetical *natura naturans* be summarized more or less *mutatis mutandis* as a tendency essence in the images of nature of successive societies without the form of the movement or even content of the movement of what is designated as the process of nature having been finally determined. Even landscape painting and nature literature—both full of memories from the pre-mechanical connection to nature and both immersed in objective material—as well as geography, which has remained qualitative, have been able to collect many components and basic forms of nature that have not been flattened much in the desert of quantity, or in the emptiness of formalism of our reductive physics so that they can occasionally even stand there as coded forms of signatures, signatures of forms of a meaning that has not yet come or that has been thwarted. Thus, there is a problem of heritage here, too, the old Paracelsus and Böhme problem of a "signatura rerum," and theory of expression of nature. No concrete philosophy of nature will leave that up to landscape painting or poetry or the curiosità memory of the much too romantic philosophy of nature. At the same time, there is an illumination from this non-*curiosità*, from the indelible: the inherited foundation of *humaniora* and that of the images of nature cannot have any other foundation as a utopian one in order ultimately to be the inherited foundation. Indelibility means indisposability; it means that possibility of another determination that has not yet been carried out. In other words, it means utopia: the utopian as fundament of the indelible is also valid here. It determines the fundament of the quality of heritage in the images of nature. It possesses its substance in the existing contents of the tendency essence nature, in the latency essence world matter, and their outcome has not yet been decided. And just as urgent as, if not more urgent than, the problem of the humanistic cultural expression in regard to the heritage of images of nature is the problem of revelation (*Wahrmachung*). But with a difference: even the classless society cannot speak the decisive word about concrete heritage of the images of nature in immediate response. For human beings, if they grasp themselves as producers of history and comprehend it without ideology, without false ideology, if they sublate the purely external necessity of history that has previously happened to them, are not yet mediated in the beginning of this act with that which is being produced and with the purely external necessity of the natural occurrence. Therefore, there are many more undetermined things from the earlier images of nature that remain left over and more dependable than from the images of culture and works that refer to the metamorphosis and the identification of human content. This is why the indicated problem of heritage lasts longer in the images of nature and is valid—as much a problem as it is a particularly objective call for a solution. "Doesn't the kernel of nature live in the hearts of human beings?" Goethe asked. It only lives in those hearts that will know themselves, and, to be sure, will know themselves down to the production or the natura naturans-cause of the entire enigma-phenomenon world and its many forms.

## The Wish-Landscape Perspective in Aesthetics: The Order of Art Materials According to the Dimension of Their Profundity and Hope

The word has another intention from the very beginning if it aims very far. It is intense, has an inkling that has not become fixed anywhere or touchable. For four hundred years poetic expression has maintained a perspective, and it is false to designate this essence, which cannot be dismissed merely as romantic. It is even more false to want to exclude the wish movement and that which is tendentious and remains tendentious from art in the classical and imitative manner. Here the will in art falls asleep, and art "reaches its goal everywhere." Thus, art is not supposed to contain its own wish-landscapes and cannot be arranged according to them as their most powerful objects. The basic feature of bourgeois classical aesthetics that originated in this way is not hope (and as a result, the aroused will); rather, it is contemplation (and as a result, passive enjoyment). Here beauty eradicates material in an illusionary way through form, and to be sure, through form that is indifferent to the material, even to the tendency of the material.

The pure aesthetics of contemplation begins with Kant's concept of "the impartial pleasure of the plain conceptual image of the object," whether this is materialistically present or not. Such aesthetics is made metaphysical in Schopenhauer's works when impartial pleasure is expanded to mean the initial release of the individual from the will to life. Of course being (*Sein*) remains dreadful here while seeing is blessed, sublime in the "pure mundane eye of art." Thus, classical aesthetics limits the relationship of beauty to pure contemplation and limits beauty itself to its purified forms—and Schopenhauer's "pure mundane eye" belongs completely to classical aesthetics even in the sedate reception of music. It limits the object of the beautiful to an area that is fully devoid of the interests of present and future existence (*Dasein*). Here art always acts as a pacifier; it is not an appeal, not even a song of consolation. For even the latter has the restlessness of the will as a prerequisite. Here the world is legitimated all over as an aesthetic phenomenon, and, to be sure, uniform, on a level of idealistic and thus beautifully formed perfection. The damage of a plain desire to contemplate goes so far that even the "wreath of the beautiful" in Hegel's aesthetics hangs in the ethereal realm of contemplative appeasement, despite the fact that he opposed formalism with an aesthetics that was more substantial, historically more relevant and varied. A certain kind of formalism, consequently abstract illusion (with uninterrupted, and therefore preferably antiquated closed thinking), is an omnipresent danger wherever the aesthetically grasped reality with all its richness, with a few categories that almost always remain the same, is interpreted to an end and reduced into relaxed schematics. Such a woven concept of plain contemplation is a danger, even for many Marxist aestheticians, especially where they still appear to be so realistic on the basis of a constant, closed semi-concept of reality. Even in Lukács' work there is still an abstract illusion of idealistic shaping at work, a schematization that is foreign to dialectical materialism. And foreign to the theory of an unfinished world and the actual richness of reality, namely, reality that is in *process and open*, especially in view of its totality. This is why a substantial and material art with all its theory cannot avoid being a packaged art, an art with perspective, an art of reality instead of presumed process. Consequently, a substantial and material art with all its theory cannot avoid being an open art and also one of a kind in which there is an *actual portrayal of the tendency and latency of its objects in an anticipatory illumination driven to an end*.

Due to this anticipatory illumination, art is not at all a totality, but rather only a perspective about something, an elaborated perspective of the portrayed objects themselves in regard to the immanent completion of these objects. Thus, we have Lessing's statement by the painter in *Emilia Galotti*, a utopian and entelechical statement: "Art must paint like malleable nature—if there is one—imagined the picture to be: without the waste which the resistant material makes unavoidable, without the ruin against which time fights." Art lays the groundwork and is influential as anticipatory illumination, as an immanent, completed anticipatory illumination in contrast to the religious. This is precisely why this anticipatory illumination can be attained, why art drives its material in actions, situations, or forms to an end, brings everything to an expressed resolution like suffering, happiness, or meaning. The statement achieved in this way is, to be sure, less than the subject in one point, namely, in regard to its direct tangibility, but it is at the same time always more than this, namely, in regard to its immanent ability to be implemented, its concentrated and essential implementation. Such an expression is the opposite of an idealistic corrective. Naturally, it is also the opposite of mere reproduction of an approximation after the fashion of the so-called total perfection of the real—as though the world, which is supposed to be changed in all other cultural functions, were an unattainable masterpiece for art. Instead, it is the groundwork, the objectively real possibility for this, such as a forest, which is effectively portrayed, a dramatic action of history, which is effectively portrayed (to be sure, its essence outdoes its object)—these works are only effective as art works in that they can and must go beyond the subject in attainable anticipatory illumination.

Anticipatory illumination itself is the attainable in that the métier of driving a thing to its end occurs in the dialectically spread and open space in which any object can be aesthetically portrayed. Aesthetically portrayed here means more immanently achieved, more genuine materially, more essential than in the directly natural or directly historical appearance of this object. Here we have the program of the aesthetically attempted anticipatory illumination: how to complete the world without the world being exploded as in the Christian religious anticipatory illumination, and without disappearing apocalyptically. In other words, art drives world figures, world landscapes to their entelechical border without causing their demise. It is only the aesthetic illusion that detaches itself from life. On the other hand, the aesthetic anticipatory illumination is precisely what it is because it stands on the horizon of the real itself. But this means content, utopian and real content, not the content of an illusionary abstract appearance (*Abstrakt-Schein*) in which polished dilettantism is consumed. Obviously this means that the anticipatory illumination is ordered according to the dimension and status of its utopian meaningful subject, and instead of the impenetrable enjoyment of art, it provides a *connection to knowledge* at the very least, and it provides a connection to the *material of grasped hope* at the very most. This connection is of such a kind that it is inescapable and unavoidable, so that even classical aesthetics could not get around it in the end and began to express it even though in an objective and idealistic way. So when Schiller defined "beauty as freedom in illusion" in the *Kallias Letters*, he brought a substantial meaning into the abstract illusion, even if freedom could only be the same thing in it as that which has escaped for play. And in Kant's works the sublime goes beyond formalism (even if beauty does not) in which the aesthetical as mere "as if" of contemplation is presumed to be other than it is. To be sure, even the sublime remains this "as if," without a supposed desire for existence originating here, without having the aesthetic thought of as a possible determinant of being in any way. In spite of this, there is a statement in the *Critique of Judgment* that contains desire and interest: "Sublime is what a capacity of the intellect proves is only the ability to think and to exceed any kind of standard of the senses," and, in regard to the object, "Sublime is this nature in those of its appearances which lead to the idea of its eternity when one gazes upon them." And here eternity is nothing but that which carries with it the presentiment of our future freedom according to which the sublimities are to be classified with the capacity to desire. In other words, according to the way they break through the formalism of pure abstract illusion.

What was called *sublimity* by the *old aesthetics* is indeed especially suited for the penetration of impartial pleasure. If anything was in a position to compel the classical harmonizing concept of beauty to be concerned about itself and to doubt itself, then it was the category of the sublime that served as the point of demarcation for the Greeks as well as for great religious art, because an undeniable element of the sublime is dread, that which dialectically changes in an uplifting way. And this latter element assigns the will to itself objectively on the subjective side, just as on the objective side it assigns material profundity to itself. This is why Goethe could say that trembling (*Schaudern*) was the best part of humankind. This is why in sublimity there is an objectivity that leaves its mark in this play as well as the same objectivity that leaves its mark on the highest faith, namely, the presentiment of our future freedom, which is by no means destined to be insignificant or endowed with insignificant content. All this came out already in classical aesthetics as soon as the category of the sublime was touched upon, or against the agreement, when classical aesthetics was touched by the sublime in the area of impartiality as well as pleasure. Even on the level of a much more urbane concern, such as that in which trembling was considered the best part of humankind, the abstract appearance became untenable. An intervention of the subject constantly revealed itself. Goethe distinguished such intervention among the objects that produced a poetic effect. He never emphasized any of the closed abstract illusions. Rather, he focused on those that were representative or symbolical insofar as they converged upon a *material profundity that they held in common*, just so long as this profundity with its unity and comprehensiveness (*Allheit*) in the poetical effect defines itself and makes a demand upon itself. With this it becomes evident that the element most hostile to impartial harmony postulates the following: *the objective perspective in the defining direction of the object itself*. It is also promoted at the point where sublimity does not interrupt the formal tapestry of the impartially produced pleasure, where emotion does not reach into the depths in order to feel the monstrous. Where the closer tendency involvement, the latency ingredients of a time, are portrayed on and in its human figures, situations, themes in a manner with perspective and entelechy. This is something that Goethe demanded in a completely objective way: "In art and science as well as in deeds and action everything depends on grasping the objects in a pure way and treating them according to their nature."

"It is precisely because of this genuine quest for reality, namely, for the entelechical and full reality, that Goethe made another significant reference, one that concerns the already manifest fullness of the real: "Probability is the condition of art, but within the realm of probability the highest must be delivered, that which otherwise does not emerge" (*Aufsatz zum Relief von Phigalia* [*Essay Concerning the Relief of Phigalia*]). And the background of perspective, *the golden ground of art*, is and remains—in keeping with the category of anticipatory illumination—a real possible wish-fulfillment landscape; this landscape lies in the windows of art, even though it has such different qualities and hierarchies. It includes that art, which is always immanent, illuminated by a world that is not yet there and as Faust-heaven. That is, it stands as attained identity of the object with the content of human impetus in the anticipatory illumination. But also within this broad series, realism in art is not a descriptive or explicative stocktaking. Rather, it holds up a mirror of immanent anticipation in an activating way. It is tendentious, utopian realism.

All of this prevents beauty from being received and enjoyed in a serene way. Wanting is already a precondition of receiving, so that this can be something that concerns the individual human being. To maintain people and to maintain a fire, both can and should be related. The last thing that could be possibly removed from the *process of creating itself*, from the production of the beautiful, was the inspired will. Also from the pathos of producing, from that which had been inscribed within the bourgeois world from the beginning, the different way of the bourgeois desire to contemplate was thwarted, the formal desire to contemplate. From this vantage point, art seemed to be active revision, a revision that certainly expands the world and essentially increases it. The French revolutionary architect Ledoux called this kind of builder, who produces this kind of art, a rival of God. And long before this, the humanist Scaliger took the word poesy in a literal sense to mean ποιετν in a Promethean sense: the poet is a "factor," an "alter deus." Accordingly, Scaliger defined the poet not as one who repeats given material but rather as another god who creates and establishes: "Videtur poeta sane res ipsas non ut aliae artes, quasi histrio, narre, sed velut alter deus condere." The comparison of the artist with Prometheus began in 1561, at the time of Faust, when Scaliger's poetics appeared, and it continued through Bacon to Shaftesbury, Klopstock, the *Sturm und Drang* writers, Herder, and the young Goethe. A designation of the will, without a doubt. A designation of genius in which courage to *creator spiritus* appears. However, it is not the pacifier of a pure, receptive, and contemplative world-eye as in the classical definition that came later: "Freedom in appearance" does not become illusion when viewed from the production side; rather, it is objective substantiation of the portrayed in the sense of proximity to humanity to which art leads and brings the world in its way. In its way—as in the indicated way of the aesthetic anticipatory illumination. Here the essential, which has not yet emerged, is moved an important step closer to its full realization (*Geboren-werden und Sein*) in that it is treated without illusion as process and existing (*seiend*). Also from this vantage point there is no formalism to which its autarchical perfection of form is the only perfection. The landscape of hope, even in the image of horror, is much more the aesthetic omega. Hegel called this objectively-idealistically eternity in mortality. Here is means, utopian-realistically, the human identity in the other, in the driving *alteritas*. That is the same as the *designation of the goal* on the strength of the symbol in contrast to the allegory that is expressed as the connection of identity in the other and is different—as *designation of the way*. Art in its way is *just as completely allegorical in its kind,* just as it remains obligated to follow the way of the prevailing goal, *obligated to the symbolical* (according to the unity and general public, which is ultimately one only as humane). Whereby, as art, it reproduces, if necessary, the distance from the law that is immanently just as it dares to create a paradise out of other objects that are immanently driven to an end and made into something, made positive and possible as anticipatory illumination. Only since Marx is this no longer a risk but an attainable part that must remain completely in the anticipatory illumination.

# Art and Utopia

## The Creation of the Ornament

In the Early Days

We start, however, from the beginning.

We are down and out and no longer know how to play. We have forgotten. Our hands no longer know how to construct things.

The flintstone had also been flattened in about the same way. All around us it seems as if craftsmanship had never existed and was never to be handed down. Instead, we paint again like savages, in the best sense of the early days, of the unsettled, the nonchalant, the concerned. Because dance masks were also carved in such a way. It must have been about that way when the primitive humans put their fetishes together, even if nothing but the need to talk about it has become the same again. So both are separated simultaneously and clearly and help us, force us to turn the cold instrument really cold, so that one realizes the goodly amount that still must be warmed.

Technological Coldness

At first, however, nearly everything looks empty to us.

But how could it be different and where should the vital, beautifully formed utensil come from when nobody knows anymore how to live permanently and has forgotten how to keep his home warm and solid?

But this is not merely due to trivial things. They are not based on the fact that the employer has become unknown and anonymous. Let us take, for instance, the study in the home as our point of focus. With the gainfully employed there is a set of needs, tasks, and graphic problems. He enters his room only in the evening to relax, read, or welcome male guests. Or he is a writer or a scholar, perhaps comparable to the Faustian dweller of the study. But, in fact, what is offered for sale or in all the designs remains hopelessly stuck in what is generally called the gentleman's room decorated in a bourgeois way. Therefore, one could say that there is much greater room for purchase than the empty products and choices allow. So it is not so much the consumer but the producer to whom all the unattractive stuff refers. And it is not the producer alone but the machine that he uses that has the misery and incisive murder of imagination on its conscience; this murder of imagination forces all museums to terminate the holdings of applied art works with the 1840s.

The machine knew how to produce everything so lifeless and inhuman in detail, just the way our new housing districts usually are. Its actual goal is the bathroom and the toilet that are the most unquestionable and the most original accomplishments of this era, just as rococo furniture and the Gothic cathedral represented the decisive pieces of art of those epochs. But now washing-up reigns. Somehow water flows from every wall, and the magic of modern sanitary facilities merges imperceptibly as an *a priori* ready-made machine commodity into the precious products of the industry of that era.

One should, of course, think long enough and frugally. Even more since we have no choice, and the old craftsman will not come back. And we certainly do not want to select the new ones; their sight is so horrible that nothing can be grafted onto them. Often they are just the most shabby philistine scoundrels with all the characteristics of the middle class in decline, greedy, fraudulent, unreliable, impudent, and sloppy, who occupy the place of the distinguished old masters as small businessmen. But if they, too, are fighting a losing battle, then a human, so to speak, *warm* commodity production by machines cannot succeed either. The transition period and capitalism developed technology, at least in terms of skills and use, largely for the purpose of inexpensive mass production with high turnovers and big profits and not really, as pretended, to ease human labor or even to improve its results. We really do not know what seemed such a relief about the rattle of the looms, about the night shift, about the terrible pressure of the constant rotation speed, about the derivation of pleasure experienced by an individual who always works only on parts and never can enjoy the comprehensive process, the finished products. We do not know what was eased or even improved in contrast to earlier production that was more accommodating with the home and workshop side by side and a small quantity of honestly produced handwork. A totally different technology, not for profit but humanistic, would have to come, and a completely different technology for purely functional purposes, without any of the junk of commodity production and mechanical substitutes of the earlier artistic goods would have to be invented: relief should come and limits at the same time, transformation of the functional form of the machine's spirit, appearance of freed, purely expressive colorfulness and profusion, detached from finery, from the old luxury. All honor to the grand élan, but all that it generated, which is not itself servicable or *functional* (like locomotion or steel production)—the entire spewed-up garbage of *static* substitute products will be packed away one morning. And the exploitative means of production of these substitutes that destroy culture will have to stand together with the cannons in the same peculiar museums of pernicious legends. I repeat: certainly one should think long and hard and be concerned with industry, for here in this breathtaking step, in this acceleration, unrest, and enlargement of our circle of action, there are great spiritual and intellectual values ready to be put to use. But all this must be considered in terms of the technological that views the machine as a functional facilitation for relief and does not involve the flimsy mass stuff of the factories, or even the terrible desolation of a *complete* automation of the world.

But, if we delimit everything in this way, the cold instrument will not be questionable everywhere. Then, of course, there are times when hatred against the machine changes. Here Marx is right in regard to the socialist craftsmen. At the very least one would like to be thankful for the sober coldness, the solemn comfort, the usefulness and the functional as the honest future, as the major mission of the machine; one would like to be thankful in the name of the other for the expression freed from hardship and style. Loss of taste, the intended beginning of the primitive, that which is purely objective function no longer leads to the beautiful old land we were used to. But conscious functional technology might lead to significant liberation of *art* from style, from anachronistic stylization and also from empty functional form, for neither the consumer nor the manufacturer is the *decisive* factor alone in the enormous change of civilized visibility. Rather the machine must also be taken into account. And the machine as well is a link in the continuing chain; decay as well as hope are only the opposite appearances of the spirit that has moved on, one that has been threatened but perhaps also vanished into wider circles. The conditions of the potentiality of the machine and its pure application ultimately belong to the history of philosophy, closely connected to the conditions of the potentiality of an anti-luxurious expressionism.

## Functional Form and Expressive Exuberance

Unfortunately, one pushes here and there from the bottom to emerge from the hardness. Basically it remains true: obstetric forceps have to be smooth, nothing less than a pair of sugar-tongs. So one tries to loosen everything with *colors*, no paste-ups, no need to prim with scabby or ulcerous replacements as it had been done before. Nevertheless, the plain rectangulars seem, as they are polished, to vanish already, glazed bricks mediate, attractive vistas might reappear at some point, factory wares are decked with flowers. But all this rarely happens anymore. It certainly does not happen anymore at the right end. The lost land is cultivated, but it only conceives and blossoms sparsely if at all. Its returns are little more than stones.

Indeed, it remains questionable whether artistic commercial things, individually decorated and luxurious, could ever again be created around us. After the rupture of a vital productive tradition, after the burst of power with which the machine commenced action and awaited the results—it was possible to create commercially beautiful things, the truly beautiful, the beauty of static instruments. Yet this success was not much more than colorfully painted concrete. Even in the most theoretical case, with the purity of material and the clearly constructed functional form, it seems that only the *stylistic minimum* is attainable in a large leap forward. That minimum showed in the first framework furniture even before all stylistic beauty. Thus, after the depletion of the great styles, it appeared in the Biedermeier Epoch one hundred years ago for the last time. It is not coincidental that most of all the sober designers, who are wanting in ideas, do not go beyond this. Concrete cannot be set in flames. It is sane in a different manner, and without it no useful modern house can be built.

And also the well-furnished machine aims to perform those tasks in a reduced amount of time whose artistic honor emanated from their difficulties, their size—as Ruskin taught us in his enchantingly sentimental way—and from the expression endowed in it by human hands. There will never be any expressionist houses built if one attaches great importance to unified form. It is impossible to produce all of the rectangular shiny functional forms in an abundantly ornamental way, to break up and cover the firm windows, elevators, desks, the telephones with Lehmbruck's, with Archipenko's curves. The only contiguity, and in this instance only a seeming one, lies in places for celebrations, in exhibition halls, in the theater, particularly when this space, as it is with Poelzig, shines onto the stage itself, into the separated magic of its semblance. And also the dome seems to be something always separated, a structure that reaches into sacred architecture. But otherwise the new art is not able, despite its temporary cubistic auxiliary forms, to paint on the functional instruments, the functional buildings. It is not able to cover in an "ornate" way. It is contradictory to the purpose of the new art to transform facilities in a passionate way, the new art whose value, the postulated essence, lies particularly in the insensibility, in the passionless practice, in the purely useful purpose, in the fortunate clear sobriety of the *nonessential*. The maximum of artistic attainment that can be achieved by the machine and its pure functional forms is therefore the leap to Biedermeier as the basic stylistic minimum and only after all styles have run their course—so long as all instruments have not vanished and are not transformed to purely functional facilities that can be socialized. But these remains, which do not have to be philistine or bucolic, ultimately form a superfluous emblem that is not oriented according to the clean mode of the machine spirit, as one can see. This is why the functional form cannot expand stylistically, and this is why engineers' structures must pay attention—also in respect to the Biedermeier, which might suddenly expand these structures—to constructive similarities that the skyscraper tries to show with the Birs Nimrud, and the solemn movie theater facade with the oldest geometric architecture, which had emerged from a different geometry. No antagonism is less incompatible than the one between an artistic pretentious constructiveness, which falsely slides over to stone, to the Egyptian, and the totally different maturity nowadays: the purely spiritual, musical expression demanding the *ornament*.

Only when the functional form limits itself to its own doing will this
other side reveal itself in a carefree and also open style. Comprehended release, comprehended discharge, cleansing what had been
mixed up impurely with commercial life, with arts and crafts, with
eudaemonistic style until now, all this comes together in a mutually
beneficial way: marching separately, fighting united. The birth of
integral technology and the birth of integral expressionism, accurately kept apart from each other, arise from the same magic: complete void of ornament on the one hand, utmost superabundance,
ornamentation on the other hand, but both are variables of the same
exodus. So, one should take the opportunity in an honest way and let
the living change wherever it alone should do so. One says for good
reasons that the oppressed Russian peasant must have been a saint to
become a decent person at all. Or, according to Lukács, a modern
architect needs the qualities of Michelangelo's talent just to draw a
table in a successfully beautiful manner. But it should be added that,
like children or peasants, a dilettante, who is needy, pressed by the
troubles of life, but whose talents cannot be compared to the least
gifted of the old masters, can nevertheless create works due to the
strange atmosphere of this epoch that are unskillful, without style, but
expressive and distinct, works that have nothing in common with the
*objet d'art* of masterful jewelery or with so-called artistic enjoyment.
This is the way to take that Klee and also Marc wanted to demonstrate. And it is the same goddess who contributes the need for the
applied arts, the technically enormous and successful relief, the expressionistic abundance. The flashing of fierce and enigmatic signs, a
sudden encounter of all ways in that overgrown, inconspicuous side-
path that turned into the main road of human development, that was
also the clandestine direction that already allowed Karlstadt, Savo-
narola, and the other iconoclasts' rage against the eudaemonistic art
when the secularized, stylistic Renaissance began—at random, but
for reasons of the pure light, the undissembled expression, the broken
compromise, the intellectual straightforwardness. Henceforth the
arts remained aloof from use and abstained from the inferior call of
taste, the pleasurable formation of style of the lower existence. *Big
technology* was to reign, an easing, cool, bright, democratic "luxury"
for everybody, a reconstruction of the planet earth striving for the
abolition of poverty, the hardship taken over by machines, centralized automation of the unessential, making leisure therefore

possible. And *great expression* was to reign, decoration was to become profound again and to guarantee pure ornaments of solution to the voice of inner concern instead of the silence of outward care.

After the practical sphere is secured firmly enough from the aesthetic sphere in regard to confusions, compromises, shift, this is the place to point to an existing relationship, which already irritated all use in its own era, to point to a latent, savable, determined spiritual meaning within the *history* of applied arts. Also in this instance, of course, a chair is only meant to sit on; it merely refers to the resting person. And a statue is made to be looked at, or rather it rests upon itself, is concerned with its own glory, and is indifferent toward all relations that are part of the surrounding life. According to the changed perspective of the observer, to the process of rotation, the obvious, the psychologically and socially embedded difference between applied and nonapplied art is determined, that which makes for high art. Everything ready for use, everything that remains floor and armchair, or, in other words, everything that is occupied by an *actual* self experiencing life, is categorized according to applied arts. In contrast, forms that draw one's gaze upward, that rise to the beams and remain above the work created by humans and thus are transformed into the throne or shrine for the body of something superior, something godlike, these forms are only occupied by the *symbolic* self learning about the inner and therefore belong to high art. And since applied art works surround us usefully, it has always been their aim to be comfortably luxurious, to maintain elegant perfection and to attract style in terms of taste as well as in terms of conscious formation in accordance with *objet d'art*. It is one of the characteristics of the applied arts to stop certain elements of decoration and construction and stabilize them as time and measure, elements that exceed the applied arts by movements of expression. The entire middle epoch of classical Greece and half of the modern age, i.e., apart from the Baroque, the modern age has been framed in a "classic" way by the Renaissance and Empire, which have essentially prepared the arts only as pleasant, nonreligious accompaniment of life, but not as the appeasement of spiritual states of misery, not as the consoling song of individualistic expression unconcerned about ugliness or beauty, not as the portrayal of the superior legend of redemption handed down to the people. Therefore, in this manner the difference between elegantly dressed-up service and high art is enormous—and it does not get less if the self, making use of it, can be in different places. What appears to the peasant as high art, the cavalier uses naturally as applied art, and many things that Louis XIV still possessed as the select commands of his personal absolutism and that emphasized his rule clearly seemed to have become and actually did become high art for later epochs. It was a high art that was significant and supposed to be mainly observed, for the social and the quasi-theological role of the self had declined. Yet, there is something *decisive* here that must be included: there is still something alive in and about the old chair that is not satisfied with comfort and points to something more than the mere person who may be resting in the chair. *Tertium datur*: There are Baroque armchairs that are too important for any use and turn the peculiar attitude, the quasi-removed mask of sitting down into something new, somewhat uncanny, like a fairy tale, a most peculiar line. It is not taste anymore, nor is it conscious, painstakingly stylized, selfrighteous immanent form, but an offprint from life is in preparation—reaching into a space where only the ultimate of pure art exists—it is already a signifying and descriptive sign, a seal of profundity and of daydream: painted as if the skin of, and carved as if the skeleton of a specter, of a spirit, of an inner figure had been transferred to it. Thus, the virtually luxurious instead of mystical purpose of Baroque insignia was only possible in times when thrones and altars mixed, when politicians formed a blasphemous alliance with the metaphysical, when Sun Kings and the theological majesty of the Roman-German Emperor emphasized ornamental art of an entirely different significance in a godlike manner. If we dissolve this alliance that was considered as such during those times by rethinking it with socialism and reformation in our minds, we would destroy this sacrilege: it would become immediately apparent that the *truly great historical applied arts* are earthly instruments and serve earthly purposes only in order to support the opulent, feudal, state church, pontifical state luxury, but even more—we must not forget the gains made in the modes of expression and the importance for architecture— they refer to a spiritual *a priori* of construction, of architecture, refer to the uselessness of building on earth for the sake of the big seal providing access to another world. Hence, this third aspect still exists between chair and statue, perhaps even above the statue: "applied arts" of a superior order; within it stretches a genuine, a transcending carpet of purely abstract form instead of the comfortable, quasi-stale, purely luxurious carpet of daily use, assembled from resting-places. In these other "applied arts," which are firmly perceptible in a particularly expressionistic way, the linear, arabesque-like ornament occurs as an overture—as the genuine carpet and the pure form, as a more easily successful but thereafter exemplary corrective for the transcending form, for the seal, for the removed, multi-dimensional, transcending ornament of new painting, sculpture, and architecture. There is no danger anymore that Egypt's dull world of stone, which is somehow intended from a constructive point of view, might effect the completely different kind of earnestness, the unearthly, expansive abstractness of expression. It is rather that a new exuberance appears that grants strongest, yes, most decisive participation in rememorizing the metaphysical and yet external ornament to Baroque—discredited by luxury—even to the *dance masks*, to the *totems*, to the *carved joists*, to the *Gothic shrines* that are much further in the past.

## The Background of the Will to Art

We always liked to see ourselves as open-minded. Therefore, from the early days on, we began carving consistently. We worked with wood. One did not have to be skillful. Whatever impressed or worried people was exorcised by a few strokes or even in a right angle.

But the feeble body cannot live in isolation and reaches for a bowl. Thus came the instrument that had to be handy and convenient. The flintstone was smoothed on purpose, hence in a jagged way. The earthware jug was molded to be handy. The material and the immediate purpose alone determined everything. That is a world of its own, and it leads increasingly to the outside, away from the expression of the inside, toward the material alien to the self. The inner measures were still incorporated into the earliest carvings, enlarged the arms and the eyes according to the rank given to them, and the will for magic that rose to the surface endowed our faraway face with masks. On the other hand, in the initial functional form, which was in accordance with the material, the path from the human to what belongs to the human has been abandoned. The stone, the structured clarity, therefore something initially Egyptian, something elemental again works in creative work.

## Greek Is Pleasing

However, the vital artistic element, which was the purpose of our quest, does not rest; it moves. Thus, the fabrics and the pitchers were at least covered with bands and friendly clear lines. Some kind of frugally decorative life sprang up, a playful geometricizing regularity. But first of all, in a truly vivid empathy, the constructive functional dimension blossomed from underneath, the *Greek* style, whose traces can be found everywhere, even without any real mediation. The Greek smile was, of course, still social and moderate. It did not begin to rival the stone with inner splendor yet. Still, it wanted to be both, wanted to be vital and tamed, understanding and symmetrical, picturesque and architectonic at the same time and thus become pure "sculpture." In its amphitheaters Greek art turned into a mere harmonized landscape. In its temples it turned into mere facade, into a eudaemonistic balance between life and strictness. This balance took place *in front of* the depth of both life and strictness, and thus it gained neither inner expression nor the power of outward space.

This is why one only enjoys what is beautiful and takes, uses what one likes. The shoots and the acanthus blossom; the tree stumps support the form. Elastic soft Ionic cushions are laid between column and entablature. But also egg-and-dart molding and fret lead their stricter line, lead through their quasi-inorganic quality, and the stone's spirit is at least triumphant as symmetrical, as a harmless, nobly decorative kind of geometry. Hence, on the one hand, the Greek figure is so lively that Pygmalion wants it to be his lover, no matter whether it is made from ivory, silver, bronze, clay, marble, or even flesh. But, on the other hand, the figure is so well-balanced, so full of Euphrosyne (i.e., cheerfulness) and proportion that it meets the unity of the block halfway at least. That is why the Hellenic torsos make a better impression than the originals from which those parts were knocked off, which, according to the spirit of the material, had to be knocked off. The Venus de Milo is only "perfect" as a torso. In contrast, the damaged statue of Chefren, which had already given everything to the stone, and for completely different reasons the statue of an apostle in Reims, which truly arose from the material in its vitality, its wealth of expression, both these figures appear merely as debris in their state as torsos. They do not even allow for those non-artistic elegiac associations as ruins do. In a few words: Greece and the Renaissance, too, stand on the same undevout, eudaemonistic, unserious, and undecisive ground. What is so considerably distorting about Dürer, who was so profoundly influenced by Italian art, is the combination of ruffled folds, angular features together with rectangular walls and doors. All this was mastered by the Greek style through an extremely peculiar decrease of richness and rectangularity at the same time. It became smooth, harmonic symmetry *ante rem*. The Greeks withdrew in that sense, arranged a world for themselves in which they could live, where they could evade the chaotic terrors but also the earnestness of decisions at any time. Here everything was subdued, mixed from the vegetal and the solid in such an Apollonian way that the calm weather of sheer beauty could develop, the shaped facade. Perhaps there was only something analogous to Greek Sophrosyne (i.e., composure) in the distant discipline with which an artist in China encompassed his much more extravagant and much more determined life lines. Greek Sophrosyne composed the form, the continuous cosmos so rapidly that even Chinese culture, to which wisdom in its most relevant form appeared as grace, was tactful, rhythmic, Tao-like, and also this culture was tempered after the fiery abundance of its own heroic-Orphic early days to become the luxurious, purely and simply aesthetic style. The Greeks remained alive even in the Christian Middle Ages, below all the Gothic glow, amidst all the most pervasive transcendentalism. Soon after this period the forms were to be rounded and no less beautiful, and, as painful as this development was, it was certain that everything would come to a pleasant, solemn end. The parish became the solid, independent, wordly-spiritual polis; the domes of the South glistened in crystalline tracery, in towers without spires, in a broad, almost comfortable horizontal. The Thomistic doctrine was eminently aesthetic, balanced the world, abandoned the Hellenic uni-substantiality of existence, abandoned the continuously self-complementing, concentric order only to establish instead the more attractive entity of a heterogeneous harmony. In this way the Christian transition was—in regard to the multifarious architecture of the official Middle Ages—far too often transformed into a semi-antique gradation within a spiritual cosmos. Of course, in order to return to the Greek column, to return to the Greek peristyle, which turned the main colonades of the interior of the Egyptian temple inside out to be a mere showpiece, one cannot evade the seriousness, not even in the artwork. And since design

dominated, in the functional form as well as in the consciously stylizing will to art, the Egyptian rigidity operated as the danger of
complete, uninterrupted construction at the end of any "style,"
especially when it reached the *serious point* of composure or rest.

## The Egyptian Will to Become like Stone

For as soon as we start to build the regular forms come up again.
Nothing seems already so indelibly inscribed in gypsum as the power
to make its worlds "Egyptian." And the Egyptian strictness comes
also constantly close to the Greek proportion, even if the feeble life
ripples and warms itself. That is: the construction of the *tertium
comparationis* evolves between functional form, style, and Egypt, even
though the depths of the connections is extremely different. It is from
these depths that the total facade arises, the recurrent functional
form, form in general, the absolute spirit of stone, the ultimately
unamiable geometry figuring as *Egypt*, as the total domination of
inorganic nature over life. Also here man looks ahead but sees himself
dying, hides in the grave. After death he comes to the nether world,
which is the land the sun passes by night, or at the most, if he had lived
a virtuous life and passed the judges of the dead, he comes to the
Westerners, to the deceased and reanimated Osiris, the lord of the
dead. But the departed one, the glance to the other side, never leaves
the world, even when such profound figures as ech, the bird of the
souls, or ka, the personal protective spirit, the human genius reveal
themselves from afar: still though, in all Egyptian figures and faces
nameless fear of death prevails, and there is no other salvation than
the affirmation of death, the suppression of inner life, the will to become like stone. The famous way that leads through alleys of rams and
Sphinxes, through colonnades toward the sanctuary is indeed only a
"path" and thus, so to speak, a purely pedagogical matter; a dead,
fixed quietness essentially remains as an overall impression, an overall
essence of the Egyptian sacred art. Only the columns still assume
plant motifs; as a whole they are geometrized bundles of papyrus and
lotus stems. The capitals show clearly the bud and the opened flower
of that mystical growth that are the signs and agents of resurrection.
But the pyramid, the pylons, the Egyptian temple, god's house continue in themselves the more strictly the purely inorganic landscape,
they are life-denying, straight, cubical with an enormous fanaticism

of rigidity. And the interior of that architecture abandons everything that blossoms all the more, everything that is mortal but is nevertheless the inner realm of life. The pyramid is a shrine, as Hegel says, wherein a deceased dwells; the sanctuary of the innermost temple space is nothing but a tomb and between its walls the bark, the colossal statue of the cosmic god oppresses and overwhelms. Even if the look enters through increasingly smaller, darker rooms the most eerie chamber, its narrowness is not the inward of the human soul but merely the contrasting space, the paradoxical space for the more absolute oversized and statuary stone of the god, the god of the sun, Ra, the highest of all. He, who is always visible through figures of beasts and humans and through all the minor gods of Egypt, is in the spirit of an absolute astral myth. The secret of the Christian sanctuary is of a completely different kind and is far from proximity with the inorganic rigidity, far from proximity with the life-denying, macrocosmic cubicity. Even the oversized Christos Pantokrator of the Byzantine apse bends over to the people. In the center of his creation he is a servant, the head of the human empire, and the most sublime sign disappears, is only visible as a miniature, as a distant figure of the dove of the holy spirit.

We said, though, that purpose and style, no matter how much the latter may demonstrate its false vitality, lead to the essence of stone. Or rather, to say it directly: even if the functional form, as a completely unartistic, purely negative random feature of cleanness, does not come close to Greek style, certainly the *nearest*, which comes objectively after the functional form and represents it with a leap in the artistic realm: the kind of Biedermeier, as well as the *topmost*, which comes after the constructive style: the rigidity and cubicity of Egypt, are firmly close to Greek style, close to style in general. And Greek style is always situated between the kind of Biedermeier and Egypt in the eudaemonistic center. The one, which is the style of Biedermeier, is already noticeable in the earliest flintstone tools. It draws its pure, practical line through the styles of the Renaissance, Regency, Louis XVI, and Empire, only to remain finally, so to speak, on the bottom, after the gradual abolition of styles at the beginning of the nineteenth century. As stated before, I am talking about a stylistic minimum in general (that is why it can be combined with all styles). The other, the Egyptian, penetrated first the Aegeans and lastly the Empire style, with the formal opportunity of influencing Empire by

the expeditions to the pyramids, and it forms, as Biedermeier represents the inferior limit against the non-artistic condition, the superior
space of the transcendental relation of Greek style and, therefore, of
style in general. But Egypt is continually betrayed by the functional
form, when the latter does not limit itself and aspires to stylishness.
This betrayal can only be avoided by maintaining life. It can be
avoided only if the sober triangle of the gable, only if the pure
roundness of the arch that is not only chosen from a worldly devout-
ness but also formed by the severity of death, only if the entire
ambiguous symmetry of the Greek and the classic style in that fuzzy,
homeless, shallow, abstract immanence are kept in their place. This
immanence does not convert to Egypt, to the winterland, to the land
of the dead, to the winter of the world, as it is called in the old occult
scriptures, and does not convert to the place of the purely inorganic
sphere of values, only due to its indecisiveness. For Egypt remains the
notion as well as the fulfillment of complete, uninterrupted shape, of
the *meaningful* construction and immanence of stone in general, dictated by the spirit of the material itself, not by stylizing efforts. Only
Christian life penetrates the stone in a serious way. In this instance
even the *external space* might become Gothic, and the angelic saluta-
tion in the gallery of the Church of Lorenz in Nuremberg had been
created precisely to celebrate the space where it hangs, to make the
space sing and to become the focus, particularly by hanging in the
center, of the internal sounding of the church's spatial body. Whereas
even in the Romanesque, Byzantine style, yes even in the horizontal
Gothic style, a final, strange possibility of Egypt reoccurs, transferred
from astrology to the open mysticism. It might reoccur wherever
gravity and order still appear as essential substance of the figuration.

The Will to Become Gothic like Resurrection

But the inner life, as it drifts toward itself, glows again even more
strongly. It makes its figures entangled, winding, placed in front of
each other, piled on top of one another. Here it is important to
remember the early days, to think constantly in terms of carving. One
works with wood in order not to flatten anymore, not to immure with
stone anymore. The inner essence exposes itself, and that which is
curious, that which moves like something that is brewing, that which
is scrolling becomes its unpretentious expression.

There already where nobody is yet, this vital clue smolders upward toward us. It is the same force that takes effect in lava, when molten lead is poured into cold water, in wood veining, and first and foremost in the quivering, bleeding, tattered, or curiously conglobate forms of the internal organs. Even today, African tribes keep their gods of life carved in wood, and their rituals are passed on in shafts, in rattles, in house beams, in thrones, and in idols. Their will for magic, their passion to transmute, to push their way into the upper realms of procreation produced, first of all, the mask, which elevates the progenitor daemonically, the always organic abstract totem and taboo. It suggests our far-off face, but Christ does not shine yet, only the glowing demon of life reigns in these creations of imagination, in these dark, sculptured systems of fertility and power—but this one does it absolutely. Even more so, Nordic as well as Oriental peoples never forgot the absoluteness of the carving, of the wood, and of the spirit of life. In the art during the time of the mass migration and in a fundamental way during the *Gothic* period the Nordic-Oriental symbiosis took place, the organic, psychical yearning manifested itself truly as the ornament. We know the entanglements, the serpentine bodies, the sea horses, the dragon heads bent toward each other in the Nordic lineations. There is nothing that could be compared with this uncanny pathos derived from the vitalization of the inorganic. Therefore, if now there is still any possible salvation behind the rejected, worn-out styles, then it can only happen through the resumption of those almost completely forgotten organic lines. Everything that shall blossom and luxuriate has to learn from those pre-Gothic figures. There are no whirls, no extravagances, and no architectural power with the profound organic rules of those extravagances that would not breathe with their heads in the wild, cloudy air of this organity filled with all the drifting, all the musical presentiments, and the infinite. Moreover, since Worringer's fortunate und pregnant presentation there is no more doubt that in these ornaments of intertwined signs and animals the concealed Gothic style is simultaneously given in the Baroque and its aftermath.

But the foliage amalgamates much more differently than the Greek. The most curious decoration covers all surfaces and ripples over the walls in order to dissolve them. We saw that the *Greek* line only met the living in its outward appearance, being the unmysterious, epidermal organic chemistry visible to everybody, and in its

light, elegant rhythm determined by an internally animated harmony. We saw that the *Egyptian* line is only rigidity, and *Sophrosyne*
(i.e., composure) turns into geometry. This is true insofar that here
only stone is thought of when dealing with stone, and not the flesh.
This is according to the spirit of the material, which is the spirit of the
desert or of the Alpine landscape and that of the enormous temple of
the dead of inorganic nature. Led by the form of the stone, the
mysterious-unmysterious way goes outward for the Egyptians. Here,
in this eternal pattern of all absolute constructive architecture, a long
forgotten groundwater rises, a belief in granite and the cosmology
emerges that quasi-unfolds and turns back many pages; it happens in
a way that a kind of mineralogy of higher ranks, a kind of second
natural philosophy connects to the sphere of the arts above all souls.
The *Gothic* line, on the other hand, retains the hearth. This line is
restless and uncanny like its figures: the bulges, the serpents, the
animal heads, the watercourses, a tangled criss-cross and twitching
where the amniotic fluid and the incubation heat sit, and the womb of
all pains, all lusts, all births, and of all organic images begin to speak.
Only the Gothic line carries such a central fire within itself in which
the most profound organic and the most profound spiritual essence
come to maturity. But this is very alien to the feeble Greek life, and at
the same time it is the most extreme contrast to the Egyptians as the
masters of death, as the gaze to which god appears more as a wall than
as a hand, as the land that Joseph had been sold to, as the spirit of the
cosmic myth devoid of people, deserted by the Jews in order to see the
huge grape from Canaan. Egypt stratifies, the Gothic style creates;
Egypt remodels the cosmic system in a constructive way, the Gothic
style moves productively and symbolically toward the embrace, toward the winding realm of the souls. Egypt, which grasped the stone,
is the spirit of the grave, the spirit of the total form, of total constructiveness by reasons of the material. Egypt is the perfect descriptive
*formal sign* (*Formzeichen*) for a perfect clarity of strangeness, a clarity of
pressure and death. Egypt is the artistic congruence with the tomb,
with the cosmic myth. The Gothic style, on the other hand, which
grasped life, is the spirit of resurrection, the spirit of the serving
formula, of lowered, fragmented constructiveness, as a merely inferior
definition of the object. The Gothic style is the imperfect *expressive-*
descriptive *seal* (*Siegelzeichen*) for an imperfect collective and fundamental secret, for a symbolic ornament and symbolism that is in itself

fermenting, incomplete, functional. The Gothic style is the artistic indication of the living space (*Lebensraum*), of a storm brewing on the horizon of the problems of collectivity as of all approaches to the myth of logos. Therefore, it is not the bright and shallow-structured Greek line, but only the Gothic one, the essentially adventurous, long-sighted, functional line that is the perfect life, that is the ultimately pure realm of the functional form, *the free spirit of the expressive movement as such*. And, only in conjunction with the Gothic line could Egypt, the constructed stone, during all meta-stylistic periods, be cut through. Thereby the Romanesque, the Byzantine, the Arab-Indian, the Gothic, and also the Baroque, except for its non-inherent stylistics, represent the rising triumph of the organic exuberance over the crystal.

This is why the inward human being cannot want anything else but the infinite line without being self-deceptive. Along this line, woodland wanders into the desert, into the crystal and degrades the crystal to a mere accessory that has cooled down a long time ago. In its first Nordic existence the infinite line had been a wild blossoming and pushing away from everything without knowing where to go; only as the Gothic line did it become in this sense the real, not only organic, but organic-spiritual transcendence, when the great, the all determining star of the Son of Man could rise up above its swelling flood. The means of stone are broken up, the total formality, the important, absolute constructiveness is dismissed, is a solely strengthening, supporting formula for the work (garment, clustered columns, cross-vault), or at most the form is the prius of the foreground in the observed Gothic object (arbitrary stretching, denaturalization of the model, winding openwork). A most profound object reigns, expressed in organic abstract seals, in the sense, that Gothic art—and whatever is connected with it in a wider sense—gives expression to an exodus of the outward material otherwise only known in music.

Hence it works and ferments in the stones to bloom together with us, to have our life. For it is impossible to vent oneself if one builds with the forces of the Son of Man within oneself. The law had not yet created a great man, but freedom hatches the true giants and extremities. Thus, it is also Egypt itself—as the model of the sealed storage of the false god—that leads toward those figures where, finally, the organic, the organic abstraction takes place again. In no other way can the inside that is turned outward, the organic of a higher level,

happen, the excessive ornament and the gentle reunion of the self that
will become the Ego: *as the Gothic entelechy of all the fine arts*. The human
being, not the sun, not geomantics and astrology, but the human
being in his deepest inwardness, as Christ, became here the alche-
mistic measure of all constructive things. If one looks long enough into
it, into that blossoming and its passage, one can see the flow of one's
innermost soul, and the soul wanders around in there, turns toward
itself. Here, that nice *warmth* prevails wherein the living soul does not
suffocate. It is the warmth of the beloved and the light that emanates
from the flower, from the lucerne of all maids, the nice warmth
wherein the living soul is overcome by humility and devotion and is
held in the Gothic Virgin's arms, just like the child Jesus himself. The
Gothic will to decorate the choir, the entire inner space in a more
and more glorified way, the Gothic high tendency in all its abundance
dematerializes all mass: now all the craving pictorial plates found
their place; mesh and loops of unprecedented stonemasonry and
craftsmanship proliferate in crockets and chapters, the glowing
windows are pierced with tracery and rose, curvature arises, not
vaults, and a dynamic pathos is pushing upward with all parts. In the
nave it pushes additionally into the depths of the choir. Sin and
atonement, the glistening devil's beauty and the realm of the gentle,
bent, calm soul meet so closely in the enormous dome of figures. They
turn it into the petrified journey of the Christian adventure. But *light*
also searches, spreads, and burns in these stones, in this ornamented
column, in this house of the human heart. We are not repudiated
anywhere, nor is more than a reflexive tribute given to the inclusive
force of the material. The wall is defeated. The colorful windows open
up into an unmeasured landscape. We are standing amidst love,
surrounded by the heavenly legions, yes, the robes and miens of the
saints assume all space comprising forces within themselves. It is a
ship made of stone. It is a second ark of Noah flying toward God. The
spire of the steeple transforms into the finial as the mystical larynx
that receives the word of the Son. And above all these miracles—
"How does each step take me far!"—"That is a profound secret, time
turned into space!"—above all this endless tangle of lines, there is
Mary smiling so sweetly and wisely as if the graves would light up, as if
the distant mystical chambers would prepare themselves and stand illuminated as the *restitutio in integrum* for the most inferior being. Many
things are certainly not formal about these domes, about these creations

of domes after the human figure, but it is the informality between our hearts and our world. Here, too, the breakthrough wants to succeed: the forms of the only art yet to come, of the organic, of the metapsychic eidetic kind present themselves and culminate all together in the lineament of the secret human form. The only essential aprioristic object of that art is the yet still flowing, indeterminate decoration and signature of immediate humanity.

The Picture of the Innermost Form

This may be the way to get home, and therefore it seemed so desirable that the point, which is supposed to be effected by the new, colorful seriousness, is not technically masked. But also concealment should not happen anymore because of a different strictness, an all too random disregard for the excitement within one's own heritage, within impressionism—its unrest and its loosening of formality that took place after all, its subjectivizing of the conception of the world that at least exists, even if it is placed low and has remained reflexive and devoid of expression. The path of the modern age, of the erupted, irresistible, mystical nominalism has to be followed to the end if the Egyptian shall not reinstall itself as something hollow, false, and empty, or if even the equally past affiliation of the historical Gothic shall be reinstalled instead of the aprioristic.

For one thing separates us distinctly and strongly from that. We have become more ego-like, more searching, more homeless, assuming more of a form *like a current*. Our collective self appears so near. The sap of the new compositional expressions springs much less than before from the fountains of means, of the life of form. Forming is no longer the only support. It is not even particularly necessary anymore to speak, to make oneself visible.

In this way, somehow, even *colors* have retreated, the primary ambition in painting: to create with it, to translate into it, to model with it. Although one would like to see clearly and possibly without relief, it is not important. Kokoschka paints in gray, in brown, in cloudy purple, with all the colors of the earth. And when Marc and Kandinsky use more distinct colors, we no longer enjoy the color as such. It is rather for the substance of excitation that the purest and crassest luminosity is chosen and composed. Marc is even aiming at a theory of harmonious colors, and on the whole, an indulgence in

clear, surfaceless local colors becomes fashionable instead of atmo-
spheric dimness. It is that peculiar emotional value of the single color
as well as the emotional value of its compositions: hate, ardor, wrath,
love, secrecy, representative of the entire aura, in which the landscape
of the soul is situated. Thus, Däubler has this to say about those colors:
"Remnants from violent yellow reach into blue inevitabilities." This
is the coloring power and, at the same time, the limit of its being
chosen, for here the color has to serve like it never did before. The
color may be diffracted in its own pleasure, in its own life of form
as often as desired. And the pure picturesque, which many
impressionists—in an unclear manner—prided themselves to have
found again, necessarily withdraws facing the necessity for statement.

It is true though that the *process of drawing* forcefully pushes us
forward again. The sightful devotion to the quick, vulgar impression
is over. And it cannot be denied, since Marées, thinking in *drawing*,
the new way of thinking in planes, seems certainly to aim even deeper.
Indeed, the less we look for color as such, the less we look for the line as
such, unless it is dense and in itself expressively condensing and not a
clearly outlining one. Take, for instance, Rousseau or Kandinsky,
when trembling or horse riding appears as a short, imposing curve, or
when revenge appears as a zigzag arrow form, or benevolence as a
blossoming flower. The contours sharpen and are charged in a sculptural way in Archipenko's work. Or, when Däubler translates
Boccioni's striding people into language, they are no longer stationary people who can occasionally step out, but they stride, and the
striding dominates the body, which comprehends itself as something
physical: "Knuckles want to burst out, soles of shoes drag space,
breasts symbolize the human microcosmos snuggling between the
signs of the zodiac. In our heads we roll an entire world through our
veins: the human is much too much, but with our motion we
irresistibly break into living geometries. On our shoulders and thighs
we carry a not yet expressed crystallization of space into our striding
rhythm." Thinking in planes. The new thinking in cubes and curves
also seems to tend to go deeper when in the most direct depiction. And
cubism is the consequential expression of that new, eternal space
magic. It started with the simple partitioning of things, with turning
up their nonvisible planes into the picture plane. One of Picasso's
early paintings bears the revealing title: *Partitioned Violin*, but soon,
what had merely been played with and tried out changed into real

experience. The peculiar attraction appeared that belongs to the partitioned plane, that can already be sensed in the layout plans of sites and buildings. It is the attraction of active, subtle partitioning, of balanced scales, and of the bare, active linear creature as such. It is the conscious will to recreate the knowledge of size, volume, and weight, to recreate the knowledge of that secret attraction, of order, and of statics that regulate the space as a combination of quadratic and cubistic equilibria, even against the slightly deadened planar arabesques. This is something different from and more fruitful than pure functional form and engineering, or the final false memories of the Egyptian death chamber, and it points toward the heavens. Not only Marées and Cézanne are painters who think in terms of space, but the Sistine Madonna also has some cubistic spatial life, as Techter points out so courageously and so correctly. Cézanne referred to spatial thinking in his famous words about the cone, the cylinder, and the sphere within the composition of a painting. The Sistine Madonna, on the other hand, seems to be surrounded by spatial relationships that resound from far away. Moreover, it seems to be surrounded by a heavenly spatiality that is virtually passed on to us. Things are cubistic not only because they are well-proportioned—according to which every picture of the past and more so those of absolute styles would figure as cubistic—but the curiously mixed Raphael reveals more in that direction than can be studied with the much more important Leonardo. In fact, objects are not only placed in space, but space is placed within things. Space is active and may certainly form an unprecedented foundation like the Roman Pantheon or even the Gothic cathedrals.

But it is, indeed, true that many things are inferior, and one should continue *to disrupt the drawing*. The drawing can and must provide stability so that the transitoriness of a great, widely resounding feeling, not only a momentous one, has its physical position. The drawing may also signify a minimal concrete definition as all suggestive forms do. But much too often, the already obvious has lived and consolidated itself here in a quadratic way and disguised its banal world with cartons, boxes, and cubes from which there is little to learn even if there seems to be so many layers. Besides, the futuristic movement—being the craze for ecstacy, dynamics, and an all-pervasive time-liness—disturbs the circles of the vain and burned out old forces, particularly in the cubistic works, just like Kokoschka and Picasso destroy the preceding belief in plain color. The motion of the line and the least expected meaning of fairy tales in the drawing occur and thus transposes the cubistic or otherwise useful statuarism to a mediating, solidifying formula or to the form of the most minimal definition of the objects in the course of expressionist ego formation, of expressionist ego projections. That motion is the strongest reaction against all that which seems to be self-composed, against all that which seems to be self-portraiture and "absolute" painting. Furthermore, if we usually have the impression that certain well-known remains, an eye, a violin clef, or just a number are continually in the cubistic picture, as if against their own will, then Braque, Derain, and other painters of the Picasso school are able to show that we wish to see, through all distractions of cubism, these object-like relations especially in the most abstract predicate of the art work—thus not only in the beginning, as the last witnesses of an emotional farewell to the world, and not only personal. Therefore, these curious pictures can be understood as the most agonizing auxiliary constructions whose concentrated abstractness will again be unraveled in a newly gained object relation and object symbolism. Hence, if one wants to create a more profound form of depiction than painting reaching into itself, into the spatial silence—as the cubists cultivated it against the excitement and elementality of impressionism—then it is totally impossible in a literal sense as pure composition made out of planes and weights. And on a large scale it is only conceivable insofar as it is impossible to conceive of a cube as ornament. In other words, a cube is not continuous but seeks to serve as *figure of significance*. That is the case according to a structured transparency that only begins with the realization of form without being identical with it or even being somewhat continuously accompanied by its stylishness and its joy in constructing. The latter is still present in impressionism, and in cubism it is again a totally geometrically hypertrophic joy in constructing.

But then, can we build at all and erect arches above us? Here, the introduction of a higher level of thinking in arts and crafts must ultimately prove successful as it has already been shown above with the Baroque chairs. It is likely that, according to the extraordinary quest for expression, certain conversions in the practical arts and then in sculpting and architecture will triumph over pure painting. Hence, under a future aspect a Sheraton chair or the unworldly curve of some

Baroque cabinets may contain more aesthetic features and meaning than the sweetest Perugino or even more prominent illusions in art history. This future aspect we find beyond the practical arts in a narrower, socially dominated sense and in the sense of style, and thus also beyond the ornament in a one-dimensional, non-transcendental sense. Many things already point in that direction, and those that are long gone or have never been understood reemerge—like the dance masks, the totems, the carved house beams, the ornamental strips, the tabernacles, like the notion of a sculpture—also carved out from the inside—of a Negro, Nordic, Gothic, Baroque kind, the nameless body of a sculpture that figures as architecture. Architecture, which is threatened so much by clear-cutting and functional form and has even lost that way, is thus always investigated as the interior of the home space that is supposed to be sculpturally well-cultivated, supposed to be approximated. With painting and with sculpture, architecture continues to figure in a more humane construction space, and more so today, as the anticipating expression of a "tat twam asi"—there you are. This architecture figures as self-encounter within the painted objects and encounter with them, close to music that is no longer frozen.

Our Secret Creative Signature

So we search for the creator who allows us to confront ourselves in a pure form, who allows us to encounter ourselves. His fresh gaze kneads things so they are no longer recognizable, and, like a swimmer, like a cyclone, it whirls right through whatever is there. Flowing water, old trees, or even a dark mountainous lake are beautiful to behold. But it is enough to possess all these things in nature where we can enjoy all that is unreproducible about air, about the estimation of spatial openness and other things much better than all the art lover's pleasures can ever communicate. Besides, the slide and the movie have been excellent substitutes as photographic means for those people who want the impression of nature without any deformation. The cinematograph is the best art gallery, the substitute for all the great general art exhibitions of the world. That should be clear to all those who, with each expressionist painting, must ask what it represents, and thus hell can shrink and resemble a street corner for their

eyes, that become a mere photographic plate. Already since van
Gogh, this had clearly changed. Suddenly we are involved, and this
involvement is exactly what is painted. Certainly, it is still a visible
tumult. There are still railings, underpasses, iron beams, brick walls,
but suddenly all that overlaps in a curious way. All at once the
discarded cornerstone strikes sparks. That which is drawn in all
appearances, that which is uncomprehensibly related and lost to us,
that which is near, faraway, like the Sais quality of the world, all this
comes to light in van Gogh's paintings as it does in Strindberg's work,
too. In Cézanne the expressionist revolution is clear as well—perhaps
even more profound than in van Gogh's work—more hidden and
somewhat covered by the strong, purely picturesque facade that
makes Cézanne the last great modern stylist. For these are no longer
fruit, not even fruit molded out of color. Rather, all that is conceivable in life is to be found here, and, if those fruits should fall down to
the ground, the world would be set on fire. Cézanne's still lifes are
already a kind of heroic landscape, and moreover, they are charged
with mystic weight and a yet unknown, nameless mythology. There is
good reason why the still life appears at this point in time, for the
ceremonial art works of the past and present world that depicted
closed cultures have come to an end. And no romantic pattern or even
a theosophy of the zodiac can bring them back again. In contrast, the
"still life" has not only remained practically the sole picturesque
object, but is and can be superior to all cultures in its escapism and
intensification of small things. After all, the new tableau is at best only
a seal and not an ideogram totally identical with our innermost
intensity, with our innermost collective and basic secrets like the
conceivable ultimate music and the conceivable ultimate metaphysics. In particular, the object becomes a mask in this new tableau,
becomes an "idea," turns into a deformed, denaturalized mode of a
secret excitement moving toward some goal. The human soul and the
essence of the world converge. Suddenly I can see my eyes, my place,
my position: I am that drawer myself and the fish, the kind of fish
lying in the drawer. For the gradation vanishes; the path between the
picturesque subject and the depicted object becomes level. The object
is to be reborn and recapture its essence, its inner principle, its
potentiality of all of us and not only its objective substantiality. My
dancing, my morning stars sing and all transparent formations of this

kind reach the same egoistic architectural horizon and also the same subjective ornament of their entelechy: to be a trace, a sign of Makanthropos, to be a seal of its secret figure, of its hidden emotional Jerusalem.

Here, nothing is left that can be borrowed from the outside. The soul does not have to accept alien prescriptions anymore. But the soul's own need is strong enough to attract the cortex and marks to assume its own position, the pictures only become our *own* emergence at a different place. Van Gogh still pointed the way out of ourselves. In his work the objects still speak, no matter how intensely they speak. But it seems as if they speak by themselves and not as an echo of the human. Then suddenly we alone resound from the objects. It is different with the new expressionism, where only the human being exists as a Kaspar Hauser figure using the objects merely as memory signs of its stubborn origins or as punctuation marks for keeping or storing its continuous recollection. Thus, the objects become the dwellers of their own interior. And, when the visual world seems to decay anyway, to empty out its own spirit, seems to become noncategorical, then the sounds of the invisible world want to turn into pictures in and about the visual world: the disappearing facade; the increase of richness; the development of woodland; an influx and outpouring of the objects into the crystal woodlands of the ego; creative and deepest eruption; universal subjectivism within the object, behind the object, as an object itself whereby the external object disappears to the degree that it reappears equal to one of the five hundred gods of Canton in the temple of the hidden inner Canton. Here, the strangely familiar pictures may appear to us as mirrors of the earth in which we see our future like the masked ornaments of our innermost form, like the adequate fulfillment that has finally been recognized, like the self-presence of eternal meaning, of the egos, of the we, of the *tat twam asi*, of our glory vibrating in secrecy, of our hidden godly existence. That is the same as the yearning finally to see the human face. Thus, there are no other paths of dreams for the magic picture than those on which the Sesenheim experience might happen, where one comes to meet oneself. And no other relation to an object can occur than one that reflects the secret contour of the human face all over the world and connects the most abstract organic with the longing for our hearts, for the richness of the self-encounter.

## The Conscious and Known Activity within the Not-Yet-Conscious, the Utopian Function

The intended look ahead is finicky, not dreary. This look requires in advance that the presentiment be sane and also not be gloomy as if it were stuck in the basement. That presentiment, in its dusk, is not meant to become aware although it may be directed toward tomorrow. Since science is absent, something hysterical and something superstitious have settled here as well. Certain psychic conditions like clairvoyance, the second sight, and that kind have been described as presentiments, or, more precisely, stupor. But that is degeneracy, whereas the real presentiment, of course, cannot reach down nor does it want to. Given that the so-called second sight still exists, something tricky is inherent; there is also a proximity to cramping and other endowments that do not provide much hope. Such things belong to that ailing sensitivity (the sensitivity of an open wound) that, in legitimate cases, only anticipates a change in weather, but here it pretends to anticipate fires and deaths. And here it fits the genuinely unconscious, deteriorated, atavistic, the expired of this kind of presentiment so that it refers only to events that already happened a thousand times before, that will happen tomorrow or the day after time and again. After all, a somnambulistic presentiment might be, at best, some degenerate leftover of the animal instincts, but here the instinct is really stereotypical. The animal's activities, although appropriate for a particular condition, become immediately contradictory as soon as the animal is confronted with a new situation and is forced to anticipate something unprecedented. The egg deposit, the nest building, the migration are carried out by instinct as if a precise "knowledge" of the future existed. But it is merely the million-year-old fate of the species where that future takes place. It is a substantially old, automatic future. Therefore, it is the mentional false one where nothing new happens. Many things about the physical instinct still seem to be in the dark. The research on signal systems is still not complete. The life of the impulse image in the instinct has not been unraveled—assuming there is one—including the sense of direction given to the impulses. A lowering of the threshold of the human presentiment, as substantial as it might be, will make it hardly possible to relearn the activity that, in the animal instinct of precaution, seems to possess the past, the present, and the future still tightly connected. It is this activity of the species that dominates in relation to others. Yet, nothing is more certain that, in this case, the future that folklore tells about, as it is in prophecy, is a totally false one, a repetition, a prearranged plot in an everlasting cycle. The instinct-future and the related atavistic presentiment starts and absorbs the same thing time and again on the same level. Therefore, the productive presentiment, even in the form of so-called intuition, is something entirely different from instinct that has become aware of itself. This presentiment does not remain gloomy and tricky or even dense. It is strong and healthy from the beginning. It is openly aware of itself, particularly as something not-yet-conscious. In its alertness it shows the zest to learn. It reveals the ability to look around while foreseeing, to have circumspection, even to be cautious in pre-caution. Starting with youth, with a period of transition, with production, the real presentiment feels at home in the most upright human conditions, not in the animal or even parapsychic condition. The German peasants of 1525, the masses of the French Revolution, the Russian Revolution certainly had, aside from the slogans, some kind of image of the revolutionary impulses; the "Ça ira" meant direction finding. But the impulse images were attracted and illuminated by a real future locus—by the realm of freedom. The so-called ability to foresee death or even winning lottery numbers is obviously of a lesser productive rank. One of the strongest somnambulists, the prophetess of Prevost, said in her pronouncements edited by Justinus Kerner in the early part of the nineteenth century, "The world is a circle for me. In this circle I could go forwards and backwards and see what there had been and what there was to come." Romanticism and Hegel, too, knew and honored the presentiment solely in that atavistic, super-stitious sense that has become totally trivial today. There is only a sense for the old world where the only new thing is the cockcrow, the one that can be heard in the graveyard and that is part of the spook. None of these midriff-prophets, from Sibyl to Nostradamus, has an understandable word to say about the future in their predictions that goes beyond the already known, not a word to say that is not just a rearranging of what we already know. In contrast, Bacon, who is not a prophet but a remarkable utopian, saw an amazingly genuine future in his *Nova Atlantis*. And that was solely based on his awareness and sense for the objective tendency, for the objective real potential in his era.

The look forward becomes even more powerful the brighter it becomes aware of itself. The dream in this look becomes quite clear, and the presentiment, being the right one, will be obvious. Only when reason starts to speak, then hope, which has nothing false to it, will begin to blossom again. The not-yet-conscious itself has to become *conscious* of its own doings; it must come to *know* its contents as restraint and revelation. And thus the point is reached where hope, in particular, the true effect of expectation in the dream forward, not only occurs as an emotion that merely exists by itself, but is *conscious and known* as the *utopian function*. All this is discussed in the thirteenth chapter of my book *Das Prinzip Hoffnung* (*The Principle of Hope*). First the content of hope represents itself in ideas, essentially in those of the imagination. The ideas of the imagination stand in contrast to those of recollection, which merely reproduce perceptions of the past and thereby increasingly hide in the past. And in this instance the ideas of the imagination are not of the kind that merely combine the already existing facts in a random manner (the sea of stone, the golden mountain, etc.), but carry on the existing facts toward their future potentiality of their otherness, of their better condition in an anticipatory way. The imagination of the utopian function that is determined in this way differs from mere fantasy in that only the former possesses an expectable not-yet-existence; i.e., it does not play around in an unoccupied potentiality and does not go astray but anticipates a real potentiality in a psychical way. At the same time, the difference to the waking dream that is stressed so often as a really possible anticipation gains new clarity; in mere wishful thinking the utopian function is not at all present, or it only flashes up briefly. With the figure of Ulrich Brendel in *Rosmersholm*, Ibsen touchingly sketched a mere planner, who was subsequently unproductive. On a much lower level, Schiller's Spiegelberg in *The Robbers* is not moving at all, for he is more a type of utopian braggart. On an incomparably higher level, Marquis Posa is also similar to this type because of the great manner in which he makes abstract and pure postulations. Ever since antiquity, pure wishful thinking has discredited the utopias in a political and practical way as well as in announcing what might be desirable: it has made it seem as if all utopias were abstract. There is no doubt but that the utopian function can only exist prematurely in abstract utopianizing, i.e., predominantly without a solid subject supporting it and without reference to the real potentially. Hence, it is easy to go astray when there is no contact with the real forward tendency, toward the better condition. But, we should bear in mind that the philistine's widely held and fully developed platitude of daily life, his narrow-minded empiricism is just as dubious as the immaturity (the fanaticism) of the underdeveloped utopian function. In short, the alliance of the big bourgeois and the empty-minded practitioner is on the whole dubious because they have not only rejected the antici-patory in its entirety but have even despised it. This alliance formed in opposition to any mode of conceiving more desirable conditions, especially those that would carry us forward. Thus, the alliance increased and centered on nihilism, especially nihilism that was capable of articulating something anti-utopian like the following: "In the wish *Dasein* (existence) projects its *Sein* (being) upon possibilities which not only have not been taken hold of in concern, but whose fulfillment has not even been pondered over and expected (!). On the contrary, in the mode of mere wishing, the ascendancy of Being-ahead-of-oneself brings with it a lack of understanding for the factial possibilities .... Wishing is an existential modification of projecting oneself understandingly, when such self-projection has fallen forfeit to thrownness and just keeps *hankering* after possibilities" (Martin Heidegger, *Being and Time*). Such words doubtlessly sound as if a eunuch would blame the child Hercules for being impotent when applied to immature anticipating. Needless to say, the real struggle against immaturity and abstraction, insofar as they were connected to the utopian function and potentially still are connected, has noth-ing in common with bourgeois "realism" and guards against the practitioner. What is important here is the imaginative gaze of the utopian function, loaded with hope; it is not corrected by a parochial perspective but solely by what is real in the anticipation itself. There-fore, that gaze is corrected by the only real realism that is the only one because it grasps the tendency of reality. It grasps the objectively real potentiality toward which the tendency strives. The real realism is at home in those qualities of reality that are utopian themselves; i.e., they contain future. The designated maturity of the utopian function—untempted by distractions—also designates the sense for the tendency of philosophical socialism in contrast to the bad "sense for facts" of the socialism that degenerated into empiricism. The point of contact between dream and life—without which the dream would only be abstract utopia, and life only yield triviality—is given in the utopian capacity that is set on its feet. This capacity is connected to the real potentiality and surmounts the specific existence (*das jeweils Vorhandene*) tendentiously not only in our nature but in the nature of the entire exterior world. It is here that the apparently paradoxical term of concrete utopia seems to be appropriate. Hence it is an anticipatory utopia, which is not at all identical with abstract utopian reverie, nor is it directed by the immaturity of a merely abstract utopian socialism. Concrete utopia designates precisely the power and truth of Marxism, which pushed the cloud in the dreams forward without extinguishing the fire of the dreams but rather strengthened them through concreteness. It is in such a manner that the consciousness-knowledge (*Bewusstsein-Gewusstsein*) of an intentional expectation has to prove itself to be the intelligence of hope—amidst the immanently ascending, material-dialectically exceeding light. Thus, the utopian function is the only transcending one that has remained, and it is the only one worth keeping: a transcending one without transcendence. The process is its position and corollary, the process that has not yet delivered its most immanent factual content that is still pending. Consequently, the process itself is expectant and has an objective presentiment of the not-yet-developed as something not-yet-well-developed. The awareness of the frontline position is the best illumination for it; the utopian function, as the comprehended activity of expectation, of a hopeful presentiment, keeps the alliance with everything dawning in the world. Thus the utopian function knows about explosive powers since the utopian function itself is a condensed form of them: the utopian function is the unimpaired reason of a militant optimism. Therefore, the consciously illuminated and knowingly explained *active substance* (*Akt-Inhalt*) of hope is the *positive utopian function*; the *historical substance* (*Geschichts-Inhalt*) of hope, first represented in ideas and encyclopedically explored in realistic conclusions, is the *human culture in respect to its concrete utopian horizon*. The combination *Docta spes* (education and hope), as the expectation in reason and reason in expectation, operates on these findings. And in this combination it is no longer the examination that predominates and that, since ancient times, only refers to what has already developed, but is the process attitude of participation and cooperating that predominates. Therefore, since Marx, the process attitude no longer ignores the open process methodologically, nor is novelty alien to the material anymore. The sole theme of philosophy has been set in the topos of an unsettled regular developing field in the representational intervening consciousness and in the realm of knowledge. It is only Marxism, together with science, that discovered this topos—in fact with the development of socialism from utopia to science.

### The Utopian Function Continued: Its Inner Subject and the Countermove against the Bad Existence

But without the power of an "I" and a "we" in the back, even hoping becomes flat. There is nothing soft about the conscious, known hope; rather, it has a strong will: this is the way it should be; this is the way it has to be. The inclination to wish and to want bursts forth with zest, the intensity of excess, of surpassing. The upright gait is a prerequisite, i.e., a will that cannot be overruled by anything that has been. The uprightness is the will's proviso. This peculiar point, where the subject can stand and from where it reacts, is designated abstractly in the stoic self-consciousness: when the world collapses, the debris will hit an undaunted person. The point is abstract in a different way when designated under the prerequisites of an intellectual pride, within the transcendental ego of German idealism and no longer by the pride of virtue. Here the self-consciousness has changed into the act of a perceiving creativity. Already in Descartes, knowledge appears partly as a manufacture, i.e., as the manufacture of its object. Of course, the prerequisites of intellectual pride had been terribly inflated with the semblance of their absolute making; reason does not at all dictate nature's rules. The world of this epistemological idealism is also not at all a utopian one. On the contrary: the main ambition of the transcendental subject was particularly to create the existing world of rules, the world of mathematical, scientific experience. Nevertheless, the transcendental subject of Kant and Fichte knew how to postulate ethically beyond a bad existence (*Vorhandenheit*), although in an abstract way, void of content, in conjunction with German misery. At least Kant, who should not at all be confused with Neo-Kantianism, built a nicer world by way of postulation, one that was, according to Goethe, based on the spontaneity of the will, a world that was not satisfied by the mechanistic experience of existence (*Vorhandenheits-Erfahrung*) and that did not decline. Therefore, the stoic self-consciousness and German idealism even more so reveal the indication of the peculiar point, although thoroughly damaged by abstractness, from which the subject guards for itself the *freedom of a contradicting countermove against the bad existence (das schlecht Vorhandene)*. In spite of the abstract formal indication of such a subjective factor, it was at least recognized. At that time it represented philosophically the citizen (*citoyen*). In this way, from *Sturm und Drang* to the people's spring (*Völkerfrühling*) of 1848, each bourgeois-revolutionary demand in Germany was still connected to the subject of idealism. But the subjective factor became a reality, not just in one's mind, when it was first grasped socialistically, that is, with the development of proletarian class consciousness, free of ridiculous idealistic pomposity. The proletariat understands itself as the active antagonistic contradiction to capitalism, consequently the one that gives the bad developments most trouble. The subjective factor that was equally real mediated the objective factor of the social tendency, of the real potentiality (*Real-Möglichen*)—against all abstraction and the corresponding boundless spontaneity of the consciousness. Therefore, the act of knowing better became that surplus, which consciously continued, directed, and humanized the path of the world that had already begun, its "dream of a thing," as Marx said. The objective factor alone is not sufficient. Rather, the objective contradictions constantly call for the mutual interplay with the subjective contradiction. Otherwise the false doctrine of objective automatism, which is ultimately defeatist, would take hold. According to this doctrine, the objective contradictions alone would be sufficient to revolutionize the world. Both factors, the subjective as well as the objective, have to be understood in their continuous dialectical interplay, inseparable, impossible to isolate. Certainly the human part of action has to be kept from being isolated, has to be guarded against the evil putschist activism that explodes and contains an overly subjective factor that believes it can skip the laws of objective-economic regularity. And Social-Democratic automatism is no less damaging since it spreads the superstitious belief that the world will be good all by itself. In short, it is impossible to manage without a subjective factor, and it is equally impossible to neglect the profound dimension of this factor, its countermove against the bad existence, its mobilization of those contradictions inherent in the bad existence in order to overcome that existence, in order to bring it to the point of collapse. But the profound dimension of the subjective factor helps form the countermove because the latter is not merely negative but also *contains the force of anticipatory accomplishment in itself and represents this force within the utopian function.*

Now the question is whether and to what extent the anticipatory countermove is connected to mere embellishment; in particular, when mere embellishment—although it outshines everything—is not a countermove at all but only a dubious polishing of what is already there. And it does this not with any revolutionary mission but with an apologetic one that is intended to reconcile the subject with the status quo. Above all, this intention fulfills the *ideology* in times that are no longer revolutionary but are still on the rise since they still stimulate the development of the productive forces in a class society. The status quo is covered up by the glitter of a deceptive harmonization, or, at best, a premature one, and it is surrounded by a lot of smoke or incense of false consciousness. (The rotten ideology during the decline of a class society—in particular, during the present decline of the late bourgeois society—does not fit here, of course, since this ideology is already knowingly false consciousness. Hence, it is fraud.) Moreover, in ideology there are certain features of concentration, perfection, and meaning in the status quo. When they refer mostly to *concentration*, they are known as *archetypes*; when they refer mostly to *perfection*, they are known as *ideals*; when they refer mostly to *meaning*, they are known as *allegories* and *symbols*. The intent to embellish the status quo in so many different ways is not a way of the bad existence. Embellishment does not want to detract consciously from the bad existence. Therefore, it does not want to detract deceitfully. Rather, the status quo is supplemented, admittedly in a manner that is predominantly idealistic and certainly not dialectical explosive, or real. Still, this is accomplished in such a way that a peculiar or figurative anticipation of what is better is not missing—an anticipation in space so to speak, not in the future or in time, or only figuratively so. And now the question has become more concrete: whether and to what extent the anticipating countermove is connected to mere embellishment. For in ideology—unlike archetypes, ideals, allegories, and symbols—there is no countermove to be found; rather, there is a surpassing of the status quo accomplished by its embellishment, concentrating, perfecting, or meaningful exaggeration. In turn, this exaggeration is impossible without a distorted or transposed utopian function, just as it is impossible to be at the outer margins of the status quo without the "dream of a thing" being irregularly glimpsed. But if the original utopian function is to be kept concrete, at least in parts, detectable in those improper improvements, then the distortions and abstractions that are not entirely terrible have to be able to be confronted. The specific relations of production make clear why the specific ideologies and the improper improvements have occurred. But the specific confusions in the humanity of specific relations of production make it necessary to borrow from the utopian function to be able to create the aforementioned supplements with their cultural surplus in any way at all. The ideologies, as the dominant ideas of an era, are the ideas of the ruling class, as Marx noted so strikingly. But since the ruling class is also alienated from itself, the projection of a world without alienation that compensates and surpasses the present, aside from representing the usual interests and welfare of the bourgeois class, was valid for humanity in general and was incorporated into the ideologies that mean culture for the bourgeoisie. It is obvious that this function stimulated the revolutionary ideologies of the rising classes almost entirely. Without the utopian function it is impossible to explain the intellectual surplus that went beyond the status quo and that which had been accomplished, even if that surplus is filled with illusion instead of anticipatory illumination. Therefore, all anticipation must prove itself to the utopian function, the latter seizing all possible surplus content of the anticipation. As will be shown, it also seizes the content in *interests* that have been progressive at one time, in *ideologies* that have not completely vanished with their respective societies, in *archetypes* that are still encapsulated, in *ideals* that are still abstract, in *allegories and symbols* that are still static.

## The Connection of the Utopian Function with Interests

A cool gaze does not prove itself by making understatements. But such a gaze wants to set things right, and it can do this. Moreover, it does not want to lose a sense of proportion. It dissolves deceptive feelings and words, wants to see the subject, aspiration, impulse as they are certainly not cut into shreds. Certainly, the economic impulse in present commercial life, which is rotten to the core, has become purely vile, and the only solid thing in it is ruthless meanness. The greed for profit overshadows all human emotions, and that greed does not even take time out for breaks like bloodthirstiness. It is also an established fact that in early, comparatively more honest times of capitalism the interest in profit was not constituted by the most noble human impulses. Due to the threat of failure, a powerful egocentrism was always active in commercial competition. Had these motives lessened and had altruistic motives taken their place, the entire capitalist mechanism would have stopped, as Mandeville's *Tale of the Bees* so cynically and truthfully demonstrated. And yet, would it not have been at least slowed down by a fair majority of the entrepreneurs at that time if the egotistical motive had fully revealed itself as it was? What if the egotistical motive had fooled itself with something more noble and communal that was thus purely subjective and different from conscious crudeness? What if it had dreamt of something subjectively almost sincere? That is why the condition of the real egotists of those days cannot be dismissed when looking at the situation of the artificial bees, a situation in which altruistic excuses and arguments also had to be made in order to make so-called honest profits in an honorable, seemingly humane way. Due to this situation characteristics of false consciousness, which were subjective, came to light in the "selfish system" of Adam Smith, and those characteristics were not wily and filled with discord, as so often found in Calvinism, but subjectively honest and harmonious. They were the characteristics of the conviction, of the good conscience of the respectable merchant and entrepreneur who, in fact, believed in honest gains. First of all, in the interplay of supply and demand, he thought of himself as a kind of benefactor of the consumers. Of course, he thought mainly of the solvent consumers, those with whom he could make money by selling the products of labor gained from the surplus value pressed from the workers. But the good conscience gained strength by supposedly relating the capitalist interest constantly to that of the consumer, making the customer satisfied. The good conscience of mutual advantage was also eased by *embellishments* since everyone was regarded as a free trader of increasing exchange power whose unmistakable self-interest was compensated by the general commercial interest that was developing everywhere. Throughout all this, the capitalist economy appeared as the only natural economy that one had finally discovered. And it was this economy that Smith praised ceremoniously as utopian. Thus, interest itself was influenced in a utopian way, or rather the false consciousness of interest, but it was quite an active one. The exploitation led by voracious dealers who were not at all burdened by bourgeois ethics could doubtlessly have gone on the same way without embellishment. The gentlemen of the East India Company did not include any kind of a utopian function in their business. It would only have harmed them. But the average manufacturer in the beginning of the industrial revolution still needed and cherished the belief in the greatest possible fortune found in the largest numbers. He needed this belief as the link between his egotistical impulses and benevolent ones that he dreamt of and pretended to have as Smith noted. And that was even more true at that time since the cynical selfishness was attributed most of all to the nobility, especially the debauched among them (compare the contemporary novels by Richardson). In contrast, the rising bourgeois businessman needed "virtue" to make profit more industriously from others as if he were making it for them. And even when it came to the last battle against feudal obstacles, the bourgeoisie, a class possessing little heroism, had to pep itself up energetically with utopian ideas. Otherwise, the bourgeoisie would not have fought itself—and in many instances it did not fight—but would have had mainly the men from the surrounding countryside fight its battle. This is why the bourgeoisie felt closely related to the Gracchi and to Brutus. This was certainly the case during the high times of bourgeois liberty of 1789. Thus, the rising class that was economically coming into its own also needed a subjectively broad passion within its confused feelings at that time in order to "conceal from itself the limited bourgeois substance of its fight," as Marx pointed out. Here, self-deception was complete. The private enterprise person of the human rights, the abstractness of the citizen (*citoyen*) as a moral person was not understood. This could not be understood at that time. Nevertheless, the self-deception did reveal something anticipatory. In particular, it revealed human characteristics, even though they were abstractly expressed and used in an abstract utopian way. Yet not everything was deception in the interests of the citizen (*citoyen*). Otherwise it would not have been possible to refer socialistically to the human rights of the human being who does not have private enterprise as the only thing in mind. Nor would it have been possible to refer to the citizen whose promises can only be kept in a socialist manner then. And, indeed, they can be kept. This is why there was a surplus contributed by utopian thought that existed within bourgeois aspirations. The social attitude, morally abstract in the citizen, i.e., abstracted from the real individual human being, must be united with humankind's own forces that are not bourgeois individualistic anymore. At that time, this attitude, which was called "virtue" then, was still present. It was present in the energy and surplus. Otherwise, how could somebody—except for the true Jacobin—like Jefferson be honored? Hence, a different, more solid characteristic, which went beyond the progress that was to be immediately promoted, could already have an effect in the impulse, if the latter was a progressive one at its time. It is possible to inherit morally that characteristic, in the same way as it is possible to inherit culturally those forms manifested in works, the surplus of the actual ideological consciousness. There were many times that good things and even the best were wanted in the past, but for the most part they were not realized. And since the wants do not achieve their goal, they move on in the process of liberation to receive their due, in this case within the capitalist society. The utopian function saves these parts from deception. In this way, everything humanitarian feels increasingly related.

## The Encounter of the Utopian Function with Ideology

A sharp gaze does not only prove itself by perceiving but also in a way that it does not see everything as clear as water. That is, not everything is so readily clear but sometimes is present in a state of ferment, as a formation process to which the sharp look is particularly appropriate. This unfinished process is most prevalent and most mixed in ideology insofar as ideology is not exhausted by the time its era has come to an end. This is also true with the merely false consciousness about its era that has accompanied all past civilizations. Certainly, ideology itself is a product of the division of labour, of the separation of physical and intellectual work that arose in the aftermath of the primeval community (*Urkommune*). It was only then that a group, which had time for imagination, could deceive itself, and, most of all, others by means of that imagination. Since ideologies genuinely belong always to the ruling class, they justify the existing social conditions in denying the respective economic roots, the exploitation. That is the case in all class societies, most significantly in the bourgeois one. Although in the ideological formation of these societies, there are three phases with a very different order in values, with a different task for the intellectual, much too intellectual superstructure: the preparatory, the victorious, and the declining phase. The preparatory phase of an ideology helps its own base that has yet to stabilize itself by confronting the decaying superstructure of the old ruling class with its own fresh and progressive one. The class, which then comes to power, sets the second ideological phase by securing its own base that has come into existence by determining its political and legal structure, by embellishing it politically, legally, and culturally—and by omitting preceding revolutionary impulses here and there with a more or less classic "equilibration." The embellishing and institutionalizing processes are supported by a harmony between the productive powers and the relations of production even though this harmony is only temporarily attained. Afterward, the decaying class sets the third ideological phase by perfuming the putrescence of the base and also by phosphorescently rechristening the night as day and the day as night. All this occurs as the credulity of the false consciousness vanishes almost completely so that there is almost complete conscious deception. Certainly, in class society the economic base is clouded by an interested false consciousness, no matter whether its illusion can be divided into such categories as ardent, classic, or decadent, or can be divided to represent a state of ascent, blossom, or made-up utilization. In brief, since no kind of exploitation can reveal itself openly, the ideology is, *in this respect*, the sum of ideas with which a society justifies and glorifies itself with the aid of false consciousness. Yet, whenever one thinks of culture, is there not *another side* of the ideology that appears—already recognizable in the morally and substantially different quality of the three phases? The ideology is, indeed, not *totally* identical with false consciousness and with the apology of a mere class society that has been better days. Concerning the critical side, Marx stated in *The Holy Family*: "The 'idea' makes always a fool of itself insofar as it is different from 'interest,'" and with this sentence he was refering to the way that French materialism had begun to perceive itself. La Bruyère, La Rochefoucauld, and especially Helvétius made clear that well-understood personal interest is the basis of all morals. But Marx also continued at the same place, "On the other hand, it can easily be understood that every massive, historically successful interest, when it enters upon the world stage for the first time, in the form of an 'idea' or 'conception,' goes far beyond its actual thoughts and mistakes itself for the human interest as such." That is how illusions are produced or "what Fourier called the tone of each historical epoch." But since the illusion that is constituted in this way—except for the blooming flowers with which a society decorated its cradle—may possibly contain those art works that, as Marx reminds us of the Greeks in the *Introduction to the Critique of Political Economy*, "serve, in a certain respect, as the norm and the unattainable model," the problem of ideology is best approached from the side of the *problem of the cultural heritage*. This concerns the problem why works of the superstructure, even after the descent of their social basis, continue to reproduce themselves in the cultural consciousness. In particular, the difference in content between the three phases cannot be omitted, not even if the continuously effective *Tua res agitur* is extended to the emerging revolutionary epoch of one of the hitherto existing class societies. It is especially then that the actual *phenomenon of the cultural surplus* that dwells on the other side becomes visible. As the phenomenon of art, science, and philosophy that is fully developed and has a bearing on the future, we encounter it in the classic epoch of a society rather than in its revolutionary one where the direct utopian impetus concerning the status quo and pointing beyond the status quo is much stronger. The fruits of art, science, and philosophy always reveal more than the false consciousness that a society has about itself and that it uses for its local embellishment. In particular, the fruits can be lifted from their initial social-historical ground since they are essentially not bound to it. The Acropolis admittedly belongs to the slave-holding society and the Strasbourg cathedral belongs to the feudal society. Nevertheless, they did not vanish with their base and, in contrast to the base and to the relations of production that may have been progressive at that time, they do not carry anything lamentable with them. It is true that the great philosophical works contain things more tied to their times that make them ephemeral. All this is due to the specific social limitations of comprehension, but these works also reveal the true classicism, which does not consist of balance but of eternal youth with new perspectives. They reveal this classicism particularly because of the high level of consciousness that makes these works distinguished and that makes it possible to look deeply into the future, into the essential. The fake problems and the provincial ideology were settled and buried in the *Symposion, Ethica*, and even in *The Phenomenology of Spirit*. In contrast, eros as substance, the substance as the subject, stands at the center of all changes as the variations of the goal. In brief, the great works are not as deficient as they were during the time of their origination, and they are also not as excellent as they were when they first appeared. Rather, they discard their deficiencies and original excellence and reveal that they have the capacity to achieve an intended later excellence. What is classic in all classicism is presented to each era as a revolutionary romanticism, i.e., as a task leading forward and as a solution that comes toward us from the future and not from the past and that speaks, addresses the future and continues to appeal as full of future. But this is only the case, even with more limited works, because ideologies are, *in this respect*, not exhausted by the false consciousness of their basis and equally not exhausted by the active work for their respective bases. In false consciousness itself, which is supported by the ideology of the class society, there is no quest possible for the surplus, and in the ideology of the socialist revolution, in which false consciousness does not take part at all, a quest is not necessary. Socialism as the ideology of the revolutionary proletariat is generally true consciousness in respect to the movement that is comprehended and in respect to the tendency of reality that is apprehended. Marx made an interesting comment to Ruge in 1843 about the relation of true ideology to the anticipation within the false consciousness of the former ideology that is not entirely false: "Our slogan has to be: the reform of consciousness not by dogmas but by analyzing the mystical consciousness that is still vague about itself. Then it will become clear that since long ago the world has the dream of a thing and the world only has to have consciousness to really possess the thing. It will become clear that it is not a matter of a great connecting line between the past and the future but a matter of the *fulfillment* of the thoughts of the past." The class ideologies, too, in which the great works of the past are situated, lead precisely toward that surplus. They go beyond the stationary false consciousness that is called culture and continue to have an effect that becomes the substratum of the cultural heritage that is to be appropriated. Now we realize that it is precisely this surplus that is produced by nothing else than the *effect of the utopian function* within the ideological formations of the cultural side. False consciousness alone would not be sufficient to gild over the ideological covers and disguise everything. False consciousness alone would not be capable of producing one of the most important characteristics of ideology, i.e., the premature harmonizing of the social contradictions. Ideology is less comprehensible as the medium of a continuous cultural substratum without an encounter with the utopian function. All this obviously exceeds the capacity of false consciousness that cannot invigorate or apologize for the specific social basis. Therefore, without the utopian function, the class ideologies would have only managed to achieve an ephemeral delusion and not the models of art, science, and philosophy. And it is precisely this surplus that forms and maintains the substratum of the cultural heritage, the morning that is present not only in the early period but more so during the full day of a society, even partly in the twilight of its decline. All hitherto existing great culture was the anticipatory illumination of something accomplished insofar as the anticipatory illumination could be incorporated into the images and ideas at the zenith of an epoch that was rich in perspective, and thus the images and ideas were not only valuable for its own epoch but went beyond it.

No doubt, the dream of a better life is perceived through all of that in a very broad sense. Or, put another way, except in its usual, mere depreciatory sense, the utopian is used not only in the aforementioned anticipatory sense but also as a function, in a comprehensive sense. Clearly, the breadth and depth of the utopian is above all not limited to its most popular feature, i.e., the utopian state, when viewed *historically*. Correspondingly, the dream of a better life reaches far beyond its social utopian origins—namely, it reaches into each kind of cultural anticipation. Each plan and each form driven to the limits of perfection came in contact with utopia and gave, particularly to the great works of a culture, those that take effect in a continuously progressive way, *a surplus reaching beyond their mere stationary ideology*. This was nothing less than the substratum of the cultural heritage. The elaboration and expansion of the power of anticipation that had been understood in a comprehensive way was begun in my book *The Spirit of Utopia* (*Geist der Utopie*, 1918). Here I dealt with products, ornaments, and figures which until then had been dealt with completely outside of a not-yet-arrived in reality, although they belong to it and are concerned with its articulation. The parasitic enjoyment of culture comes to an end with a greater understanding about the more adequate direction we should take toward identity and the responsibility for it. The works of culture arise strategically. But the question remains, whether and to what extent expression and attack could or should transfer the utopia without unneccessary misunderstandings to intentions and interests that do not at all come from the past. Those intentions and interests are situated completely in the present and are new, yet they have occurred within the development of socialism from utopia to science. As a matter of fact, the history of terminology knows of several of those extensions of former meanings of words, including the partial reduction of negative meanings attached to words. For example, the word romantic is a case in point. An even greater distinction has been made between the meanings of the concept of ideology itself. On the basis of that distinction, Lenin could call socialism the ideology of the revolutionary proletariat. And nevertheless, the power of anticipation, with its open space and its object that is to be realized and realizes itself, remained almost totally outside of terminological corrections and extensions as was the case with the concepts of the romantic in "revolutionary romanticism," or ideological in the "socialist ideology." As mentioned before, the power of anticipation has been called the concrete utopia in contrast to the utopian and the merely abstract utopianizing. The category of utopian function reigns objectively, and thus this is in accord with concepts mainly in the fields of technical, architectural, or geographical utopias but also in all those fields that finally center and centered around the "at all" (*Überhaupt*), the "actual" (*Eigentliche*) of our volition. Of course, all this happens with knowledge and the retreat of *utopianism* that has been finished off and with knowledge and the retreat of *abstract utopia*. But what remains then is the unfinished dream forward, the *docta spes*, which is only discredited by the bourgeoisie, and which can be seriously called utopia, in a well-thought-through and well-applied contrast to utopianism. In its brevity and its new poignancy, this expression means the same then as the *methodical organ for something new, an objective physical condition of what is coming.* Thus, all great works of art have implicitly, although not always explicitly—as in Goethe's *Faust*—a utopian background, which is understood in such manner. From the standpoint of the philosophical concept of utopia, these works of art are not ideological jokes of a higher form but the attempted path and content of known hope. It is only in this way that utopia fetches what belongs to it from the ideologies and explains what is historically progressive and continuously having an effect within the great works of ideology itself. The spirit of utopia exists in the ultimate predicate of all great expressions, in the Strasbourg cathedral and the *Divine Comedy*, in Beethoven's music of expectation and in the latency of the *B-Minor Mass*. The spirit of utopia is in the despair inherent in the *Unum necessarium* as something lost, and it is in the *Hymn to Joy*. The invocation as well as the credo are absorbed by the concept of utopia in a totally different way, by the concept of the known hope, even if the reflex of an ideology tied to a specific time is specifically absent from the invocation and credo. It is especially in this way that the critical enlightenment is complemented by the exact imagination of the not-yet-conscious, and thus the latter shows the gold that is not corroded by *aqua regia* and the good content remains. It rises when class illusion, class ideology has been destroyed. Therefore, after the termination of class ideologies, culture will have no other loss than that of decoration itself or harmonization that concludes everything in a false way. Until this point, culture could only have been mere decoration for the class ideologies. The utopian function withdraws the affairs of human culture from that stupor of mere contemplation. In this way utopian function paves the way to those peaks that have been conquered and that provide a clear view of human contents.

The Encounter of the Utopian Function with the Archetypes

A deep gaze proves itself by becoming doubly abysmal. Not only downward, which is the more easy, the more literal way to get into the ground. But there is also a depth upward and onward and that depth takes in the abyss from below. Then, backward and forward are like the movement of a wheel that simultaneously immerses itself and scoops things up. The real depth happens in any case as an equivocal movement: "Sink then! I could also say rise! It doesn't make a difference," Mephisto shouts to Faust. He even shouts it where a delight in that which has long gone shall begin, with Helena. And it is not only Mephisto who shouts that, who is an intriguer, a dangerous master of the equivocal meaning; it is the ambivalent meaning itself that shouts through Mephisto: it is the archaic as well as the utopian relation of pictures. Therefore, the utopian function has quite often a double abyss, the abyss of contemplation amidst the one of hope. But this can only mean that, here, the archaic frame is in part prepared for hope. To be more precise, hope is in those archetypes still generating concern that remained from the time of a mythical consciousness as a category of imagination, hence a not-worked-through, non-mythical surplus. Consequently, hope has to take care in a utopian way, except for the continuously meaningful ideologies, for those archetypes wherein something still not-worked-through is around. Hope has to add those archetypes to utopia in the way that, *mutatis mutandis*, meaningful progressive ideologies are added to it. Here it is clear that this cannot only be carried out from below, from sinking, but essentially from above, from the survey while ascending. This is certain time and again: that which has been exclusively pushed downward, that which can be found in the subconscious is in itself only the ground from which the night dreams emerge, and sometimes it is the poison that effects the neurotic symptoms: what is below can mostly be dissolved into what is known; it is not the rising drawn forward. Therefore, it carries basically only an apathetic latency. In contrast, hope and presentiment contain the potential treasure from which the great daydreams come and that do not age over long periods of time. That which is onward and above cannot be dissolved anywhere into the already known and the already developed. Therefore, it has basically an inexhaustible latency. When Faust, equipped with the elixir of youth, sees Helena in every woman, then the archetypal beauty Helena detaches herself totally from the archaic. She already moves upward in the archaic. But, the archetype can only be called upon from a utopian standpoint, and only from the survey while ascending, not during pure meditation. The utopian affinity in archetypes becomes visible if occasion arises. What Eurydice was in the Orcus of the past, the person who did not fully live her life, only Orpheus is able to find, and only for him is it Eurydice. It is only the utopian in some archetypes that enables their fruitful citation when looking forward, not backward. That has already occurred in the apparent interlocking of the phantasmagorias and in the dissolution of that appearance. All those rationalisms concerning mothers, *as those who are still giving birth*, show a light shining in from utopia, even during romanticism with the yearning graves and underworld lantern. The particular brooding in archetypes, and especially that, shows their incompleteness. But the warmth that realizes the business of maturation is not situated in regression. The archetypes themselves have been discussed already, with regard to C. G. Jung, but this arch-reactionary designated the whole thing in a false way, purely as darkness. The archaic appears like Timbuctoo in Zurich in Jung's writing. The term archetypos itself is found first in Augustine, where it is still an explanatory paraphrase for the Platonic eidos, thus for every form of species. Romanticism was the first to relate the ancient expression to a conclusive and illuminating categorial system of a pictorial objective kind oriented toward specific, compact events. Thus, in Novalis' works, Romeo and Juliet become the archetypes of young love; Antony and Cleopatra become the archetypes of the more mature, more interesting love; Philemon and Baucis, including their cottage, are seen as the group picture of the very old, irretrievable marriage. According to Novalis, the extraordinary harmony of all elements in those archetypes is decisive. In Philemon and Baucis, the harmony goes as far as "the smoked ham which hangs in the chimney." But what was far more decisive was the peculiar nimbus that was added to the harmony of the elements, a nimbus like the one around landscapes, with a successful architecture of the situation and its meaning. The beginning attention to resemblances in fairy-tale materials, in types of conflict, in types of salvation, in recurring "motifs" did a lot in pointing to the archetypes. The comparative history of literature opened up a plethora of such elements. There is, for instance, the extremely impressive motif of recognition (*Anagnorisis*), which archetypically unites subjects so far apart as Joseph and his brothers in the Bible with the encounter of Electra and Oreste in the Sophoclean tragedy. First of all, the mythology seemed to contain all the primeval situations (*Ursituationen*) and their ensemble. That is certainly a terrible exaggeration, in full accordance with what is reactionary about romantic archaism, but Karl Philipp Moritz's or even Friedrich Creuzer's studies in mythology contain indeed an abundance of archetypes by virtue of an attempted categorization of the "motifs." Here the archetypes appear as symbols. Creuzer unmistakably categorizes their archetypal characteristics as four elements: "the momentary, the total, the unfathomable of their origins, the imperative." And before this, he himself explains the momentary, also the pictoral-laconic, by an archetype: "That which is stimulating and stunning at the same time is connected to another quality, to brevity. It is like a suddenly occurring specter or like a flash of lightning which, all of a sudden, illuminates the dark night, a moment which occupies all of our existence" (Creuzer, *Symbolik und Mythologie der alten Völker*, [*The Symbolism and Mythology of Ancient Societies*], I, 1819, pp. 118, 59). Creuzer called those laconisms symbols in a romantic sense, the appearance of an idea. It would have taken only little hypostasis of an already eternally evident idea to see the archetypes also in the form of the allegory and not only in that of the symbol. The allegories are indeed, in their true form, i.e., before the classicism of the eighteenth and nineteenth centuries, not at all concretized definitions, that which one likes to call cold and abstract. Rather, the allegories also contain—in the Baroque period, unlike the Middle Ages—archetypes. They even contain their majority, namely, those of their impermanence and their multitude. The fullness of poetically operative archetypes dissolves right in the allegory that is still situated in the *Alteritas* of profane life, whereas the symbol is generally related to the *Unitas* of a meaning. That is the reason why the symbol essentially forms the religious archetypes, or why the archetypes are religiously formed. Bachofen, who was greater than Creuzer and an accomplished mythologist, not only discovered the nature of archetypes of the ancient peoples as being completely immersed in religion, but he also tried to organize them for the first time. They appeared sequentially in hetaerism, matriarchy, and patriarchy: in the hetaeric ornaments of reed and marsh, in the matriarchal ones of ears of corn and caves, in the patriarchal ones of laurel and solar orbit. The intent was to develop a social-historical as well as a nature-mythical order of all archetypes. Thus, they were not comprehensively catalogued—except in the hypothesis of the three sequences—neither in their allegorical nor in their religious-symbolic form and relationship. Nevertheless, that which is decisive in a utopian way illuminated, particularly through the works of romanticism, the archetypes as having little or nothing in common with romanticism and their pure, ultimately even transcendent idealism, despite their original Augustinian affinity with the prototypes in the Platonic sense. As follows from the previous examples, the archetypes are predominantly essentially situational categories of condensation, predominantly in the realm of poetic depictive imagination, and they are not generically hypostatized categories like the Platonic ideas. The archetypes of romanticism, or rather, archetypes as how they were understood by romanticism, were connected with the Platonic ideas solely by so-called recollection even if in a manner that makes the differences between unchangeable ideas noticeable too. In Plato, the recollection, the anamnesis, belonged to a primordial situation in which the soul found itself in primeval figurative heaven. In romanticism, on the other hand, the recollection moves historically, goes back into primeval times within time itself, becomes archaic regression. The fact that this could become possible shows how, even if there is no proximity to the Platonism of the heavenly ideas, romanticism misunderstood the archetypes in their relation to the utopian function. It is only when they are completely kept in regression that the archetypes alter the utopia into a backward, reactionary, and ultimately eventually into a diluvian one. Then they are more dangerous than the usual smoke screens of ideology. For while the latter only divert from an understanding of the present and its real driving force, the archetype prevents the development of an open attitude toward the future by expelling backward and by keeping everything in backward expulsion. Not all archetypes are ready for a utopian treatment, even if this is a real treatment and not reactionary utopianism as so often in romanticism. The entire sphere, which is often so vital and lucidly powerful on a grand scale in poetry, also in philosophy, is mistaken by the pathos of sheer archaism. As stated before, only those archtypes are ready for a utopian treatment that still have something not-worked-out (*Unausgearbeitetes*), something relatively unfinished (*Unabgelaufenes*), something indelible (*Unabgegoltenes*). Characteristically, it was especially those archetypes used up during feudalism that were the most favored in the regression that corresponded to the political reaction, as if the archetype, the token, were merely the abandonment to the past and not also—like the storming of the Bastille—an emblem of the future in accordance with the true utopian function. As the romantics used to say, the archetype is something in which everyone who is poetic will recognize oneself time and again as life moves on.

That is why, at this point, a new separation begins so that the true friends recognize each other and stay together. Only the utopian sight can find what is congenial to it, and this is an important task in contrast to bleak capitalist murder of the ornament even within thinking. First, the putrefied archetypes have to be separated from the utopian, the really *indelible* (*unabgegoltenen*) archetypes, i.e., by assigning them to the anachronistic past. But, it is obvious that the existing archetypes of the freedom situation or those of the pleasures of brightness are not bound to that kind of past. They have escaped it, or at least they are exterritorial in relation to it. This is not the place to examine the archetypes. As will be shown later, they belong to a new region of logic. They belong to the table of categories concerning imagination. As we have seen, they can be found in all great poetry, in

myths, in religions. Indeed, they belong to a truth only with their
unsatisfied part that is a veiled depiction of the *utopian tendencies within
reality*. The land of milk and honey is one archetype with an unsatisfied tendency-latency underneath the fantastic mask. So is the battle
with the dragon (St. George, Apollo, Siegfried, Michael), the winter
demon, who wants to kill the sun (the Fenriswolf, the Pharaoh,
Herodes, Gessler). The liberation of the virgin—and of innocence in
general—held captive by the dragon (Perseus and Andromeda) is a
related archetype. The era of the dragon, the realm of the dragon
itself is an archetype, when it appears as the necessary phase before
the final triumph (Egypt, Canaan, the empire of the Antichrist before
the beginning of the New Jerusalem). The trumpet signal in the last
act of *Fidelio* is an archetype of superior utopian rank. It is condensed
in the *Leonore* overture, which announces the salvation: the arrival of
the minister—he stands for the Messiah—embodies the archetype of
the revenging-redeeming apocalypse. It is the ancient thunderstorm
and rainbow archetype. To be sure, this is an archetype in the very
old manner, but in this instance it is still related completely in a
concrete manner as in Marx's statement, "When all inner conditions
are fulfilled, the German day of resurrection will be announced
through the blare of the Gallic rooster." In these examples one can see
in a purely immanent way that what is utopian about archetypes is
ultimately not at all determinable within archaism. Rather, it moves
most usefully through history. And above all, not all archetypes have
an archaic origin. Some of them only occur within the course of
history like the dancing on the ruins of the Bastille—a new, touching
original picture distinct from the archaic round dance of the departed
by a totally new content. The music of that new dance is Beethoven's
Seventh Symphony. Therefore, it is none that sets the mood for the
Asphodel meadow [which haunts the shades of the heroes]. It is also
none that sets the mood for orgiastic celebrations of Spring and
Dionysius. Even archetypes of obvious archaic origin have rein-
vigorated themselves and have changed time and again through
historical transformations. Even the trumpet signal in *Fidelio* could
have barely had its pervasive, genuine effect without the storming of
the Bastille, which provided the model and the persistent background
for the music of *Fidelio*. The thunderstorm and rainbow archetype, to
which the signal and the salvation referred, was endowed with an

entirely new origin only by that storming: the archetype changed from the astral myth to the history of revolution. Although an archetype, it had its effect without any trace of archaism. So, finally, not all archetypes are simply condensed images of archaic experience. Time and again, something productive arose from them that increased the existing content of the archetypes. This is like in the past, when the utopian, the reutilization (*Umfunktionierung*), which understands *how to liberate the archetypically capsulated hope*, intruded in the ancient as well as in the historically new archetypes. If the archetypical were completely regressive, there would be no archetypes reaching for utopia while utopia reaches back for them. Then poetry would have advanced in a way dedicated to light and dealing with the old symbols. Then imagination would only be regression (*Regressio*). The imagination, destined for progress, would have to beware of all images, also of allegories, of symbols that spring from the old mythic ground of imagination. Only the petty empiricist mind (*Realschul-Intellekt*) would stand up for the old mythic ground of imagination, and since that is a dreamless mind, it would stand against the imagination. But *The Magic Flute*—to use a piece of imagination that is unquestionably humanized—employs almost exclusively archaic allegories and symbols: the leader and king of the priests, the empire of the night, the empire of light, the water and fire ordeals, the magic of the flute, the transformation into a sun. Notwithstanding, all these allegories and symbols—among them those in which formerly no humanity was celebrated in their sacred halls—have proven useful for the enlightenment. Even in Mozart's fairy-tale music, as a non-demonic temple, they truly came home. Thus, the productive utopian function also draws images from the still valid past insofar as they are ambiguously fit for the future, despite all the spells within them, and it makes these images useful since they are the expression of what has still not happened. It makes them useful for sunrise. In this way, the utopian function not only discovers the cultural surplus as something that belongs to it, but also fetches an element of itself from the ambiguous depth of the archetypes that is an archaically stored-up anticipation of something not-yet-conscious, of something not-yet-accomplished. Or, to use a dialectical archetype, the anchor, which here sinks into the ground, is simultaneously the anchor of hope. That which sinks down contains that which comes up, or can contain it.

The same twofold nature, characterized by all that which is mentioned above and qualified for utopia, finally reveals and proves itself when the archetypes clearly change into *object-like ciphers*. These ciphers have depicted the archtypes according to nature anyway, as in numerous condensed images (still waters run deep, it is lonely on the top), as in the thunderstorm-rainbow archetype, as, of course, in the light and sun image of *The Magic Flute*. These kinds of archetypes are not at all merely formed from human material, neither from archaism nor from later history. Rather they show a piece of the twofold scripture of nature itself, a kind of real-cipher (*Realchiffre*) or real-symbol (*Realsymbol*). A real-symbol is a symbol whose subject of meaning (*Bedeutungsgegenstand*) is still concealed from itself, concealed in the real object and not only from human perception. Therefore, it is an expression for what has not yet become manifest in the object itself, but is an expression for what is signified in the object and through the object. The human symbolic image is only a substitute depiction for that. The real-cipher is made recognizable by lines of motion (fire, lightning, sound and so on), by shapes of outstanding objects (the shape of a palm tree, the shape of a cat, the human face, the Egyptian style in crystals, the Gothic style of woodlands, etc.). This way, a sharply formed part of the world appears as a group of symbols of an object-like kind whose mathematics and philosophy are both still missing. The so-called morphology is only an abstract caricature of that, for real-ciphers are not static. They are figures of tension. They are tendentious figures of the process, and above all, in this way, they are just symbolic. This touches on the problem of an object-like utopian theory of figures. Therefore, it ultimately touches on the forgotten (Pythagorean) problem of a qualitative mathematics, of a renewed qualitative philosophy of nature. But here we can see already that even the object-like archetypes that have changed into real-ciphers—found in the vast aquarium of nature, even more in the formation of human works—are only illuminated through the utopian function. The archetypes have, of course, their next existence certainly in human history, i.e., insofar as archetypes are what they can be: the concise ornaments of a utopian content. The utopian function saves this part from the past, from the reaction, also from the myth. Each reutilization that happens this way shows the indelible part of the archetypes, and renders it recognizable through change.

The Encounter of the Utopian Function with Ideals

An open gaze proves itself by the way it turns to something. This gaze has a goal in its mind that, since the days of youth, has seldom been lost to sight. Since that goal is not at hand but a demanding one or an illuminating one, it operates as a task or as a point of orientation. If the goal seems to contain not only something desirable or something worth aspiring to but also something simply perfect, then it is called an ideal. Each goal, whether it is attainable or not, whether it is foolish or something objectively meaningful, must first be conceived in one's mind. But if the goal is an ideal, it is distinct from the customary goal by the emphasis on perfection. It cannot be lowered by anything. Otherwise, active striving and willingness are abandoned, or they become diverted in an empirical and clever way if the conception of empirically stringent counter reasons (*Gegengründe*) penetrates the conception of the goal. In contrast, the conception of the goal as ideal has a continuous effect, a decision of volition in the direction that cannot be abolished. The decision becomes the goal itself if it cannot attain the goal since the unattainability is accompanied by a bad conscience, at least by a feeling of failure due to the objective incapacity to cancel the goal. The ideal of the conceptualized ideal, i.e., the ideal object, has a demanding effect. It seems as if it had a volition of its own, which is issued to the human being as an obligation. The customary goal as well as the ideal goal demonstrate the characteristic of a value, and the sheer illusion of value is found in both. But while that illusion can be empirically corrected in case of the customary goal, it is significantly harder in the case of ideals because of their reified demands. If an object appears as an ideal one, then salvation from its demanding and sometimes demandingly enchanted spell is only possible through a catastrophe, but even that does not always come true. Idolatry of love is a misfortune that continues to cast a spell on us even when the object is understood. Sometimes, even illusionary political ideals continue to have an effect after an empirical catastrophe, as if they were—genuine. The formation of ideals engenders in the process its own power, a power that interfuses the somewhat bright and mature conviction about the ideal as something perfect with much darker impulses. Therefore, the formation of an ideal may contain a great deal of false consciousness, of archaic subconsciousness, on its enthralled and illusionary side. Something like this already occurred with regard to repression in the Freudian sense, which is different from Adler's psychology of power—it concerned the overcompensating formation of the governing ideal. In Freud's work, the superego is the source of the formation of the ideal, and the superego itself, with all the threat and obligation that emanates from it, is supposed to become the internalized father. The ego relates to the superego as the child relates to the parents; their commands remain effective in the ideal-ego (*Ideal-Ich*), in every ideal command (*Ideal-Gebot*) in general, and the parent's commands exert moral censorship as the conscience. Hence, this theory of the ideal leads only backward toward the father and, provided sufficient perforation, leads back to the patriarchal-despotic era. Accordingly, Freud left out all non-threatening, all bright aspects of the ideal; the ideal is also totally confined to moral aspects. Adler's theory of overcompensation tries to explain the actual bright aspects. At the same time, this theory, in regard to what might overcome the governing ideal, is only directed toward the past, toward the former "Tom Thumb situation" (*"Däumlingssituation"*). Here, the governing or personal character ideal should not be a recollected-imprinted goal but chosen in a relatively free way. Individuals finalize themselves by turning the character mask into the ideal mask to reach the feeling of over-evaluation (*Überwertigkeit*). According to this theory, of course, all ideals are limited to moral ones. Ultimately they are limited to personal, vain ones. More objective ideals, for example, artistic ones, are completely missing. Even alternative ideals of the proper lifestyle, those from the pre-capitalist era that are still extant in our time, as solitude or friendship, as *vita activa* or *vita contemplativa*, have no place in that psychology of pure competition. When purely personal ideals set the limits, then also ideal situations, ideal landscapes remain incomprehensible, homeless. Thus, Freud and Adler only revealed the stifling spell on which the formation of the ideal can be based: with Freud it is the spell of the father; with Adler it is, at least, the spell of inferiority. Neither route is open or leads from here to the surplus-qualities or the surplus-images. Everything remains an obligation; half of the conceptualized goal is more tolerated than hoped for.

But, in the process, the willingness that looks for towers and that mounts them, too, is not at all exhausted. The formation of the ideal is not at all limited to obligations and the spell. Besides, it has its more liberated, its brighter side. Even if this brighter side shows strong negative features—substitution, disproportion, abstractness, and in the nineteenth century one can add the mendacity of the ideal—all these features are not connected to the darker or more sinister elements of the formation of the ideal. They are not connected to the obligation imposed from above, the spell, the pressure of the superego, the turn against all living creatures in general. The factor that is appealing here arises from lofty *perfection* itself. The free characters of daydreams are distinctly marked by this brighter side, particularly the voyage to the end, where fairly infinite things happen. Even if real travel itself is not undertaken, or if it only remains in the image of the ideal as the embarkation to Cythera, which is in any case a purely erotic ideal: the end is always intended, and it is a completed one. Now, it is not only easier to feel perfection, but it is also more inviting to think about it than the average cultural categories. That is the reason why the ideal was conceptualized much more clearly than the ideologies—which is self-evident due to the interested, disguising character of the ideology—and also much more clearly than the archetypes. Thus far, we do not have a definition or diagram of the archetypes, whereas we have several for the ideal. They cover such common terms as the ideal housewife, the ideal Bach baritone, etc., elevated terms that deal with the ideal of the supreme good. There are the dominant ideals of the proper lifestyle that stand in sharp contrast to each other. There is a copiously nuanced theory of the estimation of values (*Wertwägungslehre*), a theory of the criteria of the ideals reaching from the Sophists and Socrates to Epicurus and the Stoa. In Kant, the ideal is to be found in various places, where the pressure is located as well as in the final destination (*finale Richtungseinheit*), and in hope; Kant called the philosopher himself a teacher of the ideal and philosophy, instruction about the ideal. The ideal reappears in the categorical imperative of the moral law as pressure, even as attack: human dignity, which requires respect for that law, stands in contrast to all elemental impulses. But then, the ideal appears in Kant as the final force of destination so that the latter does not require anything itself. On the contrary, it is required, namely, in the postulated trinity of absoluteness: freedom, immortality, God. Likewise, the ideal appears as hope, namely, as the truly supreme good of practical reason. That supreme good then is supposed to be the link between virtue and bliss, which is—of course only in approximation—the realization of a kingdom of heaven on earth. Then, the ideal appears again in Kant's

aesthetic as the ideal of a natural perfection, thus without any supreme good, and, in this case, with the most instructive contrast to the
ideal of moral pressure. In the arts, Kant turns away from the latter
ideal since an obligatory attitude generally proves in art to be feeble
in any case: there is a thundering ethics, but commensurately there is
only pedantic aesthetics. Kant does not want such aesthetics. For him
the artistic genius is not at odds with his natural impulses as is the case
with the moral person. On the contrary, the genius, "as nature, sets
the rule." The genius is an intelligence that operates like nature. And
all that which is made beautiful in accordance with the aesthetic ideal
is defined as the "perfect embodiment of an idea in a particular
appearance." Thus, perfection unfolds as a hope for the future in
Kant, the formal teacher of the ideal, but who is thus a particularly
abstract radical teacher. Perfection unfolds as hope for the future in so
many ways, in different aspects, in those of the spell and, above all, in
those of the starlight. Kant's aesthetic notion, the "perfect embodiment of an idea in a particular appearance," moreover, shifts from a
formal idealism to an objective idealism. Therefore, this concept of
the ideal ultimately touches upon the idea that, through Aristotle,
had been developed from Plato's generic form, and that is situated
beyond the appearance and located in the goal or the entelechy
within the appearance. In Aristotle, the entelechy, which cannot
completely reveal itself in individual things due to impeding extra-
neous causes, becomes visible in sculpture, also in poetry. In this way,
aesthetic depiction of the ideal becomes something that simultaneously emanates from imitation and makes things beautiful according to an entelechical goal, i.e., shows what should happen according
to the nature of the object. Therefore, we have the famous Aristotle
quote about drama as being more philosophical than historiography.
And ultimately, it is that finalizing character of perfection of the
aesthetic ideal that lets Schopenhauer as well as Hegel follow Kant's
"perfect embodiment of an idea in an individual appearance." There
is a great deal of Aristotle in Schopenhauer: "Depending on whether
the organism manages to overmaster those deeper layers of the
powers of nature expressing the objectivity of the will, it becomes the
more perfect or the more imperfect expression of its idea, i.e., it stands
closer to or farther from the ideal to which the beauty of its species
belongs." And Schopenhauer continues with a clear touch of the
utopian function (in the static outer limits of the species): "Only in

this way could Greek genius find the prototype of the human figure and establish it as the canon of the school, as sculpture; and it is only such anticipation that enables us all to depict beauty where nature really succeeded in individual cases. This anticipation is the ideal; it is the idea in so far as it, at least for half of it, is acknowledged apriori and becomes practical for the arts by complementing aposteriori that which is given by nature" (*Werke* [*Works*], Griesbach, I, pp. 207, 297). Hegel allows for ideals only in art and not in the general reality, especially not in the socio-political reality. Insofar as Hegel is a philosopher of the restoration, he considers ideals mere chimeras of an imagined perfection. Whereas art, as a form of contemplation, is based on nothing else than ideals for Hegel, on oriental symbolic ideals, Greek classical ideals, occidental romantic ideals (honor, love, faithfulness, adventure, belief). The aesthetic manifestation of the ideal clearly in itself recalls Aristotle, especially the entelechy: "Therefore, the truth of art shall not be a mere correctness to which the mere imitation of nature limits itself, but the exterior must agree with an interior that agrees with itself and thus can reveal itself in the exterior. Art uses its true concepts and restores harmony to what has been tarnished in the usual existence by contingency and by superficiality, and it discards everything that does not comply in its appearance with that harmony, and thus only through that purification does it bring about the ideal" (*Werke* [*Works*], XI, pp. 199ff). Obviously, the ideal is not at all regarded here as being indifferent in relation to reality or as an insipid embellishment—like the fraudulent contrast between poetry and prose and finally between culture and civilization, which could be maintained. But a stronger degree of reality itself is thought of, a degree of reality with a particular perfection in actual fact intended in the process of appearance, even if this stratification is nowhere admitted in Hegel as a not-yet-developed in reality. Nevertheless, the ideal shows a much more genuine anticipation than most archetypes wherever the superego, the regressive father spell (*Vater-Bann*) or fixed images of a merely imitating overcompensation are not in action. And the utopian function dealing with the ideal becomes less of an explosion than a correction through the mediation with the concrete movements searching for perfection in the world, with a material tendency for the ideal.

Indeed, aside from both internal and especially external tendencies, only some high-sounding phrases remain. Obligation, demand, pressure belong to the ideal as spells, but as we noticed, disproportion, noncommittal abstractions, nonhistorical immobility threaten the ideal's freedom and its intended perfection. In addition to that which the nineteenth century brought with it, came the lie: truth, good, beautiful as bourgeois phrases. Fontane portrayed a bourgeoisie with ideals embodied by the wife of a wealthy merchant, Jenny Treibel, née Bürstenbinder, who did honor to her kind. She also did honor to her surroundings: "They constantly liberalize and sentimentalize, but all that is a farce. When they have to show their true colors, then they say: gold is everything—and that's it." In most of his dramas, Ibsen fervently revealed how the proclaimed bourgeois ideal had nothing in common anymore with bourgeois praxis. *The Doll's House, Ghosts,* and *The Wild Duck* are all variations of the ideal-phrase theme, and it would have taken very little to bring out the comic features of these solemn, almost tragic plays. Gregers Werle in *the Wild Duck* is precisely the Don Quixote of the bourgeois ideals amidst a degenerated bourgeois world, and Relling's cynicism is not just cynical when he called those ideals not merely lies but lies to live necessary for average people. Rather, he also unmasked the holy aspects of the late bourgeois ideals as swindles. The limitation is that Ibsen himself still believed in the bourgeois ideals. He wanted to believe in them, and he tried to present them in the dramas following *The Wild Duck* in a way that they cannot be criticized by Relling. Yet, there were no new worlds to be found, in Ibsen or Fontane. Instead the old one was immanently denounced with its imbalance between theory and praxis, with its pervasive hypocrisy. Critical realism provides enough to perceive this. Neither a study of ideology nor even a utopian function is necessary. But the utopian function, having apprehended the material tendency, is of course necessary so that the ideal with its disproportionate bourgeois existence is not seen as a unity. Thus, the ideal can be lifted from its previous mode of existence, from abstractness, possibly from immobility. First, it must be lifted from the abstractness that is disconnected, inadequately universal, suspended without power. The abstractness is essentially formal. The content has stolen itself away from real life or confronts it directly in idle grandiose words. Since the ideals did not mediate themselves through any tendency, undialectical immobility joined the abstractness. Both of them increased the illusion of values. The latter was supported by an attitude that put the ideals into a showcase for timeless edification. Abstractness and immobility together then constituted the so-called ideal principles as orientation points for words, not for actions. Such formal principles flourished largely in England and became the religion of dead slogans in North America. The American Declaration of Independence and then the American Constitution contained their rights to life, liberty, and the pursuit of happiness; their principles of liberty, justice, morality, and law were still conceived from the citizen's standpoint—the principle of property rights, less illuminated by Bengalese light, is of course not to be forgotten as a basic principle. But now, all this stands immobile, and the only real principle, the basic economic principle, allows the contents to be opportunistically used, mainly the liberties, because of the formal abstractness and immobility of the other principles. The ideal that is formed in this way cannot and will not provide a theoretical contrast to the opportunism of content that is an opportunism leading to total reversal; it cannot because of its formal misleading universality. It will not because of its stupor and inflexibility. This weakness was immense in Germany at the time of Luther, double-entry bookkeeping, and the dualism of work and faith. In the Calvinist countries, the ideal remained at least a verbal point of orientation, even a formal and democratic point of orientation for modes of dealing soon to be dropped. Mendacity developed as a tribute of vice to virtue. In contrast, the ideals were placed so far above the world in Germany that they could not come into contact with the world. The only contact was through eternal distance. This point of orientation could only result in the creation of stars that were too distant to be within reach. Therefore, they were stars of volition and not of action. Out of that emerged the phantom of an endless approach to the ideal, which means the same, the transfer of the ideal into an eternal aspiration for it. Thus, the world remained in a desperate state. The moral ideals were suspended far away in heaven. One did not even long for the aesthetic ideals but merely enjoyed their magnificence. The leap from infinite volition to mere contemplation was that easy; for even the endless approximation was contemplation, only disturbed by the semblance of constant activity, by acting for the sake of acting, *ut aliquid fieri videatur*. Even when a concrete sense for the ideal developed in Germany, at the point of realization, it was only the seamy side of the infinite non-realization, namely, total peace on earth as in the case of Hegel. Here the infinity of the approach toward the ideal disappears, but with it also all the approaches toward the ideal by *human effort* disappears. The world process as such becomes the self-realization of ideal purposes, which are established in that world process, and the human is a mere auxiliary; ultimately the human is just a mere philosophical spectator of ideals that are supposedly realized anyway. All this, of course, keeps the ideal powerless no matter whether there is an infinite approach to the world or too much coincidence with the world that is allegedly an ideal world. In both cases, the immobility of the ideal prevails with perfection that is already complete in itself; the utopian function has to prove itself precisely against that completeness. But this proof differs from that found with archetypes, which are much closer to the material but certainly more prone to sibling rivalry. It is precisely the *intended perfection*, all of its confessed anticipation, that makes the ideal accessible to a utopian treatment. The archetypes encapsulated the anticipation, and the latter has to be freed. In contrast, the ideals demonstrate how the anticipation is abstract and static and how the anticipation has only to be corrected. Very often, the archetypes show hope in the abyss and the abyss in the archaic. Then the archetypes are like buried treasures in the myth itself, and one St. John's Day those treasures will rise and bask in the sun. The ideals, on the other hand, show hope from the beginning during daylight, on the ascending side of the daily round. The renewal of most archetypes has Möricke's verse of Orplid on its side: "Ancient waters rise renewed around your hips, child!" The appearance of an ideal, however, is signaled best at daybreak by Browning's *Pippa*: "Your flow of time, long, blue, clear, flowing festively which strongly protects and blesses the earth, I feel it, all this will be mine." Certainly, there are also archetypes that do not dwell in the abyss. The dancing on the rubble of the Bastille gave the clearest example of that. And, conversely, the archetype is like the image of the mother in Isis-Maria, which is simultaneously a deeply rooted ideal. But, in general, the ideal exists purely at the front, so much so that its final image appears rather too far than too sunken. It is not without reason that the abstract utopias, as abstract but nonetheless as utopias, are essentially filled with ideals and significantly less with archetypes, not even with those of a clear revolutionary sense. The isolated island on which utopia is supposed to be located might be an archetype, but the ideal figures of perfection aspired to have a stronger effect as being a free or structured development of life. Therefore, the utopian function must essentially prove itself in the ideal in the same way as it has to prove itself in the utopias themselves, i.e., in the way of concrete conveyance with the material tendency of the ideal in the world. It is impossible that the idealistic can be instructed and corrected by mere facts. On the contrary, it is essential to the idealistic that it maintain a tense relationship with that which has merely become factual. Still, if it is worth anything, the idealistic has access to the world process of which the so-called facts are reified fixed abstractions. In its anticipations, if they are concrete, the idealistic has a correlate in the objective content of hope of the tendency-latency. This correlate makes possible *ethical ideals as models, aesthetic ideals as anticipatory illuminations that indicate a potential realization.* Such ideals, then, corrected and directed through the utopian function, are those of a humanly and adequately unfolded substance of the self and the world; therefore, they are all *transformations of the basic substance: the supreme good*— which might, at long last, summarize and simplify the entire nature of ideals. The ideals relate to that supreme substance of hope, to the potential substance of the world like means to an end. Therefore, there is a hierarchy of ideals, and an inferior ideal may be sacrificed for the superior one since the first will come to life again in the realization of the superior ideal. For example, the highest modification of the supreme good in the socio-political sphere is the classless society. Hence, ideals like freedom and also equality relate to that purpose as means, and they gain their substantial value (*Wertinhalt*)—which is particularly multivocal in the case of freedom—from the socio-political supreme good. It is in such a manner that the supreme good not only determines the content of the ideals of means (*Mittelideale*), but also varies the ideals of means according to the needs of the supreme content of purpose and, if necessary, gives a temporary justification of the aberrations. Also, the superior modification of the supreme good in the aesthetic sphere is the immanent anticipatory illumination of a humane perfect world. Consequently, all aesthetic categories have a relation to that goal and are the modifications of that goal—as *l'art pour l'espoir*. And clearer than in the archetypes, the response of the subject to what has become bad (*schlechte Gewordenheit*) reverberates in the ideals, the tendential response to the insufficient, in favor of what is appropriate for humanity. This is why Marx says that there are no ideals for the working class to be realized. This anathema certainly does not pertain to the realization of tendentious concrete goals but only to the realization of abstract, imposed goals, of ideals without contact to history and the process. For both Marx and Lenin socialism itself became a concrete ideal for the next stage to be achieved, an ideal that through its systematically conveyed solidity encourages more than the abstract ideal. And the politically supreme ideal, the realm of freedom as a political *Summum bonum*, is so closely connected to consciously produced history that it constitutes, as a concrete one, history's finality or the final chapter of the history of the world. For an anti-*Summum-bonum* or resignation (*Umsonst*), which is a possible alternative, too, would not be the final chapter of that history, but its cancellation. It would not be finality but the exit to chaos. Either there is, despite human labor, death without retreat in the process, or there is, because of human labor, the realism of the ideal in the course of the process— *tertium non datur*. The freedom of the utopian function has its activity and the ideal of its own in objectively signifying and setting free the not-yet-developed "being as an ideal" (the supreme good), which develops with real possibilities in the gray of dawn, at the front line of the process world.

The Encounter of the Utopian Function with the Allegories and Symbols

What remains is the concerned gaze that clearly proves itself even with what is not yet clear. Here, the latter is that which is not yet clear, not only signifying its own matter but at the same time signifying something else. If this occurs in poetic language, then the words might well be sensual and contemporary, but they reverberate as if in a large hall. The proverb presented itself at first as multi-leveled and significant insofar as it knew how to become allegorical. It even prefers to be that way. "Still water runs deep." This is already an allegorical expression, and that expression intensifies in the great poetic simile. "Poems are like stained glass windows." Goethe's great simile reflects best the dark-and-light of its own matter's significance and at the same time the significance of something else. Such a sentence is a perfect allegory. Of course, allegory is full of the not-yet-clear of itself, and this is why no allegory can be perfect. Allegory is, by definition, ambiguous; i.e., the matter from which its illuminating simile is taken—here the stained glass window—is not clear at all. The subject matter contains several meanings, even such meanings as do not comparatively refer to poems, and, above all it points beyond itself, in the poetic reference as well as reference to transparency, between dark and light. Thus, no allegory is perfect. If it were, if its reference (*Fortbezug*) were not one that leads in all directions and also along the same line to other matters again and again, then this kind of expression would not be allegorical but symbolic. The allegory would be perfect although the perfection that is thereby achieved would still remain something that is objectively not clear yet, something shrouded within the obvious. It would remain as something obvious that is still shrouded. In this sense, allegory possesses a kind of wealth of imprecision as against the symbolic. Thus, its kind of allegorical language does not go as far as that of the unhesitating and yet floating symbol and the unified point of its connection. Of course, this must not be confused with the other qualitative distinction, which, for a little more than a hundred years, has been made between allegory and symbol in a totally false manner. According to this distinction, allegory consists merely of sensualized or sensually decorated concepts, whereas symbol is based for the most part on so-called immediacy. Or, as Gundolf later said so foolishly about Goethe after having turned him into something like Stefan George, the young Goethe expressed his "primordial experiences" (*Urerlebnisse*) symbolically, whereas the older Goethe could only reflect upon his so-called "experiences of cultivation" (*Bildungserlebnisse*) allegorically. This qualitative distinction is not only meaningless in regard to Goethe, but also follows the conventional, false opinion about allegories common since romanticism. It was made on the basis of easily understood semi-allegories, even the simple illustrated abstractions that, during the period of the rococo and Louis XVI—as figures of virtue, of truth, of friendship, etc.—were the only conscious remains of the allegory phenomenon. The romantic devaluation of the allegories lacked the experienced knowledge of real allegories, as in the Baroque period with its orgy of emblems, as in the Middle Ages, as in the early Christian patristic period. In its prime, allegory was not at all the sensualization of concepts, or the decoration of abstractions. Rather, it was just the attempt to reproduce the meaning of a thing with other meanings of things, especially on the basis of the opposite of abstractions, i.e., on the basis of archetypes that unite the meaning of the specific allegorical elements. And the archetypes also provided a basis for the omnipresent meaning (*Bedeutungs-Durchklang*) of the symbolic simile: this simile was not to function in the archetypes of transit and transience but of a strict universality or final meaning. Therefore, it is obvious that the aforementioned qualitative distinction between allegory and symbol, as the only legitimate one, cannot be confused with the qualitative distinction between decorated abstractions, even those of the most fixated kind, and the real theophanies. The difference in rank is rather within the same field of archetypes. Allegory contains the archetypes of transience so that their importance is always based on the *Alteritas*, whereas symbol always remains attributed to the *Unitas of a meaning*. And with regard to problems of the encounter of the utopian function with allegory and symbol the category *cipher* has to be emphasized in both allegory and symbol, which is the shaped meaning of the allegorical and the symbolic linked together in the archetype, a meaning that also *really occurs in the objects*. Accordingly, allegory gives a cipher of specific detail to a meaning that is equally laid out in detail—the multitude, the *Alteritas*—which exists in transience and which even exists in a shattered state. On the other hand, the symbol gives a cipher of a specific detail to the unity of meaning that appears transparent in detail—the multitude, the *Alteritas*. Thus the symbol is directed toward the *Unum necessarium* of an arrival—the landing, the gathering. It is not directed anymore toward provisionality or toward ambiguity, which are sent back and forth. This intention toward an arrival engages the symbol, in contrast to allegories, which shift around in blossoms, which devote themselves to the constant undecidedness of the way. Ultimately, this is the reason why the allegory is essentially at home in ornate art and in polytheistic religions, whereas the symbol essentially belongs to the great simplicity in the art of the henotheistic and monotheistic religions.

So, anticipation is important in both allegory and symbol since anticipation makes itself heard in both of them. It is at the same time something sealed that reveals itself and something revealing, something opening that is still sealing itself since—particularly in the symbol itself—time has not yet come, the case has not been won yet, the pending cause. The meaning is not yet clear and not yet decided. Therefore, there is an encounter based in the material itself between the utopian function and the allegory as well as the symbol. It is the

objective signifying process where the utopian function meets itself. I
repeat: Every simile that remains in the multitude, in the *Alteritas*,
depicts an allegory like "Suddenly there stood the oak tree in the fog,/
a towering giant,/ where darkness with hundreds of black eyes/
glances from the shrubs." But if the simile talks unity, anything
central at all, if the simile converges toward certainty that is in its
initial stages of evolving even if it is still covered, then symbolism is
clearly encountered, like "All mountain peaks are silent." The form
of both allegory and symbol is dialectical. Goethe referred to this in a
term that was itself dialectically tense. For him the form was a "public
secret," a lasting interlocking of something revealed and something
veiled, something that has not yet shed its cloak. This is the case—in
all real and thus in all objectively true allegories, even symbols—
because the "public secret" not only provides the means for understanding people, for instance, due to their insufficient comprehension,
but also because it provides real qualities of meaning (*Realqualitäten
der Bedeutung*) for the outside world, which is independent from
people. Here the examples are the tendency figures of that which is
characteristically typical signifying itself in its specific appearances
and the entire world experiment concerning dialectical forms of
existence in regard to their still latent central figure. It is also intruc-
tive to compare this real publicity of a secret with Goethe's realistic
revelation of the world (*Welt-Eröffnung*): the entelechies that develop
alive in the world are altogether those many allegories and symbols
that are objectively present and alive. Ciphers of this kind are also to
be found in reality, not only as allegorical and symbolic descriptions
of that reality. The reason why there are such real ciphers (*Real-
Chiffren*) is due to the fact that *the world process itself is a utopian function,
and the matter of objective potentiality is its substance.* The utopian function
of conscious human planning and change only represents the most
advanced, the most active position of the aurora function (*Aurora-
Funktion*), which circulates in the world; i.e., it represents the nocturnal day where all real ciphers, all process figures (*Prozessgestalten*)
arise and are to be found. This is why the allegorical formation of
figures and the symbolic formation of goals reveal all things that are
transient as a simile, but as one that has a real course of meaning of its
own. Therefore, every appropriate simile is also one depicting reality,
to the same degree as it is full of objective utopian function in its
direction of meaning (*Bedeutungsrichtung*). And in its form of meaning

(*Bedeutungsgestalt*) it is full of real ciphers. Here we can see the final difference between symbol and allegory: the symbol turns out to be the attempted transition from simile to equation, i.e., the attempt to generate one identity between inwardness and outwardness. And in keeping with the truthfulness of this statement, it must be pointed out that the *Unum necessarium*—the supreme good—of the substance of such identity has always appeared only in the voice of a *chorus mysticus* and not yet with that adequate predication, that objective accomplishment, which is the ultimate goal and the final task of the enlightenment of the world. Yearning, anticipation, distance, concealment that continues to endure—these are destinations in the subject as well as in the object of the allegorical and symbolic. They are not destinations of any lasting kind but tasks to illuminate increasingly what is still uncertain in the allegorical and symbolic. In short, they are tasks for the increasing dissolution of the symbolic. But, in particular, the cognition of the tendency, including the awareness of its latency, has to do justice to the public secret.

## The Artistic Illusion as the Visible Anticipatory Illumination

It is said that the beautiful provides pleasure. It might even be enjoyed. But that is not reward enough, for art is not food. Art lasts after it is enjoyed, and even in the most delightful cases art continues to exhibit itself in a "prepainted" landscape. The wish dream reaches out for the indisputable better, and while doing so, it is something beautifully *shaped*, in contrast to the wish dream that has already become mainly political and operatable (*werkhaft*). Yet, one must ask whether there is something more than some illusionary play in those beautifully shaped creations? Is there something that is extemely artistic, but that, in contrast to the childlike, does not prepare for anything serious and means something? Is there any face value in the aesthetic chimes or sounds, any message that can be endorsed? Paintings enter less into this question since color has only a sensual certainty, and besides, color makes much less a claim on truth than words. Indeed, words not only serve poetry but also truthful information, and language provides more sensitivity for the latter than color, even as a drawing. Of course, all good art shapes and finishes its subject matter in a beautiful way, depicts things, people, conflicts in beautiful illusion. But what are we *honestly* to say about the way things are ended, about their maturation, in which only things that are invented are allowed to mature? What can we say about an abundance of material that is communicated in an illusionary way, in appearances (*Augenschein*) and sound (*Ohrenschein*)? What is the significance of Schiller's remarkable prophetic statement that what has been felt as something beautiful will come toward us one day as the truth? What is the significance of Plotinus' statement and later Hegel's that beauty is the sensual appearance of the *idea*? In his positivist period, Nietzsche confronted that assertion with a decisively more massive one, that all poets lie. Or, the arts make the vision of life more bearable by covering it with the veil of impure thinking. Francis Bacon sees the golden apples in the silver bowl as closely connected to deception (*Blendwerk*). They belong to the traditional *Idola theatri*. He compares truth to bare, bright daylight where masks, masquerades, and festive processions of the world appear only half as beautiful and majestic as they do in the candlelight of the art. Accordingly, artists are devoted to illusion from beginning to end. They have no proclivity for the truth; rather, the opposite. Premises for this antithesis of truth versus art can be found throughout the Enlightenment, and these premises made the artistic imagination suspicious when confronting a sense for facts. They were the *empirical* objections against the melancholy and flattened features, against the golden mist of the arts, and they were not the only ones that emanated from the Enlightenment. Next to these empirical objections there were the *rational* objections, which initially belonged to the Platonic theory of concepts and its especially famous, especially radical hostility toward the arts. In the calculatory course of reason during the bourgeois modern age, these rational objections made themselves fashionable again. This happened at a time when, according to Marx, there was a specific hostility toward art by capitalism in the nineteenth century—with the *l'art pour l'art* and the declaration of war by the Goncourts against the "public" as counterattacks—that was unable to leave its mark. But the ludicrous inquiry of that French mathematician, who asked, "What does that prove?" after seeing Racine's *Iphegenie*, is appropriate here. This question may seem ludicrous and also narrow-minded. Yet, it is, as a *purely rational* question, in keeping with a specific and great tradition of alienation from the arts and in keeping with the empiricist tradition. It is significant that, in all great systems of reason in the rationalistic modern age, the aesthetic component is ommitted. The ideas in the aesthetic component are not deemed worthy of scientific discussion. During the period of French classical rationalism, the most important theories of art were concerned with poetry and with art *techniques*. Descartes was only interested in the mathematical aspects of music. Otherwise, neither in Descartes nor in Spinoza could one get the idea that art was included in the system of ideas and objects. Even the universal Leibniz used very few examples from the arts. For instance, there is a reference about the harmony enhancing effects of shadows and dissonances, but he used this because it served him for matters of much greater importance, namely, to verify what was the best of all worlds. For Leibniz, the harmonic beauty is a kind of indication of the scientifically discernible harmony of the world, but it is only a confused allusion, and therefore the truth can do without it. Consequently, the aesthetics of rationalism originated very late in a strange way: it became a philosophical discipline in the hands of the Wolffian philosopher Baumgarten and began with clear contempt for its object, even with an apology for the existence of its object. The aesthetic object was the so-called inferior capacity of cognition that was effectual in sensual perception and its projections. And even if beauty represented perfection in this area, it was not comparable to the value of conceptual cognition and its comprehensive clarity. The *rationalistic* degradation of the arts was in keeping with the empirical positivist position. And yet, this is not all that is to be said about the groups hostile toward art. The hatred of art became really glaring when it was based not on reason, but on faith, in the belief in the establishment of a *spiritual* truth. Then the hatred of art moved in its attack from the golden mist of art, which was usually the target of the empiricists and rationalists, to superficiality; beauty succumbs completely to the insubstantial exterior and therefore diverts from the essence of things. "What is good about imitating the shadows of shadows?" Plato asks and thus makes his theory of concepts intellectually almost blunt. On the other hand: "Thou shalt not make unto thee a graven image, nor any manner of likeness, of any thing that is in heaven above, or that is in the earth beneath, or that is in the water under the earth" is what the fourth commandment in the Bible commands and gives the key word for the hostility toward art in regard to Jahweh's invisibility and the prohibition of all idolatry. Hence, art in general became glistening, ultimately Luciferian perfection, which hindered the truly non-glistening art, and which even repudiated it. This was *religious* and *spiritual* hostility toward the arts. The equivalent in morality was logically a rejection of the all too great visibility of the "work" and a turn toward the invisible genuineness of their "character" (*Gesinnung*). Puritanism in such a comprehensive sense—reaching back to Bernhard de Clairvaux—finally culminated in Tolstoy's monstrous hatred of Shakespeare, culminated in the hatred of the bastion of beauty in general. Even in Catholicism during the time of Pope Marcellus, a *Horror pulchri* led to the planned prohibition of the rich church music. And this horror, applied to what was visible, gave Protestantism the bare God who, in a moral belief, wanted to be worshipped through the word that is the truth. Thus, the claim of truth against beauty occurred in various forms—empirical, rationalistic, spiritual, and religious. Although these different claims on truth—subjectively the spiritual claim was one too—were disunited and so contradictory, they found a basis for unity in their serious intention to combat the game of illusion.

This issue has always moved the artists as well, especially since they took themselves seriously. In particular those artists, who refrained from dabbling with the arts in an isolated or decadent manner, felt committed to the question of truth. In the descriptions and stories of great realistic writers something beautiful also wants to be graphically true in a sufficient manner. It wants to be graphically true not only on the level of sensuous certainty but also on the level of wide open social relations, of elementary processes. This is how legitimate Homer's realism is, which is a realism of such complete accuracy that almost all of the Mycenaean civilization can be brought to mind with it. And Alexander von Humboldt, the natural scientist,—not a French mathematician—concluded from the 37th chapter of *Book of Job* that "the metereological processes taking place in the clouds, the formation and dissolution of the mist with different directions of the wind, the play of colors, the generation of hail and rolling thunder are described with individual plasticity. Also many questions are posed which our present discipline of physics knows how to formulate in scientific terminology but which it cannot solve sufficiently" (*Kosmos III*, Cotta, p. 35). This sort of precision and reality is certainly part and parcel of all great writing, often of expressly spiritual and religious writing as in the imagery of the psalms. And the demand of significant realism to counter all superficiality and also all extravagance has been acknowledged by art itself to the honor of Homer, Shakespeare, Goethe, Keller, and Tolstoy. In recent times it has been the novel that has satisfied this demand, rising to great heights as if there had never been a distrust of *Magister Ludi* and his games in the name of veracity. And yet, the artists, and even the most practical ones, have not *settled* the question of aesthetic truth. At most they have enlarged it and made it more precise in a desirable and significant manner, for realistic work of art in particular reveals that it is as an *art work*, that it is somewhat different from a source of historical or scientific knowledge or even discoveries. Precious words are peculiar to the art work, and they compel what is so strikingly signified by them beyond its given position. Telling stories is peculiar to the art work acting between persons and events in a way extremely alien to science. It is the telling of stories and also the artistry (*Kunst-Fertigkeit*) through which the empty space between what has been concretely observed is filled with what has been invented and that gives the action a well-rounded shape. But a semblance of rounding things out, rounding them over (*Überrunden*), is quite obvious in even the most realistic art works, especially in literary prose. The great illusion has a total effect that cannot be "outdone" in those art works that do not present themselves as primarily realistic, be it that they consciously romanticize along with or beyond the existing conditions (*Vorhandenheit*), be it that they fructify far beyond a mere "subject" the myth, which is the oldest nutrient of the arts anyway. Giotto's *Raising Lazarus from the Dead*, Dante's *Paradiso*, heaven in the last act of *Faust*, how do they relate—beyond all realism in regard to details—to the question of philosophers concerning truth? These works are certainly not true in the sense that they are borne out by all the knowledge that we have gathered from the world. But what is the meaning of the enormous impact of these works in form and content in regard to the world and legitimate issues? Here the question by that French mathematician "What does that prove?" reemerges surprisingly on another level and cannot be avoided even if we dispose with mathematicians and farce. To put it differently, the question about the truth of art becomes philosophically the question concerning the given reproductive potentiality of the beautiful illusion, concerning its degree of reality in a reality of the world that is not one-dimensional, concerning the place of its object correlate. Utopia as the determination of the object, with the degree of being (*Seinsgrad*) of the really possible

(*Realmöglichen*), presents a particularly rich problem for corroboration in the light of the iridescent phenomenon of art. And the answer to the aesthetic question about truth is that artistic illusion is generally not only mere illusion but one wrapped in images, a meaning that only portrays in images what can be carried on, where *the exaggeration and the telling of stories (Ausfabelung) represent an anticipatory illumination of reality circulating and signifying in the active present (Bewegt-Vorhandenen)*, in an anticipatory illumination, which portrays things in a specifically aesthetic immanent way. Here, individual, social, and also elemental events are illuminated that the usual or sharp senses can barely detect yet. It is due to the fact that the anticipatory illumination is attainable in this way, that art propels its subjects, figures, situations, actions, landscapes to the end, that it expresses these things in sorrow, in fortune as well as in meaning. Anticipatory illumination itself is attainable by virtue of the fact that the craft (*Metier*) of *propelling something to the end takes place in a dialectically open space*, where all objects can be aesthetically portrayed. To portray aesthetically means to be more immanent and accomplished, to be more elaborate, more essential than in the direct and sensual or direct and historical presence of this object. This elaboration, as anticipatory illumination, also remains an outward appearance, but it does not remain fantasy. Rather, everything that appears in the art images is sharpened, condensed, or made more decisive, and this is rarely shown by reality that is experienced. This decisiveness is based in the subjects themselves, makes the art with a substantiated illusion recognizable when looked at in the theater as paradigmatic institution. This art remains virtual but in the same sense as a mirror image is virtual; i.e., it reproduces an object, outside of itself, in all its depth onto a plane of reflection. And the anticipatory illumination, in contrast to religious illusion, remains immanent in all transcendence. The anticipatory illumination expands, as Schiller defined aesthetic realism using Goethe's works as an example, it expands "nature without going beyond it." Beauty and even the sublime are thus representative for a not-yet-developed existence of things, representative for a totally formed world without external coincidence, without unessentials, without incompletion (*Unausgetragenheit*). Therefore, the program of the aesthetically attempted anticipatory illumination is, How *to make the world be made perfect without exploding the world and without letting it apocalytically vanish as in the Christian-religious anticipatory illumination* (see also Ernst Bloch, *The*

*Spirit of Utopia*, 1923, p. 141). Art, which possesses various concrete figures at all times, seeks this perfection only in those figures, with totality as something special that is regarded in a penetrating way. In contrast, religion seeks the utopian perfection in the totality, and salvation places the individual case completely within the universal, places it into "I will make everything anew." The human being shall be born again here; society shall be transformed into the *Civitas dei*; nature shall be transfigured into the divine. Art is different because it remains rounded. As "classical" art, it loves the sailing around the existing coasts. Even as Gothic art, which crossed all boundaries, it contained something balanced, something homogenized. Only music, performed in open spaces, has an explosive effect, and that is why the art of music has always something eccentric in regard to the other arts, as if music were only transposed to the level of beauty and sublimity. All the other arts pursue the depiction of the pure carat value in individual figures, situations, and activities in the world without blowing the world up. That is why there is the complete visibility of this anticipatory illumination. Thus, art is non-illusion, for it has its effect in an extension of what developed (*Gewordenen*), in its formed, more suitable realization (*Ausprägung*). This can be seen in the writing of Juvenal, who, in order to express all possible frightening elements of a tempest, called it "poetica tempestas," in Goethe's profound remarks on Diderot's *Essay on Painting*, in which he pitted concentration as realism against naturalism that merely reproduced things as they are: "And so the artist, grateful to nature which also created him, returns a second nature to nature but one that is filled, one that is imagined, one that is humanly perfect." But at the same time, this humanized nature is one that is more perfect within itself, not in the manner of the sensual appearance of a finished idea, as Hegel taught us, but in the sense that it moves toward an increasing entelechical realization, as Aristotle pointed out. Even this entelechical or, as Aristotle also said, that which is typical and brings about completion is recalled in Engels' statement that realistic art is the depiction of typical characters in typical situations. The typical in Engels' definition does not mean, of course, the average but that which is significantly characteristic, in brief, the essential image of an object that is decisively developed in exemplary stages. Thus, the solution to the question of aesthetic truth lies in this direction: *art is a laboratory and also a feast of accomplished possibilities* plus the experienced alternatives within it while the performance as well as the result take place in the manner of the substantiated illusion, i.e., of the worldly completed anticipatory illumination. In great art, exaggeration as well as telling stories are most visibly applied to tendentious consequence and concrete utopia. Whether, of course, the call for perfection—we could call it the godless prayer of poetry—becomes practical to some degree and not only remains within aesthetic anticipatory illumination is not for poetry to decide but for society. Only a mastered history with an intervening countermove against inhibitions, with a decisive promotion of the tendency can help the essential, within the distance of art, become more of a phenomenon in dealing with life. Of course, this is the same as properly developed iconoclasm, which does not mean the destruction of art works but the intrusion into them, in order to fructify what has been, not only typically but paradigmatically, therefore exemplarily preserved in the art works. Wherever art does not play into the hands of illusion, there beauty, even sublimity, is that which mediates a presentiment of future freedom. Often rounded, never closed, Goethe's maxim of life is also valid for the arts—with the accent of conscience and content placed ultimately on openness.

## The False Autarky; the Anticipatory Illumination as Real Fragment

Often rounded: it does not suit a beautiful picture to present itself unfinished. What is incomplete is external to the picture, does not belong to it, and the artist who does not finish his work becomes unhappy about this. That is completely right and self-evident insofar we are dealing with the sufficient formative power. The source of artistry is skill, which understands its subject and thus wants totally to nurture it. Of course, for the sake of the intimate nurturing, we have to pay attention to the threat by that kind of artistry that does not stem from skill but from the component of *mere illusion*, which is inherent even in the anticipatory illumination. The temptation of satisfied contemplation and its portrayal is sufficient for mere illusion, whether that which is portrayed is as imaginary as it might be. The imaginary or what has become imaginary can lend a particularly decorative roundedness to the mere illusion, one in which the seriousness of the matter least disturbs or interrupts the beautifully coherent play. Due to the fact that mere illusion lets the image live together particularly easily in a particularly irreal way, it guarantees that pleasant superficial coherence, which does not display any interest and presence of an object beyond the blank illusion. Disbelief in the depicted object can even be an aid to the smooth illusion, more than skepticism. Renaissance paintings show that in their depiction of the ancient gods the painters did not have to be afraid of not having sufficiently dealt with the sacred. The same is evident not much later in mythologically rounded poetry. In the *Lusiads*, Camoëns lets his goddess Themis say very ironically and yet in the most flowery verses that she herself, as well as Saturn, Jupiter, and all the other gods who appear, are "conceited fabulous creatures, who are conducted to the mortals by blind delusion and only serve to provide fascination for the songs." Although, in this case, the mythological substance has been retained through the use of the beautiful illusion, which was added to the possible allegories of an anticipatory illumination. This was accomplished by means of that completed fullness invited particularly by the illusion that is continuous. And finally, there is another invitation that comes from the side of the *immanence without the explosive leap* (*sprengenden Sprung*), as it exists for all the arts, not only for antiquity or the ancient classical art. In particular, the art of the Middle Ages provides several examples for a rounded aesthetic satisfaction despite the religious transcendental conscience. The Gothic style contains this conscience, but within itself there was an equally peculiar harmony deriving from the Greek classical balance. In the early works of Lukács he quite perceptively, although in an exaggerated way, noted that "the church became a new polis ... the leap became the gradation of the earthly and heavenly hierarchies. And in Giotto and Dante, in Wolfram von Eschenbach and Pisano, in St. Thomas and St. Francis the world became round again, easy to survey. The abyss lost the threat inherent in its actual depth, but all of its darkness, without losing any of its black-shining power, became pure surface and thus fitted itself easily into a closed unity of colors. The cry for redemption turned into a dissonance within the perfect rhythmic system of the world and thus made possible a new equilibrium no less colorful and perfect than that of the Greeks: the equilibrium of inadequate, heterogeneous intensities" (*The Theory of the Novel*). However, the German secessions of the Gothic style, like those of Grünewald, are not affected by this kind of perfection. But this hypostasis of the aesthetic looks at us, even if not in full classical strength, all the more consistently from the Middle Ages, which remained determined by the Mediterranean. And therein is a harmony and a completeness of coherence that is not only idealistic but that, according to its last origins, stems from the great Pan, the prototype of all roundness. Pan is the one and all of the world and had been honored as that wholeness that does not lack anything. Hence, the ultimate temptation to nothing else than roundness, but hence, Greek equilibrium as the secular manner of the entirely pagan, and thus *the conception of the world without a leap: the astral myth.* In that myth the cosmos was really "decoration," i.e., balanced beauty; it circled continuously and *Hen kai pan* a circle itself and not an open parable. It was a sphere and not a process fragment. Therefore, there is a reason why art is very often pantheistically based on those far too rounding (*rundenden*) figures, and conversely there is a reason why a system that fits together completely has a pleasing effect even outside art. The pleasure in the sensual appearance, in the living attire of the god, certainly contributes to that pantheistic aspect, but the harmonic undisrupted nexus, the "cosmos" even without "universe," entices one more strongly to that pantheistic aspect. All these are the different reasons why a veritable artistry, an autarky of the apparent completeness can live in the art work, an exaggerated immanent completeness that first conceals the anticipatory illumination. But it is also true—and that is the decisive other, the decisive truth—that all great art shows that which is satisfactory and homogeneous about its work-coherence and where it is ruptured, unsealed, unfolded by its own iconoclasm, wherever the immanence has not been pushed to formal and substantial completeness, wherever that great art presents itself as still being *fragmented.* There, an objective, a highly objective hollow space with an *un-rounded immanence*, is opened—totally incomparable with the sheer coincidence of the avoidable fragmentation. And particularly there, the *aesthetic utopian meanings* of the beautiful, even of the sublime, reveal their conditions. Only what is broken in the art work silenced by the tone of the gallery that has made it into a mere *objet d'art*, or, better yet, only the already formed openness in great art works, provides the material and the form for the great cipher of the actual (*Eigentlichen*).

Never being closed, it fits the all too beautiful particularly well when the veneer breaks—when the surface turns pale or becomes darker, as in the evening when the light shines obliquely and the mountains emerge. The shattering of the surface just as the shattering of the merely cultural and ideological circumstances in which the works had been situated uncovers the profundity wherever it is. What is meant here is not the sentimental ruins and also not the kind of torso that, as often in Greek statues, keeps the figures closer together, produces greater unity and sculptural rigidity. Although that kind is possibly an enhancement of form, it does not necessarily reinforce the cipher, which is what counts in this instance. The reinforcement of the cipher happens only through the cracks of decay in the very specific sense that the decay has in regard to the *objet d'art* and as the transformation of the *objet d'art*. In this way, a *belated* fragment develops instead of ruins or the torso, namely, a fragment that can do better justice to the substantial depth of art than completion (*Beendetheit*), a completion that the work might exhibit on the spot. Thus, all great art becomes a belated fragment in the course of decay toward the essential, even totally self-contained art as the Egyptian, for the utopian ground blossoms in which the art work was planted. If the appropriation of the cultural heritage must always be critical, then this appropriation contains the self-dissolution of the *objet d'art*, which has become a museum showpiece as a particularly important element, but also contains the self-dissolution of the false finality (*Abgeschlossenheit*), which wants to have the art work in the right place and which makes more of a museum piece out of it. Such insularity takes a leap, and a sequence of figures arises, full of open, seductive symbol formations. And it arises even more when the phenomenon of the belated fragment connects with the fragment that *is created in the art work itself*, i.e., not in the usual, even shallow sense of the fragmentary as something unskilled or completed at random, but in a concrete sense as that which is not concluded despite supreme skill, that which *is transformed through the utopian pressure*. This is the case with great Gothic art, sometimes also with Baroque art, which has with all its powerful works a hollow space and behind that a fruitful darkness. Thus, the fully developed Gothic art, despite the presence of Pan, conducts a fragment of the central incapacity-to-finish (*Nicht-Enden-Können*). It is fitting when fragments develop in the usual sense of discontinuation, but it is unusual when the *Ultimum* appears, implicitly even though this is the only legitimate sense. Thus, Michelangelo left more fragments than any other great master, and this should give us cause for thought because it was the métier in which he was most adept, in sculpture, not painting. In painting he finished all the things he had started, whereas in ornamented columns, also in his architecture, he had pushed aside many half-finished things, which he never pulled out again and which he bequeathed. Vasari alerted art history to ponder the small number of Michelangelo's completely finished works and to ponder even more so when one considers that the huge dimension of the intended goal totally corresponded with the strength and nature of this genius. But that which corresponded to the huge dimension in Michelangelo himself, his own understanding of his overpowering nature and how to overpower a task, resisted the roundness and perfection of art in such a way that nothing of what had been carried out could become adequate or even perfect. Thus, perfection is driven so deep into whatever there is that it becomes a fragment. Such a fragment then is nothing less than an ingredient of the non-temple-like (*Un-Tempelhaften*), of the nonharmonic cathedral-like (*Kathedralischen*). It is conscience: the Gothic style still exists *post festum*. The depth of aesthetic perfection itself sets the unfinished in motion. In this respect, the non-fragmentary in Michelangelo in the customary sense, the figures of the Medici tomb, and the dome of St. Peter's Cathedral extend into that immensity that is the standard for the ultimate in the arts. Here we find the legitimate basis of the objective fragmentary for all works of this ultimate kind, in the *Westöstliche Diwan*, in Beethoven's last quartets—in *Faust*, in short, wherever the inability to finish produces something great. And if one searches for the ideological reason that continues to be effective for such an inner iconoclasm in great perfect art and particularly there, then this reason lies in the pathos of the process, in the eschatological conscience, which was brought to the world by the Bible. In the religion of the Exodus and the realm, totality is solely a totally transformed and explosive one, a utopian totality. And in the face of this totality, not only our knowledge but also our entire previous development, to which our conscience refers, appear as a patchwork—as patchwork or objective fragment especially in the most productive sense, not only in the sense of the limitation of the species or even in the sense of resignation. The phrase "See, I will make everything anew" in the sense of the apocalyptic explosion reigns above all that and influences all great art with the spirit after which Dürer named his Gothic creation *Apocalypsis cum figuris*. The human being is still not pervious. The course of the world is still undecided, unended, and so is the depth in all aesthetic information: *this utopian element is the paradox in the aesthetic immanence. It is the most thoroughly immanent to itself.* The aesthetic imagination would have enough conception in the world without that potential for the fragment, more than any other apperception, but ultimately there would be no correlate. For the world itself, as it lies in malice, lies in incompleteness and in the experimental process away from malice. The figures that this process generates, the ciphers, the allegories, and the symbols, in which the process is so rich, are *altogether fragments, real-fragments themselves through which the process flows unevenly and through which the process proceeds dialectically toward further forms of fragments.* The fragmentary is also valid for the symbol, although the symbol does not relate to the process but to the *Unum necessarium* within the process. But the symbol also contains the fragment especially through that relation and by the fact that it is only a relation and not an attainment. The real-symbol itself is only one because it is not yet manifest in itself and for itself instead of being concealed from the observer and entirely clear in itself and for itself. It is that which makes the importance of the fragment from the point of view of art and not only from the art. The fragment is part of the object itself. It belongs, *rebus sic imperfectis et fluentibus*, to the matter of the world. The concrete utopia as determination of the object (*Objektbestimmtheit*) presupposes the concrete fragment as determination of the object and involves it, even though it may undoubtedly be the ultimate sublation. All artistic and religious anticipatory illumination is concrete only to the degree and measure that the fragmentary ultimately provides the level and the material for this, to constitute itself as the anticipatory illumination.

## The Matter Concerns Realism, All That Is Real Has a Horizon

To stick to things, to skim through them, both are wrong. Both remain external, superficial and abstract—as something immediate they remain tied to the surface. The sticking adheres to that surface anyway. Skimming through things has the surface in its own open interior as well as in the other, the merely evaporated immediacy to which it escapes. Still, skimming through things is more typical of a superior type of human than taking things as they are. Above all, sticking to things, even as a conscious act, remains shallow, i.e., empiristic, whereas imagining things or dreaming can become restrained when it becomes conscious. The shallow empiricist like the effusive enthusiast is always suprised by the flow of the real that both do not comprehend. As a fetishist of the so-called facts, the empiricist remains obstinate, whereas the dreamer may be teachable. In the world, it is only reification that conforms to the empiricist's notions, the reification that captures individual elements and solidifies them as facts, and the empiricist is bound to it. In contrast, skimming through things is at least movement. Thus, it reveals a behavior that does not have to be fundamentally capable of being unmediated with real movement. In regard to the formation process, skimming through things involves art even though with a lot of illusion, with a lot of dubious escape toward an intentionally untrue dream-illusion. But the concrete adjustment of skimming opens pictures, insights, and tendencies in art and not only in art alone that happen simultaneously in human beings and in corresponding objects. In particular, that which is concrete does not derive from the groveling empiricism and the corresponding aesthetic naturalism that never moves forward from the establishment of what is factual to the exploration of what essentially happens. In contrast, the imagination, as soon as it emerges concretely, knows how to bring to mind not only sensual exuberance but equally the relations of mediation in the really experienced (*erlebniswirklichen*) immediacy as well as behind it. Instead of the isolated fact and the superficial coherence of abstract immediacy, equally isolated from the entirety, the appearances relate to the entirety of their epoch and to the utopian totality that is in process. Through this kind of imagination, art becomes knowledge, i.e., by means of striking individual images and total paintings (*Gesamtgemälde*) of a characteristic and typical kind. Art investigates the "meaningfulness" of the appearances and brings it to realization. By means of such an imagination, science grasps the "meaningfulness" of the appearances through concepts that never remain abstract, that never cause the phenomenon to fade or ever lose it. In art and also in science, "meaningfulness" is the specific of the general, is the respective instance for the dialectically typical coherence. It is the respective characteristically typical figure of totality. And the actual totality, where also the comprehended epochal entirety of all epochal elements is again an element itself, reveals itself particularly in the broadly conveyed great works only on the horizon, not in a broadly developed reality. Everything vital, Goethe says, has an atmosphere around it; everything real by virtue of being life, being process, by possibly being the correlate of the objective imagination, has on the whole a horizon. There is an inner horizon, which stretches vertically so to speak in self-darkness (*Selbstdunkel*), and an outer horizon of large breadth in the light of the world (*Weltlicht*). Both horizons, in their background (*Dahinter*), are filled with the same utopia. Consequently, they are identical in the ultimate. Where the prospective horizon is omitted, reality appears there only as a has-been, as a dead one, and it is the dead, namely, the naturalists and empiricists, who bury their dead ones here. Where the prospective horizon is continuously kept in sight, reality appears there as what it is concretely: as a network of paths (*Wegegeflecht*) of dialectical processes that take place in an unfinished world, in a world that would be totally unchangeable without the enormous future, the real possibilities within it. This includes the totality, which does not represent the isolated entirety of each part of a process, but which represents the entirety of the matter that is pending in the process in general. Therefore, it is a matter that is still tendentious and latent. This alone is realism. To be sure, it is not accessible to schematism of any kind that knows everything in advance, and that considers its uniform and formalistic pattern to be reality. Reality without real possibilities is not complete. The world without future-bearing (*zukunftstragende*) qualities deserves as little regard, art, or science as the world of the philistine does. *The concrete utopia stands at the horizon of every reality; the real possibility encloses the open dialectical tendency-latency until the very last moment.* The unconcluded movement of the unconcluded matter—and movement is, according to the profound words of Aristotle, "unfinished entelechy"—is ultra-realistically traversed by that dialectical tendency-latency.

# Marxism and Poetry

Nowadays a dream has a hard time in the world outside. That is the lament particularly of those writers whose inner life is not in mere disarray. They distrust sheer private humbug, and they have the will to express their common truth. They are thus led to socialist thought, which alone provides them with direction. But many writers touched by Marxism tend to consider themselves handicapped by this cold touch. The inner life does not come out well this way: the feeling and careful desire to articulate it are not always noticed. Each flower figures as a lie, and the intellect appears dried out or, if it has any juice at all, it is acidic. Many a pen becomes helpless by writing fiction while wanting to write the truth, or by looking for subjects that do not only let themselves be described or even narrated, but, in an honest way, let themselves be colored in an imaginative way or their story be continued. Those who are handicapped say that Marx stole their good conscience of invention. It is amazing how much Marx is blamed for everything. But even a good story often no longer knows where to begin.

Not long ago it seemed easier to start. That was the time when feeble talents dressed themselves up. Now the more gifted ones draw what they can from the dream. Thirty years ago bells still resounded everywhere. Dehmel praised the *working man*. Poets made off to socialism like going off on adventure, none for the better. There is no doubt about it: the competent but small battle cry for revolution exaggerated its virility, excluded objects that could have invigorated it. Marxism keeps greater distance from experimental poets, especially those with grotesque imaginations, than the cynical bourgeoisie, which accepts them as clowns for their private amusement and understands or misunderstands them as diversions. The "need of the moment" does not favor the broader, more creative and real poetic production any more. The motto for our day is, Make the most of your opportunities! Journalism or worse appears more readily to be tolerated: people as well as plots are conceived in accordance with flat, prearranged clichés. Naturalistic directness is praised as a manner of writing and as subject matter, the simple realism that kills the spirit, love, and the same without much ado. Such writing and subject matter confine reality mainly to what has become real for the proletariat these days, and neither acknowledges any historical remains nor any dream, even if it existed objectively. Thus, many young people, who have the strong urge to compose, to tell tales, to express their inborn imaginations, to temper them and have an effect, face the revolution as if it demanded the sacrifice of all imagination whatsoever just as the obscurantists demanded the sacrifice of intellect). Hate all of Proust, even Kafka: "Leave everything behind" appears as a permanent inscription above the door to Marxism.

But it is a distorted concern and in the long run no concern at all. Especially not when the confusing of teacher with disciplinarian, learning with draining the mind of imagination might ultimately stop. Sobriety and knowledge remain the spice of good dreams. And, if the dreams cannot bear knowledge, then they are self-deception or swindle. Marxist terminology leads beyond private or homeless curiosities. It is *real* and *great* and does not extract the true poetic correlate. Marx once called it the "dream of a thing" in the world. Marxist terminology connects, directs, and corrects the surplus of the writer's material, connects him with the *surplus of tendency and latency* that reality produces about the so-called facts. Naturalism may describe these so-called facts. They are as valuable and as superficial as naturalism itself. Genuine realistic poetry deals with *process*, isolating and manipulating the facts. The process requires a precise imagination to portray it and is connected concretely with the imagination. Once one has tasted Marxist criticism, all ideological hogwash becomes repulsive, and one will discard it. The true poetic aura, the only one remaining and possible, imagination without lie, appears all the more distinctly and does not envy any former era for its subjects. Marxism remains as clarity, non-deceptive even poetically. It sheds light on the bourgeois writers of decline such as Green, Proust, and Joyce, who reflect the mixed darkness and bleakness of the time. Marxism monitors and certifies their crypto-dialectics for posterity. Marxism predicted the capitalist "frigidization" of existence long before the first fascist was born, and now the fascists have increased it by necrophilia à la Benn. The Marxist writer does not adhere to archaic methods of nothingness when he deals with nihilism but to the dialectical process. In Western Europe the subjects of the dialectical process are still at least subversive and fermenting. But in the Soviet Union they are open and active, open to change. They are so abundant, and there is so much fresh material that literature could readily drown in subjects than die of thirst.

Therefore, the concern of writers, to be red and also mature, is distorted and is in the long run no concern at all. The time will come when the art of writing a story is no longer suspicious and when a mind with ideas will almost be busy not to have any; when having imagination is no longer a crime or treated largely as idealistic, as if there were no subjective factor at all; when the surface of things no longer stands for their totality, their cliché no longer for their reality; when little red Babbit's world no longer determines everything he ever saw. The long lasting praise of a realism, castrated by classicistic formulas, as the only genuine one is, from a Marxist point of view, an anomaly, both narrow-minded and dilettantish. But if one chooses to accept Marxism, then it opens gates to poetry where the bleakness, solitude, and disorientation of late capitalism are pressing concerns. It shows movement and landscape being newly formed that lose nothing of their abundance and aspirations through exact topography. Instead of sterility and the non-existence of problems, which had become a stigma of the congealed, bourgeois-rationalistic Enlightenment (from Friedrich Nicolai, the publisher, to the philistine of culture who claimed to know everything and to have advanced magnificently far), Marxism shows countless problems of motion and incompleteness within a reality whose tendency and utopian backgrounds require more geniuses to express it than there are muses. The so-called poetic journalism and the so-called literature of the fact, praised between 1921 and 1929, are receding now. The problem of heritage moves forward, the heritage of Pushkin, Tolstoy, the great realism emerging from great poetry, certainly not through the imitation of epigones. Even apparent irregularity gains objective space as in times when mountains turn around. Then even the "golden dragons and crystal spirits of the human soul" appear, says Gottfried

Keller, the realist, in *Ursula*, part of the *Züricher Novellas*. Keller was not influenced by Jean Paul for nothing; he speaks of times of change when mountains move. The world was not built by schoolteachers, neither its poetry nor its forming-transforming forces that provide the basis for a poetry of universal style. Marxism's sole theme is that of forming-transforming, and it scares away the dreamers but not the precise imagination. It is this imagination, which is dialectically trained and mediated with tendency and latency of existence, with those time-spaces of real possibility. In brief, if imagination can find at best only hollow spaces in the late capitalist world in which to hide, it can find subjects, work, and blessings to help it in the socialist world, the more the better. The imagination is no longer the social outcast.

The poetic inner life does not disclose at all what it is. That question is as idle and abstract as the related higher one about the meaning of the "human" as such, the so-called universality of it. Nevertheless, the "human" genuinely does exist within Marxist thought as the "oppressed, alienated human being." This way of thinking is the most real one, and Marxism does not know any other way than the real, i.e., human beings historically determined by class. The Marxist concept of the "human," related to the poetic one, is not completely absorbed by its hitherto existing historical appearances so that it is still floating in them and seems unfulfilled. The poetic concept, although it is only comprehensible as it is expressed, only exists that way. There is no doubt that all inner life, especially when it is "spiritual," is dangerously close to idealism, both overlapping with each other and almost more with objective idealism than with subjective. But Lenin noted, "Philosophical idealism is nonsense *only* when viewed from the standpoint of crude, simple materialism. When viewed from the standpoint of dialectical materialism, on the other hand, philosophical idealism is a *one-sided*, exaggerated, extravagant inflation of one feature of knowledge." Thus, it is mere "one-sidedness," but not nonsense or total non-reality. After all, it is a relative and peculiar kind of reality that belongs as one of the "features of knowledge" to the inner life of poetic consciousness, given that it is not completely detached from material existence. At the very least, "idealism" exists at the starting point of anything "human," and also in all "formative, constructive, and creative forces." When this factor is not put to use, it can only lead to non-expression, non-creation, and non-representation. It is only in this way that the undeniable reality of human products would subsequently be little more than idealism in reality. Here consciousness and existence, ideology and base have a mutual effect on each other. The "poetic" never entered the formations of ideology formally or without contents of its own so that it overlaps with mere "false consciousness"— without "productive additives" of its own. Ideology has been created by the "poetic" in the superstructure of former civilizations. The poetic is not just a formal treatment. It is also an objective piece of work with material that leads to its condensation and brings out its essence. It shows itself most clearly in dramatic form through experimental isolation and elucidation of the conflicts, through intensification of the figures so that they capture the role of their characters and reveal their essence only when *driven to the very heights* in a poetic way. Thus, Lessing's phrase becomes clear: "On stage we do not want to learn what this or that person did, but what everybody might do with a given character under certain given circumstances." Thus Aristotle's famous phrase, which was obviously Lessing's reference, also takes on significance: "The historiographer and the poet do not distinguish themselves from one another through the use of verse or prose. Their difference consists in the fact that one expresses what really happened; the other one, what might well happen. Therefore, poetry is more philosophical than historiography because it shows the universal more." Consequently, the poetical depiction of the essential is based on something fundamental that does not appear at all so clearly in the empirical substance or has not become obvious in any way whatsoever. The subjective factor of the poetical is then the midwife of the artistic anticipatory illumination. Given the amazing superiority of philosophical truth—in particular, the truth given by Aristotelian poetics in preference to poetry rather than to so-called naturalistic history—it becomes clear at the same time that the case of realism is not as simple as it seems to the elemental or schematic *Weltanschauung*. Or, not everything remains idealistic—in the sense of the unreal—which is added to the subject while it is being driven away; rather, the most important element of reality might comply with it—the not yet lived possibility. In such a manner meaningful poetry makes the world become aware of an *accelerated flow of action*, an *elucidated waking dream of the essential*. The world wants to be changed in this way. Therefore, the *correlate of the world* to the poetically appropriate action is precisely the *tendency*. To the poetically appropriate waking dream it is precisely the *latency* of existence. And especially today the poetically precise dream does not die because of truth, for truth is not the portrayal of facts, but of processes. Truth is ultimately the demonstration of tendency and latency of what has not yet developed and needs its agent.

There is childhood or the fairy tale as material that constantly refreshes itself. There are the rebellious dream images in oppressed classes or the barely reutilized treasures of cheap and popular literature. The uprisings of the people await their realization in "red" epic poems, in the kind of "historical" poetry that the bourgeoisie did not have and could not have. There is the history of heresy, a storehouse of brothers, enemies, symbols, which concern us in a powerful way— and which are poetically almost undiscovered, despite the Faust material. In our own time there is a world with fighting, corpses, victors, horrors, dangers, decisions, with the gloom and gaiety of Shakespearian dimension. There is a kind of nature to which no response has been given since Rimbaud, and, without an evocative qualitative language of latency, there is no answer whatsoever that can be given in a poetic way. All that, of course, denies the beautifully completed coherences in poetry since they are only possible idealistically. On the other hand, when observed from a Marxist perspective, reality is more coherent than ever, but only as *mediated interruption*, and the process of reality as such, traced by Marxism, is still open, therefore objectively fragmentary. It is only because of the really possible that the world is not made into a sophisticated book, but into a process dialectically mediated, therefore dialectically open. And realism, too, reveals itself poetically time and again as created in a rough and extended way. One might even say that wherever realism appears as a complete portrayal of reality without interruption and openness, then it is not realism but rather the remains of the old idealistic structure of beauty as such. Whereas in terms of realism, in particular, one finds significantly less "complete, coherent reality" in Goethe's *Wilhelm Meister* and in Keller's *Grüner Heinrich* than neo-classicism would like. There, too, we find Shakespeare everywhere, this one and only classical stumbling block of the real. Only the artificial and abstract viewpoint produces continuity—it does not objectively engender breaks in style, which has led to montage. There is a fine saying by a French poet that applies to all art that does not try to pass off cheap imitation for genuine reflection: a masterpiece never looks like one. In any case, great poetry is driven more to extremities, built with more that is essential than its subject *ante formam*, but that is why the dawn and the sea are beyond that fortress. That is why there is the sea of the process in which the depths of reality are most incomplete. Marxism relates to this so closely that it could provide access to this *subject pending in process*—minus ideological lies, plus concrete utopia. That is, access to poetry that has nothing in common with self-satisfaction and illusion, nor with false, i.e., artificial, classicism. In contrast, there is genuine classicism, as Goethe says, the classicism that is often rounded out but never closed. Creative poetry never approaches truth without pressure or demands; it toils toward the end and seeks to transcend even if the manner is not beautiful. All great writers want to become like Faust.

In many of these writers, especially in Brecht, there is even a bit of restless contempt for art and therefore the desire to destroy the saying that all poetry is false. Therefore, Marxism is the weapon that first gives the imagination a guilty conscience and also the same weapon that heals the affected imagination. The disenchantment of the lies, the separation of appearance from the potential, aesthetic anticipatory illumination will enhance the function of poetry, which feels itself as a force of production, and make poetry even more meaningful. Marxism does not in the least separate the world from the freedom of inner life, nor does it, as Sartre once did, posit the inner life as simply isolated. On the contrary, Marxism wants to create a new interplay between the world and the inner life and overcome alienation and reification. This intention is completely realistic, but surely not in the sense of a banal or even schematic cliché. On the contrary, Marxist reality means: reality plus the future within it. Marxism proves by bringing about concrete changes that are left open: there is still an immeasurable amount of unused dreams, of unsettled historical content, of unsold nature in the world. Those who have taught through poetry have rarely found any subject more excellent than our adventurously moving, latently expectant world—the most real thing there is.

# The Fairy Tale Moves on Its Own in Time

Certainly good dreams can go too far. On the other hand, do not the simple fairy-tale dreams remain too far behind? Of course, the fairy-tale world, especially as a magical one, no longer belongs to the present. How can it mirror our wish-projections against a background that has long since disappeared? Or, to put it a better way: How can the fairy tale mirror our wish-projections other than in a totally obsolete way? Real kings no longer even exist. The atavistic and simultaneously feudal-transcendental world from which the fairy tale stems and to which it seems to be tied has most certainly vanished. However, the mirror of the fairy tale has not become opaque, and the manner of wish-fulfillment that peers forth from it is not entirely without a home. It all adds up to this: the fairy tale narrates a wish-fulfilment that is not bound by its own time and the apparel of its contents. In contrast to the legend, which is always tied to a particular locale, the fairy tale remains unbound. Not only does the fairy tale remain as fresh as longing and love, but the demonically evil, which is abundant in the fairy tale, is still seen at work here in the present, and the happiness of 'once upon a time,' which is even more abundant, still affects our visions of the future.

The young protagonist who sets out to find happiness is still around, strong as ever. And the dreamer, too, whose imagination is caught up with the girl of his dreams and with the distant secure home. One can also find the demons of old times who return in the present as economic ogres. The politics of the leading 200 families is fate. Thus, right in America, a country without feudal or transcendental tradition, Walt Disney's fairy-tale films revive elements of the old fairy tale without making them incomprehensible to the viewers.

Quite the contrary. The favourably disposed viewers think about a great deal. They think about almost everything in their lives. They, too, want to fly. They, too, want to escape the ogre. They, too, want to transcend the clouds and have a place in ths sun. Naturally, the fairy-tale world of America is more of a dreamed-up social life with the kings and saints of big business life. Yet, even if it is deceiving, the connection emanates partly from the fairy tale. The dream of the little employee or even—with different contents—of the average business-man is that of the sudden, the miraculous rise from the anonymous masses to visible happiness. The lightning of gold radiates upon them in a fairy-tale-like way. The sun shines upon them from commanding heights. The name of the fairy-tale world is publicity (even if it is only for a day). The fairy-tale princess is Greta Garbo. Certainly, these are petty bourgeois wishes with very untrimmed, often adulterated fairy-tale material. However, this material has remained. And where does one ever really get out of the bourgeois style of living? Yet, there is a certain surrealistic charm in presenting old, fairy-tale materials in modern disguise (or, also, in divesting them of their apparel). It is precisely the unbound character of the fairy tale that has floated through the times that allows for such developments, such new incar-nations in the present, incarnations that not only occur in the form of economic ogres or film stars.

Cocteau's modernization of the great fairy tale of longing, *Orpheus and Eurydice*, is an example of this, an especially glaring one: Orpheus wears horn-rimmed glasses; Madame la Mort wears an ancient gold mask and a Parisian evening dress. The scene is a Parisian town house. A mirror becomes the entrance to the underworld. Everything is different from ancient times, and everything is retained, enlivened, nothing disturbed in its radiant longing. The eroticism keeps old traits of the fairy tale even in depictions of much narrower and questionable kinds and knows what to make of Eurydice. Typical also in this respect (despite all the *kitsch*) are two plays by Molnár, a dramatist, who knows how to use *Fata Morgana* in a refined if not a cunning manner, and who also understands her survival after disillu-sionment which is often dangerous and unwarranted. The first play is called *The Guardsman*, the second, *The Wolf*. Both deal with the genuine fairy-tale world of a petty bourgeois young woman of today, a world in which almost every part is false and nevertheless the whole is true. In *The Guardsman* the wife of an actor is disappointed by the everyday life with the man she formerly idolized, and she continues to dream of another kind of Lohengrin. But the actor, though somewhat unctuous in appearance, is kind and likes to undergo changes, and he fulfills her dream wish. He disguises himself as a chivalrous count in a sufficiently fabulous manner. A sublime game of love commences, sublime infidelity to her husband, sublime fidelity to the ideal incarnated by him, and the disillusionment, partly sensed in advance, partly not sensed, and certainly not desired, is caused by the husband actor who reveals his true identity. This lands the petty bourgeois woman right back to the beginning, without a lesson learned, with a Chopin nocturne and dream that is unanswered and continues to move on. In *The Wolf*, the fairy-tale dream is even cloaked by technical stage devices in a real dream: it anticipates the party at which the wife of a lawyer is supposed to see her former lover. And it fills the four fairy-tale scenes for the dreamer: scenes in which the lover seeks to appear as a triumphant general, as brilliant diplomat, as famous artist, or also just as a humble servant who is gradually humiliated because of his broken heart and obliged to carry out the commands of his mistress. Again the disillusionment (none of the four is to be found in the original of the dream) does not cancel the idolatry of the fairy-tale projection. On the contrary, the fairy-tale prince continues to live, and the sobriety of reality pops up again only in the form of a crying fit. However, if one turns from here, that is, from the old story that remains eternally new, to the really new and newest history, to the fantastic changes of technolgy, then it is not surprising to see even here a place for forming fairy tales, i.e., for technological-magical utopias.

Jules Verne's *Journey around the World in Eighty Days* has by now become significantly shortened in reality, but *The Journey to the Middle of the Earth* and *The Journey to the Moon* and other creative narrations of a technological capacity or not-yet-capacity are still pure formations of fairy tales. What is significant about such kinds of 'modern fairy tales' is that it is reason itself that leads to the wish projections of the old fairy tale and serves them. Again what proves itself is a harmony with courage and cunning, as that earliest kind of enlightenment which already characterizes *Hansel and Gretel*: consider yourself as born free and entitled to be totally happy, dare to make use of your power of reasoning, look upon the outcome of things as friendly. These are the genuine maxims of fairy tales, and fortunately for us they appear not only in the past but in the now. Unfortunately we must equally contend with the smoke of witches and the blows of ogres habitually faced by the fairy-tale hero in the now. The fairy-tale hero is called upon to overcome our miserable situation, regretfully just in mere fairy tales. However, this takes place in such tales in which the unsubjugated often seems to be meant—tiny, colorful, yet unmistaken in aim.

# Better Castles in the Sky at the Country Fair and Circus, in Fairy Tales and Colportage

Little duck, little duck,
Hansel and Gretel need some luck.
No way to go, no bridge in sight.
Take us across on your back so white.

Hansel and Gretel

Then we went back to bed. But I didn't sleep. I lay in bed awake. I thought of help. I struggled to reach a decision. The book I had been reading was entitled *The Cave of the Robbers in the Sierra Morena, or the Angel of the Oppressed*. After my father had come home and had fallen asleep, I climbed out of bed, crept out of the room, and got dressed. Then I wrote a note: "I don't want you to work yourselves to death. I'm going to Spain. I'll get help." I placed this note on the table, put a piece of dry bread into my pocket along with some pennies from my bowling money, went down the stairs, opened the door, took a deep breath again and sobbed, but very, very softly so that nobody could hear. Then I walked without making a sound until I reached the market place where I followed the Niedergasse out of town toward Lichtenstein and Zwickern, toward Spain, country of the noble robbers, the helpers of those in distress.

Karl May, Mein Leben und Streben<br>(My Life and Strivings)

If sailor tales to sailor tunes,
    Storm and adventure, heat and cold,
If schooners, islands, and maroons
    And buccaneers and buried Gold,
And all the old romance, retold
    Exactly in the ancient way,
Can please, as me they pleased of old,
    The wiser youngsters of today:

So be it, and fall on! If not,
    If studious youth no longer crave,
His ancient appetites forgot,
    Kingston, or Ballantyne the brave,
Or cooper of the wood and wave:
    So be it, also! And may I
And all my pirates have the grave
    Where these and their creations lie!
            Robert Louis Stevenson, *Treasure Island, To the Hesitating Purchaser*

It is not uncommon that random wandering, random hunting expeditions of the imagination flush out the game which methodological philosophy can use in its neatly ordered household.

                                                                Lichtenberg

Toward dusk may be the best time to tell stories. Indifferent proximity disappears; a remote realm that appears to be better and closer approaches. Once upon a time: this means in fairy-tale manner not only the past but a more colorful or easier somewhere else. And those who have become happier there are still happy today if they are not dead. To be sure, there is suffering in fairy tales; however, it changes, and for sure, it never returns. The maltreated, gentle Cinderella goes to the little tree at her mother's grave: little tree, shake yourself, shake yourself. A dress falls to her feet more splendid and marvelous than anything she has ever had. And the slippers are solid gold. Fairy tales always end in gold. There is enough happiness there. In particular, the little heroes and poor people are the ones who succeed here where life has become good.

The Courage of the Clever Heroes

Not all of them are so gentle that they simply wait for goodness to come. They set out to find their happiness, the clever against the brutes. Courage and cunning are their shield; intelligence, their spear. Courage alone would not help the weak very much against the mighty lords. It would not enable them to knock down towers. The cunning of intelligence is the humane side of the weak. Despite the fantastic side of the fairy tale, it is always cunning in the way it overcomes difficulties. Moreover, courage and cunning in fairy tales succeed in an entirely different way than in life, and not only that: it is, as Lenin says, always the existing revolutionary elements that tie the given strings of the story together here. While the peasantry was still bound by serfdom, the poor protagonist of the fairy tale conquered the daughter of the king. While educated Christians trembled in fear of witches and devils, the soldier of the fairy tale deceived witches and devils from beginning to end—it is only the fairy tale that highlights the "dumb devil." The golden age is sought and mirrored, and from there one can see far into paradise.

But the fairy tale does not allow itself to be fooled by the present owners of paradise. Thus, it is a rebellious, burned child and alert. One can climb a beanstalk up into heaven and then see how angels make gold. In the fairy tale *Godfather Death*, the Lord God himself offers to be the godfather in a poor man's family, but the poor man responds, "I don't want you as a godfather because you give to the rich and let the poor starve." Here and everywhere, in the courage, the sobriety, and hope, there is a piece of the Enlightenment that emerged long before there was such a thing as the Enlightenment. The brave little tailor in the Grimms' fairy tale kills flies in his home and goes out into the world because he feels that his workshop is too small for his bravery. He meets a giant who takes a rock in his hand and squeezes it with such strength that water drips from it. Then he throws another rock so high into the air that one can barely see it. However, the tailor outsmarts the giant by squeezing a piece of cheese into pulp instead of a rock, and next he throws a bird so high into the air that it never returns. Finally, at the end of the fairy tale, the clever tailor overcomes all obstacles and wins the king's daughter and half the kingdom. This is the way a tailor is made into a king in the fairy tale, a king without taboos, who has gotten rid of all the hostile maliciousness of the great people. And when the world was still full of devils, there was another fairy-tale hero, the youth who goes forth to learn what fear is. He resists fear all along the way. He sets corpses on fire so that they can warm themselves up. He bowls with ghosts in a haunted castle, captures a bearded old man, who is the head of the evil spirits, and thus wins a treasure.

The devil himself is often outsmarted in the fairy tale. A poor soldier tricks him by selling his soul under the condition that the devil fill the soldier's shoe with gold. But the shoe has a hole, and the soldier puts it over a deep pit. Thus the devil must drag sack upon sack filled with gold until the first cry of dawn. Then he dashes away, the victim of a swindle. So, even shoes with holes in them can serve for the best in fairy tales if one knows how to make use of them. This is not to say that mere wishing and the simple fairy-tale-like means of achieving a goal are not mocked. But this mockery is enlightened, and it is not discouraging. In times of old, thus begins the fairy tale about the frog prince, when wishing still helped—the fairy tale does not presume to be a substitute for action. Nevertheless, the smart Hans of the fairy tale practices an art of not allowing himself to be intimidated. The power of the giant is painted as power with a hole in it through which the weak individual can crawl through triumphantly.

*The Magic Table, The Genie of the Lamp*

Even good things in a form in which they have yet to be seen lend their support. In particular, wish instruments of the most comforting kind are magically offered to the weak. Here the Grimms' fairy tale *The Magic Table, the Ass with Gold, and the Cudgel* contains a highly significant meaning: a protagonist, a poor disowned son, becomes apprenticed to a carpenter, and, when his time of apprenticeship has been completed, he receives a table. It is nothing to look at, but it has a special feature. If one says, "Table be covered," it covers itself at once with delicious food, which no cook can match, and a large glass of wine stands next to it. Then there is a miraculous ass, who spouts pieces of gold from his rear end and his mouth. Finally, there is the cudgel that jumps out of a sack, the magic weapon without which the poor person cannot exist in the world, even if he were to become rich and happy. The magic of the magic table has many a correlate in the magic-wish storehouse of fairy tales: the flying boots in Wilhelm Hauff's story of little Muck and his walking cane as divining rod; the piece of wood in the fairy tale *Said's Destinies*. Here, among the shipwrecked, the piece of wood changes itself into an oracle of Delphi, whom Said rescues and brings to shore quicker than a flying arrow. The Grimms' fairy tale of *Brother Lustig* has a satchel from which the brother can magically obtain everything he may ever desire: roast goose, eight devils. Finally, after he has thrown the satchel up into heaven, he manages to have himself sent to heaven, too. The Grimms' fairy tale *The Water Nixie*, which contains a gigantic cudgel that jumps out of a sack, enables two children to throw a brush against the evil nixie, then a comb, and finally a mirror. The brush turns into an immense hill with thousands of teeth, and then the mirror into a mountain of glass so slippery that the nixie cannot climb over it and must abandon her pursuit.

Play and magic together have carte blanche in the fairy tale. Wish becomes a command. There is no difficulty in carrying it out. Neither is space or time divisive. In Andersen's fairy tales there is a flying trunk that lands in the country of the Turks, and there are magic boots that carry a judge back into the fifteenth century. In *1001 Nights* a magic horse flies and arrives in heaven, and it is right there that the most powerful force that fulfills wishes waits with folded arms: the genie of the lamp. It is most significant that the richest of all fairy tales, *Aladdin and the Magic Lamp*, is based upon nothing but utensils for wishing for what is not available. Smoke-works are ignited. The deceitful uncle murmurs mysterious words, and suddenly the cave opens up. There are hidden treasures which are piled up in the name of Aladdin. An underground garden appears, and the trees are covered with jewels instead of fruit. The slave of the ring and the genie of the lamp step forward—both representative of hallucinated pri-mordial wishes for power, for power that is not limited to certain goods as in the fairy tale *The Magic Table*. Rather, the genie of the lamp brings his master everything, anything his heart desires. The genie of the lamp provides countless treasures, physical beauty, and courtly art on command, elegant speech as well as elegant wit. He builds a castle overnight, the most glorious the world has ever seen, with treasure chambers, royal stables, and an armory. The stones are made out of jasper and alabaster, the windows out of jewels. It is an easy command to carry out. And in the very next moment the lamp transports the palace from China to Tunis, then back to its old place without the carpet at the entrance to the castle, even moving at the behest of the wind. Also, the magic slate that provides the deceitful uncle with knowledge about everything that happens in the world cannot be overlooked: "But now, on a day to remember, he conceived a sand table, and he spread the figures around and studied the sequence of their movements attentively. And in the very next mo-ment he determined the sequence of their movements, the mothers as well as the daughters."—It is the same geometrical table whose power enabled the magician in Tunis to learn about the faraway treasure in China that Aladdin obtained. Nothing but countless ways to fulfill wishes, nothing but *via regia* to attain in the fairy tale as quickly as possible what nature itself outside the fairy tale refuses to grant human beings. In general, the technological-magical digging for treasures is the fairy-tale component itself in this type of fairy tale, for the discovered treasure symbolizes above everything the miracle of the quick change, of sudden luck. Astuteness and smoke-work are necessary in the Aladdin fairy tale. Astuteness alone is sufficient in Edgar Allen Poe's *The Gold Bug*, a secularized fairy tale about treasure hunters, and also in Stevenson's *Treasure Island*. But it is still the treasure in these semi-fairy tales (which turn into adventure stories) that makes for tension and provides the turn of events. It is the very touchstone, which unlocks life and allows its splendors to be acquired. In this way the technological-magical fairy tale sets possessions as its goal only indirectly and out of need. It sets the transformation of things that are the available utility goods at any time as its goal. Instead of painting the short covers, which one has to stretch for, it portrays an old bed of nature. It intends—in order to designate the home territory of all the magic tables and also of the magic again with one fairy tale—it means to be the land of milk and honey. With milk and honey in it, it sounds moreover as if one were already hearing a social fairy tale, as if one were already hearing a state fairy tale, simpler in the goods it provides, but even more nourishing than the others.

"Love of my heart, I shall carry you away upon the wings of songs."

The youth who wanted to go forth to learn about fear dreamed only weakly at first. Even the brave little tailor won the princess almost unintentionally because she just happened to be on the way during his journey. All the heroes of fairy tales find their happiness; however. not all of them are drawn to it so clearly in dreams of happiness. Only the heroes of the later literary fairy tales (*Kunstmärchen*), which are not inferior in quality, or of the legends that resemble fairy tales (by various authors such as Wilhelm Hauff, E. T. A. Hoffmann, Gottfried Keller) are also psychological fairy-tale figures, particularly of a dreamlike-utopian nature. For instance, in Hauff's tale about little Muck: he left home to *search for* happiness. In particular, it was his dream of happiness that he pursued. "When he saw a piece of glass on the ground that glittered in the sunlight, he picked it up and put it into his pocket with the belief that it would change into the most beautiful diamond. If he saw the dome of a mosque in the distance glistening like fire, or if he saw a lake shining like a mirror, he rushed full of joy to the spot, for he thought he had arrived in a land of magic. But, alas, those deceptive images vanished when up close, and his fatigue and hunger, his growling stomach reminded him very quickly that he was still in the land of mortals."

In another curious type of fairy tale there is the student Anselmus from E. T. A. Hoffmann's *The Golden Pot*, which was announced as *the romantic* "fairy tale of the new age." Anselmus, too, has his head full of dreams, and the world of spirits is not indisposed toward him. This is, in fact, the reason why he is extremely awkward in real life. "So, as has been suggested, the student Anselmus, sank in a dreamy brooding which made him insensitive to every outward contact with common life. He felt that some unknown thing was moving within him and calling forth an ecstatic pain which is nothing but the yearning that reminds man of the loftier existence promised to him. He was happiest when he could meander alone through meadows and forests, completely freed from all that bound him to his meager life, so that he could find himself again, as it were, in the manifold images which arose from his soul." And so Anselmus managed to win the tingling Serpentina, even though he had to do battle with streaks of bad luck and combat hostile forces that disguised themselves as bad luck and even worse. Serpentina appeared in the blue room of palm trees, in the strong triad of bright crystal bells, and he demonstrated that he deserved her. Anselmus succeeded in reaching Atlantis, where he settled down with the daughter of the prince of light on a knight's estate after he had long since possessed a dairy farm there, a dairy farm in dreams, as property of the inner meaning. Such was Anselmus, the student from sunken Germany. And, as is fitting, all the other wishful-thinking characters of the literary fairy tale are aligned with him like the legendary figures made out of Don Quixote's stock. Especially if they possess Quixote's strong imagination but not his power for action.

The knight Zendelwald in Keller's legend *The Virgin as Knight* is the dreamiest example of this kind of hero. This is why he was so incompletely indecisive and knew nothing about things that transpired in his presence. And, of course, his more familiar world was filled with wishful thoughts about the world and women that he conceived in his desolate castle. "When his heart and soul were in accord about something—and this always happened with complete intensity— Zendelwald could not bring himself to take the first decisive step toward concerte action since the matter seemed expedited as soon as he was clear about it within himself. Even though he liked to talk to himself, he never spoke a word at the very moment that might have brought him happiness. But it was not only his mouth, but also his hand which his thoughts superceded. This happened so much that he was often nearly defeated by his enemies in battle because he hesitated to deliver the final blow as he had already envisioned his opponent already lying at his feet." Then some news reached the dreamy knight that, even though it came to him from the real world, corresponded quite a bit to the thing that was occupying his imagination at that time. During one of his infrequent trips he had seen the Countess Bertrade, a young, extremely beautiful and rich widow. He had been at her castle and had fallen in love with her. However, he had departed without saying a word. While Zendelwald spent many months thinking only about the faraway countess, he received news that the emperor had announced a tournament and was going to offer the countess as bride to the winner, firmly believing that the holy virgin would intervene and direct the one deserving of her hand to victory. After awhile the knight finally went forth to enter the tournament, but he then fell into his old routine of imagining and conceiving things. He anticipated everything according to his wishes and worked everything out in his dreams. "Step by step the adventure took place in his imagination and took the best turn of events. He already began to have sweet imaginary conversations with his beloved days on end as he rode through the verdant summer countryside, and he invented such beautiful things that her face blushed out of pure joy. All of this took place in his mind." Since thinking hinders the deed, however, the knight arrived just as the tournament had already ended, and everything would have been in vain for him if the Holy Virgin had not filled the gap between wishful dreaming and reality. It was she herself who actually fought in the tournament disguised as the knight Zendelwald. There is even more to this: the tardy dreamer was astonished to see his own body as victor and bridegroom next to the beautiful countess, and he became tortured by a crazed jealousy and rushed through the throngs of people to see his double and rival. However, his likeness disappeared from Bertrade's side just as the

countess turned toward the real Zendelwald and continued the conversation without having noticed the change in persons in the least.
"Zendelwald did not know what was happening as Bertrade spoke
familiar words to him which he answered now and then without
thinking. Yet, they were the words which he had spoken once before.
After awhile he realized that his predecessor must have been conducting the very same conversation which he himself had imagined
and invented during his journey." So the knight became happy with
the countess. It was from his own dream as if from his own fairy tale
that this happiness emerged and became real. Real like in a fairy tale.
The Virgin Mary, herself a religious dream, helped a dreamer,
inclined to the most tender and almost destructive wishful thinking,
to reach wonderland. Of course, neither the weak Zendelwald nor
Anselmus came out of their introverted realms, nor did they come out
of that realm where the fairy "legend" provided them ground to
stand on.

"Quick, let's go to the corridors of the hallway. I know the most
beautiful place there."

And yet, this kind of morning realm is not only enjoyed from within.
The glittering pieces of glass that little Muck stuck into his pocket illuminated a way outside of him as well: they lit up the *outside field* where
they lay. For sure, long before the essence of the wish-projections
begins to flow, the wishes are aroused by the fairy-tale qualities of
nature, especially by clouds. It is there that the distant mountains first
appear, a towering and wonderful foreign land above our heads.
Children believe that white-capped clouds are ice mountains as
though Switzerland were up in the sky. There are castles there, too,
taller than they are on earth, of ample height. For the young this
yearning belongs undoubtedly to concrete existence, and the setting
sun reinforces it by the direction the sun takes. In Lagerlöf's fairy tale,
*The Journey of Little Nils with the Wild Geese*, the youth sets forth with
the glittering and singing birds toward the south, where the heavenly
castle stands on earth, where the blissful islands Wak-Wak are at
home in the sea. For even the first picture that most human beings
have of the sea stems from the distant sky and leads in that direction.
This is to say: the cloud is not only castle or ice mountain to the fairy-
tale gaze, but is also an island in the sea of heaven or a ship, and the

blue skies on which it sails reflect the ocean. If faraway realms are over our heads, if the air of heaven with its clouds is not limited by the earthly coasts, or if they reflect them, then all fairy tales submerge this in a gigantic water above in which the blue heavens emerge, and the journey continues without difficulty toward the coast, which intervenes in this fantasy toward the morning star. In all of this there are still astral-mythological remains that have an effect right up through the fairy tale about the star money. But the fairy tales that fly higher and higher than the birds hardly need them, just as they can do without the Christian heaven.

Even without all that, the fairy tale has its wondrous views, and if they are wondrous, they carry out the splendor of their own nature in an extremely comical way, and everything smells of poesy here. This is the way they took shape in the fairy tale in Gottfried Keller's novel *Green Henry*: they are used like messages to stimulate Frau Margret. She is like another Little Muck with pieces of shinning glass and uncertain utopia, which does not need to feel ashamed if it contains something more beautiful than the mundane world. Frau Margret lives underneath the flotsam and jetsam of her rummage and antique shop. Missing things rise up and make themselves heard. Daylight itself is illustrated with pictures from faraway countries and from unholy books: "Everything had a meaning for her and was alive. When the sun shone through a glass of water onto the brightly polished table, then the seven colors playing with another were for her a direct reflection of the splendors that were supposed to be in heaven itself. She said: 'Don't you see the beautiful flowers and wreaths, the green countryside and the red silk scarves? Those golden little bells and those silver fountains?' And whenever the sun shone through the room, she made an experiment in order to look into heaven a bit, as she put it." It is the *realist* Keller who took down and recorded this childish nonsense. Nevertheless, the desire to reach the sun in an innocent soul is captured here, and this desire fulfills everything alive and is embellished by the nonsense. When the faraway realm roars like the sea in the shell, it may look like the harbor light in the prism, like Frau Margret's odd wondrous light, and the fairy tale has nothing against this. In fact, it is possible that its dream makes charts, in other words, that it conceives a formal map of its coasts. In addition, the outside field is inviting. It is from there that its dream moves and from which its dream selects the images of the imagination that have been stamped by experience in a fairy-tale way, records and orders them.

In his dream fairy tale *The Brushwood Boy*, Kipling has his boy conceive this exact type of a map, and he takes a journey on it. Hong Kong is an island here in the middle of the "sea of dreams," and on its coast lies Merciful Town, the charitable city, "where the poor may lay their wrongs away and the sick may forget to weep." In the dream the Brushwood Boy rides the 30-Mile Trip with the girl he has thought of since his childhood. He rides with the Brushwood Girl of his dreams through the dunes and steppes, through the dusk of the wish geography, through "the valleys made out of miracle and irrationality." Even later, when, as a grown man, he becomes a colonial officer and is confronted with the reality of East Asia, the dreamland does not become invalid. Policeman Day wakes him regularly to take on the bad reality. Despite this, the dream map does not fade in the real world. The images of the hero's wishes is mixed in this fairy tale with the plain nocturnal dreams in such a way that he compels them to become the representation of his own daydreams, to become India, the land of his wishes, and the princess of his wishes emerges from the dream. Moreover, the beloved in Kipling's fairy tale does not only become the woman whom a lonely man conjures, whom he decorates with dream jewelry and accommodates in Fata Morgana, but the Brushwood Girl also exists in concrete form. She encounters her hero in her own identical wish dream. So, in the end the two subjects of the dreams discover themselves as real and rediscover their India in a real love mysticism. A real India of a higher order, one to which the dreamed-up India was a promise and the cause, the stuff of the imagination, the indismissable background, beyond the Orient itself, way beyond the bank of the hallway, a fabulous outer world itself through which the fairy tale is able to establish a connection more readily with the available things in the outside field. The Brushwood Boy is at home there. The jungle absorbs there and clears the way for looking toward a land beyond (*Ausland*), which is nothing but native land and home in the fairy tale. South Seas, turquoise green skies, the archways of a bazar, the mysterious house—all of this Oriental scenery surrenders to the fairy-tale wish with great affinity and absorbs it. The reason for this is by no means simple: certainly most of the material of fairy tales stems from the Orient, especially from India, and is inclined to return there. Even the nature of the fairy tale, particularly the clouds and castle made out of the sky, even the German fairy-tale forest border on the Orient. To be sure, the indicated rebelliousness in many of the Grimms' fairy tales culminates there as well as the miraculous occurrences, the adventure and scenery of the magical realm. They make the archtypical splendor of *1001 Nights*. This splendor may also lie on the island of Hong Kong or even in the imago of the Brushwood Girl, the miraculous woman. The most introverted fairy tale contains this piece of an outside place. In the Indian Ocean of dreams, in the image, which takes off from faraway and departs on a trip.

## The South Seas at the Fair and Circus

For the young, the faraway realm can also take off in a very sensual way and be present. In colors and shape, raw like meat, colorful like the little tags that Italian butchers stick on the meat. The *sideshows* at the fair do not originate here, nor does their magic, which is continually dusted off and revealed anew in the repeated performances of the sideshows. The magic operates as if abnormal and foreign. Yet, it is ordinary and full of swindles, but it is still more substantial than the trouble that the philistine causes for the age-old joy of young and old people. So these boat-like shows set sail and are carried by the South Seas for the simple soul and the uncorrupted, complicated soul, too. The tent-boats weigh anchor for a short time in the dusty cities. They are tattooed with pale green or bloodthirsty paintings in which votive pictures projecting rescue at sea disasters are mixed with those of the harem. The motor drives the orchestration with foreign, fatty, inhumane, breathless-sluggish sound. Sometimes it is connected with a dancing wax lady screwed down next to the entrance. And she dances with sudden contortions, moves with twisted gestures of screweddown wax that turn into dance, and she throws her head back from time to time. Eventually she comes to a halt and trembles in this position right behind the barker, who fears nothing. The type of world extolled here has the secrets of the bridal bed and also of the miscarriage at one end and the secrets of the bier at the other end. "The lady will reveal her beautifully built torso. You will see the secrets of the human physique." But also: "Professor Mystos will bring an Eygyptian mummy back to life at nine o'clock, the exact hour at which the person died." Strange human creatures and their art offer themselves to the spectators in nothing but peepshows of abnormality. The sword swallower and fire eater, the man with the untearable tongue and iron skull, the snake charmer add the live aquarium. Turks, pumpkin men, fat women, they are all there: "Nature has dealt out the stuff of its body in such an extravagant way that, when the body had spread to its most perfect form, it weighted 400 pounds." And, in addition to the abnormal faraway realm, the fairytale realm reappears continually and also that of the horror story: the oriental labyrinth, the jaws of hell, the haunted castle. That is the fair, a colorful, peasant fantasy. To be sure, in the large American cities it has become increasingly automated with loudspeakers and amusement centers. However, the land of wishes from the medieval South Seas, so to speak, has remained. And it maintains itself out of the Middle Ages, which go much further back, right to the fair of a higher order, in the kind of show of the *Circenses* without any curtain at all. For, as the miracles of the sideshows are assembled altogether under one roof, in a ring, and as the menagerie breaks out from here, the coliseum or the circus now originates from the South Seas. Of course, the feature of the wax figure cabinet cannot be present here, that suspended animation, that mechanical organ, because everything in the circus is alive. And, in contrast to the fair, which operates with concealment, with stage, showcase, and curtains, the circus is fully open. The ring brings everything with it.

The circus is the only honest, down-to-earth honest performance. A wall cannot be built anywhere in front of spectators who sit in a circle and surround the performers. Nevertheless, there is estrangement. The death-defying leaps are the most extreme a body can produce, but it does bring them off. Magicians perform, but without magic. Made as if by lots of gypsies in a green wagon, older than the oldest reader can remember, perhaps even pre-historical, the art of the circus is the locale without backrooms, with the exception of a cloakroom and stables, and the stables can be visited during the intermission. Everything happens in the brightly lit ring, on the trapeze underneath the roof, and, in spite of this, it is magic, its own wish-world made out of eccentricity and precise ease. The types have changed very little over the years—the stern, comical, and athletic. They are set just as the types of animals that one gets to see: the elephants, lions, trotting horses, which promenade around the ring, the ringmaster with whip, and the stablemaster in the entr'actes, the bareback rider, the tightrope walker and other high flying acrobats, half sylph, half on the verge of death, the animal tamer, and the strong man, who breaks chains. The fact that the circus has become popular amusement without intermissions (*Volksvergnügen ohne Pause*) has been accomplished with the help of clowns who perform during the intermissions. The clown types range from the glittering and powdered ones of the Elizabethan Age to the tramp with the round red nose and smiling mouth painted black and white, to the king of poverty, the dumbbell. These are all the figures from the coliseum, which has become a friendly place, and so it is only appropriate that the skits or pantomimes form the second part of the circus. The performance is introduced by the most beautiful music of this kind, by Fucik's gladiatorial march, and it closes with the march *per aspera ad astra*. Even today the circus still represents the most colorful mass show or picture of sensation. It is Arabian fantasy in the most cheerful Roman arena.

All that which is mirrored in the sideshow or tent is very rarely mirrored again. It cannot be mirrored surrealistically even though the wax figure is dipped in horror and the glittering clown juts out into unknown territory. Only Meyrink extracted his own fairy tale from this, made his own colportage out of this world—an elective affinity, comical, poorly written, uncanny, everything together. This was the way Mohammed Daraschekoh's oriental panopticon was described: "The motor at the entrance slowed its tempo and powered an instrument like an organ. There was a jumpy, breathless music—with loud and muffled sounds at the same time, something strange, something softened as if the tones were being made under water. The smell of wax and smouldering oil lamps was in the tent. The program number: Fatima, the pearls of the Orient, was over, and the spectators drifted back and forth or looked through the peepholes at the walls decorated with red cloth and a roughly painted panorama which depicted the storming of Delhi. Other people stood silently in front of a glass coffin in which a dying Turk was lying and breathing heavily, shot through the bare breast by a bullet from a rifle—the edges of the wound were blue and gangrenous. When the wax figure opened its lead-colored eyelids, the crackling of the watch springs penetrated through the box." Everything was contrived, yet the horror was here nonetheless, again powerful in its impact, in the impression and in the relation to it, and the dream lights, which connect to the fair and circus, were not absent either. Meyrink's book *The Golem* is a fairy-tale colportage about the fair just as his novel *The Green Face* is also a colportage sprinkled with the spectacle of the circus. In its colportage, *The Golem* treats nothing more and nothing less than the secret sideshow to which back payment helps. There is the tooting music, which comes in from the street, the moonlight at the end of the bed, a pale painting, which looks like a piece of fat, the room without a door, somewhere in the city of Prague, with the Golem as inhabitant, the ledge made out of stone in the Golem room. It is the ledge to which the guest clings and looks and looks and then falls, for the stone is as slippery as grease. Also, a beautiful Miriam walks around, a wax dream of perfection, and her house stands in the light of morning, no admission like the sideshow with the secrets of Greece that bars visitors sixteen and under, like the sidereal life. The strange mixture out of Jakob Böhme and joking, which this type of writing appropriates, can disgruntle the reader. Such a style can be traced up through surrealism, and it is connected to the ambivalent, two-headed completely allegorical genre. The paintings of Dali and even some of Max Ernst move in a similar mixed atmosphere of levity and seriousness, coziness and horror. The model for all of this is provided by the wax figure that moved in a humorous way and is at the same time stiff as a stick. Meyrink and the entire magic of the fair, depending on the degree, are nonsense, and no performer or author leaves us with any doubt about this.

However, there is a yearning, which resides here, that is itself not nonsensical, even though it is shrill and fraudulent, cheap and un-controlled. It is the yearning for a constellation in the world, made out of esoteric and weird things, the yearning for the curious as objective quality. Of course, Dali and Meyrink together had been surpassed—something that has been self-evident anyway. But what is not so self-evident is the contemptible and brutal manner in which they are dropped when compared to a great writer who knew how to handle droll, strange, and humorous elements that were grim, and who may have yielded to these elements and subjected himself to a metaphysical curse. This writer is Gottfried Keller, and his *Dream Book* (*Traumbuch*, 1848) dealt with the matter under discussion, which is a matter that never receives full discussion, in the following manner: "I entered a wax museum. The gathering of great figures looked pitiful and neglected, and I was overcome by a horrifying loneliness.

So I rushed through the figures into another room where there was an anatomical collection. Almost all the parts of the human body had been artfully portrayed in wax, most of them in sick, terrible conditions, a most strange general assembly of human conditions, and they seemed to have convened to write an address together to the creator. A great part of the honorable gathering was formed by a long series of glass cases which contained the shapes of the evolving human being from the smallest embryo to the fully developed foetus. These shapes were not made out of wax but were natural specimens and sat in alcohol in positions of deep contemplation. This pensiveness was all the more striking as the little fellows actually represented the hopeful youth of the assembly. But suddenly loud music with drums and cymbals could be heard in the room of the tightrope walker next door which was separated only by a thin wall. As the rope was being crossed, the wall trembled, and the silent attention of the little people vanished. They began to shake and dance to the beat of the wild polka which could be heard over there. Anarchy set in, and I don't believe that the address was ever completed." Such was the writing of the young Keller, and again his humor is striking: there is depth to his sarcasm and ambivalence as well.

The age-old pleasure of people, in no way simple and no way decadent, is preserved in the fair, wanders within it and outside. There is a piece of frontier here, set at reduced admission, but with preserved meanings, with strange-utopian meanings, conserved in a brutal show, in vulgar crypticness. It is a world that has not been sufficiently investigated for its specific wish areas. In particular, it is that "oddity," the kind that was last called such during the Baroque period, that keeps itself above water here, above land.

The Wild Fairy Tale as Colportage

Even in the fairy tale things do not proceed gently from the beginning. There are giants and witches in it. They block the way. They make the protagonists spin the whole night through. They lead people astray. In contrast to the much too gentle or precipitous blue sky, there is a kind of fairy tale that is very rarely considered as such. It is a wild kind of turbulent fairy tale. It is very rarely recognized not because it degenerates easily into trash, but because the ruling class does not like tattooed Hansels and Gretels. In other words, the turbulent fairy tale is the adventure story. The best way that it continues to maintain its existence today is as colportage. Its face bears the expression of a neglected crude creature, and this is the way it often appears. Nevertheless, colportage consistently reveals traits of the fairy tale, for its hero does not wait as in the magazine stories, until happiness falls into his lap. Nor does he bend down and pick it up as though it were some bundle thrown at his feet. Rather, its hero remains related to the poor swineherd of the folk tale, the daring protagonist, who sets corpses on fire and slaps the devil over the head. The hero of colportage shows a kind of courage, often like that of its readers, that have nothing to lose. And an affirmed piece of do-nothingness emanates from the runaway protagonist who does not end up dead. When he returns, he has the aroma of palms, knives, and swarming Asian cities around him. The dream of colportage is: never again to be trapped by the routine of daily life. And at the end there is: happiness, love, victory. The splendor toward which the adventure story heads is not won through a rich marriage and the like as in the magazine story but rather through an active journey to the Orient of the dream. If the magazine story has something from the unspeakably dissolute legend, then colportage is the last but still recognizable grow of the courtly romance, of Amadis of Gaul. This is where the praising of deeds comes from. It was characteristic of the ancient heroic poems such as the *Waltharlied*, in which the hero defeats ten knights at one time, or the legend about King Rother and Strong Asprian, who throws a lion against the wall with such force that the lion breaks into pieces. This is where the passion directed against the philistines comes from, against a life that already has two feet in the grave at age twenty, against cozy homes and juste milieu. The genuine fairy-tale aura of a wild kind originates here. The Stevenson world of "heat and cold, storms and winds, of ships, islands, different types of adventures, or marooned people, treasures and pirates." And the entire group, especially where it ends without excuse as it were, that is, without literary finesse, has the smell of a common hussy about it. This smell is ambivalent. It can point to members of the Ku Klux Klan and fascists and endow them with a special kind of attraction. Or, it can also point to the unjustified mistrust of the calm bourgeoisie against too many campfires of poor devils. Every adventure story breaks the moral of "work and prayer." Instead of praying, cursing is the dominant feature. Instead of working, the pirate ship appears, the protector not in the pay of the king. The robber romanticism reveals in this way another face, one that has spoken to poor people for ages, and colportage knows all about it.

The leader of the robbers had a falling out with the authorities. Often his enemy is the same as that of the common people, and this is why he frequently has supporters among the peasantry. So there is a great deal of substance behind the Italian, Serbian, and especially Russian tales about robbers that were handed down over the centuries and that differ markedly from the reports of the police. Schiller's play *The Robbers* with the motto "In tyrannos!" is only the classical literary form of a phenomenon in which the robber and Brutus could change their shapes. There is a raw, yet honest substitute for revolution here, and where else can it express itself but in colportage? If only Schiller, the genius of this genre, had become more dedicated to it, then this genre would have become something other than the degenerated courtly novel and treasure-hunter story. The Ku Klux Klan and fascism set only the criminal and wild abortions of the genre into action. In contrast to this, there is the tremendous goal in the wilderness: incarceration and liberation, the killing of the dragon, the rescue of the maiden, cleverness, breakthrough, revenge—all these parts belong to the freedom and splendor beyond the wilderness. It is not fascism but the revolutionary act in its romantic time that is a kind of *Volksbuch* that has become alive. This is why plays about rescue emerged right before and after 1789 and Schiller's *The Robbers*. One can call the plays fairy tales about rescue. Prisoners were dug out of caves just like treasures were dug out of the ground. And here it is important to note that the text to *Fidelio* is the sharpest and most thrilling colportage, as is well known, and belongs to the theme of liberation. Dark dungeons, pistols, signals, rescue—things in the more refined literature of the new kind never appear by themselves. These things produce one of the strongest possible tensions available: that between night and light. Accordingly, a re-evaluation of this genre is especially evident on the strength of its highly legitimate wish-image in its mirror. Here, missing meanings are fresh everywhere, and those that are not missing are waiting, as in the fairy tale. The happy ending is fought for and won. Nothing remains of the dragon except the chains. The treasure hunter finds his dream money. The separated lovers are reunited. The fairy-tale-like colportage is a castle in the sky par excellence, but one in good air, and insofar as this can at all be true about plain wish work: the castle in the sky is right. In the final analysis, it derives from the Golden Age and would like to stand in such an age again, in happiness, which pushes forward from night to light. This kind of happiness is such that it will cause the bourgeoisie to laugh on the other side of its face, and it will cause the giant, otherwise known as the big banks today, to believe in the power of poor people.

# Building in Empty Spaces

## New Houses and Real Clarity

Obstetric forceps have to be smooth, a pair of sugar-tongs not at all.
Ernst Bloch, *The Spirit of Utopia*, 1918

Today, in many places, houses look as if they were ready to travel. Although they are unadorned, or precisely because of that, they express their farewell. Their interior is bright and sterile like hospital rooms, the exterior looks like boxes on top of mobile poles, but also like ships. They have flat decks, portholes, gangways, railings; they shine white and to the south, and as ships they like to disappear. Western architecture is so sensitive that for quite some time it has indirectly sensed the war that is the embodiment of Hitler, and it gets ready for that war. Thus even the form of a ship, which is purely decorative, does not seem real enough for the motif of escape that most people in the capitalist world of war have. For some time now there have been projects in this world to build houses without windows, houses that are artificially illuminated and air-conditioned, that are completely made of steel; the whole thing is like an armored house. Although during its creation, modern architecture was basically oriented toward the outside, toward the sun and the public sphere, there is now a general increasing desire for an enclosed security of life, at least in the private sphere. The initial principle of the new architecture was openness: it broke the dark cave. It opened vistas through light glass walls, but this will for balance with the outside world came doubtlessly too early. The de-internalization

(*Entinnerlichung*) turned into shallowness; the southern delight for the world outside, while looking at the capitalist external world today, did not turn into happiness. For there is nothing good that happens on the streets, under the sun. The open door, the wide open window is threatening during the era of Fascisization (*Faschisierung*). The house might again become a fortress if not the catacombs. The wide window filled with a noisy outside world needs an outside full of attractive strangers, not full of Nazis; the glass door down to the floor really presupposes sunshine that looks in and comes in, not the Gestapo. And certainly not with a connection to the trenches of World War I, but definitely with the Maginot Line of World War II, even though it was futile, the plan of a subterranean city developed— as a city of safeguard. Instead of skyscrapers, the projects of "earth-scrapers" invite, the shining holes of groundhogs, the rescuing city that consists of basements. Above, in the daylight, on the other hand, the less real but decorative escape plan of a flying city occurred, utopia-ized in Stuttgart and also in Paris: the houses rise as bullet-like forms on top of a pole, or as veritable balloons they are suspended from wire ropes. In the latter case, the suspended buildings seem particularly isolated and ready for departure. But also these playful forms only demonstrate that houses have to be dreamed of, here as caves, there on top of poles.

But what if under such conditions a jump toward brightness is to be demonstrated? That has indeed been tried in architecture, but with the *affirmedly* uncomfortable desire for many windows and equally sterile plain houses and instruments. Certainly, those things presented themselves as the cleansing from the junk of the last century and its terrible decorations. But the longer that lasted, the more it became clear that the mere elimination was all that remained— within the limits of late bourgeois emptiness—it had to be that way. The longer that lasted, the clearer the inscription above the Bauhaus and the slogan connected to it emerged: Hurray, we have no ideas left. When a lifestyle is as decadent as the late bourgeois one, then mere architectural reform can no longer be shrouded but must be without soul. That is the result when between plush and tubular steel chairs, between post offices in Renaissance style and egg boxes there is no third thing that grips the imagination. The effect is the more chilling as there is no longer any hiding place but only illuminated kitsch, even if, which is indisputable, the beginning had been ever so clean, that is to say, vacuum clean. Adolf Loos in Europe and Frank Lloyd Wright in America drew the first lines of negation against the epigonic cancer. Although Wright had some hatred against the city, partly anarchistic (*anarchisteldem*), partly healthy, with the partition of the murderous meta-city into "home towns," into a "Broadacre City" and ten times as much space for everybody as one was accustomed to have. On the other hand, Corbusier praised in reverse a highly urban "dwelling machine"; he signified together with Gropius and others, even inferior creators of the New Sobriety (*Neue Sachlichkeit*), that part of engineering that presented itself as being so progressive and that was so quickly stagnant, that so quickly became scrap. Therefore, for more than a generation, these creatures of steel furniture, concrete cubes, and flat roofs stood around without a history, highly modern and boring, seemingly courageous and truly trivial, allegedly full of hatred against the empty phrases of all ornaments and yet more stuck in schemes than ever any copy of style during the terrible nineteenth century. Finally, then also in France, it was enough for the tenet of such an important architect of concrete like Perret: "The ornament always hides a structural defect." In the process a classicistic would-like-to-be, almost romantic, is not lacking, partly because of the geometric form, partly because of peace and quiet as a citizen's first duty, partly because of abstract humanity. Corbusier's program, "La ville radieuse," sought some kind of Greek Paris everywhere ("Les elements urbanistiques constitutifs de la ville"). In the Acropolis he illustrated some kind of general human spirit ("le marbre des temples porte la voix humaine"). But here Greece became an abstraction like never before as well as "Être humain," which was not further differentiated and to which the constructive elements are supposed to relate in a purely functional way. Also the urbanism of these steadfast functionalists is private, is abstract; for of all that "Être humain" the real human beings in these houses and cities become normalized termites, or within a "dwelling machine" they become foreign cells, still too organic. All this is quite out of touch with real human beings, home, comfort. That is the result, has to be, as long as architecture does not care about the ground that is not right. As long as the "purity" consists of omissions and unimaginativeness, as long as the mirth consists of ostrich policy, if not of deception, and the silver sun, which wants to sparkle here all around, is chrome-plated misery. All around here architecture appears as surface, as something eternally functional. Accordingly, even with the greatest transparency, it shows no content, no burgeon and no ornament forming blossom of some content. To be sure, this abstractness connects superbly with glass, and could be strangely created in it, ground emptiness in air and light, newly cosmic from nothingness. Bruno Taut, a disciple of Scheerbart, sketched such a "house of heaven" (see *Die Stadtkrone* [*The Crown of the City*], 1919). The floor plan consists of seven triangles, the walls, the ceiling, the floor are made of glass; the illumination turns the house into a colorful star. As the immediate successor of the "pan-cosmist" (*Pankosmiker*) Paul Scheerbart, who was the first to universalize glass architecture, Taut was supposed to rebuild the entire earth as a crystal. And as an example for the new transparency Taut quoted the lines from Claudel's *Annunciation*: "Into the waves of divine light the architect wisely puts/ The stone frame like a filter according to plan/ And gives the water of a pearl to the entire building." In addition to the most modern material, numerology also found its place in Taut's programs, with the astral ultimately succeeding the colorfulness. Thus an Egyptian adventure from the nothing arose, and it arose in vain. Parallel to that, a Gothic style deriving from nothingness spread, with rays and beams of no content gushing up like uncontrolled rockets. Pure functional form and unconnected exuberance thus act dualistically, but also complementarily, in a way that the machine style cools down and is relieved, but the imagination becomes even more homeless and comes out all the more. Whereas in the old architecture, particularly the three principles mentioned by Vitruvius, the *utilitas* and the *firmitas*, which were never missing, intersected with the *venustas* or the imagination and therefore in detail as in general decorated the entire structure, functional form and imagination do not come together anymore in the decay process, not even if the latter was an enormous, often significant one, as with some Expressionist painters—as painters, not as architects. Connection to more than the surrounding bourgeois nothingness or semi-nothingness was certainly sought. Mostly it was called half engineer-technical, half without real rhyme or reason, a connection to the "laws of the universe": but as interesting as the results in painting, also in sculpture, might have been, the ways of Taut and Scheerbart in architecture remained fruitless. Architecture cannot at all flourish in the late capitalist hollow space since it is, far more than the other fine arts, a social creation and remains that way. Only the beginnings of a different society will make true architecture possible again, one that is filled at the same time constructively and ornamentally by its own artistic volition. The abstract engineer style will not, under any circumstances, become qualitative, despite the phrases that its literati add to it, despite the deceptive freshness of "modernity" with which the polished-up death is presented like morning glory. Today's technology, which is itself still so abstract, does lead out of the hollow space, even as it is fashioned as an aesthetic one, as an artistic substitute. Rather this hollow space penetrates the so-called art of engineering (*Ingenieurkunst*) as much as the latter increases the hollowness by its own emptiness. The only significant thing in all this is the direction of departure of these phenomena generated by themselves, i.e., the house as a ship. Certainly, further elements of change are also prepared in here, to the same degree as the flourishing new human relations and relations to nature of a new society are mature and clear enough to manifest themselves also in architectural outlines and ornaments. Full of heritage, without historicism, even more so—as is self-evident by now—without the infamous copies of styles, the knotty romanticism of the *Gründerjahre*. Therefore, it is absolutely right to be against the extremes, box or kitsch: cleansing of all that has still been preserved, preparation to cultivate and channel all emerging sources to gain architectural exuberance. All this is preceded by the radical distinction between architecture and machine. And also the relatively most interesting thing of today and yesterday, i.e., the utopia of the glass building, needs shapes that deserve transparency. It needs configurations that retain the human being as a question and the crystal as an answer that has to be mediated yet, an answer that still has to be opened. Maybe then the architect will give his work "the water of a pearl," but also at last, a lost, less transparent cipher: the architectural exuberance *in nuce*—the ornament.

## City Planning, Ideal Cities, and Again Real Clarity: The Penetration of the Crystal with Fullness

If connected with others, houses do not look ready to travel anymore. The good architect needs groups, plazas, a city. The city shall no longer need to vanish, it shall have long-term planning. That is one of tomorrow's hopes, and where tomorrow already dawns, it is today's.

But that hope is as old as architecture itself, remains inscribed in it and self-evident. Therefore, urban planning is not at all limited to modern times. Even though it is often to be found then, it appeared already in the last century and thus also intersected there in a peculiar way. To be sure, the bourgeois society is calculating and organized around the profit principle, but due to the anarchic economy, it is also a disarranged society, one of economic coincidence. Therefore, it is particularly the industrial cities and the residential districts of the last century to which we owe the great courage of construction speculators, the absolute lack of reflection and of planning. The only thing homogeneous is their dreariness, the chasms, the desolate line of streets leading into nowhere, the kitsch of their own style of misery or stolen ostentatiousness; the rest of the layout, nevertheless, is anarchic like profiteering on which it is based. In the process the so-called developed cities of the pre-capitalist era in particular did not at all spring up at random due to the mode of production that was still regulated. Antiquity passed on distinct city planning, from the time before Alexander, the rash founder of cities from the Nile to the Himalayas. From the beginning deliberate precaution distinguished the architect, even in striking proximity to the socially constructive. Aristotle mentioned such an architect called Hippodamos, namely, in a striking duplicity of architectural and political planning: "Hippodamos, son of Euryphon of Miletus, who invented the sectioning (*diairesis*) of towns and who cut through the Piraeus ... was at the same time the first who, without being a practicing politician, undertook to say something about the perfect state constitution" (*Politics II*, cap. 8). Hence the contact of architectural and political planning is that old: the aforementioned Hippodamos had also planned a *diairesis* on the state ground for the purpose of the cult, the public service, of private property and had his development plan almost socially based. Moreover, the excesses of planning were not missing that have always been part of the caesarean madness and that took their building craze into account, and yet it was a planned and methodical madness. Alexander and his architect Dinocrates dreamt of carving out the entire cape of Athos and turning it into a colonizable colossus. On the left hand, the mountain statue was supposed to carry a town; on the right hand, a basin was to accumulate all rivers of the mountains and flow into the sea as an antique Niagara. That was an urban fantasy that also in terms of thorough reflection, not only in terms of extravagance, was not paralleled by any constructive-Baroque or neo-feudal kind. Although it was half geomantic, then of an astrological nature, city planning existed when Augustus let Rome be transformed from bricks to marble, and then when Constantine turned Byzantium into the capital of the Empire. Last but not least, the Middle Ages, claimed by romanticism and its restitution as being particularly "instinctive," was rich in city planning *sui generis*. The early medieval settlement was centered around a castle with precise premeditation; the colonial towns in Southern France, in Eastern Germany even displayed a regularly repeated planning. Of course, all this remains true, despite all the individualistic accident as then exploded in the construction anarchy (*Bau-Anarchie*) of the nineteenth century: only capitalist calculation, that other side of the commodity society, let rational urban utopias emerge in particularly great numbers. That stood in a pathetic-constructive contrast to the same economic anarchy of which calculation, as an abstract law dealing with accident, is itself a part. Especially before the French Revolution, when the mass of small and medium-sized individual entrepreneurs was still not emancipated, when the period of manufacture established a general, comprehensive regulating bureaucracy, the planned design succeeded, the checkerboard, the ring—in brief, a formal urban calculation of planning and new foundation. All this, no matter how wild the cartouche bulged from a certain building, no matter how bold the group of buildings placed along the winding *veduta*: the ground plan of the individual Baroque building was as symmetrical as the designed group of buildings. Here the Versaille garden and Descartes reigned, not Galli-Bibiena; only rococo suspended that symmetry. The checkerboard design of a Baroque foundation like Mannheim stood in contrast to the organic-excessive style of Baroque architecture in an almost non-synchronous, almost classical way. Goethe, who otherwise despised the Baroque style, said in *Hermann und Dorothea* that the Mannheim layout was built bright and friendly. This was the same tension that was in the cultivated conversations of Baroque society itself: the most interesting topic was human passions, and there was only one competitor: the interest in mathematics. The engineer who built fortresses joined with the architects of castles and churches: many of the major Baroque architects, Hildebrandt, Balthasar Neumann, Welsch, Eosander, came from the field of functional military buildings, and they kept on managing these areas along with their architectural fantasies. The Baroque style amazingly tolerated that simultaneity of inebriation and bourgeois calculation, of Counter-Reformation and military geometry; the latter succeeded as a recourse to Renaissance patterns primarily in city planning. Here we find the same contrast everywhere that also contained the mechanization of the conception of the world culminating in the seventeenth century toward the excessive, organic Baroque ornament. Certainly the mathematics of that era was also a dynamic one, the concept of the mathematical function pervaded, the fluxion and differential calculus, the *veduta* of something infinite. But in Descartes, as in Spinoza, the conception of the world itself was inorganic, basically a mechanical one; thus the Baroque philosophy reigned also in the construction plan with crystal clarity if possible, *more geometrico*. Hence, next to the organic redundancy in sculpture, architecture, and also poetry, the mathematical facade rose, i.e., clarity, i.e., the crystal. Yes, we might say that next to the "Gothic style" of Baroque construction stood the "Egypt" of the intellectual Baroque (*Denkbarock*), most strikingly in Spinozism. These crystal structures connected very easily with all tendencies for order, the Hispanizations in neo-feudal Baroque. That is even revealed in the differences of the utopian architectures as they occurred in the novels dealing with state concepts (*Staatsromanen*) of the Renaissance and then in those of the Baroque. While the liberal social utopia of Thomas More decorated its superior state with individual houses, with low buildings, with loose garden cities, one hundred years later Campanella's authoritarian utopia displayed apartment houses, high-rises, a completely centralized city plan. Here—with concentric walls, with cosmic wall frescoes, with circular structures in general— the mathematical exact measure as such prevailed, in consequence of the other, even astrologically determined utopia of order (*Ordnungs-utopie*). But beyond that, ever since the city planning of the Baroque, the overall geometrical became the keyword of each bourgeois ideal city and has remained the calculated city. This is true except for those eras that did not know any city planning at all anymore, i.e., the second half of the nineteenth century, when city planning was not only thwarted by individual profiteering but completely abolished. Nevertheless, until then and again in the monopoly capitalist period, in a so-called controlled, imperialist economy, a cult of regular structures, buildings, and urban maps bordering the Egyptian reigned over and over again. At the same time it excluded, except for some swerving luxury in the streets of the fashionable residential districts, any contact with the Gothic urban map, with the crooked-ness, with the deeply comfortable fullness of the old German towns. The bonds that were not provided by the capitalist society were meant to be replaced or newly created by the geometry of the city. Now that geometry became the *utopia of the entire newer bourgeois city structure*. That will immediately become clear when we examine individual cases of some of its significant examples. On the whole, these examples contain the contrast to the economy of accident, namely, with an increasing anarchy of the latter, but these examples equally and increasingly contain the apologetic affirmation of their alienation and soullessness. In the best of cases, i.e., solely in the program external to the uncovering realization, they contain the *problem* of a crystal city (*Stadtkristall*) behind which the concrete order—the order applied to what?—presses through or is still hidden.

Thus there was definitely a search to give a clearer frame to the unorderly life. The earliest design of this kind was created in 1505 by Fra Giocondo: the ideal city is circular; in the middle is a round square with dome constructions, and from this square the streets are radially arranged. In 1593, Scamozzi, the architect of the Proc-uracy on St. Mark's Square, designed a regular urban polygon (*Stadtpolygon*) with corresponding gates, with equal halves and quarters—Palma Nuova near Udine was later built that way. In 1598, in Vasari il Giovane's work the *Citta Ideale* became a combina-tion of rectangular and radial structures: in the middle is the main square with axial buildings; eight radially arranged streets start from there with gates as their aims. Other streets are arranged in a rect-angular network. Piranesi (1720–1778), who was only appreciated much too long as the etcher of Roman ruins, used early classicism to provide the ideal city, not only in its design but also in its streets of houses and its decorations, with the symmetry that became increas-ingly absent in bourgeois society. Soviet architecture even adapted certain elements and city planning utopias of Piranesi—the Soviet architect Sidorov called him "penseur dans la domaine de l'archi-tecture"—particularly arcades and public squares, tower structures and the proportion of heights. Maybe the most peculiar designer of futurist settlements that can be found in all of utopian architecture is the French revolutionary architect Ledoux, who has only today been fully appreciated (see Kaufmann, *Von Ledoux bis Corbusier* [*From Ledoux to Corbusier*], 1933). He did not make classicism as representative as the Empire style did, but he made it more multifarious. Ledoux (1736–1806) designed the ideal city Chaux, namely, *a priori* as a community structured by vocations. Thus the building formation is broken up into smaller groups, and it is integrated at the same time; the modern pavilion system appeared. Instead of an inner city formation and endless peripheries, Ledoux designed park areas everywhere with work centers and the "corresponding architecture," which expressed their utilization. The ideal city contained various types of buildings in accordance with the vocations of their dwellers—the houses of the lumberjack, of the field guard, of the merchant, and so on. The ideal city even contained a "house of passions"—a kind of temple of sexual emancipation—a "house for the glory of the women," a "house of harmony." But with the geometry, with the stereometry of these houses the relative partitioning has its limitations; superior to the partitioning is the characteristic utopia of order in all modern age city planning. The geometric allegory, which Ledoux bestowed on his constructions, pointed to this kind of utopia of order as a geometrically directed, persuasively Egyptian one. Therefore, despite the pavilion system, a military geometry predominated that recalls Campanella's city, where not even the astrological allusions were missing. The woodcutter dwelt under a pyramidal roof, the field guard in a spherical house that depicted the globe, the "ville naissante" as a whole was surrounded by an ellipse corresponding to the planetary orbits. In this way the pathos of the bond emerged in Ledoux's ideal city too—and in a surprisingly anticipatory way amidst the French Revolution. Ledoux called the architect "God's rival"; that is a tremendous self-consciousness of human creation; but the world that he wants to form in such a Promethean way nestles within the orders of a cosmos that is seen as complete, namely, as a geometrically complete one. Just as Piranesi connected classicistic motifs with the ideal urban geometry, Ledoux took Masonic-Egyptian ones: their content was a utopian collectivity, though he himself was stuck in the body of a crystalline, much too crystalline urban utopia. The "tuning in with the cosmos," which in the works of Taut and Corbusier still arched over the purpose of human architecture and its shapes, this secular astral myth that was touched not only in phrases but also in the idolatry of an external frame, thus in the urban utopias, demonstrated to the entire modern age its effectiveness. Within the *capitalist calculation* it demonstrated its effectiveness mathematically. In the *feeling contrasting the increasing anarchy of economy and culture* it demonstrated its effectiveness based on sentimentality. Therefore, it resulted in the attraction toward the crystal as the closest contrasting strictness, resulted in addition to calculation and calculus in the power of geometry, which at least seemed to be stripped of spreading human confusion. Moreover, recently there is a particularly alienating motive, which is basically the *only original* one. It is *engineering as architecture*, which has a significant utopian effect. Now it is engineering into which architecture as the real art has been incorporated and from which it has to reemerge on the threshold of a concrete society. What it means here is the new combination of the old utopia of crystallization with the *desire to disorganize*. This kind of combination is precisely related to the abstract technology itself with which the new architecture is so closely linked and provides also disorganization *sui generis* for the crystalline urban utopia, which is a disorganization well-known from neighboring technological areas. Thus the house without an aura, the city map made of affirmed lifelessness and distance to people, made from cones of rays as such or other imitations of projective geometry, corresponds to the machine that no longer resembles the human being. Functional architecture reflects and doubles anyway the icy realm of commodity world automation, its alienation, its labor-divided human beings, its abstract technology. As much as technology might possibly advance into the non-Euclidian, architectural space demonstrates, insofar as it advances into "abstract" composition—particularly in glass structures—the unmistakable ambition to depict empirically an imaginary space. Expressionism experimented with it by generating stereometric figures through rotating or swinging bodies, which at least have nothing in common with the perspective visual space (*Sehraum*); an architecture of the abstract, which wants to be quasi-meta-cubic, sometimes seeks structures appearing to be similarly remote, not organic anymore, not even anymore meso-cosmical. Of course, the space of these bodies of rotation remains as Euclidian as any other, and the so-called un-Euclidian pan-geometry (see Panofsky, *Vorträge der Bibliothek Warburg*, [*Lectures of the Warburg Library*], 1927, p. 330) provides positive ways for architecture also in the symbolic allusions. The only thing that remains important is that the crystalline dominates in all city planning since the Renaissance including that of the otherwise organically drifting Baroque. It seeks cosmic connections, but it also looks for some daring of extra-organic remoteness, although—as is in technology—still without any material contact despite all the "turning in with the cosmos." Nevertheless, in those instances where expressionism did not only, as it so often did, throw excess of pure subjectivity into the void, it experimented also with the problems of object-like, highly abstract forms of the works, which provided profound expression for the human subject, a "forest of the crystal ego" (*Ichkristallwald*). In a more certain and legitimate way, i.e., connected with a still rising bourgeois society, mannerism not only confronted the Baroque with the utmost subjectivity of "mood" and expression and simultaneously contrasted it with the strongest boldness in statuary modeling (Correggio, Tintoretto, El Greco, but also as early as Michelangelo) but drove the latter into the Baroque. And today, as is already well-known, the incredible problems of a *"Gothic style" within the crystal* arises, in a way as if the entire nature of the crystal in spatial art (*Raumkunst*), instead of eventually only leading into the Egyptian clarity of death, *malgré lui*, was a particularly keenly darting humanity. Therefore, as an upshot, or better as the problem of an upshot, we have: *How can human fullness be rebuilt in clarity? How can the order of an architectonic crystal be penetrated with the true tree of life, with the human ornament?* A synthesis between the architectural utopia of Egypt, on the one hand, and Gothic, on the other, is impossible; it would be a foolish, epigonal fantasy. But there is a genuine third possibility, which has not appeared anywhere yet, above rigidity and exuberance, in housing projects as well as in architecture. Just this is the power of Marxism to posit order as the end so that human fullness gains space. In Marxism the contents, which emerged in all former abstract social utopias in alternative ways, i.e., subjective freedom (More) or constructed order (Campanella), are mediated not synthetically but rather productively and thus raised to a third, the constructed realm of freedom itself. Also in regard to the orders of nature, Marxism is far away from subjectless-undialectical depiction, hence from that "tuning in with the cosmos." The concrete tendency is rather the humanization of nature. Thus the space architecture of a classless society will hardly remain abstract crystalline, in contrast to the anarchy of the ecomony (which then will have vanished). In the old city plannings, in the works of Piranesi and Ledoux, a sense for space occurs sometimes, a completely new one although classicistically encapsulated. Yet, it leaves abstract crystal form or those devoid of people far behind. A non-formalistic glass sculpture or glass architecture also reaches, as mentioned before, into unknown forms of construction at times, forms of space. They penetrate in there, curious curves and stereometries penetrate with a seemingly cosmic expression, but in reality it is human. Here the human sense of anticipation starts from the center of the crystal, perhaps mediated by it but certainly only through it. This sense of anticipation starts with an extroversion toward the cosmos; however, in its bend backward, it moves *to the lineament of a home*. Architecture as such is and remains the attempt to produce the human home—from the given purpose of dwelling to the appearance of a more beautiful world of proportion and ornament. According to Hegel's truthful and not only idealistic definition, achitecture sees its purpose in shaping inorganic nature in a way that it as an artistic outside world becomes kin to the spirit. The spirit means the human subject, which is still searching for what can be called related to it. In different societies this subject (*Wesen*) always builds different corners, arches, domes, towers of an earth that focused on the human being. Thus the architectural utopia is the beginning and the end of a— geographic utopia itself, all this search for precious stones on the face of the geode Earth, the dream of an earthly paradise. Great architecture wanted to present itself as a constructed Arcadia and even more. And if it carried something mournful, some tragic mystery, as in the Gothic style, it was only to bring it to the difficult euphony. Might is the wealth derived from a few basic elements, mighty the alternative between a columned hall in Karnak and Sainte Chapelle in Paris, between our picture of home here, truss and light there. But protective circle, pre-built home: *that is what the basic outlines of a better world mean in respect to their realization in architecture.* Here the aesthetic figure emerges as an encircling one, in such a form that all other fine art forms have their place and rank in it: the paintings on the wall, the sculptures in the niche. The encircling provides home or comes in contact with it: all great constructions were *sui generis* built into the utopia, into the anticipation of a space adequate for human beings. And the thus erected humanity transposed to rigidly significant spatial form is, as a task, equally a moving of the organic, of the humane into the crystal as well as and above all the penetration of the

crystalline with stimulus, humanity, and fullness. When the conditions of the order of freedom are not partial anymore, then the path
will finally be open again for the unity of physical construction and
organic ornament, open to the gift of the ornament. The path will be
really open for the first time without having to alternate, to mix or to
isolate time and again that which—no Egypt here, no Gothic there—
is termed the crystal or the tree of life. The crystal is the frame.
Indeed, it is the horizon of peace, but the ornament of the human tree
of life is the only real content of that overall peace and clarity. The
better world that the great architecture forms and depicts in an
anticipatory way consists of the stones of life as a real task *vivis ex
lapidibus.*

# On Fine Arts in the Machine Age

1. It is certain that we do not suffer anymore from plush. Rather we suffer from a little too much glass and steel and from a little too little of that which decorates. But whenever there is too much decoration, and when that occurred, too much, much too much was covered over and made terribly slick and ostentatious. For not only in war but more so in the lie, the muses are silent. The semblance purchased in this way always takes shape accordingly. No purchase at all would be more preferable.

2. Dishonest things are kitsch, which we are not lacking even today. Its actual source and its souvenir—which still exists for the Russians up till today—was the German *Gründerzeit* after 1871. These were the times of plush, although it was already a machine age. But it was the era that was least willing to acknowledge that it was much more masked with a lot of stolen pomp, funny and uncanny, from earlier days. A lot of doilies everywhere, floating portières, including buffets that looked like castles and next to them leaning halberds with thermometers in the shafts. The women around were like Gretchen at the court theater and Franz Lenbach painted the directors according to rank as if his name were Tintoretto. On the outside, where one at least could not build without iron, especially at train stations, the parallels were Gothic chapters on top of cast iron columns; even an already completely finished steel construction of the halls, as, for example, the Frankfurt central station, had a portal of a palace á la Palladio built in front of it—lies everywhere.

3. Enough of that. The change that is brought about is, as is well known, swift. Hoijotoho does not have the odor of the wide world

anymore, and also the Stalin style has run its course. For a long time the functional form held sway, from van de Velde, Frank Lloyd Wright to Corbusier. The scabby and ulcer-like ornaments, as Adolf Loos called them, fell off. They could not be pasted back on again, and the plain transportation box or egg box as the building, which had "Hurrah, nothing comes to our minds anymore!" as its only head decoration, does not have to be the final word against the former scab. It does not have to be the final word in regard to the peculiar *interweaving* (*Ineinander*) that our era shows—seemingly unconnected —in its technical-architectural *cool reservations* (*Kühlungen*), but then also in its picturesque-sculptural *fantasies*. There was a hypocrisy of the New Sobriety (*Neue Sachlichkeit*). There was and is a pure functional form reified to be a goal in itself. In architecture there was and is an iconoclasm against the ornament unheard of thus far. And in spite of this: Paul Klee was teaching right then at the Bauhaus, and simultaneously, on a much wider scale, the Folkwang Museum in Essen opened with a clarity all around, full of a lot of expressionism, with congenial folklore and exoticism. But not only at the same time but also in the same space, so to speak; how strangely does a new world of pictures and sculptures go together with tubular steel chairs and concrete walls, throwing out all ornaments from the functional space (*Gebrauchsraum*) and having purely ornamental objects in frames and on pedestals that are completely devoid of luxury. Thus the *ad hoc* ordered Chagall painting in the steel and glass lobby of the new Frankfurt theater appears to be the least inappropriate thing. And it is really not the masquerade as once had been the plush halberd wrapped arround a thermometer or also like the Renaissance portal to hide the railroad tracks.

4. What is it then that appeals to us differently, that lets torches burn in today's water? It is obviously not downright masquerade or even double-entry bookkeeping. Even the snobbish philistine cannot expect any improvement, anything decorative from Franz Marc to Max Ernst, from Archipenko to Henry Moore. Although something that might link technology with the new shock of the arts is decisively very different from that which was the homogeneous and uniting former style. That was when the most simple tool was as beautifully built as the most precious one, when the lace cap of a Burgundian noble lady looked equally Gothic as a pinnacle at a cathedral, when

a stroke of writing was as Baroque as a volute, and when the bow of notables to each other showed the same form as the exterior flight of stairs in front of an *ancien régime* palace. All that was gone in the hiatus between the functional form and the expressive exuberance, also gone if one set one's mind at ease by thinking that a stylistic image of our time is a pluralistic one (and thus reducing the antagonisms to dust). It would be more true to address the style of this epoch, also the bourgeois style in transformation and particularly this one, as the international train station style. But that is not sufficient for the given, highly paradoxical analogy between glass house and ultraviolet; then both would be only dissolved for the sake of departure, even for its own sake. Instead, it is true for both at least as a task and their problem: march separately, fight in unity. Thus, instead of a dualism, the perspective of a possible division of labor between the technological-anonymous and the visionary-articulate arises, arises in the open space ahead.

5. In the past, the external life was more beautiful for some people, but also then it was certainly not more comfortable. There is no need to talk about the difference between the pinewood torch and the light bulb. That difference is representative for all improvements of this kind. There is no doubt that the technological age has caused a lot of damage in bodies, lives, peace, and nature, and not only because it is still badly administered. It outgrows the people and provides them with total lethal weapons for their antagonisms, but nevertheless, during times of peace, the technological age is the least alien to relief. The iron works painted by Adolf Menzel look more grim than the modern factory, and the stagecoach is closer to the discomforts of the stone age than the automobile, a very recent invention, to the discomforts of the stagecoach. To be exact: *relief from the unessential* was approached in a technological way. Thus, the question was posed, what if by this a specific *space of expression of the essential* would have been opened up, a space freed from all luxury dealing with the unessential? Are not the relief and artistic novelty that have been brought about variables of the same exodus? Thus, are they not far beyond the mere train station style, at least in the long-distance train and the abstract perspective of the best paintings? Hence there is a place for art works that—according to a phrase of the *Blaue Reiter* around 1910—are no longer *objets d'art* but expressions, or rather,

visible-invisible expeditions toward the essential. During expressionism that kind lived beyond its means, but during the entire period of a denatured way of the arts there was and is enough swindling of mere explosion. That was no different than any other epoch of change, thus the more during a period of transformation that came so abruptly. This transformation could hardly have brought about relief and pushed off itself into the detached without the aspired, the ornament-free sobriety of the dwelling-machine. This happened even with protest from the former ensemble of culture, one that had with increasing necessity become imitational. Therefore, the answer to the old ornamental task of the arts brought painting and sculpture totally to the locus of the exodus of the heresy—which is exactly the heresy of the essential.

As mentioned, for the present the new houses are, without any ornaments, very dismal. Here little is left that is in harmony with the fullness, even the rigidity of the old architecture. Glass and steel make things pale instead of causing them to flourish. But it is rather the beginning of something different from the demise of great old things. The actual end of architecture was not brought by the engineer but rather by the Wilhelminian times. It declined in Wallot's *Reichstag* building, not in the relief without decoration, even if it was for the time being a very monotonous relief. But that which marches along on a separate way, i.e., the new painting and the new sculpture, despite all the inherent imagination, and perhaps because of all that imagination, is said to be the "end of all art." That, of course, if it is said in such a general way, has already and always been the battle cry of stagnation, uttered by those whose own minds came to a standstill. They are the ones who called for Bruckner when Schoenberg was played and who were the calves of those cows who called for Haydn when Bruckner had been played for the first time. Thus they are the people who react and who, on a theoretical terrain, were characterized almost analogously by Lichtenberg, who stated that when Pythagoras found the theorem that is named after him, he made a sacrifice of one hundred oxen to the gods; since then all oxen tremble when a new theorem is dis-covered. This is the case also with "the end of all art," if used in an ironic way and given a totally different meaning. Why should Franz Marc's, Kandinsky's *Blaue Reiter* not have had the right more than half a century ago, instead of going down the customary main road that had become a matter of imitation, to go down a narrow one that had until then been insignificant in order to turn it, as one used to say, into the new main road? The end of art in Klee's *Angelus novus*, in Max Ernst's *Zitadelle*—these cipher formations are rather the end of that museum supplement within the regular cultural perspective that is ranked and arranged in a culinary way. Such an end might be the beginning of information that pours light even onto the pictures of the old great days, which have become unrepeatable and inimitable. And the light might pour through their decayed excellence. And such an end causes, aside from that, also the cleansing of Homer and Goethe from the red pedantic teacher in favor of the classicism that is to be recited in an *open* way. So much here for the significant new area that happened or might happen to a self-repellant art since the technological relief pulled away from the reified gala perspective, from the historical gallery tone. Thus the new area made the new cipher formation of the essential to be the only task that was still artistic, still novel.

6. In the process there is no lack of more related ways, divided and yet viewing each other. The workbench cannot teach an old authority on art, but more than ever can it teach an artist. To make, to create, the new environment of this new making and its framework might be used abundantly by the new arts, even for very different reasons. Even material stemming from the past was discovered and used in this way, the ball of wire, the ribbed iron cast around cavities. But first of all the framework itself had been inscribed into the blueprint of the body that has been purely organic until now, or it had been written on the body. And a different nature took place more so in landscape painting, technically wounded as well as rebuilt, still with the decline in spirit, with the attempted distillation of rivers, mountains, plains, turning them into a pure linear creation in the sense of a map. It is not so rare that behind all this stands the reconstruction of the planet earth, with a crystal clear intention in the sense of the quite rational "city crowns" (*Stadtkronen*), the "planetariums" by Taut and Scheerbart. Thus in the sense of crystal formations, in this case of the architectural kind, and obligated to the new stereometries of the functional form with a fantastic sudden change. Furthermore, the artistic montage was derived from modern technology as a device in a world not at all complete anymore or unmistakably stratified. In

this sense the montage was used, the exchange of parts and elements from one ensemble with those from another. All that which was well arranged was broken up, cancelled, slanted. It was an exchange that was known thus far only in the grotesque, but now this exchange stretches from the early photo paste-up (photo montage) to the most abrupt use of alienation by Brecht, which seems to come from some totally other place. Something far-near, near-far spellbound in Chirico's uncanny still life at the fireplace, to the left a billow rolling into the room, to the right the jungle as a wall. That which is in close approximation in the experienced reality and in regular nature is thus separated by many miles through montage. That which is many miles apart is moved together and inscribed on the plane of the picture through montage. Something analogous happened with Joyce in literature; i.e., one day in the life of the advertisement salesman Bloom equals 24 years of Odysseus. Also the docks in London's Eastend and temple courts of India glittering with water fountains change places; they also have their intersection at the same place, as interchangeable concordance. Accordingly the specifics of modern technology also effect the artistic rendering in a manifold way, particularly when the latter is not only experimenting in a subjective way but has to meet the requirements of such a described spellbound reality. All this is done so that our world, within what is essential at the present, is infused with horror and hope, half in pieces, half a figure, which first forms itself in the frame in a concrete significant way or comes on the pedestal.

7. But certainly the ways of making remain: here inventive, there formative, and in all of that different again. The artificial is not the artistic, and the tubular steel chair gave a free pass to the picture shock (*Bildschock*) to be sure, but certainly not the password. Moreover, the basic beginnings in Marc's and Kandinsky's *Blaue Reiter* were still rustic and exotic, not urban-industrial. And the creative subject, which continues to set in expressively beyond the relief, was more the inner room for a long time, the musical inwardness that drapes the visible more than the technical external cunning. But the machine age, which let the fine arts be repelled, was nevertheless presupposed, for the exterior of another, which did not exist at all, of a dimension that resounded specifically in a subjective manner. The objects themselves could thus appear artistically as the dwellers of

their own inner country, as the "disguised ornaments of our innermost figure." And especially toward the cosmic side of the objects the external world was first of all denatured so that the outward would equally appear as the inward. That is precisely why the relation of the fine arts to nature, despite all subjectivity, was never as unfriendly as modern technology. In contrast, a Goethean "naturalization" (*Naturierendes*), even an allegorical-ornamental "forest of ego crystals," as a world of expression is obviously alien to such technology. Ever since Galileo there has been no natural science, and thus technologically—despite all "formalizing"—no conceivable "signatura rerum." Even in abstract painting a tuning into the figurative is unavoidable, even if one does not associate it with Marc's "organic" pantheism. The result is the constant creation of ciphers, i.e., the dissecting, blending, mutual illuminating of things, that puzzles as well as wants to point toward something: toward ornaments without ornamentation, toward written pictures, toward objects as if made from signatures. That comes unexpectedly in succession to the Shakespearean phrase "The artist gives a tongue to the trees, finds writing in the brook" (whereby the tongue is just as expressive as writing that finds, copies, and makes the cipher emblematic). But also there, the cipher itself figures as one that points further ahead, that gives further meaning in a world that is unfinished and open. Thus this new kind of honest pictorial information is not only, as is certainly often the case, made out of inefficiency, but also from an open horizon that is charged with the not-yet and with what is only possible. Let us close by staying with the self-understanding of such artists themselves and by quoting the Russian-American sculptor Gabo, *What way beyond the machine age*: "If this art should survive any longer period of time, or if this art should grow into something which might be taken as important by the coming age as the old arts were for their age, then this is only attainable if the artist of the future is able to manifest in his medium a new imago, in painting or in sculpture, so that it expresses the true spirit of what the present mind tries to create and what will be the receiving imago of life in the universe." Or, as Franz Marc expressed it in much simpler terms, devoted in a utopian sense to the exodus of the imago as well as to the imago of the exodus, "Painting is our surfacing at some other place."

# On the Present in Literature

If you want me to show you the vicinity, you must first climb to the roof.
Goethe, *Westöstlicher Diwan* (*The West-East Divan*)


For the Day

It is easy to live for the day. All lazybones do that and legitimately those who have finally taken a rest and enjoy in a relaxed way what is offered to them. The more eventful the better since then it is easy to forget what happened before and since unconnected impressions can be grasped in a particularly fresh way, in a virtually raw way. And in the same way as one might live for the moment, although distracted and in a completely fleeting way, in a completely superficial way, one might write oneself equally easily and superficially into the day without worrying. Then, too, we pick and discard, every day anew and wilting whatever might happen during the day's events. If this kind of day-picking was not effortless, then there would not be that many newly written newspapers. However, good things take time and some of it has to be in the newspapers, at least in those that are not filled with clichés. And taking time lets you gain distance from a thing in order to see it better.

A Shadow Due to Lack of Distance

For without distance, right within, you cannot even experience something; not to speak of representing it, to present it in a right way—

which simultaneously has to provide a general view. In general it is like this: all nearness makes matters difficult, and if it is too close, then one is blinded, at least made mute. This is, however, only in a strict sense true for a precise, on-the-spot experience, for the immediate moment that is still in the dark as a "right-now" that is lacking all distance. But this darkness of the moment, in its unique directness, is not true for an already more mediated right-now, which is of a different kind and which is a specific experience called "present," be it at home, in public, in the political arena, and so on. Nevertheless, something of the darkness of the immediate nearness is conveyed—if the difference has become clear—to the more mediated, more widespread present by necessity, i.e., an increased difficulty to represent it (in comparison with the portrayal of times long since gone, of past blocks of time). By not seeing the difficulty, precisely as one of the battlefront, it does not disappear. On the contrary, then one misses that which is the most important thing: to begin to transcend that difficulty of nearness in a Marxist way. We are talking about *portraying*, as mentioned before, not about recalling and for the moment not even about the analysis of the situation and the action determined by the need of the moment, directed and made possible by this analysis, which is a Marxist one. We are talking about an actual *formed portion of time (Zeitstück geformter Art)*. Today such a portion of time presupposes more precisely than ever an established analysis of the situation; both certainly do not coincide. Only non-artists, although they are writing, do not notice any difficulty in regard to nearness to the very end, and also young artists, in the beginning, certainly do not notice the shadow due to a lack of distance when they, in a truly revolutionary mood, declare war on their era, or, even on the contrary, when they are absolutely positive about a good, emerging era. When the 25-year-old Mayakovsky gave a copy of *War and Peace* to the 28-year-old Prokofiev for a trip and wrote in the book, "To the chairman of the music section of the universe—by the chairman of the poetry section of the universe," then a proud *Sturm und Drang* coincided wonderfully, closely related, and appropriate to a new era. But the problem of the concrete right-now never ceased to be relevant in the long run. In the area of landscape painting, this problem meant, Where does the "foreground" end, and where does the "landscape" begin? In poetry it meant a particularly focused creative power. As we shall see, it requires very specific means for its artistic realization, which are critical or utopian or combine both. If the actual material in its dimension was enormous, if it was progressive only at a heavy cost, then temporal distance to it was always the case. Even novels about World War I, which were only halfway broad enough, needed a distance of about ten years from the time of the war. *War and Peace*, the most comprehensive *period novel* (*Zeitroman*) of them all, needed a distance of half a century from the events to be so fresh and to have such little resemblance to a "historical novel." But then there was also *Anna Karenina* simultaneous with its material. Actually, in the past there was a relatively large number of excellent simultaneous novellas, novels, plays. However, the difficulty of nearness existed for them, too, and always made it difficult, although the degree of difficulty varied according to the writer's intensity, according to the power and the transparency of the social material. Nevertheless, even a moderate picture of the present had an effect, and an important one like *Simplicius Simplicissimus* did not need a lot of distance to be a mirror for the Thirty Years' War and the postwar period, even to laugh about it. "Grab right into the full flow of human life, and whatever you grab, you'll find it interesting." This maxim, which is not only realistic but quite conscious of how to make use of its time, is a very smart one. Not only the frail form of the present period novels proves that but also the opulent form of the past ones. With regard to this point: in which cases does nearness make it more difficult to be creative and by what means has that difficulty been so strikingly overcome in many cases? What attitudes of a writer and which conditions of something actually present have to be especially developed and recognized so that the nearness might even give wings to the work? Particularly the latter is the question now. Let us examine our affairs. Poetry is not entirely within the hollow space (*Hohlraum*) of the past.

## Listen to the Actual Pulse

Writing in keeping with the times is not the same as writing according to life. Since many people, who seem to listen to the actual pulse, have only heard what was marketable, not what was really going on. And only because those writers depicted widely held beliefs instead of real matters could an illusion of a period novel originate among readers, in an entertaining sense perhaps, but certainly short-lived. We are still not talking about the little scribblers. They would have even failed with the non-actual matters. Therefore, they are not part of the problem. Looking at past writers whose names have lasted, like Gutzkow, Spielhagen, Freytag, who failed in the period novel, which they had particularly cultivated, it is not their second or third rank talent that is worth considering but mainly that which might have been urgent to them and which they, due to their semi-talents, did not notice, did not use, did not shape. Gutzkow always wrote period novels in nine volumes (*Die Ritter vom Geiste*, 1850, *Der Zauberer von Rom*, 1858); Spielhagen was an equally liberal, up-to-date fighter (*Problematische Naturen*, 1860); Freytag was only liberal (*Soll und Haben*, 1860), with a social purpose, so to speak, "seeking the German people at work" (minus the workers, being himself a craftsman). All that turned out more than mediocre, already far worse than the actual novels of Immermann (*Die Epigonen*, 1836, and the more important *Münchhausen*, 1838), who very belatedly tried to emulate nothing less than Goethe's form. Gutzkow, Spielhagen, and Freytag tried that, too, in a doubly epigonal way. Immermann, being stronger, could merely show a mediocre, mostly unclear picture of his days, although it elucidated at the same time how such failure could be relatively independent, as mentioned before, of the formal size of the talent and even from the greatness (viability, transparence) of the material of the era itself. Obviously an era of social upswing provides more fruitful material than one of social decline, although life runs faster in the latter case, hence more likely escapes the view of the observer. It is equally obvious that mature, well-developed epochs contain certain "foregrounds," and to make matters easier, already as "landscapes." Therefore, they are workable on the spot as subject matter and thus portrayable. Freytag, during the empty era of German capitalist philistinism, conformed to this era, being a philistine himself, and there was nothing anyway that could detract from the superficiality of banal everyday life. But Immermann, who was not a philistine and who wanted to be close to the great spirit of classicism, saw quite explosive matters around him in the German bourgeois life of his times: smoking chimneys, the start of industrialization, a monstrous bourgeoisie along with the narrow-mindedness and reactionary attitude of Prussian feudalism. He described the literary epigonism of his era, in which the group *Junges Deutschland* (Young Germany) and even better were at the same time in revolt. This was the period when Herwegh's dictum—the days of pure poetry are over, now is the time

of aspiration—could already be heard. Nevertheless, despite his com-
plaints, Immermann, *mutatis mutandis* like Raabe later, did not get far
beyond the atmosphere of morbidity around him, not far beyond the
romantic, anti-capitalist externalized images of the capitalist "spirit
of deception," of the feudal "putrescence." "Who will be able to
name the current in which our day's vessel travels," Immermann
exclaimed in one of the reflections inserted into *Münchhausen*. But
there was also the lack of insight into the social sciences, which did not
exist at that time, that prevented one from making changes within
such "currents." For even the great Balzac, in the middle of France's
highly developed capitalism, did not understand the "current" as is
known. He was not even a romantic anti-capitalist but simply a
reactionary anti-capitalist, who sided with the Tories, although he
was against the usurers and the hyenas of post-revolutionary France.
However, he was not confronted with a bourgeoisie that, as was the
case in Germany of the same time, slowly remodeled itself from the
philistine (*Spiessbürger*) of the declining system of guilds into the
capitalist philistine. Thus there was no reason for a real romantic
protest by the artist. That is all the more reason why Balzac's incomparable art of painting the attitude of *Enrichissez-vous* (Enrich yourself) was helped by two resources that were also effective at a time
when a Marxist analysis of the situation, or analysis of the "current,"
could not be applied. These resources were *criticism to the point of satire*
and *humane utopia*; both in fact were resources not just as mere subjective additives but at their best as the detected ingredients within the
social reality itself. In a pre-Marxist sense, these resources brought
about the possibility to be within that world, to exist in close creative
presence, with a Balzacian "landscape," in which the still immediate
"foreground," and especially this one, does not appear as something
external but already with instances that point out what is important.
Needless to say, this kind of reading into those mediated important
instances in Freytag's dabbling with foregrounds and his embellishments is completely missing (and today we find even worse examples
in the present novels dealing with the East, clumsy and trashy at the
same time). Something that is grasped satirically enables the reader
to see clearly that which is close; something that is grasped in a
utopian way, the measure for the satirical that saves it from being the
sole measure, enables the reader to have a wide, full, complementary-
whole view also within the closeness. The fruit of such pre-Marxist

mastery of existence (*Seinsmächtigkeit*) within poetry might be classified under what one calls critical realism. However, by real one
cannot mean the foreground and less so the totality of all foregrounds,
but essentially the current, the landscape of the stream that is unveiled by this situational picture in this point in time itself. This is
true, even when the anatomy and physiology of the material of the
period made possible by Marxism (so that it can be absorbed in a
genetically mediated way) is still missing.

It was due to this double grasping that closeness was not always
difficult. That was particularly true in bourgeois poetry that did not
flee the present at all. There are plenty of great period pieces. Of
course, they are illuminating and penetrating to different degrees,
but all of them do away with the flat dimension of reality. They give
shape to the essential characteristics of the figures. They open up plots
that carry on, that are pushed in a poetical way toward a decision.
They pour the light, which often exists only in an idealistic sense and
which is therefore not available over indicated inadequacies and
against them. This is true for the novel as well as for the drama. Only
the patina that some of these works have acquired prevents us from
seeing them as what they had totally been during their time—their
relevance in time also as material. The more recent series includes, to
name the most concise *Recherches du temps actuel*, the period pieces of the
*Sturm und Drang*, the exemplary *Wilhelm Meister*, Balzac, Stendhal and
Flaubert, Dickens, Dostoievsky and Tolstoy, Gottfried Keller, the
experimentalist Robert Musil, and Thomas Mann, the most conscious novelist of the bourgeois present. This is more than just a long,
drawn-out series with enormous differences, but one with a unifying
theme: how to master the present in a poetical way. It also does not
matter in this context whether the average was chosen for that
purpose, as with Dickens, or the extreme, as with Dostoievsky. No
matter what the case was, they all tried to master the present despite
the increasingly stronger limitations within the bourgeois period
novel of the twentieth century, despite increasing criticism, increasing
invocation of the ideal. The socially determined lack of perspective in
the late bourgeois novel brought about even more obstacles in both
cases. This is why Robert Musil and Thomas Mann (in whose works
the revolutionary proletariat is not even marginally visible) endeavored even harder to employ the powers of critical satire and
human utopia. And it was all the more true in the major work of the

bourgeois period novel, in *Wilhelm Meister*, which is as realistic as the genre is capable of such perspective *sui generis*. The analytic understanding of the "fate of the period" (*Zeitschicksal*) is, of course, missing in this instance too. But neither critical satire nor utopia lacked their real counterparts in this novel. The attempted mastering of the present was not possible without the broad involvement with business, and since the bourgeoisie was still rising at this time, there was even an economic education of the people, not just an aesthetic education. This is particularly evident in Novalis' well-known rejection of *Wilhelm Meister*; he called the novel "prosaic and modern" and missed "that which is romantic, the poetry of nature, the miraculous." It is an embittered polemic, but it took its starting point from a romantic designation of the utopian, one that looked backward and from the blue horizon of *Heinrich von Ofterdingen*—a vaguely enhanced Tasso argued once again against Antonio as if *Hic Rhodus hic salta* were always a betrayal of the dream. Yet, it was much more true that the utopian element of *Wilhelm Meister* (together with the closely related idealistic one) not only wanted to have wings but also soles, and according to Bacon's advice, both elements wanted some lead in them so that the idealistic in particular could stand in this world, take effect, and be mediated. The actual world in *Wilhelm Meister* is certainly limited, even filtered. One cannot find material problems anywhere. Of course, it does not show any plebeian stratum. There are only well-to-do citizens, wealthy nobility in the plot (except for his own dream, the other dream, of the Blue Flower concerning Mignon and Harfner). Therefore, the utopia of an "island," of a "pedagogic province" was at least in the beginning or *expressis verbis* limited to an elite of the higher estates whose actions and morals were to be promoted. However, as mentioned before, this did not happen without real resistance by the existing elements, namely, in a Germany that was no longer backward in a capitalist way but could nevertheless remain corroded by its feudal conditions. At any rate, all pertinent criticism of those times, especially in *Wilhelm Meister*, stemmed from a consciousness of a possible better world and everything tenable in this consciousness was derived from actual tendencies, at least from those with a lasting effect of the *citoyen*, although they had been cut off. There was already a lot of Saint-Simonism inherent in *Wilhelm Meister* when Goethe interpreted the actual tendencies as leading toward industry and simultaneously had them strive toward moral and intellectual organizations. That was not only in *Wilhelm Meisters Wanderjahre*, i.e., with the medal of social respect, but already *ante rem* in *Wilhelm Meisters Lehrjahre*. Of course, given this example of a period novel in particular, it is clear that satirical criticism and the ideal utopia alone, even when there is a strong feeling for the actual tendencies of the time, no longer suffice to master the present image that has developed since then. Certainly, there are times when the satirical fits in an entirely objective way (which is the meaning of the Juvenal phrase during the Roman empire: *Difficile satiram non scribere*—It is difficult not to write satire), and there are times when the utopian goes all around in an overwhelmingly real way (all *Incipit vita nova* times are like that). Even though our era also belongs to these times saturated with grimaces and the red glow of sunrise, it is the most loath to insert the understanding of the currents that have been finally elaborated, i.e., the *economic, causal analysis of the situation and the tendency*. Only this analysis will have success in turning criticism that has mounted to satire into something truly biting, which is to say, to lead it beneath the surface of the symptoms and to make utopia concrete. As we have seen, only satire and utopia had been the ingredients that made it at all possible for a poetic mastery of the actual foreground, with the landscape of here and now not very far away. However, only Marxism, and above all only the true *Incipit vita nova* period, which coincides with Marxism and whose expression Marxism becomes, eliminates the lack of perspective due to the social circumstances. During the period of the rising bourgeoisie, this lack of perspective only allowed the formation of more or less abstract ideals, also in *Wilhelm Meister*. And at a time when the decline of the bourgeoisie began, when it was still possible for Keller to paint these wonderfully written pictures of his era, with a true or at least seemingly true national democracy and its supposed expectation that was invoked, the work ended in the melancholy of *Martin Salander*. Moreover, the understanding in a class-conscious sense was missing for one to be convinced of a present even behind the symptoms.

Up to now I have been talking about novels, but there is nothing in bourgeois *science* as well that could compare with the truly revealing analysis by which Marx and Engels captured their present, which was almost incapable of being mediated. Historically they did this in the *Eighteenth Brumaire*, philosophically in the *Communist Manifesto*. On the other hand, it is clear that, in the literature with a socialist orientation in our days, there are no comparable parallels that can match their analyses, except for Gorky, the rather lonely real poet (*Realpoeten*) of the vis-à-vis, and later Brecht. In the case of Gorky, this occurred after he became the knowledgeable, involved organizer of the proletarian revolutionary struggle and of the poor Russian peasants. But the political theater of the communist Brecht worked with a shock similar to that of the *Sturm und Drang* period. However, it was more like a cloud-sweeping storm and fury of instruction, alienated and didactic, with the attempt to illuminate the next step to take. Critical satire and utopia gain command of existence (*seinsmächtig*) on a poetic level only through Marxist clarity by becoming part of the poetic process. Here clarity certainly does not sell itself short to become a mere streetlight for the next five-year plan. Rather, clarity cuts off criticism and utopia from directness (*Unmittelbarkeit*), which existed and still exists. Thus, actual song originates, preserving the genius of capability.

## The Specific Now at Different Times

The now (*Jetzt*) moves and propels itself through each day, whenever. It knocks in all that happens, with its shortest time span, and it knocks on the door. But not every present opens up for it. The actual impulses, the socially driving pulses, do not knock in each present fresh and vital. Not every time opens up for the now and the next now that stands exactly at that moment in front of the door and that has never "entered" before. It has not unloaded its true contents with which and toward which it is on its way. These contents have not come yet, other than in fragments, at best in installments of a more fulfilled existence (*Da-Sein*). That which we call the propelling now evidently does not mean anything other than the tendencies within all that exists projected onto and atomized within the course of time. But the "point in time" isolated in this projection begins to show itself tremendously objective in every point that is *historically* labeled, that which in its proximity is not only invisible but also *halting*. Times that are socially and culturally dull crawl along also in their now-proximity, which is then paralyzed, or even suffocated. The subjective reaction to that is boredom, the objective finding is emptiness *in actu*, seemingly immobile and without history. On the other hand, there are the flowering high times of early classicism. It is worthwhile to come into contact with them, with their now, that is to say, actually to ascertain that more fulfilled now of the past. Of course, this is only possible if the specific now-time (*Jetzt-Zeit*), as, for example, our present, is in its actuality congenial to those past openings (*Aufschlagungen*). That is, if it does not stagnate like most of the Victorian, also of the Wilhelmenian, "now-time," if it also is not split up into facets and finally becomes nihilistic, as is our current West German present. In contrast, the link between *enthusiasm* and *partiality*, which takes place only during times of ascent, brings the now-time, which generates enthusiasm and partiality and which is worth it, into connection with other periods of awakening, no matter how long they were in the past and how differently embedded they were within the historical continuum. They become blasted out from that continuum, so to speak. Thus there is something else to be added to the Marxist and scientifically tendentious illumination of proximity, which is an ingredient nonetheless Marxist, that is, the concordance with past times, although times that are actually still present, with their *Tua res agitur, de te fabula naratur*. Thus a view from past times to one's own becomes possible, that is to say, from times that can be objectified, which might nevertheless concern us as a now-time, and hence they concern us and come close to us—Spartacus, Thomas Münzer, but also all formed art works of the past not solely dealt with in a historical sense or even settled in a historical sense. Such traveling along during which we sometimes change our views cannot completely coincide with that which one calls the cultural heritage. Nor does it coincide with the only true heritage (which therefore is not merely contemplative, or even a quotation or from a museum), which has the phrase prescribed that is just as well known as it is still largely undiscovered: "That which you inherited from your fathers,/ Acquire it in order to possess it." Of course, with the really indelible past there is no acquisition at all. Now-time in the past cannot be a possession: it is help and warning. Let the misunderstanding remain far away on the margins, as if the historical novel were a step toward the intended way of thinking, since the historical novel, as is said, revitalizes the past. This means that Howard Fast's *Sparatacus* may make the now-time within the past recognizable, but something like that is not really part of the entertaining historical novels with their antiquated episodes. Most of these novels deal almost exclusively more with escape and decoration than with contemplation. This is true despite or because of the colorful historicist images (*Historismen*) of the prime models provided by Walter Scott or the developmental precision contained as truth in Flaubert's *Salambô*, his most questionable work. This kind of genuine vitalization does not occur because of the writer's moving into a past, into which he must by necessity bring his present, a past that is ultimately almost arbitrary. Rather, he migrates from a past now-time into a pressent of ours and by shaping such past as something indelible.

In this way the difficult closeness becomes especially broadened, indeed, re-illuminated. Even retrogressive companions think, because of the fact that they go backward, that they have something to say in this matter. For Robespierre conjured Aristides as if his remnants were from today. Shortly after there were plenty of imitations of Christian-Germanic knights. And since big capital, which is completely unromantic in itself, had not died yet, they are still living happily today. But the genuine broadening of the now-time does not relate to that as does the original to the counterfeit; the *Montanunion* (The European Coal and Steel Community) as Carolingian Occident is so ridiculously wrong that it does not even imitate genuine points of contact. The concordances of the genuine now-time refer exclusively in form and contents to the future in the past, that which has not become, which is in process. In there we find the repressed, the interrupted, the indelible on which we can in one and the same act fall back upon while it reaches forward to us in order to develop in a better way. "And also the others return in an altered form, the dead return, their deeds want to become at one with us again. Münzer stopped most abruptly, and yet he wanted to go the furthest. Whoever actively studies him has thus the present and that which is definite about it more steady, more observable than in an event that is experienced much too quickly and has not had the steam taken out of it. Above all, Münzer is history in a fruitful sense; he and his cause and all things past that are worth recording are made to obligate us, to enthuse us, to support more and more that which is always meant to be for us" (Bloch, *Thomas Münzer als Theologe der Revolution* [*Thomas Münzer as Theologian of Revolution*], 1921, p. 13). According to this kind of "tradition" all historical concerns want to and can live only in the now-time of history, bear testimony—a warning that comes from searching, getting lost, possibly finding (*Vor-Finden*). All this touches upon the highly significant aperçus Walter Benjamin dedicated to the category of now-time (*Jetztzeit*) in his last works. Here actuality simply becomes a postulate, but, of course, not in the usual sense, chronologically actual sense, but rather in a historical, philosophically accumulative, more striking sense. H. H. Holz demonstrated that correctly by remarking that the real philosophical history is not inscribed into the linear time any longer, but that it is a kind of concentric time that in perspective wraps itself around the present. In Benjamin's words, "And basically it is the same day that reappears in the form of holidays which are days of remembering." The revolutionary, the historical materialist, "leaves it to others to exhaust themselves with the whore called 'once upon a time' in the brothel of historicism. He remains in command of his forces: Enough of a man to burst the continuum of history. . . . He understands the constellation into which his epoch has stepped together with a specific epoch of the past. He thus justifies such a concept of the present (*Gegenwart*) as the 'now-time' (*Jetztzeit*) into which splinters of the messianic time are scattered" (Benjamin, *Gesammelte Schriften* [*Collected Writings*], I, 1955, pp. 503ff.). As is obvious also in this sentence, of course, the emphasis as well as the messianic content of "now-time" will be placed senselessly on one point if it is not defined within an objective "anticipation." If the aim is to explode the continuum of history, then it certainly does not mean also to explode the context, which is called the "current," the "tendency" of history, and which is interrupted and yet, time and again, keeps going. For only within this tendency of the course, which time and again makes itself felt, cracks the crust, the corresponding points of the now sparkle and transmit each other. Therefore, to explode, in this instance, does not mean to focus on one point, not even to turn something into a monad. Rather, to explode is a liberating act that frees all essentially related, utopian moments from before and after within the respective dawning of now-time and relays their directions. Only this actual emphasis and messianic content (as Benjamin called the flowing, ultimate ending) can finally make the distinction between the partiality of the true point of the now-time and the historicism of collected dead pasts that are to be done away with again. And the respective now-time, if it really is one in this sense, understands itself either as a connecting corridor that has been prepared again, much better prepared, or even as the first stop of a time that has to be fulfilled, that is, one wherein appears what has not appeared, was not yet able to appear. "Le jour de gloire est arrivé" could therefore be the great cry of the French Revolution; the conditions for the emergence of the day related to all days like that seemed to have been met. The establishment of a new, better world, which is here always the ultimate content. That is why the now-time of this most decisive sense is certainly the most revolutionary time, also in its religious and chiliastic form. Therefore, the time "that was fulfilled," namely, the "kairos" (the right moment) of John the Baptist, belongs to this form and is hardly different from the later, apocalyptically covered feelings of deadline such as those during the German Peasants' War in regard to the year 1525. All this involves a quasi-higher *carpe diem* (makes use of the day), as if "remain though" (*Verweile-doch*), where not only the intention toward the essential had to arrive during a "supreme moment" but also all former contents of now-time would unravel in this moment. But, in regard to a poetic mastery of proximity, those borderline problems have been left out as a consequence, although they did appear also in the final verses of *Faust*. What remains important for the specific problem of a poetry of the now-time is that the contemporary person who, at a sufficiently important moment, shares in the creative process is not only the comrade of his now-time, participating in a turning point in a Marxist sense; but since this moment is understood as a turning point, it contains all the indelible corresponding elements gathered within this time that is to be shaped. This is the resource that enables now-time to be seen and yet not contemplated, thus without the loss of goal, without the loss of its frontier characteristic. On the contrary, now-time reaches an unexpected as well as legitimate resonance of the past that is none—it is actuality, seen through consideration (*Eingedenken*).

Again, Literature in the Now-Time Today

But why then is it that today the difficult closeness cannot be surmounted very much in depiction? Why are there so few good novels dealing with everyday life or with festivities? Why so few successful period plays (*Zeitstück*) dealing with a contemporary social and human conflict, at least one that is non-antagonistic? There is certainly no lack of writers, and even if there are so many important ones, well, we do not always have to have great love or a completely convincing work. Instead, even the acceptable products are few and far between today, more difficult to find at least than even the authorities would like it to be. Some people believe that those requests by the authorities, that is, the public "directives," have a paralyzing effect insofar as they provide singular guidelines for the writers. This is regarded as a patronizing manner, as if the index fingers, which cannot write, were prescribing to the writers how they are supposed to write by threatening them with utmost disfavor. Yet, even this explanation of the weaknesses of present-day writers is *in the long run* insufficient since the socialist has a goal that is so earnest, rich, and keen that it simply does not require someone out of touch wth the times, but rather someone who knows the essence and the distortion, also in order to penetrate the un-eternal yesteryear (*unewig Gestrige*) through the now. As long as we are in the midst of an era of building and reconstruction, this era can generate the highest interest in its representation and consequently in its orientation. Therefore, it can advance itself like no other era before, despite all possible institutional hindrances. At the beginning, in view of so many formerly successful period plays and novels, the question was posed: Which attitudes of the writer and which feature of the actual, specific situation have to be particularly developed and regarded so that the closeness might give wings to the work? After the attempt was made to answer this question somehow, although only in rough outline, by referring to "attitudes" and "features"—i.e., satire, criticism, human utopia— we must now pose the question in reverse: Does the "frail form of the present period novel" lack those long proven ingredients and hormones of representation? Here, contemporary literature has a quality that could not be of any help before but is now grasped in the world, namely, the Marxist situational analysis and the economic and dialectical research of tendencies as well as the concordances that ultimately can be understood: now-time. Both, situational analysis and economic and dialectical research of tendencies, should make satire, criticism, and human utopia poetically more effective, putting it more in command of reality (*seinsmächtiger*), providing that both, standing on their feet, are able to walk sufficiently and do enough.

Of course, even in this sense closeness as such still remains difficult. This is also true even if there is no obstruction of inherent developments, even when the time has come for lifting the eyes as objectively as possible. In a purely epistemological sense, the now as well as the here is that swiftly occurring immediacy. As such, it needs its very own careful cultivation, given its contents that move so strongly and are rich in mediation. Oedipus was the wisest of humans: he solved the riddle of the Sphinx concerning the "human" in general, not a specific living one and particularly not one who is standing here. But the same Oedipus was the last person to understand that he had married his mother. It was exactly the fact of being personally involved, short distance, not only the shock of the contents, that make it harder to understand. To be sure, *portraying* now-time does not require as great an effort as Oedipus required, because the writer cannot become identical with any of his figures to the same degree as Oedipus, even if a writer's poetry, according to a saying by Ibsen, should be a day of judgment upon himself. But in regard to painting the present these days, a careful writer like Thomas Mann in *The Magic Mountain* and especially in *Doctor Faustus* had to employ a distant view with great deliberation, a peculiarly tricky kind of secludedness, and even an ambush in order to grasp the now despite his well-known critical realism (or because of it, as bourgeois realism): In *The Magic Mountain*, a sanatorium high up, far from the coming events; in *Doctor Faustus*, making entries into a diary, somewhat posthumously in regard to those current events. In addition to the two overlapping periods in *Doctor Faustus*, one of the contemplating master Zeitblom and the other of the active Adrian Leverkuhn, Mann was conscious of the reader coming later (see *Doctor Faustus*, chapter 26). These are quite intriguing practices or ways of looking, and they are, of course, with a writer so distant as Thomas Mann, neither pure chance nor of minor importance to today's writers who are not so distant. There is no way of direct shipping—that is what this kind of actuality means—of these goods, to these destinations. It requires many harbors as stopping-off points, also of a *oratio obliqua*, as has never been common in any representation of the present, and perhaps not even necessary. Mann's trap-door-like, concordant copying of Luther's German, the late Gothic setting of actual coldness, greatness, and decadence demonstrates in any case how much echo, how much *vineta*, it takes to advance to understand expressions of the now-time, at least of a late-bourgeois selection of it. Although there is no social rising forced in this late amazing book by Mann, the homelessness of the transitional period is portrayed more precisely in an indirect way than in those contemporary novels attempting a direct approach and doing justice to the social ascending forces, and yet—even in the great art of Anna Seghers—they do not even come close to the other side of the homelessness: the twilight between night and the more than possible day. In an epical way, the now seems to have more potential if it contains a lot of transitory matters of historical substance. That also holds true even when favorable conditions, without troubles and limitations, bring forth the true mirror of the period. At any rate, the situation is the following in a methodical sense: a contemporary novel that succeeds in a unique way pays the price for that success by reflecting everything in a particularly complicated way on different levels of distance, and most of all: the novel's present can be more easily portrayed than a completed present, even though there is a transparently represented decadence that appears as a rise with embellished obstacles.

But how come the day was written about and set in verse all over in the past without much hesitation? The critical utopian look from the roof was enough not only to see far, but particularly to see the vicinity around the house more clearly. Today, apparently, that does not work so easily anymore, as I have already emphasized, not only because of the difference between minor writers and major ones— since there were minor ones, too, who dared to climb on the roof in the past. And if censorship is brought up, then this was almost exemplary during the feudal, reactionary times, whereas capitalism, on the other hand, was directly hostile to art and literature according to Marx. And should it be that today, even in the progressive camp, there are lesser important writers than during the good times of the bourgeoisie, there is the now-time, which is of great revolutionary concordance in the aforementioned deeper sense, although not for the incompetent but for the smaller votaries and also for Apollo's new apprentices. In contrast to the flowering *juste-milieu* or even the nihilistic decadence, there is the attraction of the socialist perspective. Yet, it seems to be particularly the absence of such a perspective that explains why even gifted writers appear to think the contemporary novel is a lead article furnished with a plot, and this is why a powerfully loaded now is so inadequately administered, disclosed, and formed by poetical praxis. This is the case, despite the wonderful possible unity of microscope and telescope in theoretical Marxism— moreover, with a telescope that is needed in order finally to see the planet earth with the maximum range, which means in this instance the study of tendencies. One would expect that it would be a plus for the writer in regard to his concrete relationship to the now. One would expect a contribution by a Marxist approach in recognizing the real laws of motion and tendencies adding to the methods of earlier period pictures (*Zeitbilder*), adding to their criticism, which was bound to the symptoms, adding to the still abstract human utopia. The fact that this is not the case might be due exactly to the "directives" and the weakness, namely, to the *too narrowly perceived presence of the perspective*. For, if this does not remain sufficiently conscious, then the criticism of the close circumstances fades beyond the pressure, and the utopian contents, instead of becoming concrete, wear down to the degree and become their opposite, that is to say, embellishment—often done in a completely irreal manner. The specific premises in regard to art have apparently not been sufficiently worked out in Marxism, and vulgar Marxism often obstructs these premises completely. But the Western world, as long as it remains barred from the future, regards only the grand hotel called sadness as the field mostly for its muse, be it a frivolous or a comfortable one. Thus the present time, which is currently in an extreme transitional period, is reduced in its perspective, the latter being its most genuine poetical feature. The mere means turn out to be reified ends in itself and are thus praised, even those means that are not always unavoidable or still necessary. *Hic Rhodus hic salta*, this ultra-solid phrase holds certainly true for every production or depiction that has a concrete relation to the now and therefore not least for literature. But particularly socialist closeness will never exist other than in conjunction with the future bearing features of reality.

# The Stage Regarded as a Paradigmatic Institution and the Decision within It

They already sit there, calm with raised eyebrows and would like to be astonished.

The director in *Faust*

## The Curtain Rises

For years now people who have been peculiarly aroused have gathered in this place. The impulses that have led them to the box office and into the windowless room vary. Some are bored and want only to purchase a place for an evening that will more or less be entertaining. A better part, which is growing today and formed by the working people, does not want to kill time but wants to use it. These theatergoers, too, want to be entertained, hence loosened up and liberated, by the performance, but not without more ado or to be merely liberated from something but to be liberated for something. Yet, the impulse for everybody is something that one can call a mimical need. This need is more prevalent than the poetic need. It is positively linked not only to the compliant or hypocritical but to the tempting wish to undergo a transformation. This desire is shared with the actor himself, seeks it through him; that is, in all instances of better quality, it can be satisfied through that which he specifically represents. Moreover, and most of all, the spectator does not want to see what the actor represents in a mimical way but that which he and the entire group of actors present in a sensually colorful and vocally exciting performance. If the spectator gets drawn into the life on stage, then he is not simply pulled away from him previous daily life as it happens to friends of mere entertainment. This does not happen even if so-called light fare is presented on stage and even if it is different from kitsch that does not entertain but merely makes one stupid. The curtain rises; the fourth wall is missing. Instead there is the open frame of the stage, and within that frame something has to happen in a pleasing way, in an entertaining but meaningful way. That is, it has to mean something. Life as it happens is voided of its restrictions that it often gets into. Remarkable and decisive people, another place, powerful fates rise up now. The spectator looks on with expectation and ready to experience things to come.

Rehearsal for the Example

But the spectator does not only remain in expectation, for the exciting, lively actors arouse him for more. They demand that the spectator make decisions, at the very least a decision as to whether he likes the performance as such. An objective play is presented so that applause and booing, with which the decision is expressed, have to be extended to the play, which provides the actor with his role in the first place. But what happens if the spectator, who is not a teenager or an idolizer of stars, does not perceive the actor other than as a medium for the dramatic figure within such a plot? The displeasure, expressed in this instance, or the applause in the middle of a scene—they differ greatly from the silent or even passionate position on literature assumed by the reader. Only by really seeing on stage what he wishes to see, or also that which he does not wish to see, is the spectator usually forced to make a statement that goes substantially beyond the decision of a mere matter of taste. Not least important in this case is that in every theater there is a formal gathering of people capable of making a decision, while in front of a book there is usually only one reader to be found. It is interesting that Brecht makes a key point out of this decision by realizing how it separates itself from the merely "culinary" matter of taste and how it also evaluates the enacted people, encounters, and actions not only according to "the way they are but also to the way they could be," and that the theatrical development of the human being "does not stem from him but is directed onto him." That is why Brecht made the decision sharp and deliberate in his directing and in the course of action, with the result that it always had to extend beyond the evening at the theater. All this was done to activate and instruct, to lead into a life that was to become active and better, into the things *that are meant to come in an unusual sense of the word.* *First*, the spectator no longer merely emphathizes with the play. He keeps on the alert and places himself in the action and its actors while at the same time he assumes a position opposite all this. Therefore, the only right way is to take "the attitude of the smoking observer" (Brecht's note for the *Threepenny Opera*), not that of the spellbound man, who resists his feelings in a wallowing way instead of *thinking* and enjoying himself, learning in an amused way. The play has to provide pleasure, more than ever before. Here dead seriousness is much more wrong than any place else: "The theater has to be able to remain something superfluous" (Brecht, *Kleines Organon für das Theater* [*Small Organon for the Theater*], paragraph 3), but the experienced pleasure ought not to let the spectator melt away; rather, it makes him instructed and active. *Second*, the actor himself does not become entirely at one with his character and the action that he imitates. "He always remains the one who points toward something, the one who does not become involved himself." He stands next to the figure of the play, even as its critic and praiser, and his gestures are not those of immediate affect but make the affects of somebody else clear in a mediating way. By this more epic than dynamic acting style—freed from all exhibition of the actor's soul or of the so-called blood of the theater—the performance will be endowed not with less but with more vitality, warmth, and intensity.In keeping with this and in regard to the effect of the epic acting style on the audience, Brecht stressed, "It is not the case—although it is sometimes said—that the epic theater, which is—as it is also sometimes said—not simply non-dramatic theater, rings out the battle cry reason versus emotion (feeling). The epic theater does not in any way abandon emotions, nor, in any way, the feeling of justice, the striving for freedom, and the just wrath. In fact, not only does it not abandon these feelings, but it does not even rely on the mere presence of these feelings. Instead it seeks to increase or to create them. The critical attitude into which it seeks to put the audience cannot be passionate enough" (Brecht, *Theaterarbeit* [*Theater Work*] 1952, p. 254). The artistic means of objective highlighting of a scene corresponds to the objectifying of the actor, which Brecht called *estrangement* (*Verfremdung*). That means: "Certain movements of the play should—by inscriptions, sound, and music and the way the actor performs—be elevated (estranged) like closed scenes from the realm of daily life, of that which is a matter of fact or expected" (Brecht, *Stücke* [*Plays*] VI, p. 221). The effect should be that of astonishment, in other words, that kind of scientific puzzlement, philosophical amazement whereby the mindless acceptance of phenomena and also the phenomena of the play stops and a questioning attitude and desire to know arise. The "advice of the actors," who know about the estrangement effect in a Brechtian didactic play, is consequently (quite with amazement as the beginning of the reflection)

You saw what's common, that which happens all the time.
But we are asking you for:
That which is not alien, find it strange!
That which is common, find it inexplicable!
What is usual should amaze you.
What is the rule recognize as misuse
And where you find misuse
Take remedial measures!

Epilogue to *The Exception and the Rule*

And in contrast to inconsequential literature, estrangment makes an especially strong appeal to thoughtfulness with anticipatory consequences. Since those things that have not been changed for a long time appear easily as being unchangeable, estrangement in the theater of portrayed life ultimately takes place in order to "remove the imprint of commonness that keeps events which can be socially influenced from getting changed today" (*Kleines Organon für Theater* [*Small Organon for the Theater*], paragraph 43). Thus we reach the *third* and last of the main concerns in regard to directing, that is, the theater as *rehearsal for the example*. Attitudes and events are to be formed and experimented with by play, whether they are fit for the changes in life or not. Therefore, one can say, the Brechtian theater intends to be a kind of realm of varying endeavors to create the right behavior. Or, in other words, it means: a laboratory of the right theory-praxis on a small scale, in the form of play, as though it were a case on stage that might provide the experimental experience for the serious case. This is an experiment *in re* and yet *ante rem*, that is, without the real negative consequences of a quasi-untested concept— see the learning play *The Measures Taken*—and with the pedagogy to demonstrate dramatically those kinds of negative consequences. Possible alternatives, too, are portrayed by this kind of endeavor, together with on-stage outcomes of each one of these alternatives—see the contrasting learning plays *Der Jasager, Der Neinsager* (*The Yeasayer, The Naysayer*). A similar *ductus*, then, shows in Brecht's late play, *Galileo*, in which the question could be explored as to whether Galileo recanted for the sake of the major work he still wanted to write. Brecht tried to create a "parable drama" with examples and decisions heightened by means of style and often simplified. And the Brechtian style discarded the abstractness of the advice to be given in an increasingly wise way. There are no simplifications whatsoever in that truly terrible form called schematism since it had already memorized the territory accessible to it with five or six formulas or with a closing filled with cheers. That is also why schematism hates all Brechtian technique. Brecht's theater looks for a mode of acting that contains only communist conclusiveness of action that is to be tested anew time and again, and this testing leads toward the goal of the active creation of the really useful and its reason.

## More about the Rehearsal for the Example to Be Sought

It is undoubtedly unusual that plays teach first by learning themselves, that the involved persons and their actions are turned upside down in a questioning and investigating way. And yet, there is already an open form in all dramas, where human beings and situations are shown particularly in their permanent contradictions. Only where a leading character, be it a character or a social function, acts in a straight and inevitable way, are there no variabilities. Othello's jealousy does not falter, and it is impossible to think of it in any other way, in all its consequences and situations in quick succession. Antigone's traditional matrilineal and persevering "piety" does not alter either. Nor does Zeus' "reason of state" that becomes socially victorious. The conflicts, in this instance, are unavoidable. Experimentation with a capacity for a different way of living, with a capacity for a different way of acting, with a capacity for a different way of terminating affairs would be grotesque even as a mere allusion of an interpretation and its stage directing. But are there not a great number of dramas with many possible alternatives? Is there not Hamlet or, in a much smaller, insignificant, and predetermined way of an alternative, Fiesco's monologue vacillating between republic and monarchy? Were there not always dramas with several possible versions—evaluations of the plot, of the ending?—for instance, Goethe's *Stella*, *Tasso* in relation to the original version of *Tasso*? In 1776, Goethe ended *Stella* in reconciliation; in the 1805 version the ending was tragic. In the original version of *Tasso*, Antonio, the prosaic person, was presented as negative, the impassioned poet as positive. In the second version it is almost reverse. To be sure, there has been no dramatics up to now—and not even the great well-rounded dramatics—with a genuine relationship of theory and praxis or even with the drama as a continuously self-correcting—interrupted by tableaus—didactic course. But even the unalterable dramas, although they were not rehearsals for the example to be sought, were nevertheless examples of a course to be finished, a good one or a bad one, one to be sought or one to be fled, with the recommended motto: *Exempla docent*. And that was above all true where the theater, with or without didactic insistence, was endowed with moral provisions. The unexpected happens, which is why Brecht wanted to be far less moralistic and pedagogic than Schiller, for instance. As author of learning plays and operas for the school, in particular, Brecht was a friendly materialist and rejected a theater that was only moralistic and nothing more than that: "Under no circumstances could it be elevated to a higher level if it is, for instance, turned into a market place for morality. Then it would have to be more concerned about not being debased, which would happen immediately if it did not present the moral cause in a pleasurable way, namely pleasurable to the senses—from which the moral cause would only benefit" (*Kleines Organon* [*Small Organon*], paragraph 3). But the rejection of blurbs and headlines, the kitsch of "visual advertisement" on stage did not handicap Brecht's program, that is, the program of the theater that educates intellectually and trains for decision-making. In that sense, this program wanted "to move the theater as close to institutions of teaching and publishing as possible." Of course, theater understands itself as a well established place for entertainment, and its influence is conveyed through poetry and not through headlines and a conformism that screams hurray. The latter, in particular, does not need to be rehearsed for the example since it already knows everything and replaces the word example with the word ideal model. Brecht meant instead a moral institution with great joy in which the depth of the intended enlightenment and impulses is to be cultivated in direct proportion to the depth of pleasure. In this instance, there is good reason to point to the sensually pleasurable theatrical illusion of the opera: progressive masterpieces like *The Magic Flute* or *The Marriage of Figaro* provide the wish-image of the most active human being along with a most noble pleasure. And like the means so are the contents of the teaching—that is, medicine and advice—mediated by the progressive theater, one of pleasure. Thus, in the play, the content appears as one to be created in struggle and having been created as one with anticipatory illumination. "Therefore, the choice of the standpoint is another main part of acting and has to be chosen outside the theater. Like the remodeling of nature so is the remodeling of society an act of liberation, and it is the pleasures of liberation that should be conveyed by the theater of the scientific era" (*Kleines Organon* [*Small Organon*], paragraph 56). So much for the theater when it appears as the house for decisive action on which and between which choices are made. As soon as the rehearsal for the example is staged the goal is clearly visible, but the stage, being experimental, that is, being a state of anticipation, tries out the ways in which to behave in order to achieve them.

## Reading, the Mimicking of Language, and the Scene

I have already stated that all proper plays are better to see than to be read because decision can be made in a less tasteful way in front of the stage and can be made in a more communal way than in front of a book. But in pathetic cases it still seems conceivable that it is good or even better for the stage play to be read than to be seen. That is the case when actors place themselves above the role, for instance, when we get the "intriguing" actor Smith on stage instead of Iago. It becomes even more unpleasant when a star actor uses poetry as a pretext to embody and demonstrate his unique personality and style of speech. Moreover, in case of less pompous performances, either because of so-called vivacity or also because of the lack of time, the actors usually talk much too fast on stage, particularly when verses have to be recited or artful sequences have to be performed. A great deal that is precious in the play is lost by such whirlwind cleaning. What reveals itself as a richer landscape during a quiet reading of the play turns in an awful way into a steeplechase. But the theater must prove that it is more rewarding in comparison to reading, no matter how much the ears and eyes gain enjoyment during the reading. The theater must be so rewarding that even the best written closet drama acts in relation to the performed drama like the shades in *The Odyssey* thirsting for blood in order to stand in reality and to be held accountable. Rarely are good dramas and never dramas true to the original produced more beautifully than when they are produced in a way true to the original. The dramas that are better for reading are, at best, lyrical plays with dialogue and repartée that lack fast action, that lack convoluted plots, appearance, exit, trouble, the noble colportage not only of the Schillerian kind but also of the Shakespearian kind that demands to be staged. There is no world in drama without the visible place for characters and the change of scenes that the actors and above all the directors bring out. And even great lyrics, insofar as they are part of the action and thus the drama, are only reflected in the scene through the movement or reflection of the mood. In short, they are reflected through the drama, to which they belong, in an introverted form. This is why—and here the inner world of the verse is not so self-evident when read as an escape from the theater— Brecht's lines are so significantly true:

About the evening heath
the Elisabethian wrote verses for us,
which cannot be reached by any lighting technician,
not even the heath itself!

And these lines are true: the lighting technician does not reach the verses because the evening heath of the Elizabethan poet has been poetically developed to its truest essence, but they are reached inside the *theater*, inside the Lear and Macbeth scenes for which Shakespeare wrote all these verses. The reaching, surpassing, and revealing of the evening heath by means of great poetry happens no doubt through the key power that such poetry exercises over nature. However, the theater shows the poetically composed heath as the ground on which *finally its own play is going to be performed.* Aside from that, only a perfect theater of this kind can ultimately realize the important pause that in the drama, does not necessarily occur between the lines but between the words, between the sentences, and between scenes. Listening, knocking, paying attention to remote calls, some expectation rests therefore primarily in those pauses, including the development or the drapery of important customs. Even the absolutely wonderful trumpet movement in Verdi's *Othello* announcing the envoy of the doge stems from the immanent form of Shakespeare's pause, be it from inside or outside the opera. Therefore, in contrast to the book, the theater has a sensual reality of experience where the unheard is publicly heard, where that which is marginal to the reality of experience becomes physically public, where that which is invented and poetically made dense (*Gedichtet-Verdichtet*) appears in truly perfect form as if it were flesh. And it is, in any event, mimicking through which poetry is represented on the level of the theater; it is *mimicking of language plus mimicking of gesture* plus the *mimicking of the aura* in the scenery created by the stage designer. Here the perimeter of the stage turns into something like a window through which we see the world change until it becomes recognizable, until the world sees and listens. Thus the theater is the institution of a new reality of experience that is not to be found anywhere in the direct sense, and that reality of experience is revealed by referential elements of the dramatic poetry.

Here, everything depends on the tone with which a role is provided. One could even say that the human being to be portrayed is a sound figure, and as such he is being born for the stage. Therefore, in the beginning there is the way of speaking (*Sprechform*), which is the difficult art of inflecting and modulating. Now, the general tone (*Grundton*) upon which the *mimicking of language* is based—this excellent term was invented by Schleiermacher, who was a preacher and also a philosopher—is not just set with the abstract outline of a figure, or even with the stereotype that has developed from it. The real general tone only stems from the disposition, the commitment, and the projected image of the figure, consequently from the possibilities to act and to exist that are opened up by the character and his circumstances. In this instance, character is not meant in a static sense of something engraved, of something carved-out; rather, here character means the destination toward an action that is yet to be created. Only in this direction does a truly dramatic sound figure develop. It will only be varied by the destination. The great director Stanislavsky cited Hamlet as an example. To wit, it is in the character Hamlet that the task is to be discovered: I want to avenge my father. But one might also discover a higher task: I want to discover the mysteries of life. But there is an even superior task to be discovered: I want to save the human race (see Trepte, *Leben und Werk Stanislawski* [*The Life and Work of Stanislavsky*], pp. 78ff.). Stanislavsky's directing develops the figure of Hamlet, including all inhibitions, according to this final "basic formula." More difficult, though, is the intended style in the mimicking of language, once the latter is traditionally determined by a certain abstract, untrue, and pathetic pitch. That is still the case in regard to Schiller. That is, it is a problem to be able to speak Schiller's verses also in a detached manner, or in a completely non-sonorous manner. That is the case in the mimicking of singing and no less in the mimicking of orchestras in regard to Wagner. In speaking, with Schiller's Wallenstein, it is hard and difficult to find a way to break through the persistent tone of the court theater, its yearning or rolling pathos. It is also hard and difficult—although in the new Bayreuth theater it seems that attempts have been somewhat successful—to remove the Baroque form of plush and victory march from the modulation of the *Ring of the Nibelungen*. This outdatedness certainly stems in part from the original works of Schiller and Wagner, the origins stemming from a rhetoric that is much too highly elevated, often maintained by force only. But the counterbalance lies also in the sharp logical power of Schiller's language, in the sharp countersubjective power of Wagnerian expression. And the reinstatement of Schiller and Wagner means, in Schiller's work, to represent the inherent speakable *piano* of what is contemplative; in Wagner's work, to represent the inherent singable *bel canto* of the infinite melody. In Wagner there is much more inherently, more from his own era, stuck in some super thunder, the overdue case of *restitutio in integrum*, which can be accomplished first by starting with the general mimicking and gradually moving to the entire structure. Therefore, in view of this, it is a more important task to make the performance of Wagner appropriate specifically to that which blooms and which is precise, that which is powerful and which has the abrupt depth of the work. Then the mimicking of gestures will follow, along with the scenery, in a non-obdurate way, no longer with thunder, the clashing of swords, and the swaying of waves. *The mimicking of gesture* itself sets the stage for the dramatic action mediated by words on the bodies of the actors, but also on the body, so to speak, of the objects. This scene can be bare, for instance, as in Brecht's plays, as in the old English and the old Spanish theater. It can be plush, as in some good examples of the former Meininger theater and the set designs of Max Reinhardt. It can above all let the play itself expand aura-like in the stage decor and settle down as in Stanislavsky's art. In regard to Stanislavsky, it has been said with good reason that he had the keys to all doors and all rooms and that he knew how to act with the same power of the master of the house in the Ibsenian room of Doctor Stockmann, in the hell of *The Lower Depths*, in the huge apartment of Czar Berendij. Closely related to the mimicking of gesture is the aforementioned *mimicking of the aura* of the scenery that develops and is created by the set-designer. Neither Calderon's theater nor Shakespeare's practiced that. Yet, despite all the bareness, indicating a cave, a forest, or a large stateroom only with captions, the necessary requisites such as the dagger or the rope ladder were not missing at all. And the allegorical set became the extension of these requisites, their imprint and expression in space, as it were. Stanislavsky's colleague Nemirovitch-Dantschenko expressed that mimicking of gesture including the scenery by saying in a somewhat pointed but not any less expanded auratic sense, "A stage production can only be called a good one if, at any point in time, the performance could continue without words and the audience would still understand what is going on." In fact, the dagger in one of Calderon's dramas of jealously and the rope ladder in one of Shakespeare's love dramas are also mimical. In Calderon, the dagger is jealousy itself in its extreme form, and in Shakespeare the morning light between the nightingale and lark is no longer the surface but the revelation of Romeo and Juliet's love and death. Such things, even when driven to their highest point, do not divert from the plot, but the homogenized aura of the objects conducts into the scene, as when Shakespeare lets his Hamlet say to the actors that "at the same time any necessary point of the play is to be considered." It is obvious that even with the well-mastered mimicking of gestures and their scenery, the spoken language remains the end-and-be-all of the play. Therefore, pantomime never gains a life of its own or comes first, but even the most perfect pantomime serves the play, according to Nemirovitch-Dantschenko. But from the point of view of mimicking, theater is the sculpture of poetry at its best, and it is one where, even with the strongest movement geared toward mimicking, the sculpture is not neutralized.

## Illusion, Honest Appearance, Moral Institution

The old question is to what and for what purpose does the stage really elevate. The stage works with make-up and, in general, mainly with means and lights that are intended to make believe. Therefore, the stage is more illusion than any other form of art and in particular because the stage lets its illusion, despite the separating perimeter, become a real experience. To be sure, that gives the theater its simultaneously enchanting and illusory power, but it also underscores the illusion so strongly that it is like no other pure art form. For the person not kindly disposed to the theater, the illusion of the stage might resemble more the appearance of a wax figure—and that happens quite often and not only among critics of the theater—than the elegant transparent appearance of a painting that bears no real experience. In addition to that, there is the so-called transformation of the actor hero or the actor martyr. If we consider what real hypocrisy means, the term comedian stems from this. Indeed, the difference between moral and theatrical appearance was already clear at the time when acting was not yet an "honest business." The comedian pretends while the actor transforms himself; or rather, he makes the role that he plays truly recognizable. By virtue of performed poetry, the stage presents itself as the governing force of something that is not real experience within poetry. Thus, the connection with the wax figure or with the so-called living pictures, with illusion in general, is missing. Nevertheless, the question remains on the level that is appropriate: Is the theater, if not bedazzlement, at the very least nothing but *illusion*? In bourgeois aesthetic usage this notion does not have anything pejorative about it. Thus it refers also to something that is not real in an external sense, and something that is pure, decent appearance as it were but had nothing in common with any kind of anticipatory illumination. In this sense illusion was extended to all art forms, also the so-called pure arts, but always with the implications stemming from the illusion of the theater. E. von Hartmann, for instance, in his book *Philosophie des Schönen* (*The Philosophy of the Beautiful*), which is three-quarters petty trivia and one-quarter a resumé, claimed that illusion is the characteristic of all art, and he defines it as the "subjective correlate for the objective aesthetic appearance." But then there is nothing real about this illusion. Ever since Kant and Schiller's definition of beauty as the freedom from real appearance, one can detect this approach in almost all the works of aestheticians. This appearance as a useful one becomes only beautiful "as soon as it is detached from the reality that generated it and thus also from the *reality* of the purpose of that which it is serving, and as soon as it is transfigured to pure aesthetic appearance" (E. von

Hartmann, *Philosophie des Schönen* [*The Philosophy of the Beautiful*], 1887, p. 174). But the surprise follows closely, of course not in E. von Hartmann's work, but in the work of Schiller, who was the best Kantian aesthetician. For if indeed freedom from the *reality* of purpose was the objective correlate for the subjective illusion, then not even the theater illusion is an illusion. In fact, this illusion may be the very least one, as we shall see soon, even if Schiller himself called it a "beneficial illusion." However, here this beneficence neutralizes its illusionary character decisively, once and for all. "The theater, regarded as a moral institution," is what is meant here: "We shall be given back to ourselves. Our feelings will awaken. Wholesome passion will shake our slumbering nature and our blood will well up anew."—In the same sense, the alleged mere illusion settles in reality, refreshes it, and points toward a stronger one, a reality that can be set free. The effusive declaration by Schiller, quoted above, sparked his early essay about the program of the theater, which is rooted so little in illusion, the theater regarded as a moral institution, consequently not at all free from reality. But if the theater is such an institution and in that it is, then the character of illusion is incompatible with it, because no illusion activates the realizing will and the will to reality. Certainly the theater as an illusion had to correspond to the ways of a bourgeoisie that severed reality from art and ideal completely, much beyond Kant. However, it is true that art as illusion would be and remain a lie all the way, in a moral and an extra-moral (*aussermoralisch*) sense, that is, in its intention to deceive as well as in regard to the impossibilities generated by that kind of art. In contrast, the existing appearance of the theater is in no way an illusionary appearance but more an *absolutely honest* one—appearance "as the extension of that which has developed, in its formed and more appropriate shape." The play of the appearance does not quiet down; rather, it is able to influence the will of this world in particular, to influence its real possibilities—as a paradigmatic institution.

However, in order for it to be effective, one should not forget about the beautiful illusion (*schöner Schein*) in this institution. Although the stage is not illusionary, it does not show the pointed finger of instruction in its coat of arms. Wherever that figure appeared, there was plenty of bourgeois and puritanical hatred for the arts, at least some distancing from art at work. Unfortunately, this kind of distancing was also employed by socialists, as if the theater were not for pleasure but a Sunday school (attended by nothing but naughty boys and model boys). I have already demonstrated how Brecht, in particular, recalled the theater as a place for training, the same writer who had been the first to praise the consciousness-raising stage instead of the merely culinary one. But in Brecht the theater was not supposed to be an *undecorated* moral institution and certainly not an obstrusive one. On the contrary, also here, the moral is conveyed via pleasure as the "most noble function that we have found for the theater." But Gottsched's pedantry implanted on the German face of the moral institution has not died out that quickly. Therefore, time and again, tolerance must be requested for the light with happiness. That is the reason why Goethe declared his allegiance to the beautiful and cheerful illusion in his essay "German Theater" (*Deutsches Theater*): "From its primitive and yet weak beginnings, almost like a puppet theater, German theater might have gradually worked through various epochs to become strong and just, had it been in southern Germany where it was really at home and could have made peaceful progress and could have developed. But the first step took place in northern Germany by people who were shallow and incapable of producing anything, a step not toward something better but toward a so-called improvement." And after Goethe judged Gottsched's reforms with reservation, after he expressed his views about the Hamburg dispute whether a priest is or is not allowed to go to the theater, he continued and alluded to the title of Schiller's early work: "This dispute, fought by both sides with a lot of passion, unfortunately forced the friends of the stage to declare themselves for a moral institution, whereas the theater is actually only dedicated to a sublime sensuality.... The writers themselves, good, brave men from the bourgeois class, did not object and worked toward this purpose with German uprightness and rigid minds without noticing that they perpetuated Gottsched's mediocrity." In keeping with this sharp plea Goethe wanted the famous Aristotelian catharsis directed at the character of the drama and not at the theatergoers. Nor was it to be transposed to them. There is no doubt but that all this in Goethe's work is not an Aristotelian reaction against the common good of the German bourgeois enlightenment but his antipathy toward secularized sanctimoniousness, which even attached itself to the moral institution that eventually became a negative theater. Likewise: Apollo without the muses and Minerva without Epicure would suit the materialism in the arts much worse than they had suited idealism in the arts during their times. But what Schiller had in mind with his moral institution was a flourishing theater instead of Gottsched's home-made plainness that became moral utilitarianism. Schiller wanted a scene that was to become a tribunal. Only then, through the richness of the scene, could the theater serve morality. As is so often the case in the arts, the highest form of morality is to come about. The isolated perfection of this can be seen in *Hamlet*, in the scene where the drama within the drama forces the royal murderer to reveal himself. The social revolutionary moral institution can be found in Schiller's *Kabale und Liebe* (*Love and Intrigue*) and in *William Tell*, in Goethe's *Egmont*, and in Beethoven's *Fidelio* furnished with the loud music of Brutus. This moral institution is not only a tribunal, for the ways of salvation, at least the signs of its light, appear above the judged one, even over the victorious one and thereby over vice causing a repulsive reaction. German classicism on the whole was the attempt to develop a complete, unfragmented human being out of a society fragmented in classes. This attempt, built purely on the belief in an aesthetic education, was of course a very abstract one, but it also, undoubtedly, put some significant models up on stage. Among them are those that are only now finding their true task, without any abstraction or even with effusive misery. Therefore, the honest appearance of the theater, like the illusion, is the very least thing that is detached from the *reality* of the purpose. The honest appearance is rather the advancement of the task through pleasure.

## The False and the Real Actualization

Good plays are reproduced on the stage but never the same as they were. Therefore, for every new generation there has to be a new staging, several times even. The changes in the production must be particularly drastic when another social class takes its seats in the theater. But even if the theater does not stay unchanged, that is, if it does not remain junk, then it is also not a coatrack where you can constantly hang up new clothes. This means that the characters and places of an old play cannot be completely and radically "modernized." In any case the costume of the era in which the specific play takes place remains. That was no contradiction at all for the Baroque stage that dressed its ancient heroes according to fashion and also had them act in this way. Indeed, the Baroque theater portrayed ancient heroes; however, the plays were not ancient ones but dramas written at the time. Thus the Baroque theater did not distort any of the ancient dramas when it transposed their subject matter onto its own bourgeois courtly figures and conflicts. Much later Cocteau's *Orpheus and Eurydice*, written in the 1920s out of far lesser creative reasons, though out of even more deliberation, wore polo shirts and horn-rimmed glasses. This also was accomplished without being offensive. However, there is nothing more tactless and nonsensical than playing *Hamlet* dressed in tailcoats or, to refer to less extreme examples, to place the first act of *The Tales of Hoffmann* in a chrome-nickel bar; or to dress Schiller's robbers in proletarian attire and have Spiegelberg wear the mask of Trotsky. All this is snobbish; at the very least it is an exaggerated backlash against a way of playing historical theater that is outdated anyway. True is only what is self-evident; i.e., all theater is of its own times: it is neither a true-like masquerade nor a pedantic game of fun set up by philologists. Therefore, the scene needs a new and newly incorporated look to be embedded in it throughout the play to make it fresh again. However, this must be done in such a way that the aroma of the time of the drama and of its stage design will never disappear. Indeed, the new partiality of the view needs the character and the action to be in the right place of the ideology that is given by the play if the playwright's subject matter is to reveal hate and love, villainy and goodness in a different way. The setting that the playwright had in mind has to be altered to become recognizable, instead of being thrown away. For instance, there must be a clearer focus of the class conflicts that take place in the play and that have only now become acute. Only in this way does the theater become truly actualized and not just stylized and, just as the setting must be altered, so too the *text of the play*, which must be freshly illuminated and modeled. Aside from deleting antiquated portions of the play, it must be revised wherever it is dusty or underdeveloped and un-finished in some parts, and here—as a *conditio sine qua non*—the writer who revises or adds to the text must be a kindred spirit of the original author or at least equal to this author. For example, Karl Kraus not only saved Offenbach's texts but also the gems of his music from the sloppy mistreatment they had undergone. For example, Brecht saw Lenz's *Der Hofmeister* (*The Private Tutor*) as a human plant (*Men-schenpflanze*) that grew out of the misery of eighteenth-century feudalism into the capitalist misery of the twentieth century. But here such revising can become precarious when impudent directors, frustrated playwrights, or sorry imitators want to use all that which has become old as crutches and substitutes for their production. Those imitators who do touch-ups in literature (for example, the closing of Schiller's *Demetrius*) are similar to those detestable restorers of castles and palaces of the last century in what was called architecture in those days. Like the architecture itself, these restorers have become more rare, whereas vigorous directors are still transposing and actualizing the text of the drama in unbelievable ways on the basis of vulgarized political "understandings" of the text. And all this is done for the purpose—even if it is ever so commendable—of making a tendency visible outside of the text instead of making it visible within it. We do not need to recall that production of *William Tell*—most uncommendable, to be exact, pre-fascist tendency—where Gessler is put into the center as the "most interesting" figure by diminishing the heroes of freedom. Or even when the comedy *The Merchant of Venice* has to make up for an anti-Semitic vulgar play. For even with the most correct tendency, the vulgar-political actualization brings the drama into a field alien to the work, *with the loss of the given dramatic contents*. For instance, this can occur when *Maria Stuart* is given the wrong setting and distorted to a degree that the play does not figure as a tragic drama any longer but rather celebrates the triumph of Elizabeth; because she, Elizabeth—due to a dramatic reconstruction without precedence—is supposed to represent rising capitalism versus Maria, who stands for what is French, Catholic, and neo-feudal. To be sure, this is not incorrect in a historical sense; however, for the given drama, in the last act, it makes matters even worse. In particular, it becomes far more superfluous than a palace restoration in the style of the 1880s. Only with a dramatic figure that is ambiguous itself, above all Hamlet, is it possible to justify the exaggeration of one of the figure's aspects, even if it is one that has been neglected until now. Here, too, these aspects would have had to be revealed by Shakespeare, and the director need only develop them. Only with this kind of development and mature elaboration does rejuvenation of the theater take place, and only for this purpose are masterworks staged with a fortunate loss of their "gallery tone," of their museum characteristics. Even Richard III does not act as if he were Hitler but rather embodies today some part of that which represents Hitler, and this becomes clearer the more he acts his own part and that of his times through Shakespeare. Something similar is true in the same play about Richmond and the beautiful day of tomorrow around him, at least in the allegorical aspect of the rescue. However, this portrayal must have many levels of meaning and cannot be a panopticon presenting something "timeless," something "human, all too human." In this instance the many levels of meaning demand that the classical drama has to be spoken and staged in such a way as to allow the drama to carry some meaning of the present. In no way is the present to be imposed on the drama. All this is based on its conflicts, which are never exhausted by time—even more, on the contents of the conflicts and the solutions: each classical masterpiece employs its conflicts and solutions to demonstrate something that surpasses its time, a *concern that goes beyond* the present. Even plays written in our days possess only a dramatical and relevant meaning (in the sense of a hint as well as an illumination) if they know how to present such concerns that go beyond the present. There is a social process (between the individual and society, even between contrasting forms of society) that stretches from the Greek beginnings of the drama into the future, into the society where contradictions have not disappeared, of course, but where they are no longer antagonistic. This process, dramatically concentrated between typical figures, makes every great play great because it is capable of new actuality, and it makes every great play relevant because it is transparent for future tasks; i.e., it functions as an optimistic tragedy. In *Rameau's Nephew* Diderot lets someone say, "Many columns were standing along the way, and the rising sun was shining on all of them, but only Memnon's column made a sound." This column stands for genius in contrast to mediocrity, but on a purely objective level the column means permanent power and actually of great plays toward the morning dawn. The actual stage production, therefore, will be set up best if it keeps to this direction. This direction is immanent in the most truthful plays, from *Prometheus Bound* to *Faust*. Such a production and direction does not need custom-made advertisement for itself but, rather, simple revelation.

More Genuine Actualization: Not Fear and Pity, but Rather Defiance and Hope

The standard for this freshness, however, has always to be actively renewed. The safest way to gain this renewal can be attained from the existence of important, new plays and from the appreciation for them. Ultimately it is gained from the great difference that arises when a socialist era's wish-image (*Wunschbild*) is pitted against one of the past. This difference becomes tangible in what Schiller called the *basis of pleasure in tragic issues*. In this essay bearing the aforementioned title and in the subsequent one, *On Tragic Art*, it seems that Schiller could still not detach himself from the Aristotelian definition of tragedy. Moreover, he did not intend to make a difference between tragic drama [*Trauerspiel*] and tragedy [*Tragödie*], both which have to move the audience to feel something. And, indeed, it was *emotion* (*Rührung*) that served as the starting point for Aristotle's famous teleology of the tragedy: it has to rouse emotions of fear and sympathy. Schiller only emphasized sympathy in tragedy. Yet, even in the Aristotelian original, tragedy shows people, first of all the heroes in it, in a state of suffering. The dramatically designed intensification of the fear of suffering, of the pity with the suffering, is supposed to free the audience, as is generally known, from this emotion. That means, the emotions are supposed to be worked off to normal levels in life through the dramatic intensification. This is the purport of the Aristotelian catharsis or purification, one that always includes moving the audience to feel something through dramatic experienced suffering. Indeed, Euripides first brought emotion (*Rührung*) into the tragedy, which is the reason why Aristotle credited Euripides for the strongest dramatic effect in the sense already indicated. But not only the specific play that generates emotion is assumed in this case, but above all an attitude that, less as a protest against fate, points to the suffering, to loss, no matter how nobly endured. All the slave societies of classical Greece and Rome did not recognize a tragic rebelliousness inherent in suffering, nor did they recognize Prometheus as the tragic model hero, or at least they did not want to recognize him fully. This is true despite Aeschylus' Prometheus trilogy and despite the knowledge that the tragic heroes were better than the gods, even better than fate. And now it is especially instructive, for the *degree of refreshing the dramatic aspects*, how the catharsis in terms of fear, and then in terms of sympathy, have become for us the most alien of the tragic effects. As we have seen, Schiller still loved the tragic effect (although with the exclusive emphasis on pity), and Lessing, earlier in his *Hamburgische Dramaturgie* (*Hamburg Dramaturgy*), defended or purified it anew (however also by reducing the fear that was supposed to be pity related to ourselves). But the enterprising and dynamic bourgeois society already understood the classical basis of pleasure in tragic issues only with misunderstandings. This bourgeois society began to put into effect a totally different wish-image theater (*Wunschbild Theater*) through the tragic hero, even through the Greek tragic hero, and it was much different from the theater that carried merely passive emotions of fear and pity. The emotion of fear had been dropped together with the tragedy of fate (*Schicksalstragödie*) in any case. And as far as pity was concerned, this kind of emotion, and that which was related to it, was much less than *admiration*. It is even possible to detect far more, entirely different things in this emotional shift, in this essential kind of actualization, that came to effect in this way. For if the tragically designed basis is no longer fear or pity, then it will not exclusively remain as admiration. The basis, and now seen as such *within the tragic person itself*, is rather *defiance and hope*. Only these are the two tragic emotions in revolutionary circumstances, and they do not surrender to so-called fate. Defiance, though, disappears in and around the *helping*-victorious, who are the heroes of the socialist society and dramatic art. This is done in accordance with contradictions that are no longer antagonistic, with substantial solidarity. More important, however, is defiance around and in the *failing*-victorious, who are the heroes of the classically transmitted dramatic art, which, according to the playwright Hebbel, touched on the big sleep of the world. And the specific hope that, in any case, carries on its proper paradox within this failure, and that constitutes the best reason for pleasure in the tragic issues, comes home without any paradox only in the socialist theater. (To be sure this is done in a way, along the lines of the last plays ["Romances"] by Shakespeare, or of Goethe's *Faust*, so that the tragic element may be sublated.) Altogether, the theater sheds light on its role as a moral and paradigmatic institution, one that is cheerful and anticipatory. That is why it is also cheerful in the tragedy, not only in the critical comedy (*Komödie*), not only in the comical play (*Lustspiel*). That is why the panoramic horizon of the morning spreads itself around the tragic heroes, even around the genuine emotion—that means around the noble downfalls of the tragic drama. When Schiller says, "That which never happened anywhere, that alone never grows old," then this sentence is without any doubt, one might say, exaggerated; and yet underneath all the pessimistic and idealistic resignation, there is a material core. However, the sentence should read, That which has *never entirely* happened *anywhere*, but which is *to come as a human event and which defines the task*, that will never grow old. The effective part of the future, therefore, provides the real measure of freshness, also in the comedy that criticizes the present; in the comic play that lets the present come to a happy end; especially in the sublimity of the tragic world. For in the effect—rich in hope—of the heroes of the tragic world, it becomes clear that their downfall is not entirely true, but that the element of the future there is uplifting.

# A Philosophical View of the Detective Novel

1. Something is uncanny—that is how it begins. But at the same time one must search for that remoter "something," which is already close at hand. The hidden "who" is in demand, but when it is told as a story, it is not highly regarded. It is seldom praised and often read, even by those who despise it—what do we have here? There must be something to this case after all.

2. What is remarkable in this case is that it has not surprised us more often. Who, indeed, is moved by such a thing more than superficially and fleetingly? The setting in which detective stories are enjoyed the most is just too cozy. In a comfortable chair, under the nocturnal floor lamp with tea, rum, and tobacco, personally secure and peacefully immersed in dangerous things, which are shallow. But it does not always have to be love at first sight, especially when it appears that thrills, even when unrequited, are hardly ever one and the same. There are more than enough bad examples, but they could not be termed "bad" unless clever and shrewd ones also existed. The latter—an example of which is the work of E. A. Poe—can function as a divining rod amidst the superficial. And not only E. A. Poe, but also the form he used, which is recognizable in the genre's worst mass-produced merchandise, endures longer, expresses more, has remarkably more recent ancestors and more profundity than many of the standardized products of which literary history is full. Why is it that the detective novel produces so many trashy bestsellers?— The romance and so-called social novel produce these as well, probably to a greater degree, without this generally being held against these genres. And if there are people who do not want to come into

contact with the detective novel in public, they are only die-hard intellectuals, who do not even go to variety shows. Here, in contrast, Lichtenberg's adage is to be taken seriously: It is not uncommon that random hunting expeditions flush out the game which method-ological philosophy can use in its neatly ordered household. This applies even more to detective expeditions, which are not so random after all. They search, observe, and follow nothing but clues along the way. Indeed, all they are is a hunt for sufficient evidence in narrative form. However, the question here focuses not on crimino-logical evidence, but evidence of its literary representation. Its form is highly unusual, that of a "ferreting out," and presupposes many determinants according to the way it has become.

3. Why, then, is the narrator who fishes in murky waters such a recent phenomenon? Above all, why does the detailed hunt for evidence appear at such a late date? The reason is that earlier legal procedures did not depend on it. Justice was dealt out in cash, so to speak, whether or not extorted. Because the *trial by evidence demanded* that evidence be sufficient for both the initial arrest warrant and the trial, criminal investigation arose with the detective in the fore-ground. Signs of all kinds, footprints, false alibis and the inferences arising therefrom, have now become as important as the old, often too-sweeping, *cui bono*. Prior to the middle of the eighteenth century there were absolutely no evidentiary trials, at least none that were deliberate. Only several eyewitnesses and above all the confession, which was called the *regina probationis*, could sustain a conviction—nothing else. Since it was seldom that enough witnesses were avail-able, torture was instituted to elicit the *regina probationis*, and its pain-ful question was the only refined one in Charles V's gallows justice. The result was that the accused was put off his guard through pain and made to say things—a torn web of lies at the cost of equally torn limbs—that no one but the perpetrator and the judge could know. The effect was unthinkable atrocity, the worthless extortion of guilt, against which the Enlightenment rebelled for both humane and logical reasons. Since then, evidence is necessary and must be pro-duced; it is the basis for proof before judge and jury in most cases. (This applies at least outside the colonies and to non-fascist jurispru-dence at home.) Even a confession does not replace or detract from the taking of evidence in a given case, since it could be a false self-

accusation aimed at protecting another or deterring the investigation of further crimes as yet unknown. To this extent, the depiction of the evidence gathering work of the detective is no older than the evidentiary hearing itself. No doubt, evidence can also mislead, culminating in judicial murders of a new narrow-minded variety, especially where it appears to fit together smoothly and without gaps. However, evidence *is* more civilized than torture and suspenseful in a different way.

Yet, the ferreting out of the necessary clues was not always narrated in a suspenseful fashion. Or *vice versa*, stories of this kind that appeared many decades later still preserved the thrills and chills of old. Thus, the old curiosity remained, to see what's cooking in the neighbor's pot, to eavesdrop whenever possible with an avid eye to gossip. A primitive interest remained in the portraits of great criminals, extending down to their ballads, pictures, and songs at country fairs. With poison and dagger as props, bloodcurdling Baroque plays in the tradition of Seneca had a lasting effect, coupled with the new-found delight in the Gothic novel, which Walpole's *The Castle of Otranto* in 1764 signaled as the other side of Pietism. There were raging storms instead of silver moons, horror instead of elegies, with Ossianic trappings at a bargain price, but also with the rainy nights and English weather scenery that still suits the detective novel extremely well. The ghost has fallen by the wayside never to be seen again, but the horror novel lends its colors to the desolate houses and trapdoors, even to docks, the East End, and flickering lamps. Indeed, a genuine criminal literature had already constituted itself a little earlier. However, characteristically, it was purely narrative and repetitive and without detectivistic snags. It blossomed in the famous collection of the lawyer Pitaval in 1734, in Anselm Feuerbach's psychologically rich *Darstellung merkwürdinger Verbrechen* (*Portrayal of Remarkable Crimes*) in 1828, in the graphically narrated *New Pitaval* by Alexis in 1842 and more. Not the least is Schiller's *Geisterseher* (*Ghostseer*), that marvelous dime novel of mystery, revelation, and new enigma. It gained broad appeal with Dumas' restoration of the recesses of the newly discovered old quarters and its underworld and especially with the crossings of Grand Guignol and French Romanticism. Here scenery is everywhere, and intrigues abound that only the skill of the detective could penetrate. But the suspense in all this was provided by the criminal and not primarily by the detective, absent as he was. Therefore, the story that includes him is entirely different from the traditional ingredients of the past; it follows the entrusted pursuit of evidence and the narrated understanding of its meaning.

The beginning of the clever end appears to have been difficult, but unfortunately became all the more easy later on. Hoffmann's *Fräulein von Scudéry* paves the way in 1819 with the noble old lady unmasking the goldsmith and saving his apprentice in an almost detective-like manner. As is well-known, the genre was rigorously developed with all of its appurtenances by E. A. Poe; the model is *The Murders in the Rue Morgue* of 1841 with Mr. Dupin as an unmistakable detective with a particularly elusive perpetrator, an orangutan. Since the end of the last century, however, the erstwhile genre of Hoffmann and Poe (rivaled nowadays only by science fiction) has been subjected to an increasing opening of the floodgates of pleasure and suspense, not to speak of the hundred thousand blanks drawn in this criminal lottery. Among the older diversions of this type, A. K. Green looms large, continually enveloping and unwrapping as with Japanese boxes of progressively diminishing size the clue buried in the last. Conan Doyle, however, became a veritable folk song, which is attributable not only to the most popular of detective heroes, but also to an almost archetypical collection of precarious situations and the surprising twist in the concluding lines of the first chapter of *The Hound of the Baskervilles*, which defies imitation. Next on the agenda was the entertainment to be had with authors like Gaborieau, Frank Heller, Oppenheim, and, of course, Agatha Christie, which is always repeatable because quickly forgotten; thrillers with and without sagacity effortlessly follow suit. Unfortunately with Wallace it is easily possible, despite a good thing like *The Sixth Sense of Mr. Reeder*, not to be captivated. Yet, despite the duds in the lottery business, despite the diehard intellectuals, and despite the modesty of this literature, its relaxed suspense is, more than ever, part and parcel of the intelligentsia. This poses a problem, as will be seen, with significantly more than just psychological or sociological roots. And literary caliber, an earmark of the genre since Hoffmann and Poe, recurs consistently, emerging most recently in Chesterton's dreamy, unsavory Father Brown, whose intuition is rooted in his Christian charity. Chesterton's paradox in this area is paid off in small change and lessons taught. In the process the detective novel, especially the average variety, has the advantage of partaking of the peculiar form of "colportage," a form that consistently preserves significations long excluded from "better" literature, and that is not to be equated with kitsch or trash. What is meant are all those familiar detective landscapes of listening, knocking, surprising, interpreting clues, and sudden illuminations, all of which make the legitimate thriller possible. Indeed, they are found primarily in that genre. Yet, their effect can be so transparent, as if a much subtler crudeness, perhaps from *The Tales of Hoffmann* or even *Fidelio*, were sounding from afar. To sum up: colportage contains significations which in part are also present in the loftier realms of poetry and philosophy. However, they are seldom so disconnected and haphazard there. The emergence of colportage at this more mundane level constitutes a double-faceted and renewed reference to an entirely different emergence. In the case at hand, it is based on the *form of the detective novel*, the Oedipal *quod erit demonstrandum* shining through like initials.

So we are now prepared for the style itself, knitting and knotting; for its *characteristics*, which are threefold, closely intertwined and full of intention. First comes the suspense associated with *guessing*, pointing itself, in detective-like manner, to the second characteristic, that of *unmasking* and *discovering*, with special emphasis on what is remote, often the most important source of information. And the act of discovery leads, in the third instance, to events that must first be wrested from their pre-narrative, un-narrated state. The third aspect is the most characteristic of the detective story, rendering it unmistakably independent of the detective figure. Before the first word of the first chapter something happened, but no one knows what, apparently not even the narrator. A dim focal point exists, as yet unrecognized, whither and thither the entire truckload of ensuing events is mobilized—a crime, usually murder, precedes the beginning. In all other narrative forms both deeds and misdeeds develop before the omnipresent reader. Here, on the contrary, the reader is absent when the misdeed occurs, a misdeed that, though conveniently home-delivered, shuns the light of day and lingers in the background of the story. It must be brought to light and this process itself is the exclusive theme. The obscure deed is not even presented in a prelude, for it is as yet unpresentable, except through a process of reconstruction from investigation and evidence.

4. *Suspense*, initially for its own sake, is characteristic of the genre. It can be crudely realized and bloody, which, however, is of no concern here. Though built on blood and bodies, no good detective story achieves its fame with such attractions: they are merely the pretense for a purely intellectual exercise with a narrative picture puzzle aimed solely at the discovery of the perpetrator. This is what draws one in and affords relaxation through its apparent opposite, namely, the reader's competition with the detective in the quest of the probable right clue. The search itself is depicted in isolation, and that is why many of the best readers read the last pages first to participate with cooler heads. Once the "who" is already known, however, the "how" of its discovery emerges more emphatically in well-made stories. "Oh, you're a non-smoker," exclaims one gentleman at a social gathering to another with whom he is supposedly unacquainted, offering him a cigarette: the reader with knowledge of the ending more easily recognizes how a slip of the tongue ruins the gentleman. A suspense that is more subtle than that aimed exclusively at the final resolution is at work here. The process reveals its quality more accurately. Only in that kind of water does one catch that kind of fish: a sporting mode of inquiry for everyone.

5. A *second* characteristic is the *act of discovery* and its *evidence*. Amidst the haste and frenzy it is important not to be rash, but to reconnoiter carefully. It is often the smallest, purely incidental signs from which the detective gleans the most salient information. This was the case, before the advent of such conscious detective stories, with *Abner the Jew* who saw nothing, in Wilhelm Hauff's story, which has the same title as the name. As dreamy as Father Brown, though for more depressed reasons, Abner insists he has seen nothing but a small gold line on the wall and otherwise trivial matters. Yet, these are sufficient for him to put others on the track of the stolen horse. In this connection it is interesting how much the position and image of the detective are *unprofessionally* enhanced by virtue of his knack for incidentals. And the position is always that of a private, virtuous person, independent of the routinized police; this was true at its inception with Poe's unemployed Mr. Dupin. The criminologist as outsider tends to be a Bohemian, an inveterate *flaneur* in his spare time, who, like Abner, only notices that which eludes others in their habits and routines. The Bohemian Holmes evinces a clearly artistic

air, with his careless division of the day, much *l'art pour l'art* in the muddle of his bachelor flat on Baker Street, his tobacco stored in Persian slippers held to the wall by an even more exotic dagger, with his playing of the violin and his love of Chopin. Not only is imagination played off against the policemen, but the new type of detective with his more refined manner of gathering evidence also offers protection for the rashly accused, the possible victims of crude routine. Thus, in almost all of these stories, this figure embodies the characteristic that, according to Radbruch, should distinguish the jurist above all: deliberation. Another interesting aspect, unrelated to the status of outsider, is the change of *method* determined *in general* by society that the respective model detectives employ in gathering and interpreting unconventional clues. This becomes fictitiously clear in the case of two of the more prominent among these sportsmen, especially adept in tracking and putting others on the track. Holmes, *fin de siècle*, utilizes the scientific-inductive method; he can tell from the mud on the soles of his visitors from which part of London they hail; he differentiates between all kinds of tobacco ashes, and chemistry is his favorite science. Agatha Christie's character Hercule Poirot, on the other hand, a product of less rational times, no longer stakes his "grey little cells" on the inductive card, but instead intuits the totality of the case in accordance with the increasingly irrational modes of thinking characteristic of late bourgeois society. Thus Bergson and totality theory have triumphed over J. S. Mill and the mere aggregation of particulars in the realm of the detective novel as well. Be that as it may, whether inductively or intuitively: the pathos of minute evidence, those inconspicuous details so often overlooked by the constables—this *micrological* perspective, as it were, remains intact and fills the valleys of this kind of literature with almost Chinese fastidiousness. How important it can be to have seen whether the letter opener on the desk was placed with the handle or the blade toward the visitor; how absolutely nothing escapes the eye of Abner the Jew except Hecuba; how decisive, on the other hand, is Hecuba's realm when in Agatha Christie's *Thirteen at Dinner* the double destroys the original's alibi by saying París (the city) instead of Páris (the Trojan hero). Numerous examples come to mind for this—literally murderous—meticulousness. Yet when these tricks become known to the police, there is a resistance to letting them become routine, let alone a pattern. Thus, when Hercule Poirot busies himself with a piece of lead pipe so thick that it went unnoticed by the police, and his companion is amazed at his sudden interest in it as if it were trivia, no one less than Agatha Christie has her hero say, "Mon ami, a focal point two feet long is just as valuable as one measuring only two millimeters. But it is impossible to eliminate the romantic view that all important ciphers have to be infinitely small." And, as the precursor Poe already forewarned, every clue *ex machina* is an error similarly "nourished by the massive reading of detective stories," expecially when used at the end so all works out for the best. The result is, as Thackeray says so humorously in *The Snob Book*, "the remedy is at hand like in the pantomime, where as soon as the clown needs something—a hot-water-bottle, a pump handle, a goose or a woman's cape—a bloke saunters in from backstage with the very item desired." To be sure, all detective novels include trivia (to the status of which the thick lead pipe has graduated) and hints, and this micrological realm is most powerful in isolation, away from the standardized perspec-tive. It also encompasses Father Brown's sudden amazement at the "sickly appearance of the marzipan figures," including the light that emanates from them. And another thing, finally, which explicitly pertains to the micrological *dimension*, is characteristic of the hunting ground of the detective: sidelights fill the surroundings and become increasingly inscrutable. It is the *man in disguise* the *inauthentic environ-ment*, veritable talmi gold, typical of this kind of colportage for over a hundred years. Benjamin mentioned it in *Einbahnstrasse* (*One-Way Street*) under the "royally furnished ten-room-dwelling;" a *Gründer-zeit* not exclusively German with aftereffects hearkening back to the "disinterred corpse of the ancestors." This is a theater more commensurate with the detective pursuit than the slums or the East End in former times: "The only adequate depiction and, at the same time, analysis of the style of furniture of the second half of the nine-teenth century is afforded by a certain type of criminal novel, in the dynamic center of which is found the horror of the dwelling. . . . This sofa is the only place on which the aunt can be murdered." In those days lace, doilies, etuis, and draperies still belonged openly, so to speak, to the bourgeois codes of behavior, decorum, and decor, to the world of cant and its crooked or easily corruptible ways. Apart from the realm of the detective in the narrow sense, it was, after all, the heyday of the pillars of society. Benjamin cites Gaston Leroux, the writer of detective stories, in this connection and praises his *Phantom of the Opera* as "one of the great novels of the nineteenth century"; Leroux had "brought about the apotheosis of this genre." And if this is exaggerated, if the "khanate of humbug" is at least to some degree passé, the fundamental characteristic of everyday duplicity that produced it, however, is not. If anything, alienation itself has increased, an alienation that holds people in opposition to themselves, their fellow humans, and the world they have created, and the concomitant chaotic insecurity of life (compared with the relative security of the nineteenth century) has added general *mistrust* to the duplicity. Anything can now be expected from anybody, consistent with the economy of exchange that now applies to faces as well and that, as in an Alfred Hichcock horror film, does not even know the direction from which the blow will come. As a consequence, the ultimate clue in the detective novel can and usually will consist in the unmasking of the most unexpected, least suspected person as the perpretrator. No doubt there were formerly periods of much speedier suspicion, but they were confined to a much smaller circle. This was the case in the days of Brinvillier the poisoner and of the fear of becoming her victim as well as that of the court (Hoffmann's *Fräulein von Scudéry* takes place at precisely this time). This was especially the case during the witch trials, the Inquisition, and the much shorter Reign of Terror. Yet, the relations between people were not a widely and diffusely affected as in the calmer, more normal, yet more anonymous times after Nazism when cunning in a double sense holds sway. Certainly, a genre such as the detective novel expresses this condition of alienation, despite the professional thoroughness and breadth of its suspicion, only through sensationally exaggerated emphasis on crime in the form of entertainment. Without this universal epoch of hypocrisy, however, this type of literature could not have, in the words of Benjamin, "revealed a slice of bourgeois pandemonium" (and not just with an obvious bourgeois label). An ancient manuscript by Aulus Gellius entitled *Noctes atticae*, an anthology from the second century A.D.—and, as will shortly be explained, not only from that century—contains the following line: "Treat your friends as if they were your future enemies." Thoroughly unChristian, this sentence reveals a part of the detective novel's *time and space* that, commensurate with the circumstances, has remained unchanged. Brecht, for good reasons a student of this type of literature, closely approximated the interchangeability of all people who have become faceless; and it is not always the bad guys who wear masks. This increasingly alienated world of masks spells good times for the detective pursuit as such, as well as for a micrology that smacks of criminalistic provenance.

Therefore, even better literature deals more than ever with the process of unmasking. The heights of this better literature have scarcely been measured against their detective content, yet, here in particular, masks drop from faces. In other words, there exist genuine *literature and science* that closely approximate this process of uncovering as such. This is not surprising in any other kind of clarification. The works of Ibsen and Freud, for instance, can obviously not be classified in the detective genre, and to do so would be blasphemy even with due respect for Poe's chase story. Nevertheless, they are structures of *detection sui generis* of the dramatic and analytical variety. They present a characteristic "fresh breeze," "a day of reckoning" for lies and stuffiness that strips off disguises. Ibsen's *A Doll's House, Ghosts, The Wild Duck, Rosmersholm,* and even his last drama are trying to bring to light what is improper for the pillars of society. In the case of Ibsen, an unsolved darkness always precedes the rise of the curtain, a flash of the past is there reminiscent of the narrative form of the detective novel. Significantly, this is no longer satire, but is effectuated through morality in the manner of Scotland Yard, as is also the case on entirely different terrain in the field of psychology. Here Freud comes to mind, his analytical research that is no longer informed by cool dissection but by a vigilance typical of the detective. The conviction that the more neatly the mask conceals, the less salutary that which goes on behind it, gives rise to a deep suspicion of draperies and facades directed at all that ideal and upright superficiality that is too beautiful or comfortable to be true. It is not necessary, nor is this the place, to deal with psychoanalysis, other than to stress the fact that the interpretations of dreams and neuroses are not the only features thereof that read like a detective story. As inadequate as it is to dig for true instincts and repressions predominantly in the private sphere and the unconscious solely as no-longer-conscious, at close inspection a reconstruction very close to the detective form emerges, of that which in Freud's words has led in the "Acherontic" of earlier times to the existing complex and resolves it as soon as it is made conscious. This is an attempted uncovering of *subjectively* false consciousness, primarily of a socially isolated, private-neurotic variety. *Objectively* false consciousness is descriptive of the normal state of affairs in any society that is oblivious to its infrastructure and whose unenlightened sectors allow themselves to be deluded by grandiose phrases (on a par with the sanctity of parental love). The mode of detection appropriate to this type of consciousness (saying "Bible" and meaning "calico," for example, and not only in the colonies), as well as to the great non-detective ideologies, is called the economic interpretation of history. Thus for Marx, the true secret history of Rome is that of private property, and a radical detective inclination claims that all ideologies are reflections of their respective relations of production—indeed (and that would certainly be the test of the hypothesis), that the ideologies develop entirely genetically from them. The illuminating power of this uncovering, discovering view of history is evident even if every superstructure cannot actually be derived from the infrastructure; a reciprocity exists, rather, with the ideologies contributing, nay, producing their own surplus. It is precisely for this reason that such detection techniques, when correctly understood and applied, have the effect of nitric acid in the testing sense: they dissolve false gold, rendering that which remains of the genuine element in formerly progressive times unmistakably recognizable—indeed, in substantial surplus transcending ideologies.

6. The *third* characteristic, finally, is that *most decisive* criterion, which separates the detective novel from all other narrative forms and makes the *un-narrated factor* and its *reconstruction* especially interesting. In the detective novel the crime has already occurred, outside the narrative; the story arrives on the scene with the corpse. It does not develop its cause during the narrative or alongside it, but its sole theme is the discovery of something that happened *ante rem*. Everywhere else the narrative was genetically present: the Alberichs rob the gold before our eyes and Raskolnikov kills the pawnbroker just as epically and visibly as he conceals everything that follows. If, however, new murders occur in the course of the detective story, they constitute yet another black mark, connected with and augmenting the darkness before the beginning, often hampering the resolution of the case. The main point is always the same: the alpha, which none of the characters appearing one after another admits to

have witnessed, least of all the reader, happens outside of the story like the fall from grace or even the fall of the angels (this in order not to shun all-too-mythical coloration). This is also alien to those narrative forms that use flashback and recoup in order to interpolate undisclosed but by no means hidden incidents at the opportune time: it is used informationally, when Isolde recounts for Tristan a part of her pre-history, or, in the grandest example, when Odysseus supplements Homer, so to speak, at the feast in the palace of Alcinous. Nevertheless, the "fresh breeze" of a mightier order attributable to the detective ethos inures to the benefit of the "ante rem" way beyond its pseudo-morphosis in the detective novel. Thus, this principal earmark of the detective story, the darkness at the beginning, is similar in an especially striking manner to some *early great works of literature*. Due to the fact that evidentiary techniques were either absent or not a topic of discussion, their method of uncovering understandably lacks or only sporadically avails itself of the special craft of the detective. The art of detection, of unearthing and reconstructing, on the other hand, is not lacking in the least. It has been said that colportage preserves meanings that have been lost or are no longer officially condoned; this is particularly true of Poe's genre, which through its establishment in classical literature is able to exchange new codes and breathing space. If Brecht's "Pirate Jenny Song," when carefully listened to, touches on very remote, even Manichaean realms, Poe's detective-form, on the other hand, touches time and again on the related realm of Oedipus. This holds particularly true with respect to that "X" that precedes the beginning, waiting in the wings, which leads from the dark pre-lude, the unknown pre-history, into the narrative.

And it does not always have to be a corpse that arrives on the scene. Other things suffice, for great literature does not depend on hoodlums and gangsters. Now, finally, their diametrical opposite, *Oedipus*, should be mentioned, unknowing murderer of his father, unknowing husband of his mother. One recalls the resulting plague inflicted upon Thebes and the interpretation of the misdeed after it ocurred by the Oracle at Delphi. One recalls as well Oedipus' increasingly pressing and urgent investigations carried out in the interest of his people and his own security from the murderer, yet thwarted by the most confounded obstacle. The hunter who is himself the prey and fails in this quest of self plies his monstrous trade until he belatedly recognizes the truth and does penitence for the perpetration of crimes in which he participates, neither consciously nor morally, but with a highly classical and a highly modern ego-identity. Multifariously disguised, the theme of Oedipus, this *primordial detective theme per se*, continued to have an effect, always criminalistic to be sure, and with the hidden antecedent. A peculiar reverberation of this theme thus appeared in the Middle Ages in Hartmann von Aue's *Gregor auf dem Stein* (*Gregory on the Stone*), transmitted by a Latin legend (the story was retold by Thomas Mann in *The Holy Sinner*). In this story the reader knows what happened behind the back of the hero in the way of incestuous birth and incestuous love, but the hero finds out, quite in accordance with the rules of detection, only in the plot and as plot itself. And then, with an even greater leap in time, society, and subject matter, an Oedipal element reappears in Fielding's *Tom Jones*, that voluminous masterpiece of reconstruction, constantly reinterpreted by its author. Here the reader discovers, simultaneously with the foundling Jones and despite many vagaries, what his dark birth was all about. And the revelation comes at the end, when, with the darkness lifted, the foundling finally sees not only who his father was, but also that which he had never questioned because he erroneously believed he knew the answer, the identity of his mother. This last discovery concerning a most unexpected lady lends a special reconstructive glamour to this detective novel without a detective. And finally, with another great leap, one recalls Kleist's strangely reduced Oedipus of *Der Zerbrochene Krug* (*The Broken Jug*), reduced to and done out of an amorous rendezvous, a comical shadow cast by the great tragic theme. Here the cryptic prelude is totally minimized, yet, for the first time since Sophocles, the judge and the perpetrator are one. In addition, the judge must exercise finesse off the top of his head to protect himself from the growing evidence, such as the lost wig— and this at the occasion of an inspection testing his judicial capabilities. Satire aimed at the patriarchal discretion of the provincial judicial system as well as the military press and its arbitrary corruptness is at work. Yet the story line itself, entirely sustained by evocations of the "ante rem" incest, is reduced to an attempted rendezous and homicide to the breaking of a jug. In short, Thebes is everywhere, shimmering threateningly through even the most distant transformations; Tom Jones, or the circumstances of one's own birth, lend an anticipated probing Kaspar-Hauser flavor to the process of detection. This is in accordance with the foundling's condition in which not only the exiled Oedipus finds himself, but everyone on earth whose world is not of his or her own choosing. And without exception, as if not only the Oedipus myth but Poe as well were the guiding inspirations. In order to develop, all plots of this type are preceded by a crime or at least a mysterious mistake that needs to be uncovered. This is the criminological knot that constitutes the Oedipal theme, the archetype for all later occurrences.

7. So much for literature: it is paralleled by even more remarkable ruminations of the speculative variety. And once again, the common denominator for everything is the process of uncovering, whereby in this case the presupposition is that a veiled misdeed precedes the creation of the *world itself*. The aforementioned phrase "fall from grace," stemming from mythology, first a dense shadow, had an effect on later concepts. Every loyalty relationship to the ancestral lord deems revolt a crime and associates chaos with it as well. However, this reactionary attitude toward retrospection is precisely what initially mobilized sensibilities for the problem of the uncanny: more so, in any case, then the carefree gaze averted from all hullabaloo, trusting, not only that God is in heaven, but that everything is well with the whole history of the world. Thus the suspicion of an accursed secret *ante rem, ante lucem, ante historiam*, of a *casus ante mundum* appeared in *philosophy* as well, in a particularly conspicuous and penetrating form: that is to say, in those passages and indeed quite partisan images of a primevally conceived revolt, outlined by Franz Baader and the late Schelling. It is important here to refer back to a dreadful primordial event, "an un-origin" as abyss with reactionary production costs but, on the other hand, curious Oedipal touches of a metaphysical nature. This *ab ovo* theme, undoubtedly in the detective category, was "immemorial," before the beginning of the world, and according to Baader and Schelling the repercussions of this immemorial element portend nothing good. Thus Baader maintains, after positing causal nexus and finiteness as the principal determinants of our world, that finiteness suggests a prisoner, the latter, however, a crime committed before the world existed for him. This world is continually linked to an original sin, spreading repercussions of misfortune, which the fall from grace only hints at with-

out exhausting it: "Through all the beauty of Nature, man hears her melancholy lament, sometimes softer, sometimes louder, about the widow's veil (!) which she must wear as a result of mankind's sins" (Baader, *Werke* [*Works*], II, 1851, p. 120). And above all: "Only a monstrous crime (!) less an apostasy than an insurrection, could cause this material revelation" (i.e., the world) "to be an institution of crisis, restraints and rehabilitation, and the persistence of this crime explains the perpetuation or regeneration of this matter" (ibid., p. 490). Naturally, this sort of thing is kindled by a reactionary ideology of calumny against the French mystagogue Saint Martin and his drawing of a parallel between *révolution* and *révolte des anges*. However, it is remarkable that a theory of primordial darkness void of any counter-revolutionary reference can already be found in Jakob Böhme, who, along with his introduction of the term "un-origin" (*Ungrund*) and its participation in Creation, became so important for Baader in later times. And further in the past, having influenced Böhme himself, the Cabala teaches just like Baader that the world is a retrospective prison. This is emphasized especially by Isaac Luria in the sixteenth century. According to him, "bereshith," the beginning (the first word in the Bible), does not mean the beginning of a *creation* but points to a capture (tsimsum = contraction) of God Himself. Of course the crime here is attributed to the captor and not to an "un-origin," "abyss" in the God of this atypical criminal mythology or metaphysics. Instead, the beginning in the Cabala resembles a type of dark, primeval Egypt that has repercussions in the world as exile, a world that demands Exodus in order to break out and dissolve the beginning. After all this, let us cite Schelling and his culminating problem of a "rupture" with God at the beginning, without which finite entities would not exist. Evil *ante rem*—precisely this represents the confluence of the detective form and what is certainly the most eccentric metaphysics. Schelling's *Philosophy of Religion*, 1804, reads as follows: "Whoever thinks he can recognize the principle of good without that of evil is making the greatest of all mistakes, for just as in Dante's poem, the path to heaven leads through the abyss in philosophy as well" (Schelling, *Werke* [*Works*], VI, p. 43). And more in the grand style, hardly inspired by Dante this time, yet again full of Oedipus and the dark antecedents of the plague in the otherwise well-constructed Thebes: "After the eternal act of self-revelation, everything in the world as we now see it is law, order and form; yet lawlessness always lurks at its foundations, as if it could once again break through, and nowhere does it appear as if order and form were at the origin but rather, that an original chaos was brought to order. . . . Without this antecedent darkness, there is no creational reality; gloom is its necessary heritage" (*Philosophische Untersuchungen über das Wesen der menschlichen Freiheit* [*Philosophical Investigations into the Essence of Human Freedom*], 1809, *Werke*, VII, pp. 359ff). In this context, the Ahriman of the Manichaean doctrine, who robbed the sparks of light or made them fall in love with his base world, has also had a visible influence on the notion of the criminal beginning. Thus, the den of gangsters erupts into the world of the righteous; it must be redressed and rendered harmless. It was therefore placed at the very beginning by the archeologists of gloom, Baader and Schelling, as if ensuing history were nothing but pure anti-crime and had no other plans, nothing else to do. All this is far removed from Hegel's totally uncriminalistic theory of origins, which, though certainly much too panlogistic, nevertheless disturbs the *Alpha* of every *Pan*-Pitaval: "The beginning is what is in itself, the immediate, abstract, the universal, that which has not yet progressed. The concrete, the rich comes later; that which comes first is the poorest in determinations." Once again, and *here* there is no escape: "Thus the original realm of immediacy is inadequate *per se* and must be endowed with the drive to develop itself further" (Hegel, *Logik* [*Logic*], II, Meiner, p. 489). And it must be added: the sorry end cannot, *per definitionem*, stand at the *beginning*, but comes later, is incurred in the story—getting into trouble, brewing. Beyond their mythologems, however, it is true that in all of the aforementioned examples of Oedipal metaphysics, an original *darkness* or *incognito* is reflected, if not a fantastically contrived *crime*. In this respect, every last investigation of origins is related to the Oedipal form, which treats the incognito basically not just as an unknown of the logical variety, but also as something uncanny, unknown even to itself. And no Oedipus has yet answered, let alone solved the only worthwhile riddle of the Sphinx: the incognito that explains why anything at all appears, why the world exists. It is also true—yet this relates least of all to a so-called primordial beginning, but solely to what is incurred along the way—it is also true that a certain clearing exists in the forest of history, and this is why both Schiller and Hegel call world history a last judgment; and what is even more certain is that there would be no process, searching, changing, and possibly healing, if there were not something that ought to be different. Obvious as well is the fact that a characteristic, homogeneous archetype runs through the entire highly multifarious hunting ethos from the Oedipal kind to the recollection of origins. It is and remains the investigation of a darkness *ante rem*, of the way it is obliged to shun the light or at least is in need of knowing the path of illumination; this principal characteristic of detection has been modified both epically and metaphysically.

So much for signs in places where they are not expected. They are all instances, they have insufficiently, nay, barely, been given their due. They extend from the stupidest of the clever detective stories up to the trial comedy, to strange mythologies of abduction, to high seriousness, which also has a place. For most people, the detective stories, the poor relatives, are the first to reveal this heuristically; this is how they were thought out. The omitted beginning in *Tom Jones* and in *Oedipus rex* is here, above all, a higher sphere because it is the lowest. And in order not to shun the strongest Oedipal transparency: is the reader of these mysteries not caught in the darkness of his undisclosed momentary being continually renewing itself? And even if the world into which the reader has chanced does not, following Schopenhauer's denunciation, look like a cabinet of monstrosities, an inn of scoundrels, or an insane asylum depending on one's viewpoint, it nevertheless looks like a precarious as well as difficult detection phenomenon, whose catchword has not yet been found. Certainly, this is an inquiry for which even the Oedipal model lacks jurisdiction. However that may be, *rebus sic imperfectis*, a principal concern of philosophy is not incorrectly characterized by its form, even if from a different perspective. Theodor Fontane concludes his semi-detective novel *Unterm Birnbaum (Under the Pear Tree)* with the following words: "And once again bore witness to the wisdom of the proverb: Nothing is spun so tight, eventually everything comes to light." This is in any case better than nihilistic songs of loneliness, which desire to know absolutely nothing, of schematic victory chants, which already know everything anyhow. The Greeks, however, called Δίχη the Just, the wisest as well, for she brought everything in time, through time, to light. This sounds very mystical, yet also has its rational aspect: light shining into a crime.

8. Item: something is uncanny, that is how it begins. Investigative uncovering is indeed only one aspect, aimed at the origin. Investigative edification is the other, aimed at the destination. There, the finding of something that has been, here, the creation of something new: this tense process is often no less labyrinth-like. And strangely enough: even edification appears in its own form of novel, in a form once again frequently sinister, then again significantly elevated, namely, in the so-called *novel of the artist*. It would be tempting to demonstrate this right here without digression by way of their contents. How rightful it is that the author of *Fräulein von Scudéry* marks this newer beginning here as well, this time dealing with the craft of genius. E. T. A. Hoffmann, a judge in Berlin, with his detective knack, actually had no problem switching over to the "Serapion principle" of the painter, musician, or poet. This is revealed openly in the music conductor Kreisler and indirectly in the student Anselmus of the *The Golden Pot* through the tiger lily and the salamandrian features of his master. After that it goes downhill: novels of manners dealing with the loose morals of artist types and their models, naked ones of course, in great detail, bacchanalian for most, in Paul Heyse's case anyway (and down below gushed the Isar). The middle range covers a broad spectrum, likewise replete with the so-called glimpse into the artist's studio, yet occasionally occupied with the ebb and flow of a real creative process. Wassermann's mediocre *Gänsemännchen* (*The Little Goose Man*) but also Rolland's *Jean Christophe*, not to speak of Werfel's *Verdi, Roman der Oper*, belong to this group. Surpassing these is the most highly successful portrait so far, Keller's *Der Grüne Heinrich* (*Green Henry*), in which the artist is left to fail in a "cypress-shaded finale" in the first version, but in reminiscent resignation in the second. Thomas Mann entered this suspicious sanctuary totally without protection, in bold counterpoint, with *Doctor Faustus* late German style, therefore as musician. The theme of this genre continues to be dawning, setting, and breakthrough, also effected by eccentrically central catalysts. A quite stirring example of the latter, despite its mediocre quality, is Werfel's *Verdi*, with the singer and her "well-balanced fragrance," with the surging *melos* of revenge from *Othello* after Wagner's death. To be sure, the *breakthrough* itself, this garish principle characteristic of the matter, is either avoided in this form of the novel or merely circumscribed in declaratory style. This presumably relates to a self-

signaling though also signal aspect of the breakthrough, which is usually only represented in music. This is the reason why this type of oceanic calm and blissful journey is more easily accommodated in an opera than a novel (this even applies to insignificant ones, such as the first act of Pfitzner's *Palestrina*). The unmistakable form evinced throughout in the novels of detectives and detection is completely absent in the novel of the artist: unless a significant way of *omitting the ending*, of *unproffered fruit* can be seen as characteristic of them. According to the portrayed *status nascendi*, this ending would have to be the *artist's work itself*, imaginary as it is (with the exception of artist's biographies in novel form). Only *Doctor Faustus* is able to master these difficulties to a degree by means of suggestive velleities. There the omitted ending, which is nevertheless latent in coruscating flashes of aurora, could have a similar meaning and correspond to the obscure beginning in the detective genre. The reason for the absence of an unmistakable form in the novel of the artist is surely the lack of great old masterpieces of this type. There are none from which the novel of the artist could develop in a secularized form, from which it could gain sustenance, regardless of their remoteness. For even Goethe's plot in *Tasso* suffers, hopes, and fails because of love and not the creativity of the artist; there is no *Oedipus rex* in this realm, illuminating and substantiating. And that, in spite of the fact that creativity and its representation are the furthest from lacking an old archetypal figure: its name is *Prometheus*. Yet, he was never constituted as the archetype of the artist in any classical work. This much as finale and no more here about the novel of the artist, and only to use its investigative-edification to stress and contrast the investigative-uncovering of the Oedipus genre. Though the novel of the artist finds itself in the same book as the detective or detection novel, it is written on another page, which in both literature and philosophy is not even half as comprehensive—indeed, its Promethean form is presumably a thing of the future. In contrast, the detective novel has given rise to more imitation, to such a degree that its mass-produced commodities are vulgar, whereas those of the novel of the artist, numerically fewer anyway, are not petit bourgeois. After this side-glance at a related genre, as its foil, let us conclude, reaching back with a much tighter, arresting grasp at the detective novel. The expedition so far has revealed something not-too-trivial in what has become trivial literature—here, too, the suspense is not stupid. And what was observed at the beginning has been confirmed: there must be something to this case after all. The problem of the omitted beginning affects the entire detective genre, gives it its form: the form of a picture puzzle, the hidden part of which predates the picture and only gradually enters into it.

# A Philosophical View of the
# Novel of the Artist

1. While reading we like to empathize with a character, especially when the character's life assumes a more colorful aspect than what is usual. A life like this does not always have to be successful, particularly not in a cheap sense. It can also affect the involved reader when there is suffering and failure insofar as this does not become lukewarm. In particular, young people, along with curious dropouts, participate in all of this as though they were its guest. Such vicarious reading is not only a substitute for real life, but can also jar readers and prepare them for something.

2. Empathizing is most effective when one is simultaneously carried away. The reader breaks out and escapes to encounter unusual people and situations, among them the artistic. During the period of *Jugendstil* the special places of escape were Paris and Munich. Unusual young people fled to these cities. "You can hear the Isar River rustle." It is in this way that the vicarious pleasure gained from reading appears itself to be artistic. Instead of the so-called higher echelons of society, the life of the artist seems to be more attractive—the successful artist and accordingly his novel of the artist. Artist—now, that is a word, that has been used for Bohemians and pop singers as well as for Hölderlin, and petty-minded people love artists even when the latter are especially anti-philistine. This is why there are trashy novels in this genre as well as peepholes to look at nude models. In former times the wives of self-important industrialists liked to read such books at holiday resorts, and they could read about tenors who were like Apollonian gods. One story about an artist has the trumpeteer of Sackingen as its hero, whereby Hoff-

mann's music conductor Kreisler is minimized as heir. But such caricatures have not had a visible effect on the *genus* (even though they themselves still live off its imagination.) Nor has the genus been effected by Heinrich Hart's hymn entitled *Cäcilie*, for which Richard Strauss wrote the music. It ends this way: "If only you knew what life means, enveloped by the divine breath that created the world ... if only you knew, then you would come to me." The good genus concerns things that are less enveloped by divine breath but are more connected to the workshop as life, life as workshop in which there is a fruit that is formed and thrives—or sometimes not. Then in the formation of such stories—and only in them—the formation is silence of the sea, labyrinth and thread, thicket and clearing—or sometimes not. *Schwere Stunde* (*Difficult Hour*) is the title of a story by Thomas Mann in which Schiller is sitting at his desk and working on *Wallenstein* during the night. Schiller arose and "moved toward the oven from where he looked over at his work with a quick and painful, strained glance, the work from which he had fled, this burden, this pressure, this tortuous conscience, this sea which he was to drink up, this terrible task, which was his pride and misery, his blessing and damnation." Such a story is a report about effort, not about licking honey on the hills of Mymettos or at parties in artists' studios. Even when genius is much more meaningful than industriousness, and even when the best is easily done, stagnation and breakthrough, effort and light belong together in this matter, along with the strange source at Parnassus over whose dangerous terrain the mediocre novel of the artist, not the mere vulgar one, endeavors to cross. The reason why the element of seduction and also the element of preparation can sustain themselves is that: they concern young disciples and entice them by the dream of the *opus magnum*. Here it could appear to many a Karl Moor *sui generis* as though he was reading in Plutarch about great people. Rolland's "heroic biographies" among others already corresponded to them. They are anecdotal like Plutarch's lives that treated experienced masters and their works. Of course, the *genuine* novel of the artist deals with imaginary heroes and works, although there are references to real life, autobiographical facts that are converted, even self-judgment. This is the way it is with Hoffmann's music conductor Johannes Kreisler right at the beginning, and this is the way it is with Mann's Adrian Leverkuhn at his provisional late bourgeois ending. One is seduced, but this happens everywhere, and it is more or less like a legal visit to the so-called land of genius.

3. It has not been very long that invitations to visit such people were sent out and that artists have seemed interesting at all. The situation was different earlier: there was nothing special to be told about them. Whereas the detective novel requires a process of collecting evidence, penetrating backward to a past crime, the novel of the artist requires recognition of and interest in the creative person who brings out something new instead of something past. The creative person's social standing belongs to all this, a more visible, particular precedence made out of the workday and future. Neither the Age of Greek and Roman Classicism nor the Middle Ages captured the life and strivings of their artists in the imagination. In fact, the Greeks disdained their painters and sculptors, whom they considered insignificant; that is, they were viewed as manual laborers because they did physical work. The tragedians were the only ones among the poets, who sweated only in a metaphorical sense, to be accorded a high rank. However, even their names went largely neglected, and certainly their lives were of little interest to anyone. This was also the case in medieval society, which had almost no feelings for that which was later to be called the glamour of personality. To be sure, the courtly *Minnesänger* and epic poets became more familiar figures to a degree. However, it was never considered necessary to invent a name for the unknown poet of the *Nibelungenlied*. And many painters and wood carvers of great works are known today only by made-up names (such as the Master of Marienleben) that art historians bestowed upon them 500 years later. We are still in the dark about Grünewald's life, and this has something indistinguishably to do with the mystery surrounding the unrecognized genius that was to arise later. Where and how was it possible for the novel of the artist as particular *aventiure* (adventure story) to be cultivated like the fabulous courtly romances or narratives of fantastic voyages? There were no arenas or lights for it, not even in the well-known choral contest (*Sängerkrieg*) on the Wartburg, which was clearly the first romantic one. There were practically no public characters in art until the estate society of the Middle Ages began to break down in the early phase of capitalism. The period of the Renaissance was the first to present real-life material of the painters from Cimabue to Titian, filled with anecdotes, somewhat

*post festum* already, about 1550, right before Italy was to be greatly influenced by Spain. Still, by this time there had already been visionary victory marches made up purely as Petrarch's *Trionfo della fama* and Boccaccio's *Amorosa visione*. And this was also the beginning of the satirical depictions that were decidedly anonymous. Of course, the satire was directed more against the humanists than against the artists. Yet, it was against their arrogant claim to be the sons of Apollo. Accordingly, one caricature portrayed them as expecting an even greater bow from the leaning tower of Pisa whenever they passed it. There is plenty of such satire because the picture of the artist that began to capture the imagination fully at that time arose only due to the victorious assumption of power by the bourgeoisie in the eighteenth century, and these artists had indeed a clear anti-feudal disposition, as can be seen in the cult of the genius of the *Sturm und Drang* writers. To be sure, the artist appeared here for the first time in the wild Apollonian genre as the canonical exception by virtue of his nature, not by virtue of his ancestry. The artist's room under the roof spouted fire. Creative fomentation soared and attracted attention. The classical period of the Greeks and Romans and the South was understood from this position, for example, in Heinse's *Ardinghello*, in a bacchanalian sense, not in a Winkelmannian one. The picture of the genius was invigorated in this way by the *Sturm und Drang* for some time. When it had long since disappeared, that is, when it had long since blown over, it was continued in all of Europe by the awe raised by Napoleon, who shared the titanic aspect with the powerful genius of the *Sturm und Drang* in incredible reality, even up to the image of the chained Prometheus on the island of St. Helena. Prometheus himself had only been recently recalled through Shaftesbury—and not as the hero who stole fire from the gods, as he was most often depicted by the Greeks and Romans, but as creator, a new maker of human beings and thus the archetype of the artist. This became most clear during the *Sturm und Drang* period especially in the early works of Goethe, then in romanticism without restoration. For example, Shelley's works are important here, particularly his drama *Prometheus Unbound*, which is in no way just a comedy. There was an aura of this kind from then on that continually endowed the image of figures. For it was at this time that the demonic aspect was added, and it was alloyed with romantic wish-terror (*Wunschgrauen*) of the artistic kind inside and out as that category that was not uncanny and that had pertained formerly only to creatures of the middle world between here and there like eccentrics, believable goblins, and spooky places, and also fanatics, witches, and conspirators. However, these kinds of things transformed themselves in the image of the artist into something elementary that came from *Sturm und Drang* in a positive way, into something volcanic deep underneath and into a light on top of the mountain that could not be missed. The artist was supposed to launch his poetic and erotic fire high into the air in an exemplary way. Of course, this did not prevent virtuosos, too, from finding a place for themselves there, especially among the late romantic audiences. Thus, Paganini, who loved to have everything set aflame around him, had a long and constant effect. All this belonged to the image of the artist that had become in great demand at that time. It was still recognizable in Wagner's Hörselberg-Tannhäuser, even in the *terminus* of the magician with the bagpipe, which Nietzsche wanted to apply to Wagner. But it was the life itself of a great poet, namely, Byron, who gave noble stuff of divine notoriety to all such archetypes. His life had an effect all by itself even without his meteoric works, which, in spite of Cain depicted as Manfred, did not intend to build tension as in colportage. Yet, whatever makes a mark first tends to remain. For example, E. T. A. Hoffmann created the first detective story in *Fräulein von Scudéry*, and then this same writer produced the first figures of the novel of the artist in the form of the music conductor Kreisler and also Anselmus in *The Golden Pot*, along with the love in these works. They found their musical embodiment in Schumann's *Kreisleriana* and in Berlioz's *Symphonie Fantastique*. All this, in turn, *came out of the life of an artist*. Pre-romantic literature could not provide much material for this subject in spite of the Renaissance or even the *Sturm und Drang*. The novel of the artist is methodically the only one in which *Sturm und Drang* continually reappeared as subject matter. "If only a creation full of nectar could gush from my fingers"—this verse of the young Goethe, filled with desire and volition, also contains the theme of birth and destiny with defeat or victory of work upon which the novel of the artist had to make for itself its optimal wish.

4. It is strange how often more trickling is portrayed here than flood. The mediocre novels like Friedrich Huch's *Enzio* or Jakob Wassermann's *Gänsemännchen* are good examples of this. In the long run the artists in these works do not turn out to be artists. They were mistaken

despite their desire, which did not come just out of thin air. In fact, they had a strong wind behind them at first. Huch's Enzio fails because he lacks either artistic training or talent or both. And when Wassermann's musician Daniel Nothafft resigns nobly after a spiteful wench has burned his compositions, he knows why, even if he does not choose death like Enzio but decides to live out his life as a quiet, wise man. The petty bourgeois *habitus* of both novels makes it clear what imitation means. Nevertheless, their characters allow one to realize what desire without capability is, what seduction is, and then folly and narrow-mindedness. In addition, one recognizes that this process, which is as genuine as it is disturbing, has very rarely been portrayed in a meaningful way with its motto "Many feel the calling, but few are chosen." It fills one of the most innocent tragedies according to that negative heterogony of purposes that demands that the work does not outdo the plan during the performance; rather, the reverse is true: the plan shrinks during performance. That is, it lives only in idle wishing, not in the flesh. Even a figure like Ulrik Brendel in Ibsen's *Rosmersholm* comes close to fulfilling the plan with numerous unwritten works, and just as he wants to pour them out, everything is empty. He had sown his seeds in his dreams. This is that ironic portrait of a *soi-disant* Raphael without hands, which is certainly meaningful. And he is noble in his way, more noble than Ejlert Lövborg in *Hedda Gabler*, the threatened one, who is successful even though he is lost at the same time. Of course, it is much different when the hero of a novel of the artist—and he is only this because he is a character that is not made up but one that is historically famous—goes his way *realiter per aspera ad astra*. For example, Werfel called his novel *Verdi, Novel of the Opera*: it was filled with nights made out of depression. However, there were also catalytic factors in it that went beyond that. Much of the novel is fictitious. Though only barely historical and mediocre, the work is not a panopticon. There is a great deal of portrayal of the late Verdi, always the Odysseus part of the production with the difficult auora that leads to the successful work. Verdi burns the ineffective score to his *Lear*, and the *Requiem*, which had been written ten years before this, seems to him to be his own swan song. However, then the other comes, the positive text, for whose sake the novel of the artist may allow itself to be written at all, to tell about proven masters and not merely to duplicate them. The adventure of the *breakthrough* occurs, the difficult midsummer day of the new work, *Othello*, which is conceived in the novel as though it were being conceived right now. Romain Rolland's *Jean Christophe* is not as historical as Werfel's work because it concerns a "contemporary" German musician, and yet it contains a notable character who is already known and somewhat strange. It is Beethoven who struggles, judges, and explodes as the measure of the citizen (*citoyen*) in music during a much greater earthly pilgrimage. This long, if not somewhat long-winded novel about a German musician named Kraft seeks more than just this. Like many other novels of the artist, it is full of sentimentality and earnestness. What is heroic is part of the scenery of creativity attached to a star, not the reverse. Of course, even that mere supplementary display of creating becomes noticeable. The biographical novels reveal this tendency time and again in contrast to those works that are completely fictitious. Rolland's Beethoven novel reproduces the act of conducting through a seventh symphony. Werfel's novel must steer an even clearer course due to the familiarity with the Verdi opera. Thus, it is in this way that the process *per aspera ad astra* is necessarily structured with norms in spite of the Lear night or the unexpected Othello lightening. This manner in which the writer can create a portrait has already been structured more than half.

5. This is why such a manner turns out better when it remains a free-wheeling one. Then its origins can emerge, and they are filled with purely invented characters that are thus first discovered and given life as in the works of E. T. A. Hoffmann. It was this artist who wrote the first genuine story of the artist, half autobiographical and experienced, otherwise imaginary. Of course, it is true that Huch's Enzio and Wassermann's Nothafft are fictitious, too, and are not listed in any history of music. However, this is mainly due to the fact that they are too general and not because they are basically developed as creative characters. In contrast, Hoffmann's student Anselmus and music conductor Kreisler embody the "Serapion principle," which emanates from them and which is both something completely and disruptively new and also a continuation of something known. They have no desire to depend on models outside of themselves. Here we find the captured and generated Imago of the artistic in the romantic period, which is portrayed by an artist who confronts himself. This also occurs with failure, with the very deep

wounds that Hoffmann received in his relationship with Julia Marc, with the unfinished musical works that Hoffmann had intended to write, with the transformation of Julia into "divine images of feminity," which continually console and reject him—with the yearning for Atlantis and the "possession of inner poetic sense," which is to be found there. It is similarly the case with the Archivarius Lindhorst himself, who has a distinct oriental character (the connection here is that the way to Baghdad from old Germany was always closer than from the Mediterranean to Baghdad.) This produces the fairy-tale atmosphere governing the Serapion principle, which does not mean Hoffmann's portrait of the artist and light of the artist is indicative here—just poetical subjectivity alone, but also its alliance with the recondite, with the sulfurous or blue remote color in the object. The insane hermit Serapion, introduced by Caprian in *The Serapion Brothers*, whose name becomes the title of the brothers' club, envisions Alexandria of 2,000 years ago in or through a German town of the present—thus, a world that is spliced with another one. Thanks to the power of the imagination, Hoffmann's Anselmus experiences Alexandria merging with the town again, the realm of Lindhorst with Dresden on the River Elbe. And this is simultaneously the celebration of the artistic process. To be sure, it is nothing but the novel of the artist as objective fantasy of itself and its world. Here Hoffmann set the tone in which the life of an artist and his oblique imagination represent themselves for the first time—with figures that stand there like notes of their own music, above all of their first sounds written and developed first in the novel. The same holds true for the fictitious works of these fictitious characters who were not at all like the transplanted characters from the history of art, i.e., from real life. Of course, in Kreisler's case, the genial protagonist of the *Kreisleriana*, Kater Murr, the crazy musician, who is hindered by his own dissatisfaction and the miserable conditions surrounding him that make him scurrilous, all of this keynote work here lies in the distant horizon. Nevertheless, Hoffmann sets his musical distress into relief as nocturnal fantasies on the piano, with works that never became anything and yet could be claimed to be better than anything known at that time as another kind of pastoral. Kreisler discusses many of these improvising composers and his own imaginary work, and here he particularly focuses on everything opposed to the philistines and his own enemies. He has himself and artists in mind when he says that "many of these unfortunate fanatics become aware of their own errors too late and succumb to their own insanity, and this can be detected very easily from their statements about art. They believe, for instance, that art allows human beings to intuit its higher principle and lead them out of the meaningless hustle and bustle of everyday life toward the temple of Isis where nature speaks to them. These crazy people have the strangest ideas about music. They call it the most romantic of the arts since its theme is mainly eternity. Music is the mysterious, the sanscrit of nature articulated in tones that fill the human breast with eternal longing, and only in music can people understand the high song of the trees, the flowers, the animals, the stones, and the water." Here we have the endeavor in Kreisler's works (which are written in this way, but which is nevertheless described quite concretely in the story about an artist). Of course, Kreisler's concrete portrayal is not to be considered the most appropriate task for a piece of music. There is much too much fantasy here intended to spite the Bamberg philistines. Nevertheless, attempts could have been made at that time to try the harmony of glass bells, Aeolus' harps, and natural sounds that were beyond the earthly vale of tears. Be that as it may, Hoffmann's novel of the artist allows (again for the first time) unwritten works to emerge as sprouts, as projects. It is not only in the indicated course of his intended works that a not-yet emerges, three-quarters of a life before the coming day or perhaps not, with whose arrival the novel of the artist is especially concerned—with the fictitious and open novel of the artist.

Therefore, nothing stands in the way of this kind of struggle, nor in the way of the depicted struggle, to investigate that which cannot be solved. To sketch buildings that were not built, to describe a musical composition technically that would have probably been possible in its time. This astonishing feat was accomplished long after Hoffmann by a novel of the artist that assumed the form of a travelogue of the imagination with imaginary reference notes throughout it. All this, among other things, occurs in one of the last of these formations with *Doctor Faustus* finally as artist. To be sure, Thomas Mann's Adrian Leverkuhn is just as different from Kreisler as is his Felix Krull from Anselmus, as the parody of the floodlight on Julia, as Phosophor, always cold, as Isis, of course, also as genius, impure, like yearning for genius. This Doctor Faustus wishes to explicate the production process totally through the incarnation of his production (and then again vice versa). There are Brentano compositions, then an "apocalypsis cum figuris" in high Dürer fashion, and finally a Faust *oratorium*. There are just as many illuminations of how to reach the black way as there are to reach the blue. Thus, this novel presents the characteristics of the fictitious novel of the artist in general and epitomizes them. Here this form becomes entirely comprehensible and instructive *as portrayal of the desire to articulate that which has never yet been heard in Apollo*—just as the young Modigliani once wrote to a friend in a more realistic way, "Io sono ricco e fecondo di germi e ho bisogno dell'opera." Just as William Blake allegorized the difference between the conservative factor and the eclectic factor in the creative process: "The cistern contains, the fountain overflows." The fact that the devil fetches Leverkuhn at the end, that disease pulverizes him, and that all the inhibitions and creative unwholesomeness of the late bourgeois period dissolve into the demonic once again, this does not hinder in the least the portrayal of the creative process. Just as it does not hinder, "without some concealment and hypocrisy," the creation, the aurora in the night, in spite of or because of this. For there never has been a late period just with decline alone. In each one there was a dialectical dawn made out of sunset and sunrise. And the latter certainly does not lack the "apocalypsis cum figuris," nor the loneliest final note, held high and long, *malgré lui*. Before the end becomes extinguished, there is the middle, in which evil has to be allowed to create in a much different way than the poor devil could give or celebrate. Here the actual theme of the novel of artist; the process of production is developed in a more penetrating way because the satiated epoch has already written and thought of everything for the artist in a classically tested form. Ambivalence, not only in a moral but also in an allegorical sense, is the keyword in the entire novel. Ambivalence as a powerful modulating, wavering creature between the abyss and the precarious rise. That which has been split asunder and flayed also emerges in a late period and rises above the cracked polish of the surface. There is a specific way to cultivate this, too. This is the reason why the novel could let Leverkuhn experiment so "elementarily" in fragments and on the boundaries of his time. This means that he *had done some torturing* on the boundaries of inorganic nature and let it exceed itself. Indeed, art conveys its objects to an even more pure, still pure region beyond themselves to a further or deeper meaning that they contain, just as the artist himself who engenders this must raise himself to a higher power in his *natura-naturans* in order to be capable of becoming an artist who engenders. Although *Doctor Faustus* maintained the basic theme of the novel of the artist like no other novel, even when it had to pay for this and became uncanonical, there is still no existing novel of the artist that has brought to life such artistic processes in a movement forward, in an until now not-yet so that the artistic process could find its *entire self-portrait*: that is, the portrayal of the desire to articulate, to form the face itself of that which has never before been heard. In this way artists have their next existence before them, the silence of the sea and happy journey, those phenomena of resistance and of a possible victory. Nietzsche once reproached accepted aesthetics (and rightly so) for being passive, namely, for being set by art consumers instead of by people who knew how to be more than receptive and know what for and against which beauty *in statu nascendi* stands its ground. Art must be grasped by the artist, not by people who experience, receive, or even categorize it. At the very least, art must be against historicism, sociologicism, and schematicism (for here there is a tendency to obfuscate the subject of art itself) and must recall the truth of a basic source. Of course, novels of artists cannot and should not set standards for aesthetics even in their most prominent examples. (Even in *Doctor Faustus* such examples are only placed in the mouths of characters as a kind of essayistic tape.) However, the presence *in statu nascendi* of art mediated by the theme of the novel of the artist would improve the art theory very much in favor of "the land of the poet" in the field of its own anticipations, and this would be very much to the disadvantage of sociological and normative alienation "regarding the object." It would not be in keeping with any kind of narrow psychology, definitely not in keeping with the particularism of *l'art pour l'art* regarding creative production and work that overlooks society, the difficulties and accomplishments of production in society in which producing occurs, and on which artistic producing is dependent for its form and contents, if not in a completely decisive way, then, however, in a comprehensive influential one. But the phenomenon of producing in that which has been produced and its position in the world must always be ready as though the given *theme* of the novel of the artist came out of the background of art itself, as the background of a creation in its own embracing sense, not only of a finished product or of a standardized object. Accordingly, the concern of that which is thematized in the novel of the artist as its partiality belongs to the general task: not to neglect the producing factor in favor of the product, not to neglect the anticipatory factor either.

6. All kinds of things appear visible about which a fictitious life and struggle can make one think. The concern of a novel of the artist as such contributes meanings here about which nothing or not enough is perceived. The subject stands here philosophically for nothing less than the depicted action of engendering, for the work on the voices of the not-yet, which sound in the creation of an art work in their own unique way and are audible and *suo modo* instructive. In each case there is a dream story that moves forward, whether it is only with a head full of crazy ideas, with a sky of youth full of veritable bass violas, however, always with the intention to give birth to a work. And, according to the subject, this extends into the colportage of a subject in spite of the little people of the artist who disturb the colportage. The subject maintains its background so very strongly that it ultimately—with a surprising confrontation between Hoffmann's *Fräulein von Scudéry* and Hoffmann's *Kapellmeister Kreisler*, i.e., a confrontation between the first detective story and the first story of the artist, which is only superficial—lets it be said that if the action of the detective story—from the beginning of *Oedipus*—is concerned with revealing a *past crime*, with revealing it, then the action of the *artist* story—from the beginning of *Prometheus*, even to the legend of the *building of the tower* of Babel—concerns itself with the *formation of the human*, with revealing this. The detective story depends on penetrating and digging up material, while the inventive story depends on revealing and shaping it in the not-yet and out of the not-yet that arises before us as that of the work. This occurs with lasting consciousness of the journey, and this is why Joseph Conrad in his *Recollections* compared the trouble of such art in particular with the effort "that one must expend when rounding Cape Horn westerly in a bitter winter." However, there is also help of a peculiar kind at hand that allows that heterogeny of purposes, understood now in a positive sense, not to shrivel or go unfulfilled during the attempt to produce a great project. Rather, it lets the plan expand during the production to include unexpected purposes and to succeed. That which becomes especially visible when the plan was at first in its infancy is like a mere

jug that is supposed to be turned on the wheel and becomes instead a Greek vase. Let us take a prominent example: Columbus wanted to find a sea route to India, a country that was already known, and he discovered America. Of course, the first plan, the youthful plan in the life of an artist, is always the great one, like the plan of the young apprentice of Sais, which Schiller used as the basis for his poem, and not without reason, for it contains the *Sturm und Drang* motif: "What do I have when I don't have everything?" The realization to be gained from the poem, which ends in a fiasco, can certainly be comprehensive, but it does not need to be exhaustive. This is true in all areas of human creation where it can be creation and is one. That which moves one in the novel of the artist itself, as one which ultimately, like the genuine Faust material, concerns all of humankind, even without the respective epithets, is the desire to break new ground, with knights, death, and the devil, to head for the envisioned utopian castle or to that which corresponds to its formation in shape, sound, or word. The increasing reports about the light that appears to shine before an individual are of utmost importance here, or as Goethe himself called it in *Dichtung und Wahrheit* (*Poetry and Truth*): "the early harbingers of that which we shall be capable of achieving." No story that is a good story about production places a period behind this element of the harbinger. Yes, this element of the harbinger, this anticipatory illumination lives right in those *really accomplishing* works insofar and in that they are accomplished. So much for the novel of the artist and the usefulness of reading it—*et hic dii sunt*, here too, there is that which spreads, there is Pandora with hope.

# The Representation of Wish-Landscapes in Painting, Opera, and Poetry

Painting is surfacing in a different place.

Franz Marc

Those writers, whom we call eternal or simply good, and who enchant us, possess a common and most significant characteristic: they walk a specific path, and they also make an appeal to us to follow them, and you feel, not with your mind but with your entire being, that they have a goal.... The best among them are realistic and show life as it is, but since every line appears to be imbued with an awareness of the goal, as though filled with juice, you get a sense of what life is supposed to be aside from life as it is, and that is what captivates you.

Anton Chekhov

Beauty is life as it is supposed to be in full reality until it has to be.

Tchernychevsky

Videtur poeta sane res ipsas non ut aliae artes, quasi histrio, narrare, sed velut alter deus condere.

Julius Caesar Scaliger

## The Hand in Motion

It does not lead to anything merely to feel in a beautiful way. It remains internal. It has no way to get to the outside. Nothing is communicated. In much the same way the interior is presupposed whenever there is any artistic creation. There has to be an ego behind the applied colors, a hand that applies. There is a feeling that passes through the hand in motion that becomes part of the painting. On the other side, a creative talent is only characterized as such when it is ordered *a priori* according to certain shapes, when it does not find anything at all in itself that is not already pressing for its well-defined place. Therefore, the craft does not come to the creative subject as something other, as something foreign to the subject, but it is the subject that girds and prepares itself. If something gets lost on the way between the ego that knows how to do something and the craft that is known, then it is not worth much. As soon as the subject has something to say, it speaks; there is always expression. So they both speak about each other. This is why a picture is also heard, not only seen. It tells about the things you see on it. And indeed, this happens right away in a friendly manner. The colorful in itself has a cheerful effect.

## Flower and Carpet

Here the hand starts delicately and meticulously; it plots lines. What the pencil draws is supposed to be clear, what the brush paints is supposed to be colorful. Light must be able to shine through. Finesse teaches and reveals capability in particular. Therefore, the best way to learn to paint is dealing with flowers and glass; every good picture has an inkling of flowers in it. And, related to this, there is a carpet in it, this bed full of balanced colors. Only beyond the pure, mastered finesse and through it do things reveal themselves as being painted. They are reborn and formed by color; flower and carpet unravel as objects, first as still lives. Then the tablecloth becomes transparent to itself, also the plate, the fruit, the meat. Such things as this cannot get enough resonating color that enables them to be linen-like, porcelain-like, and opulent. No silk that you touch is as soft and shiny as properly painted silk, no steel is more masculine, more flashing than the steel that has passed through the color blue. Similarly something that is often spread-out like a carpet is closely kept together by a color that links everything together harmoniously. Nothing is disturbing or is disturbed. Everything acts on the spot, is kin and affiliated to itself, for everything is born from color. In this instance, the color is the primeval sustance, and it brings that which is formed by it, no matter how different it is in life, to a denominator based on color. Aprons as well as cups receive their nuances from a basic white; red goes into lobsters and into roses. The still life is educated by the flower, becomes a bunch of flowers that offers itself. Unnecessary to say that the bunch itself like everything in it is of minor importance.

## Still Life Made of People

Maybe it is part of closeness in general that it is narrow and appears to have such an effect. A small area has a shrinking effect, makes a friendly *tangible* circle. It paints an existence that in real life may easily become stale, but as a pre-painted existence it is in a peculiar way a warm one. There, tame behavior has its place that contents itself in a useful manner, but that also enjoys a safe circle and being on it. Above all that is true where the circle is derived from one's own power, and the life within it is not wasted but secured and delimited, therefore demonstrates peaceful warmth. This is the case with Dutch interiors, where everything turns into a room, the streets too. A warm stove is burning everywhere, even outside when it is springtime. Vermeer, Metsu, Pieter de Hooch portrayed that kind of homey living, a "home sweet home" still without being stuffy. The woman reads a letter or talks to the cook; the mother peels apples or watches the child in the courtyard. The old lady walks in the street passing a tall wall. From beyond the wall gables peek in. Nothing else is happening. Sunbeams flow through the serene miniature. And in the actual interior the tranquility becomes what cooing doves represent in an old enclosed courtyard. A different light that penetrates it causes partitions to form. *A Mug of Beer* (Amsterdam) shows the chamber illuminated by slanting light where a woman in an infinitely calm mood pours her beer. To the right we look through an open door into the brightly flooded living room and through the window frame out into the open. The threefold penetrating light opens the narrowness and the homeliness without enlarging it. In all these paintings space takes precedence over people, but the space encloses people. Space is meant for closeness. The objects of bourgeois comfort manifest themselves quietly: the brass wall lamp with the reflector, the red tile, the brown armchair. Pure and simple orderly lifestyle is everywhere. The house is tidied up, and the spirits are high. Even the building line is demarcating. In Hooch's work the vistas do not go beyond one or two hundred meters. A grocery store of happiness appears, and in this instance it seems like a treasury. A lot of homey everyday life is painted in the Dutch genre picture, but with all its closeness it is also designed in a way as a ship's captain would see it from afar when he thinks of home: as a miniature that carries homesickness in itself. Corresponding to this, on the other hand, is the fact that maps of the world hang on the walls very often in these pictures, with the ocean that peeks in and provides all the homey comfort due to Dutch world trade. Pieter de Hooch also painted elegant rooms where ladies and cavaliers dance, dine, and play music. The colors on arches and columned fireplaces in these pictures are not as moodful. They are blue and gray. The red color of the costumes is hard. But even in the court paintings there is something lilliputian, something elfish that is protective and is protected itself. Nothing sick, nothing wild, nothing noisy, nothing disturbing can be seen in this lovely format. Nor does it seem that any trouble could peek in. The room and the window facing the street are painted in a way as if there were no disturbance in the world. The grandfather clock always strikes the evening hour. There is nothing that people could not cope with. Nothing is urgent.

Departure for Cythera

So gentle is the closeness. But part of the distant world is that it is veiled in unrestfulness: it is a world that binds that searching look and attracts people because it is *veiled*. Then the feeling is erotic longing. When painted, it is departure, a travel of love (*Liebesreise*). Therefore every depiction of the erotic distant world already expresses seduction. One of the fundamental portrayals of this kind is Watteau's *Embarquement pour Cythère*. From the outset it is clear that the title is utopian. Young gentlemen and young ladies are waiting for the bark that will bring them to the island of love. The fact that Watteau, who was an excellent, though not first-rate, painter could give such a sensitive and meaningful depiction of a wish-landscape (*Wunschland-schaft*) is due to the way leisure time was spent in his times. Rococo works in a concentrating, at least isolating, way also by artificial and erotic reduction. Watteau painted his picture three times. The first version is merely based on the impression of a stage setting, the pastoral play *Trois Cousines*—which is recalled up until Offenbach's *La Périchole*. In the first version the arrangement of the figures is still awkward. The mood is conventional. The time of the day is still indeterminate. The air is not yet charged with expectation. Also the second and the third versions appear to be conventional when they are looked at in a superficial way. That is to say, they stem from the era of the secrets of the deer parks and boudoirs that had been dealt with and exploited in a thousand ways. In this regard he used only the lecherousness of court life and an exchangeable pastime to base his work on. The latter was often more eroticized boredom. Nevertheless, in the course of time the painting looked after the right things in an extraordinary way; the archetype of the journey of love (*Liebesfahrt*) appears very clearly in this fashionable subject. Particularly the second version, the Parisian one, anticipates dream and formation of a group *in spe*: the couples are surrounded by an enchanting land-scape. The contours of the park are already disappearing. The bark of love is waiting in the silvery water. A distant mountain sits in the dusk, invisible, but the night of the island makes the movement and the anticipation of desire appear to be immanent in the picture. The third version, the Berlin version, is less perfect since the bijou in it is too obviously arranged and too well-known. Not only is the fore-ground more detailed in this version, but most of all the love boat itself with the motif of the putti floating around the sail. The bark is obviously ready. The mast with *amor*'s sail draws a clearer line at the blurring horizon. The direct coexistence of rose-red and sky-blue around the sail is definitely saccharine. It seems to be a banner of promises sent by the island of love. But also here, the departure for Cythera is only hinted at or no longer the departure itself, only with anticipated happiness. This is the difference between Watteau's pic-ture and all other portrayals of lust, particularly those in which Cythera already seems to have been reached. There is one great picture of this kind that influenced Watteau to a large extent in its form and color: the *Garden of Love* by Rubens hanging in Madrid. But the painting by this much more powerful painter provides serenity, almost like happiness as a habit. Cythera, on the other hand, has never existed, or it is gone. In Rubens' work, opulent women in a golden brown tone are grouped in front of a massive grotto structure, flanked by two couples in red and black. Above in the intervals, putti fill the space. The sticky air is charged and turns into the flesh of putti. Even the stone of the portal is auto-eroticizing, like the fountain sculpture that ejects water from its breasts: here is indulgence as an emblem, coitus as a timeless mastery. The entire garden has been altered in this sense, in a simply existential and therefore monumental way. The columns at the portal are femal thighs. Cupid is reaping. But the departure for Cythera is only alluded to where the antici-pation of desire is represented, with gardens completely other than those on the solidly existing land. That is the reason why these paintings require a state of suspension, require a sail, the condition of a cloud, a veiled expectation and its light. When the curtains part, there is not a garden of love with vivid colors and a majestic affirmation, but rather the wish-landscape *ante rem*, the woman herself as the awaiting landscape. Giorgione's *Sleeping Venus*, Goya's *Naked Maja* preserve the light surrounding Cythera. In Goya's work the light emanates undiminished from the white pillows, from the licentious and cool flesh-tone, from the vital lines: this nude, too, lies on an island. Especially the so-called impure thoughts are clearly those of these pictures themselves. They are the lustful utopian reason to which their figures lead and in which they are situated. But Cythera exists as if there were nothing in the world except for the shining and the silhouette of the woman.

## Perspective and Great Horizon in Van Eyck, Leonardo, and Rembrandt

That distance, which leaves the view unobstructed, which does not hide anything, is richer in objects. Even where the painted view lies in the mist, there is no delimitation but, rather, a standard set particularly for the *vastness*. As soon as this world, instead of heaven, began to become infinite, the wish-landscape as open distance appeared in paintings. It peered through the window and arches in blue-green, through open grottoes. That is where the long-range view from the mountains started. Everything that had been thus far attributed to cathedrals, the depth of the third dimension, now became the spatial dimension of the picture: the world as the longship. Now depth could be brought into the picture plane since it appeared as a slit through the cone of vision. In this sense, it is as if the viewer were looking through a window. The picture plane itself is like an open window. The point where the lines of perspective meet lies at infinity; the lines running in the middle section go beyond the horizon. The figures enclose something new: a centrifugal space. Thus already at the end of the Middle Ages vastness, a vastness of wish (*Wunschweite*) became clear in the Parisian Madonna of Jan van Eyck. Perspective is instrumental to an initial *veduta* that is framed by architecture. The landscape appears as a window space of the house. And in van Eyck's pictures, for the first time, the law of the vanishing point was consciously taken into consideration. The transference of objects, seen in the

depth to the plane, was started. Between the Madonna and the figure
of her donor the view goes through three arches of a stately hall, and
thus a distant land overfilled with treasures opens up interrupted and
lined by columns. It is detailed in a masterful way, occupied by all
kinds of spatial and utopian feelings that are capable of breaking up a
quasi-horizontal abyss. A town becomes visible, gables and steeples, a
cathedral, a vast plaza with stairs, a much-frequented bridge, a river
furrowed by tiny barges. In the middle of the river, on an island
smaller than the fingernail of a child, a palace rises with several small
bell towers surrounded by trees. Behind all this stretches a world of
green hills toward the horizon where snowy mountains arise, and in
the very far distance the clouds fade into the limitless sky. It is the
perfect dreamland, although it is in the extended line of realities lying
one after another. This is neither Bruges, Maastricht, Lyons, or any of
the contemporary cities one could have guessed. Rather the perspective shows a Gothic ideal city without walls in the apse of infinity.
Soon, in Piero della Francesca, also the *veduta* of *nature* would find its
place, together with the new value of the horizon of the Renaissance.
But, it was Leonardo da Vinci who provided the complete, open
original for the dream value of perspective. In *Leonardo's* work, distance together with secret colors create a space where sculptures cease
to exist, where only light structures itself into almost unknown objects. The painting *Madonna in the Grotto* portrays the darkness of the
cave, sharp edges pointed in Gothic style, but the grotto breaks and
the view wanders without any transition to a remote river valley. The
figures in *The Madonna and the Christ Child* are strictly inscribed in a
pyramid but the landscape behind them changes into a wild rugged
mountain mass, half mist, half body, an indefinable other world of
objects easy to survey. The nature of distance (*Fernwesen*) permeates
the portrait of Mona Lisa itself. It is true that the dream of the
background lets the figure in the foreground gain some corporeality,
but at the same time this corporeality is lost again. For Mona Lisa
herself reproduces the form of the landscape in the ripples of her
gown, the weightiness of the dream in her eyelids, the congealed,
uncanny, paradoxically nontransparent ether in her smile. *In this
painting the landscape is as important as the figure.* They are related if not
equal hieroglyphs. In the words of Leonardo's philosophical conception of the world: "Each part has the inclination to reunite with the
whole in order to escape imperfection. And it is necessary to know

that this very wish is the quintessence, the companion of nature, and the human being is the model for the entire world." The distant landscape's name is Mona Lisa, too, and it is—a fantastic, pointed mountain labyrinth in the most soft light, in between lakes, pale fields, streams. Mona Lisa looks from there, and she also looks into the distance, laid out toward her or complete enigma, in greenish-blue, smoky light.

But if everything is smoky in the first place, how can one see into the distance? It happens in that the dark ground out of which the painting is made alienates the things themselves and in that the light in which the objects stand seems to come itself from the background, reflecting itself. Therefore, Rembrandt, the strongest painter of the distant shining that reflects in the nearby, leaves even Saskia halfway in the dark, and the *Man with the Golden Helmet* carries his metal as though first collecting the light, even leading down into darkness. In Rembrandt's work the lustrous spots are, from a viewpoint of painting technique, never shining and attached in a virtually flat way. They are a relief where the bright color only adheres to the granular elevations whereas the sunken areas, the given close-up substance (*Nahstoff*), so to speak, remains filled with the darkness of the underpainting or with the brown glaze. The true rarity and preciousness of this light, its captivating shining illumination of the night, result from the reality of the night on the one hand, from the mere reflection of the light on the other hand. Corresponding to this is the complicated technique of dark priming and overpainting that Rembrandt pursued throughout all of his oeuvre. Its first triumph, already comprising everything, is characteristically in a painting of the Passion, in the entombment of Christ at Munich. People, even objects, stand isolated in the vastness of the dark space. The colors come solely from a mysterious reflex of inner light from within the world and from behind the world, from a paradox of final light (*Endlicht*). Therefore, the light stems neither from the sun nor from an artificial source of light. Moreover, the existing world, including some transcendental world (*Überwelt*) that is believed to exist is not at all capable of providing this light, being neither from this world nor from heaven. The distance up to now, the cosmological open perspective is extinguished by the dark space. The latter creates a circular composition of the figures, almost unstructured in itself. Only in the worldly group portraits and landscape paintings like *The Night Watch*, the site of the ruins of Kassel is the ground cut by spears, a castle, and clouds, and a scaffold with straight lines stretches into the night watch. The portraits, on the other hand, and the pictures with Christian subjects show essentially the unstructured darkness outside, the noncosmic (*akosmisch*) solitude inside. Rembrandt, who stopped painting landscapes in his later years, framed everything completely with a strongly concealing and gloomy recouped dark tone, meaning in this instance universe and infinity. Nevertheless, here, too, the darkness of the background is streaked with a golden-brown tone. The group of people stands in *sfumato* perspective; i.e., the transitions between areas are softened, black and golden at the same time. The light effects the darkness; it colors here in a chromatic manner also, penetrates from a strangely existing nowhere. Rembrandt's paradoxical light does not occur anywhere in the entire world, but it also does not emanate, despite its continuous reflections, from some old metaphysics of celestial light: it is the *perspective light of hope*, led deeply into closeness and solitude, responding to these. The open cosmic perspective is extinguished by dark space, but the light that rises up against this dark space the same way as it breaks forth mysteriously from solitude and blackness paints the truth of hope or of the shining that is not there into the dark ground of the existing world. This erratic appearance only mediated by reflexes constitutes the exotic of Rembrandt's illumination, the echo of a fairy-tale distant realm where the objects that are receptive to it or that belong to it are very closely painted. It is only in this way that the glimmer comes, as well as the love for that which shines from silk, pearls, jewels, from the gold helmet. That is where the necessary Arab-ization stems from in the portrayal of Saskia and Jews: the distant light speaks most clearly through the fairy-tale land of the Orient; a transcendental Baghdad glows in the night. And only from there, in the depth, the light does not stand as an element of the world, also not as an element of the transcendental world (*Überwelt*), but as a mystical existential expression of the figures belonging to it. The result is the absolute stillness in the Munich painting of the Resurrection, with Christ at the very bottom, shining palely, Christ, who still escaped the mythical celestial light and who is superior, the light that falls down behind the descending angel: an *ex oriente lux* that in itself stands at the entrance and is reflected from the corpse in utmost remoteness. All of Rembrandt's paintings, also the profane ones, are composed by starting from the background, and their colors—made of night, incense, myrrh, and gold—paint the perspective: a hollow space with sparks.

## Still Life, Cythera, and the Broad Perspective in Literature: Heinse, The Romance of the Rose, Jean Paul

A picture tells about those immediate things that one can see on it. And a poem perceives and can let us see what it tells in succession. That is most of all true when the poem lets itself be led by a desired kind of picture, by the still life, but then by the departure, by the great vastness. The *poetical* form of the *still life*, now, of course, seen in a completely nostalgic way, is the *idyll*. Even the tiniest detail in it is honored and good, for where there is no abundance, all things have to serve the best thing. So in Andersen's work: the pliers, kettles, and candles are alive. The room itself is a little fairy tale, all utensils dwell in it. The idyll offers modest meals, cultivates carefree conversations, contains continuous, pleasant destinies. Of course, the poem can also, in the same way as the painted still life that consists of people, carry that docile contentment with it, suited and most useful for the ruling forces. Moreover, it is not by chance that the idyll stems from the old pastoral poems, in which a gluttonous social class embellished the limited life that those people had to lead who had no choice. Indeed, they themselves did not lead his life of milk and honey, nor were they decorated, or beribboned. And yet, later, the bourgeois idyll contained space for something downright good that was only found so desirable in this Biedermeier circle. It was something homey, as if one had returned from far away, domestic peace, a rural garden "with a smooth wafting coolness. "During the day the routine life is surrounded by the buzzing of the bees, during the night by the humming of the teakettle—such as in Voss' *Luise*; also in moderation, despite the specific misfortune, in Goldsmith's *The Vicar of Wakefield*. Distance appears here only as the tea. The outward storms howl in the chimney and contribute specifically to the cozy atmosphere of home. The bad guys are reduced to odd characters and provide the salt of contentment. In contrast, the *poetic* way of the erotic *exodus*, of *Cythera*, exceeds the limitations of the enclosed idyll. The South came first to mind, lute playing, wine, friends and their girls, purple nights, columns illuminated by torchlight. This could not be found in Winckelmann and his kind but in Wieland and successors. In the eighteenth century the South was seen with those signs. Also romanticism, in E. T. A. Hoffmann's work, did not change much of this. Here Italy figured first and foremost as musical and erotic, the land of yearning for libertarian and liberated love, not of Apollonian marble. This is evident in a work of the late *Sturm und Drang* that still owes much to rococo in a strange way. I am referring to Heinse's *Ardinghello und die glückseligen Inseln* (*Ardinghello and the Blissful Islands*), 1787, a novel structured in an archeological way, also half pornographic and utopian. The wishful dream of the *ver sacrum* was dared or heated up in this novel as follows: "It went deeper and deeper into life, and the festivity became more sacred, the eyes were aglaze with tears of joy.... The most bacchanal storm roared through the hall like the thundering cataracts of the Senegal and Rhine rivers where one forgets about oneself and returns to eternal glory great and omnipotent.... Everlasting spring, beauty, and fertility of the sea and the land and wholesomeness of water and air." It is not the first lascivious but rather the first Dionysian antiquity that is portrayed in this Cythera novel. In contrast, Wieland, in whose work the graces were never without satyr but satyr also never without them, rejected Heinse's novel as a priapism (a permanent erection) of the soul. In the end Ardinghello founded an ideal state of lust on the islands of Paros and Naxos, where nothing but lust remains, where no one but this goddess enters the many caves and temples. In this sense Arcadia, ever since Theocritus the old bucolic yearned for a realm of escape, is awarded to the erotic magic islands where the hot nights were all bucolic, completely without the happiness in confines. Therefore, Heinse's Cythera could live from the much earlier pastoral poems that were blossoming again in Italy during the Renaissance, mainly from Tasso's *Aminta*, the first and also most perfect example, with fauns, nymphs, and satyrs, with an enchanted grove and the arrow of Cupid, with the cool temple of Diana, and the choir of the shepherds of the Golden Age as the era of free love. This was also the constant and enduring wish during the ever so sentimental old pastoral poetry, at least during the Renaissance; the Golden Age with ancient classical characteristics also containing Oriental characteristics. The original of the Cythera poem is located in that Renaissance the same way as the Renaissance was drawing its magic gardens from Saracen, from Saracen-Gothic memories, those where the bucolic borders the tropical, borders the non-temperate zone. The unveiled distance of Cythera contains this kind of non-temperate nature in its most well-known form; as love and only in the garden of love, in this wish-landscape of the Orient, will it blossom toward that which almost everything bucolic had been tending since the Crusades, and from which it returns adorned. Therefore, it is not by chance that the *primary Cythera book* and also everything Ardinghello-like belonging to this realm grew from conditions of the Saracen culture of love (*Liebeskultur*) and its chivalrous heritage, that is, the Gothic *Romance of the Rose*. For this primary book, more artificial than rococo and full of a paradoxical and scholastic naturalism, presents itself in its fullness only as the phenomenology of the land of love. And moreover allegories were added. In medieval graphicness, concepts are transformed into people; consequently, their interplay turns into a drama. That which seems to be cold today was at that time full of resonating references throughout the sensual world of the multifold, full of life. Now, the departure for Cythera was prolonged with all the dangers and problems. Thus it became an *ars armandi* with quodlibets from all the contemporary sciences. *The Romance of the Rose*, begun by Guillaume de Lorris, finished by Jean de Meung, from the late thirteenth century, eulogizes this path to pleasure in more than twenty thousand verses. The poet himself reaches the garden of love. Madame Leisure opens the gate for him. His heart gets wounded by Cupid. Bel-Accueil invites him to the roses, but now the intrigue starts. Around the roses a wall is being erected, Danger, and his companions are guarding the gate and with a lover's mourning. Guillaume de Lorris closes his book of longing. However, in the sequel, Genius, the "Chaplain of Nature," proposes to advance with an entire army of love. His appeal is followed and joined by Jupiter and Godfather, Venus and the Holy Virgin, mysticism of Jesus and the most funny pornographic materialism. Nature dictates the laws of human behavior, though it is something that is not based outside ourselves in heaven and in the norms of the Church but within the human being and in this, the human being's world. Genius preaches against virginity and sodomy, threatens everybody with hell who does not comply with the demands of nature and love, promises life without end in a Muhammadan, industrious Zion to those who are loyal, illuminated by Jesus and the most beautiful women. Encouraged by Genius' words and protected by Venus, the procession of love enters the garden and moves toward the hidden Virgin, who "is more perfect than Pygmalion's statue." Jealously, Shame, Fear, and other allegories of emotions set up infinite obstructions, but Courtesy, Frankness, Kindness, and, above all, Bel-Accueil (who is the son of Courtliness) free the rose of love from the fortress and put the rose of love at the lover's heart. *"Ci est le roman de la Rose/ Ou l'art d'amors est tote enclose."* The vaginal allegory of the rose provides the lust-utopian ground of the Gothic Cythera. Digressions about the human duty to procreate are interspersed. In addition, there is a great deal of satire plus astronomy, nominalistic philosophy of nature, geographical fairy tales, teachings about money and monetary circulation, about classical heroes, about the origin of obedience, about communist utopias. *"Chascune por chascun commune/ Et chascun commun por chascune."* The social upheavals of the fourteenth century cast their light ahead. This is true mainly in that part of the romance that Jean de Meung had already written for the rising bourgeoisie, with relentless questions, turning toward nature. Being a Rousseau of the Middle Ages, he addressed the feudal *ars armandi*. He talked about a primeval state through the metaphor of free love. Cythera spreads out widely in poetry, being frivolous and subversive, knowledge and subtly elegant—Cupid stands at the end of the world.

All around here is the distance, but it is one that is tenderly veiled for us. If that distance appears for itself, then it becomes a very large foreign realm dawning in itself. Its form, then, is *poeticized perspective*, in the South, and more so in the North. Oceanic feelings are part of that distance, unbounded vastness and an all fluid affirmation. When fog descends, the vastness appears as an Ossianic landscape that in its intensification has been called the utopia of Thule. And yet, it is not at all only the North, but is full of aroma, veils, half-open doors, the smoke of the Orient. Now Jean Paul though, aside from his idyll of permanent wish-perspectives, revolving panoramas, sometimes subterranean, sometimes vastly expanding, showed in almost all of his landscape the double appearance consisting of night and East, mediated here by the Bible once again. But even in Italy, even in the azure, and more so in the curiosities, the estrangements, the augustness of the world that he composed in grand allegories, he saw that being in the fog. His distance was the most unbounded of all those known to us, especially when it went into the *abyss*, when the distance continued to murmur in there, in endless beginnings: "A tower full of blind doors and blind windows stood in the center, and the lonely clock in there talked to itself, and it wanted to separate the joining waves of time with the iron rod swinging back and forth—it struck a quarter to twelve, murmured as in sleep." Then the description of an object, which does not murmur Hades, but really shouts it, the *Vesuvius of the landscape*: "The morning was dawning, and in the middle of a dark winter we began the journey to the gorge of fire and to the gate of smoke. As in a burned-down, smoking city, I passed cave by cave, mountain by mountain, and on trembling ground I moved toward a powder mill with a magazine in constant operation. Finally I found the chasm of this land of fire, a large, red-hot valley of steam, again with a mountain—a landscape of craters, the workshop of doomsday—filled with pieces of the broken world, frozen, bursted flows of hell—an enormous heap of time fragments—but inexhaustible, immortal like an evil spirit, and under the cold, pure sky giving birth to itself with twelve months of thunder. Suddenly the big steam rose more dark red than ever before, the thunder came together more wild, the heavy hellish cloud of fumes hotter—suddenly morning air floated in and carried down the flaming curtain from the mountains." The dark of night, ruins, and Tartarus from the wish-landscape of negative infinity, as the river Lethe of estrangement. But the deeper Pluto, the higher Apollo, the sun of the endless cave of Fingal that is the world. In Jean Paul's *Titan*, the hero has just this kind of distant perspective of *Apollo's Day*: "The Alps stood together like fraternale giants of the distant pre-world in the past, and they held up high shining shields of the icebergs to the sun—the giants were wearing blue belts from the woods—and at their feet were hills and vineyards—and in between the vaults formed by the vine grapes the morning winds played with cascades like with taffeta ribbons made of water—and suspended from the ribbons was the overfilled sparkling surface of the lake hanging from the mountains, and the foliage of the chestnut forests surrounded it. . . . Albano turned slowly around in a circle and looked up and down, into the sun, at the flowers. And on all the summits the noisy fires of the mighty nature were burning and in all the chasms their reflections—a creative earthquake was beating like a heart down below the surface of the earth and was driving out mountains and oceans" (*Titan*, 1st Cycle). For Jean Paul, the Italy described in *Titan* was not a concept or even confirmed presence as it was for Goethe, or even for Heinse: it remained a distance magic, and beyond it was further significant perfection—the eternal is only an allegory. And in Germany, love, the moon, and spring give to the hero of *Titan* a gaze that is at all points in time exaggerated, that is driven by presentiment and hope, as, for instance, when the gardens of a prince are exalted as a *Terra australis*: "But look down, fiery human, with your fresh heart full of youth, onto the magnificent, immense magic of Lilar! A dawning second world, soft sounds they paint for us, an open morning dream spreads out before you with its high triumphal gates, with whispering mazes, with blissful islands— the bright snow of the sunken moon lies only on the groves and triumphal gates and on the silvery dust of the fountain; and the night that springs from all lakes and valleys swims across the Elysian fields of the heavenly shadowlands where the unknown figures occur to the wordly memory like banks of the Otaheiti, lands of shepherds, groves of Daphne, and poplar islands" (*Titan*, 23rd Cycle). This form of the distant landscape obeys human beings and reflects them in an enthusiastic way of the most peculiar ecstasy, namely, identity. A utopian reception takes place through the ciphers of great nature. The Sphinx of strangeness becomes lighter, becomes bearable and sublime in mythical and yet anthropomorphic pictures. The glow of sunrise and sunset becomes a color of perspective that wants to reach far beyond the circle line of the horizon: "The enormous mystery of the universe promises to reveal the voices of the night, and in the far distance the mountain peaks, from which the human being can look deeply into the aspired other world, are uncovered by the passing fog." This is boundless cosmos, linked just as much to chaos as to infinity that never ceases to be full, that is filled time and again.

# Selected Bibliography

## Primary Sources

## I. Bloch's Works in German

*Gesamtausgabe*, 16 Bde. Frankfurt am Main: Suhrkamp, 1977. This collection of 16 volumes is also known as the *Werkausgabe* and includes the following:

1. *Spuren*

2. *Thomas Münzer als Theologe der Revolution*

3. *Geist der Utopie* (1923)

4. *Erbschaft dieser Zeit*

5. *Das Prinzip Hoffnung*

6. *Naturrecht und menschliche Würde*

7. *Das Materialismusproblem—seine Geschichte und Substanz*

8. *Subjekt-Objekt—Erläuterungen zu Hegel*

9. *Literarische Aufsätze*

10. *Philosophische Aufsätze zur objektiven Phantasie*

11. *Politische Messungen—Pestzeit Vormärz*

12. *Zwischenwelten in der Philosophiegeschichte (Aus Leipziger Vorlesungen)*

13. *Tübinger Einleitung in die Philosophie*

14. *Atheismus im Christentum*

15. *Experimentum Mundi—Frage, Kategorien des Herausbringens, Praxis*

16. *Geist der Utopie* (facsimilie of 1918 edition)

Selected Bibliography


There is also an *Ergänzungsband* (additional volume) containing *Tendenz—Latenz—Utopie*. The individual volumes were originally published as follows:

*Geist der Utopie*. Munich, 1918.

*Thomas Münzer als Theologe der Revolution*. Munich, 1921.

*Durch die Wüste. Kritische Aufsätze*. Berlin, 1923.

*Spuren*. Berlin, 1930.

*Erbschaft dieser Zeit*. Zurich, 1935.

*Freiheit und Ordnung. Abriss der Sozialutopien*. New York, 1946.

*Subjekt-Objekt. Erläuterungen zu Hegel*. East Berlin, 1949. Expanded edition, Frankfurt am Main, 1962.

*Avicenna und die Aristotelische Linke*. East Berlin, 1952.

*Christian Thomasius. Ein deutschter Gelehrte ohne Misere*. East Berlin, 1953.

*Das Prinzip Hoffnung*. vol. I, East Berlin, 1954; vol. II, East Berlin, 1955; vol. III, East Berlin, 1959.

*Differenzierungen im Begriff Fortschritt*. East Berlin, 1956.

*Naturrecht und menschliche Würde*. Frankfurt am Main, 1961.

*Philosophische Grundfragen. Zur Ontologie des Noch-Nicht-Seins*. Frankfurt am Main, 1961.

*Verfremdungen I*. Frankfurt am Main, 1962.

*Tübinger Einleitung in die Philosophie*. vol. I, Frankfurt am Main 1963.

*Tübinger Einleitung in die Philosophie*. vol. II, Frankfurt am Main, 1964.

*Verfremdungen II*. Frankfurt am Main, 1964.

*Literarische Aufsätze*. Frankfurt am Main, 1965.

*Atheismus im Christentum*. Frankfurt am Main, 1968.

*Philosophische Aufsätze zur objektiven Phantasie*. Frankfurt am Main, 1969.

*Politische Messungen, Pestzeit, Vormärz*. Frankfurt am Main, 1970.

*Das Materialismusproblem, seine Geschichte und Substanz*. Frankfurt am Main, 1972.

*Vorlesungen zur Philosophie der Renaissance*. Frankfurt am Main, 1972.

*Experimentum Mundi. Frage, Kategorien des Herausbringens, Praxis*. Frankfurt am Main, 1975.

*Zwischenwelten in der Philosophiegeschichte*. Frankfurt am Main, 1977.

*Tendenz-Latenz-Utopie*. Frankfurt am Main, 1978.

## II. Bloch's Works in English

*Atheism in Christianity*, tr. J. T. Swann. New York: Herder and Herder, 1972.

"Causality and Finality as Active Objectifying Categories," tr. G. Ellard, *Telos*, 21 (Fall 1974), 96–107.

"Dialectics and Hope," tr. Mark Ritter, *New German Critique*, 9 (Fall 1976), 3–10.

"A Jubilee for Renegades," tr. David Bathrick & Nancy Vedder Shults, *New German Critique*, 4 (Winter 1975), 17–25.

*On Karl Marx*, tr. John Maxwell. New York: Herder and Herder, 1971.

"Man as Possibility," tr. W. R. White, *Cross Currents*, 18 (Summer 1968), 273–283.

*Man on His Own*, tr. E. B. Ashton. New York: Herder and Herder, 1970.

*Natural Law and Human Dignity*, tr. Dennis J. Schmidt. Cambridge: MIT Press, 1986.

"Nonsynchronism and the Obligation to its Dialectics," tr. Mark Ritter, *New German Critique*, 11 (Spring 1977), 22–38.

"Odysseus Did Not Die in Ithaca," tr. H. Loewy and G. Steiner in: G. Steiner and R. Fagles, eds. *Homer—A Collection of Critical Essays*. Englewood Cliffs: Prentice Hall, 1962. pp. 81–85.

"A Philosophical View of the Detective Novel," tr. Roswitha Mueller and Stephen Thaman, *Discourse*, 2 (1980), 32–51.

"Philosophy as Cabaret." *New Left Review*, 116 (July–August 1979), 94–96.

*A Philosophy of the Future*, tr. John Cumming. New York: Herder and Herder, 1970.

*The Principle of Hope*, tr. Neville Plaice, Stephen Plaice, & Paul Knight. Cambridge: MIT Press, 1986.

"Theory-Praxis in the Long Run," tr. Wayne Hudson in: R. Fitzgerald, ed. *The Sources of Hope*. London: Pergamon, 1979. pp. 153–157.

"On the Threepenny Opera," tr. Sophie Wilkins in" Maynard Solomon, ed. *Marxism and Art*. New York: Knopf, 1973. pp. 576–578.

## Secondary Sources

## I. Critical Biographies and Monogaphs

Horster, Detlef. *Bloch zur Einführung*. Hannover: SOAK, 1980.

Hudson, Wayne. *The Marxist Philosophy of Ernst Bloch*. New York: St. Martin's Press, 1982.

Markun, Silvia. *Ernst Bloch*. Reinbek bei Hamburg: Rowohlt, 1977.

Münster, Arno. *Utopie, Messianismus und Apokalypse im Frühwerk von Ernst Bloch*. Frankfurt am Main: Surhkamp, 1982.

Raulet, Gérard. *Humanisation de la Nature. Naturalisation de L'homme. Ernst Bloch ou le Projet d'une autre Rationalité.* Paris: Klincksieck, 1982.

Schmidt, Burghart. *Ernst Bloch.* Stuttgart: Metzler, 1986.

Zudeick, Peter. *Der Hintern des Teufels. Ernst Bloch—Leben und Werk.* Moos & Baden-Baden, 1985.

## II. Collections of Critical Essays on Bloch's Works

Bahr, Hans Dieter, ed. *Ernst Blochs Wirkung. Ein Arbeitsbuch zum 90. Geburtstag.* Frankfurt am Main: Suhrkamp, 1975.

Böhme, Wolfgang, ed. *Das Reich der Hoffnung. über Ernst Bloch.* Karlsruhe, 1979.

Bloch, Karola and Adelbert Reif, eds. *Denken heisst überschreiten: In memoriam Ernst Bloch 1855–1977.* Cologne: Europäische Verlagsanstalt, 1978.

Bremer, Thomas. ed. *Ernst Bloch.* Munich: Text + Kritik, 1985.

Deuser, Hermann and Peter Steinacker, eds. *Ernst Blochs Vermittlungen zur Theologie.* Munich: Kaiser, 1983.

Gropp, Rugard Otto, ed. *Festschrift Ernst Bloch zum 70. Geburtstag.* Berlin: VEB Deutscher Verlag der Wissenschaften, 1955.

Horn, Johannes Heinz, ed. *Ernst Blochs Revision des Marxismus.* Berlin: VEB Deutscher Verlag der Wissenschaften, 1957.

Löwy, Michael, Arno Münster, and Nicolas Tertulian, eds. *Verdinglichung und Utopie. Ernst Bloch und Georg Lukács.* Frankfurt am Main: Sendler, 1987.

Perels, Joachim and Jürgen Peters, eds. *Es muss micht immer Marmor sein. Ernst Bloch zum 90. Geburtstag.* Berlin: Klaus Wagenbach, 1975.

Raulet, Gérard, ed. *Utopie—Marxisme selon Ernst Bloch.* Paris: Payot, 1976.

Schmidt, Burghart, ed. *Materialien zu Ernst Blochs 'Prinzip Hoffnung.'* Frankfurt am Main: Suhrkamp, 1978.

Schmidt, Burghart, ed. *Seminar zur Philosophie Ernst Blochs.* Frankfurt am Main: Suhrkamp, 1983.

*Über Ernst Bloch.* Frankfurt am Main: Suhrkamp, 1968.

Unseld, Siegfried, ed. *Ernst Bloch zu ehren.* Frankfurt am Main: Suhrkamp, 1965.

## III. Essays and Books on Bloch's Aesthetics

Adorno, Theodor W. "Bloch's Spuren" in: *Noten zur Literatur. Gesammelte Schriften.* Eds. Gretel Adorno and Rolf Tiedemann. Vol. 11. Frankfurt am Main: Suhrkamp, 1974. pp. 233–250.

Bahr, Ehrhard. "The Literature of Hope: Ernst Bloch's Philosophy and Its Impact on the Literature of the German Democratic Republic." *Acta neophilologica,* (1980), 11–26.

Selected Bibliography

Berghahn, Klaus L. "'L'art pour l'espoir'. Literatur als ästhetische Utopie bei Ernst Bloch" in: Thomas Bremer, ed. *Ernst Bloch*. Munich: Text + Kritik, 1985. pp. 5–20.

Bothner, Roland. *Kunst im System. Die konstruktive Funktion der Kunst für Ernst Blochs Philosophie.* Bonn: Bouvier, 1982.

Brenner, Peter J. "Kunst als Vorschein. Blochs Ästhetik und ihre ontologischen Voraussetzungen" in: Hiltrud Gnüg, ed. *Literarische Utopie-Entwürfe*. Frankfurt am Main, 1982. pp. 39–53.

Bronner, Stephen E. "Expressionism and Marxism: Towards an Aesthetic of Emancipation" in: Stephen E. Bronner and Douglas Kellner, eds. *Passion and Rebellion: The Expressionist Heritage.* South Hadley: Bergin & Garvey, 1983. pp. 411–453.

Dahlhaus, Carl. "Ernst Blochs Philosophie der Musik Wagners." *Jahrbuch des staatlichen Instituts für Musikforschung*, (1971), 179–188.

Emmerich, Wolfgang. "'Massenfaschismus' und die Rolle des Ästhetischen. Faschismus Theorie bei Ernst Bloch, Walter Benjamin, Bertolt Brecht" in: Lutz Winckler, ed. *Antifaschistische Literatur*, vol. 1. Kronberg/Ts.: Scriptor, 1977. pp. 223–290.

Gramer, Wolfgang. "Musikalische Utopie. Ein Gespräch zwischen Adornos und Blochs Deneken." *Bloch-Almanach*, 4 (1984), 175–190.

Hoffmann, Rainer. *Montage im Hohlraum*. Bonn: Bouvier, 1977.

Ivernel, Philippe. "'Soupçons—D'Ernst Bloch à Walter Benjamin" in: Gérard Raulet, ed. *Utopie-Marxisme selon Ernst Bloch*. Paris: Payot, 1976. pp. 265–277.

Jameson, Fredric. "Versions of a Marxist Hermeneutic: III. Ernst Bloch and the Future" in: *Marxism and Form*. Princeton: Princeton University Press, 1971. pp. 116–159.

Lenger, Hans-Joachim. "Ernst Bloch-Georg Lukács. Kontroverse um den Expressionismus." *Kunst und Gesellschaft*, 3–4 (1977), 91–106.

Massuh, Victor. "Die utopische Funktion und der Mythos" in: Burghart Schmidt, ed. *Materialien zu Ernst Blochs "Prinzip Hoffnung."* Frankfurt am Main: Suhrkamp, 1978. pp. 189–195.

Mayer, Hans. "Musik als Luft von anderen Planeten. Ernst Blochs 'Philosophie der Musik' und Feruccio Busonis 'Neue Ästhetik der Tonkunst'" in: Burghart Schmidt, ed. *Materialien zu Ernst Blochs "Prinzip Hoffnung."* Frankfurt am Main: Suhrkamp, 1978. pp. 464–472.

Mayer, Hans. "Ernst Blochs poetische Sendung: in: Siegfied Unseld, *Ernst Bloch zu ehren*. Frankfurt am Main: Suhrkamp, 1965. pp. 21–30.

Mayer, Hans. "Ernst Bloch, Utopie, Literatur" in: *Ernst Blochs Wirkung. Ein Arbeitsbuch zum 90. Geburtstag*. Frankfurt am Main: 1975. pp. 237–250.

Norris, Christopher. "Marxist or Utopian? The Philosophy of Ernst Bloch." *Literature and History*, 9 (1983), 24–45.

Oellers, Norbert. "Blochs Nähe zu Hebel." *Bloch-Almanach*, 3 (1983), 123–134.

Paetzold, Heinz. *Neomarxistische Ästhetik. Teil 1: Bloch. Benjamin.* Düsseldorf, 1974. pp. 22–129.

Phelan, Tony. "Die sogenannten 'Goldenen zwanziger Jahre': Zeitkritik und Kulturgeschichte in Ernst Blochs *Erbschaft dieser Zeit*" in: Keith Bullivant, ed. *Das literarische Leben in der Weimarer Republik*. Königstein/Ts.: Scriptor, 1978. pp. 250–281.

Reininghaus, Frieder. "Musik wird Morgenrot. Ernst Bloch und die Musik." *Spuren*, 3/4 (1977), 78–90.

Simons, Eberhard. *Das expressive Denken Ernst Blochs. Kategorien und Logik künstlerischer Produktion und Imagination.* Freiburg/Brsg.: Alber, 1984.

Solomon, Maynard. "Marx and Bloch: Reflections on Utopia and Art." *Telos*, 13 (Fall 1972), 68–85.

Tripp, Günther. *Absurdität und Hoffnung. Zum Werk von Albert Camus und Ernst Bloch.* Berlin: Ernst Reuter Gesellschaft, 1968.

Ueding, Gert. "Blochs Ästhetik des Vor-Scheins" in: Ernst Bloch, *Ästhetik des Vor-Scheins 1*, ed. G. Ueding. Frankfurt am Main: Suhrkamp, 1973. pp. 7–27.

Ueding, Gert. "Tagtraum, künstlerische Produktivität und der Werkprozess" in: *Ästhetik des Vor-Scheins 2*, ed. G. Ueding. Frankfurt am Main: Suhrkamp, 1973. pp. 7–22.

Ueding, Gert. "Begriffene Kolportage" in: *Glanzvolles Elend. Versuch über Kitsch und Kolportage.* Frankfurt am Main: Suhrkamp, 1973. pp. 163–204.

Ueding, Gert. "Traumliteratur. über literarische Erfahrungen und ihre Wirkung" in: Hans-Dieter Bahr, ed. *Ernst Blochs Wirkung. Ein Artbeitsbuch zum 90. Geburtstag.* Frankfurt am Main: Suhrkamp, 1975. pp. 251–270.

Ueding, Gert. "Schein und Vorschein in der Kunst" in: Burghart Schmidt, ed. *Materialien zu Ernst Blochs 'Prinzip Hoffnung.'* Frankfurt am Main: Suhrkamp, 1978. pp. 446–464.

Weigand, Karlheinz. "Zu Tiecks 'Der blonde Eckbert' anhand der Deutung durch Ernst Bloch," *Bloch-Almanach*, 3 (1983), 115–122.

Werckmeister, Otto Karl. "Ernst Blochs Theorie der Kunst." *Die neue Rundschau*, 79 (1968), 233–250.

Wiegmann, Hermann. *Ernst Blochs ästhetische Kriterien und ihre interpretative Funktion in seinen literarischen Aufsätzen.* Bonn: Bouvier, 1976.

Witschel, Günther. *Ernst Bloch. Literatur und Sprache: Theorie und Leistung.* Bonn: Bouvier, 1978.

Zipes, Jack. "The Utopian Function of Fairy Tales and Fantasy: Ernst Bloch the Marxist and J. R. R. Tolkien the Catholic" in: *Breaking the Magic Spell: Radical Theories of Folk and Fairy Tales.* London: Heinemann, 1979. pp. 129–159.

Zipes, Jack. "The Liberating Potential of the Fantastic in Contemporary Fairy Tales for Children" in: *Fairy Tales and the Art of Subversion.* London: Heinemann, 1983. pp. 170–194.

Zipes, Jack. "Populäre Kultur, Ernst Bloch und Vor-Schein" in: Michael Löwy, ed., *Verdinglichung und Utopie. Ernst Bloch und Georg Lukács.* Frankfurt am Main: Sendler, 1987, pp. 239–253.

Zudeick, Peter. "Im eigenen Saft. Sprache und Komposition bei Ernst Bloch." *Bloch-Almanach*, 1 (1981), 61–90.

# IV. Essays, Books, and Interviews Concerned with Bloch's Philosophy

Adorno, Theodor. "Grosse Blochmusik." *Neue Deutsche Hefte*, 69 (April 1960), 14ff.

Arenilla, Louis. "Ecology: A Different Perspective." *Diogenes*, 104 (Winter 1978), 1–22.

Bahr, Ehrhard. *Ernst Bloch*. Berlin: Coloquium, 1974.

Bloch, Jan. "Zur Bestimmung der Naturqualität" in: Michael Daxner, Jan Robert Bloch, and Burghart Schmidt, eds. *Andere Ansichten der Natur*. Münster, 1981. pp. 78–115.

Bloch, Jan. "Ein alter Tisch aus London" in: Burghart Schmidt, ed. *Seminar zur Philosophie Ernst Blochs*. Frankfurt am Main: Suhrkamp, 1983. pp. 261–282.

Braaten, Carl E. "Ernst·Bloch's Philosophy of Hope" in: Carl Braaten and Robert W. Jensen, eds. *The Futurist Option*. Westminster, MD: Newman, 1970.

Breines, Paul. "Bloch Magic." *Continuum*, 7 (1970), 619–624.

Buhr, Manfred. "Critique of Ernst Bloch's Philosophy of Hope." *Philosophy Today*, 14 (Winter 1971), 259–271.

Bütow, Hellmuth. *Philosophie und Gesellschaft im Denken Ernst Blochs*. Berlin: Ost-Europa Institut, 1963.

Capps, Walter H. "An Assessment of the Theological Side of the School of Hope." *Cross Currents*, 18 (Summer 1968), 319–336.

Capps, Walter H. "The Hope Tendency." *Cross Currents*, 18 (Summer 1968), 257–272.

Capps, Walter H. "Vertical versus Horizontal Theology: Bloch-Dewart-Iraneus," *Continuum*, 5 (Winter 1968), 616–633.

Christen, Anton. *Ernst Blochs Metaphysik der Materie*. Bonn: Bouvier, 1979.

Cox, Harvey, "Ernst Bloch and the Pull of the Future." *New Theology*, 5 (1968), 191–203.

Damus, Renate. *Ernst Bloch: Hoffnung als Prinzip—Prinzip ohne Hoffnung*. Meisenheim: Anton Hain, 1971.

Dietschy, Beat. "Eine Seitentüre als Naturzugang. Ernst Bloch's *Spuren*." Bloch-Almanach, 1 (1981), 91–116.

Eckert, Michael. *Transzendieren und immanente Transzendenz*. Vienna: Herder. 1981.

Fahrenbach, Helmut. "Zukunft als Thema der Philosophie" in: Helmut Fahrenbach, ed. *Wirklichkeit und Reflexion*. Pfullingen: Neske, 1973.

Fiorenza, Francis P. "Dialectical Theology and Hope I," *Heythrop*, 9 (April 1968), 143–163.

Fiorenza, Francis P. "Dialectical Theology and Hope II," *Heythrop*, 9 (October 1968), 384–399.

Fiorenza, Francis P. "Dialectical Theology and Hope III," *Heythrop*, 10 (January 1969), 26–42.

Franz, Trautje. *Revolutionäre Philosophie in Aktion. Ernst Blochs politischer Weg genauer besehen.* Hamburg: Junius, 1985.

Furtur, Pierre. "Utopia and Marxism According to Bloch." *Philosophy Today,* 14 (Winter 1970), 236–249.

Gekle, Hanna. *Wunsch und Wirklichkeit. Blochs Philosophie des Noch-nicht Bewussten und Freuds Theorie des Unbewussten.* Frankfurt am Main: Suhrkamp, 1985.

Gollwitzer, Helmut. "Zu Immanuel Kants und Ernst Blochs Hiob Deutung, als Exkurs" in: *Krummes Holz und aufrechter Gang. Zur Frage nach dem Sinn des Lebens.* Munich: Kaiser, 1970. pp. 239–250.

Green, R. M. "Ernst Bloch's Revision of Atheism." *Journal of Religion,* 49 (1969), 128–135.

Gropp, Rugard Otto. "Die marxistische dialektische Methode und ihr Gegensatz zur idealistischen Dialektik Hegels." *Deutsche Zeitschrift für Philosophie,* 2 (1954), 69–112.

Gross, David. "Man on His Own." *Continuum,* 7 (Winter 1970), 625–627.

Gross, David. "Ernst Bloch and the Dialectics of Hope" in: Dick Howard and Karl E. Klare, eds. *The Unknown Dimension.* New York: Basic Books, 1972. pp. 107–130.

Habermas, Jürgen. "Ernst Bloch: A Marxist Romantic." *Salmagundi,* 10/11 (Fall 1969–Winter 1970), 311–325.

Habermas, Jürgen. "Ernst Bloch: A Marxist Schelling" in: *Political Profiles.* Cambridge: MIT Press, 1983. pp. 61–78.

Heer, Friedrich. "Vision der Zukunft in Rot und Gold: Ernst Bloch." *Hochland,* 53 (1960/61), 35–52.

Heinitz, Kenneth. "The Theology of Hope According to Ernst Bloch." *Dialog,* 7 (1968), 34–41.

Hobsbawm, E. J. "The Principle of Hope" in: *Revolutionaries.* London: Weidenfeld and Nicolson, 1973. pp. 136–141.

Holz, Hans Heinz. *Logos spermatikos. Ernst Blochs Philosophie der unfertigen Welt.* Darmstadt: Luchterhand, 1975.

Howard, Dick. "Marxism and Concrete Philosophy: Ernst Bloch" in: *The Marxian Legacy.* London: Macmillan, 1977. pp. 66–87.

Hudson, Wayne. "Open System as Marxist Metaphysics." *Bloch-Almanach,* 3 (1983), 81–94.

Hurbon, Laennec. *Ernst Bloch. Utopie et Espérance.* Paris: Les Editions du Cerf, 1974.

Jäger, Alfred. *Reich ohne Gott. Zur Eschatalogie Ernst Blochs.* Zurich: EVZ-Verlag, 1969.

Kellner, Douglas, and Harry O'Hara. "Utopia and Marxism in Ernst Bloch." *New German Critique,* 9 (Fall 1976), 11–34.

Kimmerle, Heinz. *Die Zukunftsbedeutung der Hoffnung.* Bonn: Bouvier, 1966.

Kränzle, Heinz. *Utopie und Ideologie. Gesellschaftskritik und Politisches Engagement im Werk Ernst Blochs.* Bern: H. Lang und CIE, 1970.

Landmann, Michael. "Critiques of Reason from Weber to Bloch." *Telos*, 29 (Fall 1976), 187–198.

Landmann, Michael. "Talking with Ernst Bloch: Korcula, 1968." *Telos*, 25 (Fall 1975), 165–185.

Lowy, Michael. "Interview with Ernst Bloch." *New German Critique*, 9 (1976), 35–45.

Mandel, Ernest. "Antizipation und Hoffnung als Kategorien des historischen Materialismus" in: Karola Bloch and Adelbert Reif, eds. *Denken heisst überschreiten. In memoriam Ernst Bloch 1885–1977*. Cologne: Europäische Verlagsanstalt, 1978. pp. 222–234.

Mayer, Hans. "Bloch und die Heimat" in: *Ausgewählte Reden*. Frankfurt am Main: Suhrkamp, 1978.

Metz, Johannes B. "The Responsibility of Hope." *Philosophy Today*, 4 (1966).

Metz, Johannes B. "God Before Us Instead of a Theological Argument." *Cross Currents*, 18 (Summer 1968), 295–306.

Metz, Johannes B. "The Responsibility of Hope." *Philosophy Today*, 10 (Winter 1976), 280–288.

Moltmann, Jürgen. "Hope and Confidence: A Conversation with Ernst Bloch." *Dialog*, 7 (1968), 42–55.

Metz, Johannes B. "Hoping and Planning." *Cross Currents*, 18 (Summer 1968), 307–319.

Münster, Arno. "Marxismus und Tendenzwissenschaft im Werk von Ernst Bloch" in: Michael Grauer and Wolfdietrich Schmied-Kowarzik, eds. *Grundlinien und Perspektiven einer Philosophie der Praxis*. Kassel: 1982. pp. 55–79.

Negt, Oskar. "Ernst Bloch: The German Philosopher of the October Revolution." *New German Critique*, 4 (1975), 3–16.

Negt, Oskar. "Erbschaft aus Ungleichzeitigkeit und das Problem der Propaganda" in: Joachim Perels and Jürgen Peters, eds. *Ernst Bloch zum 90. Geburtstag. Es muss nicht immer Marmor sein*. Berlin: Klaus Wagenbach, 1975. pp. 9–34.

O'Collins Gerald. "The Principle of Hope." *Scottish Journal of Theology*, 21 (1968), 129–144.

O'Collins Gerald. "Spes quaerens intellectum." *Interpretation*, 22 (1968), 36–52.

Oliver, Harold H. "Hope and Knowledge." *Cultural Hermeneutics*, 2 (May 1974), 75–87.

Pannenberg, Wolfhart. "The God of Hope." *Cross Currents*, 18 (1968), 283–294.

Piccone, Paul. "Bloch's Marxism." *Continuum*, 7 (Winter 1970), 627–631.

Rabinbach, Anson. "Ernst Bloch's 'Heritage of Our Times' and Fascism." *New German Critique*, 11 (Spring 1977), 5–21.

Rabinbach, Anson. "Benjamin, Bloch and Modern German Jewish Messianism." *New German Critique*, 34 (Winter 1985), 78–124.

Radnoti, Sandor. "Bloch and Lukács: Two Radical Critics in a 'God-forsaken World.'" *Telos*, 25 (Fall 1975), 155–164.

Ratschow, Carl Heinz. *Atheismus im Christentum? Eine Auseinandersetzung mit Ernst Bloch.* Gütersloh: Gerd Mohn, 1971.

Raulet, Gérard. "Hermeneutik im Prinzip der Dialektik" in *Ernst Blochs Wirkung.* Frankfurt am Main: Suhrkamp, 1975. pp. 284–304.

Raulet, Gérard. "Critique of Religion and Religion as Critique: The Secularized Hope of Ernst Bloch." *New German Critique,* 9 (Fall 1976), 71–85.

Raulet, Gérard. "Die überwindung des bürgerlichen Wissenschaftbegriffs durch Blochs objektiv-reale Prozesserkenntnis." *Praxis,* 2 (1982), 84–98.

Reimer, A. James. "Bloch's Interpretation of Münzer: History, Theology and Social Change." *Clio,* 9 (Winter 1980), 253–268.

Reinicke, Helmut L. *Materie und Revolution. Eine materialistischerkenntnistheoretische Untersuchung zur Philosophie von Ernst Bloch.* Kronberg: Scriptor, 1974.

Roeder von Diersburg, Egenolf. *Zur Ontologie und Logik offener Systeme.* Hamburg: Fritz Meiner, 1967.

Rühle, Jürgen. "The Philosopher of Hope" in: Leopold Labetz, ed. *Revisionism: Essays on the History of Marxist Ideas.* London: Allen & Unwin, 1962. pp. 166–178.

Schelsky, Helmut. *Die Hoffnung. Blochs Kritik der marxistischen Existenzphilosophie eines Jungbewegten.* Stuttgart: Klett-Cotta, 1979.

Schmidt, Alfred. "Der letzte Metaphysiker des Marxismus" in: Karola Bloch and Adelbert Reif, eds. *Denken heisst überschreiten.* Cologne: Europäische Verlagsanstalt, 1978. pp. 62–65.

Schmidt, Burghart. "The Political Nature of Epistemological Categories: Introduction to Bloch." *Telos,* 21 (Fall 1974), 87–91.

Schmidt, Burghart. "Ein Bericht: Zu Entstenhung und Wirkungsgeschichte des 'Prinzip Hoffnung'" in: *Materialien zu Ernst Blochs 'Prinzip Hoffnung.'* Frankfurt am Main: Suhrkamp, 1978. pp. 15–40.

Schmidt, Burghart. "Die Stellungnahme Ernst Blochs als Marxist" in: *Materialien zu Ernst Blochs 'Prinzip Hoffnung.'* Frankfurt am Main: Suhrkamp, 1978. pp. 41–58.

Schmidt, Burghart, "Vom teleologioschen Prinzip der Materie" in: *Seminar: Zur Philosophie Ernst Blochs.* Frankfurt am Main: Suhrkamp, 1983. pp. 204–227.

Schmidt, Burghart, "Die Aktualität einer Naturpolitik in Blochscher Perspektive" in: Michael Daxner, Jan Bloch, and Burghart Schmidt, eds. *Andere Ansichten der Natur.* Münster, 1981. pp. 34–58.

Schmidt, Burghart, "Ernst Bloch: Die Frage nach dem Augenblick in der Geschichte" in: Josef Speck, ed. *Grundprobleme der grossen Philosophen, Philosophie der Gegenwart.* vol. 4. Göttingen: Vandenhoeck & Ruprecht, 1984. pp. 9–42.

Schreiter, Robert, "Ernst Bloch: The Man and His Work." *Philosophy Today,* 14 (Winter 1970), 231–235.

Sonnemans, H. *Hoffnung ohne Gott? In Konfrontation mit Ernst Bloch.* Freiburg: Herder, 1973.

Selected Bibliography

Strohschein, Barbara. *Tagträume hinter Schulmauern.* Frankfurt am Main: Volkhard, 1982.

Tadic, Ljubomir, Tadic. "The Marxist Critique of Right in the Philosophy of Ernst Bloch." *Praxis International*, 1 (January 1982), 422–429.

Tillich, Paul. "The Right to Hope." *Neue Zeitschrfift für systematische Theologie und Religionsphilosophie*, 7 (1965), 371–377.

Ueding, Gert. "Ernst Blochs Philosophie der Utopie" in: Wilhelm Vosskamp, ed. *Utopieforschung*, vol. 1. Stuttgart: Metzler, 1982. pp. 293–303.

Walser, Martin. "Prophet mit Marx- und Engelszungen" in: *Über Ernst Bloch.* Frankfurt am Main: Suhrkamp, 1968. pp. 7–16.

Wren, Thomas E. "An Ernst Bloch Bibliography for English Readers." *Philosophy Today*, 14 (Winter 1970), 272–273.

Wren, Thomas E. "The Principle of Hope." *Philosophy Today*, 14 (Winter 1970), 250–258.

Zudeick, Peter. *Die Welt als Möglichkeit und Wirklichkeit.* Bonn: Bouvier, 1980.

# Index of Names and Works